# THE RISE AND FALL OF THE
# GRAND ALLIANCE, 1941–45

# The Rise and Fall of the Grand Alliance, 1941–45

Edited by

Ann Lane

and

**Howard Temperley**
*Professor of American Studies*
*University of East Anglia*

First published in Great Britain 1995 by
**MACMILLAN PRESS LTD**
Houndmills, Basingstoke, Hampshire RG21 6XS
and London
Companies and representatives throughout the world

A catalogue record for this book is available from the British Library.

ISBN 0–333–63041–6

First published in the United States of America 1995 by
**ST. MARTIN'S PRESS, INC.,**
Scholarly and Reference Division,
175 Fifth Avenue,
New York, N.Y. 10010

ISBN 0–312–12674–3

Library of Congress Cataloging-in-Publication Data
The rise and fall of the Grand Alliance, 1941–45 / edited by Ann
Lane and Howard Temperley.
p. cm.
Based on papers presented at a conference which was held in Sept.
1993, Norwich, Eng.
Originally published: Basingstoke, Hampshire : Macmillan, 1995.
Includes bibliographical references and index.
Contents: Anglo-American war aims, 1941–43, the first review :
Eden's mission to Washington / Warren F. Kimball — Soviet war aims
/ Jonathan Haslam — American foreign economic policy and lend-lease
/ Kathleen Burk — The Soviet economy and relations with the United
States and Britain, 1941–45 / Mark Harrison — Churchill's Roosevelt
/ John Charmley — Anglo-American-Soviet intelligence relations /
Chistopher Andrew — Stalin, Soviet strategy, and the Grand
Alliance / John Erickson — Anglo-American strategy / Correlli
Barnett — The war against Japan and allied relations / Peter Lowe –
– The atomic bomb and the end of the wartime alliance / David
Holloway — Yalta, Potsdam, and beyond : the British and American
perspectives / Norman A. Graebner.
ISBN 0–312–12674–3
1. World War, 1939–1945—Diplomatic history—Congresses.
I. Lane, Ann.   II. Temperley, Howard.
D749.R58   1995
940.53'2—dc20
                                                    95–13886
                                                         CIP

10   9   8   7   6   5   4   3   2   1
04   03   02   01   00   99   98   97   96   95

Printed and bound in Great Britain by
Antony Rowe Ltd, Chippenham, Wiltshire

In memory of
Richard Bone
Head of Library and Records Department
Foreign and Commonwealth Office
1989–1995

# Contents

# Notes on the Contributors

**Christopher Andrew** is Professor of Modern and Contemporary History at Cambridge University. His recent books include *Secret Service: The Making of the British Intelligence Community*; *KGB: The Inside Story of its Foreign Operations from Lenin to Gorbachev* (with Oleg Gordievsky), and *For the President's Eyes Only: Secret Intelligence and the American Presidency from Washington to Bush*.

**Correlli Barnett** was Keeper of the Churchill Archives Centre (1977–95), and a Fellow of Churchill College, Cambridge. His recent books include *The Audit of War*; *Engage the Enemy More Closely: The Royal Navy in the Second World War*; and *The Last Victory: British dreams and British realities 1945–1980*.

**Kathleen Burk** is Professor of Modern and Contemporary History at University College London. She is the author of a number of books, of which the most recent is *'Goodbye, Great Britain': The 1976 IMF Crisis* (with Alec Cairncross).

**John Charmley** is Senior Lecturer in History at the University of East Anglia. His recent books include *Churchill: The End of Glory* and *Churchill's Grand Alliance*.

**John Erickson** is Director of the Centre for Defence Studies at the University of Edinburgh. His books include *The Soviet High Command, 1918–1941*; *The Road to Stalingrad*; *The Road to Berlin*; *The Soviet Ground Forces*, and, as editor, *Barbarossa: The Axis and the Allies*.

**Norman A. Graebner** is the Randolph P. Compton Professor of History and Public Affairs Emeritus, University of Virginia. His most recent book is *The National Security: Its Theory and Practice, 1945–1960*.

**Mark Harrison** is Reader in Economics at the University of Warwick. His books include *Soviet Planning in Peace and War, 1938–1945*, and (with John Barber) *The Soviet Home Front, 1941–1945*.

**Jonathan Haslam** is a Fellow of Corpus Christi College, Cambridge and the author of *The Soviet Union and the Threat from the East, 1933–1941*. He is also chairman of the international advisory group of the Russian Foreign Ministry's Historical Documentary Department.

**David Holloway** is Professor of Political Science, and Co-Director of the Center for International Security and Arms Control, Stanford University. His most recent book is *Stalin and the Bomb: The Soviet Union and Atomic Energy, 1939–1956.*

**Warren F. Kimball** is Robert Treat Professor of History at Rutgers University. He is author-editor of the three-volume *Churchill and Roosevelt: The Complete Correspondence,* and, most recently author of *The Juggler: Franklin Roosevelt as Wartime Statesman.*

**Ann Lane** is Editor of *Documents on British Policy Overseas* at the Foreign and Commonwealth Office, and author of *Britain and Yugoslav Unity, 1941–49.* The comments attributed to this contributor in the present volume are the author's own and should not be taken as a statement of official government policy.

**Peter Lowe** is Reader in History at the University of Manchester. He is the author of *Great Britain and the Origins of the Pacific War* and *The Origins of the Korean War.*

**Howard Temperley** is Professor of American Studies at the University of East Anglia and a former editor of the *Journal of American Studies.* His most recent book is *White Dreams, Black Africa: The Antislavery Expedition to the Niger, 1841–1842.*

# Introduction

Wartime alliances tend to be short-lived. They are formed in response to immediate needs, unite rivals in the face of commonly perceived dangers and fall apart once their period of usefulness has passed. So it was with the Grand Alliance of 1941–45 between Britain, the United States and the Soviet Union. Brought about by the need to join forces against a common foe, the allies found they had little else to bind them together once victory had been achieved. There were, it is true, all the grand generalities contained in the Atlantic Charter – renunciation of territorial aggrandisement, affirmation of democracy, the right of nations to self-government, freedom of the seas – but when it came to deciding what these meant in practice there was no common agreement. No wonder, once the war was over, the alliance fell apart.

Nevertheless, the struggles of these years continue to fascinate if only because we still live in their shadow. The Second World War was midwife to the birth of a new era in international politics in which a system, once dominated by the major powers of Europe, was to be displaced by an uneasy balance between the emerging superpowers. One development, already evident by the time the fighting ended, was Britain's diminishing status as a world power. Effectively, Britain was reluctantly passing on responsibility for maintaining world order to the United States. This shift in responsibility, in turn, brought with it a change in the world economy, with a new era of liberalism resulting from the end of the system of imperial preference and the substitution of the dollar for the pound as the principal unit of international exchange. As Kathleen Burk's chapter in this collection shows, the groundwork for this transformation was laid during the war. The alliance also brought new measures of cooperation in the fields of strategic planning and intelligence which laid the foundations for the postwar unified command operations which have operated in hot-war conflict since 1945 and in one sense, are a practical application of the principle of collective responsibility for world order which was advocated by the Big Three as an essential ingredient of postwar international peace-keeping.

The collapse of the Soviet Union and the consequent transformation of the postwar international system have changed historical perspectives and prompted a new revisionism which seems likely to be sustained by fresh evidence emerging from hitherto closed Soviet archives. The historiography of the alliance has gone through a series of distinct phases. The early release of American records, particularly in the form of published documents, meant that the initial histories of the alliance were written, in the absence of

British and Soviet records, largely from an American perspective moderated only by the publication in Britain of official histories and eyewitness accounts, the latter being self-evidently individual rather than collective perspectives, and in some cases essentially self-serving. The first revision of the interpretations these spawned came in the early 1970s with the release to the public domain of the British official record. At this point the American role was also undergoing a re-evaluation stimulated by the climate of critical self-questioning which developed alongside American military involvement in Vietnam. More recent interpretations on both sides of the Atlantic have attempted to synthesise these earlier works in the light of fresh archival evidence. This process is currently receiving additional stimulus with the partial release of Soviet sources and the revival of Russian and East European scholarly traditions.

The essays contained in this volume span a range of interpretations covering the politics, economics and grand strategy of the Second World War and are drawn from a diverse range of sources, including some of those now available to scholars in Moscow. They do not aim to give a collective judgement on the alliance and still less to offer a comprehensive account. Indeed some aspects, such as the role of propaganda, the relationships between the military staffs, and the role of resistance movements, are not discussed here. These papers concentrate rather on a selection of issues at the level of high policy and both individually and collectively have some statements to make about the effectiveness of the allied cooperation as a factor in winning the war and the issues which contributed to its breakdown.

The alliance owed its immediate origins to the fall of France in June 1940 which left Britain as the sole major power prosecuting the war against Germany. The French collapse forced acceptance in British policy-making circles of the premise that the resources of the United States had to be sought, regardless of the cost, in order that the war against Germany might be continued from British shores. The fruits of this quest emerged publicly for the first time in August 1941 in the shape of the Atlantic Charter. However, there is a certain irony in the fact that by this time the German offensive against the Soviet Union had already provided Britain with formidable assistance in prosecuting the war for Europe. Shortly after the Japanese attack on Pearl Harbor, which transformed the European war into a global conflict, 23 nations signed the United Nations Declaration: Britain, the United States and the Soviet Union were the principal signatories. They were bound by this declaration alone and, excluding the Anglo-Soviet agreement of May 1942, no more formal treaty existed between them.

The alliance, created by a common interest and determination to bring about the comprehensive defeat of Hitler's Germany, had also to deal similarly with Japanese militarism. The order of priorities, which gave primary emphasis to the reconquest of Europe, represented a particular triumph for

Winston Churchill. Securing American acceptance of this, which was never a foregone conclusion, marked the high-water point of British influence in the alliance, after which the American voice became increasingly dominant. Within this broad unifying aim there was a second objective, that of replacing the prewar international system, which had failed to keep the peace, with one which from the point of view of British, Soviet and American interests would achieve the security which derives from prolonged stability. The search for an international order which would meet the individual objectives of the Great Powers, however, was to prove elusive.

Several themes regularly recur in this book. Some chapters emphasise the existence of differing political systems and the misunderstandings to which this gave rise. If one allied government seeking aid from another failed to understand the process by which decisions were made by its potential benefactor and the pressures upon decision-makers within that system, it was not only handicapped in framing its request but unaware of the subtleties of meaning implicit in the response. It follows from this that the different positions occupied, constitutionally speaking, by the leaders of the alliance had an important influence on the way decisions were made. So too, of course, did the personalities of the leaders themselves. Indeed, it would not be going too far to say that the relationship between the war efforts of the three allies was centred in and epitomised by the triangular relationship between the three principal allied leaders. Thus, as the Americans assumed increasing weight in the western half of the alliance, so the centre of gravity of the alliance itself, rooted as it was in the personalities of these men, shifted from Churchill to Roosevelt. In this connection the following pages have something to say about the functioning of the democratic process in wartime, and the frequently-debated nature of Stalin's role in the Soviet dictatorship. One further theme which overarches the whole volume is the importance of precedent in shaping the alliance's policies and the perception by each ally of the other two. Several contributors set their chapters in a broader historical context, drawing particularly on the lessons learnt during the First World War and the policy failures of the 1930s.

The chapters trace three major themes and two lesser ones. The former encompass the evolution of war-aims, inter-allied economic relations and grand strategy. The latter cover the inter-allied intelligence relationship and Churchill's view of the war's immediate aftermath.

In Chapter 1 Warren Kimball examines the evolution of Anglo-American war-aims with particular reference to the discussions which took place on the occasion of Anthony Eden's visit to Washington in March 1943. He poses fundamental questions about the balance between western expectations for the postwar world and the perceptions held by British and American policy-makers of reality: in this context he is concerned with the persistently perplexing question of Roosevelt's understanding of the concept of self-determination. He also dwells on the Anglo-American debate about the nature of European problems and reviews the position taken by each as to the relationship of France with Germany and Britain. Kimball confesses his own uncertainly as to where Roosevelt stood in relation to the twin themes of internationalism and self-determination which dominated the debate about the postwar world, and, while agreeing that the Atlantic Charter had been a genuine call for a new world order, he tentatively concludes that it remains unclear whether Roosevelt had a definite plan to replace *pax Britannica* with *pax Americana*.

Soviet war-aims, on the other hand, are viewed by Jonathan Haslam as being derived from traditional Russian objectives in Europe, the Near East and Far East, combined with a commitment to communist expansion. The effect, he argues, was to define in the minds of the Soviet leadership a series of non-negotiable policy objectives and thereby create a unilateralist outlook which necessarily, and from the outset, relegated diplomacy to the margins. Soviet war-aims, unlike those of Britain and the United States, were consistent and practical. As to Stalin's role, Haslam discerns in it a degree of incompetence and, in so doing, adds usefully to the debate about Soviet policy in 1941. While agreeing that Stalin's policy was aimed at satisfying the Russian craving for security, manifested in Moscow's defiance of the western allies over eastern Europe, he argues that there are also grounds for supposing that it was dictated by the innermost needs of Stalin's own personality.

In analysing Anglo-American economic relations, Kathleen Burk argues that the American policy towards lend-lease was part of a continuum which culminated in 1945–46 in the negotiation of the US loan and had, all along, been directed towards the objective of achieving the collapse of British external economic policy. The central theme of her chapter is the motivation behind American economic pressure on Britain and Britain's desperate need for American support. In his chapter on the Soviet economy and relations with the United States and Britain, Mark Harrison uses little-explored Soviet material to establish the importance of lend-lease aid to the Soviet Union as an essential component in the Soviet victory in the war against Germany. In this interpretation, however, lend-lease is portrayed as a double-edged weapon. As the standard-bearers of world revolution the Soviets found themselves in the disconcerting position of having to rely on the world's leading capitalist nation for their wherewithal for survival, a situation that provided fertile ground for suspicion. Neither the reasons for its giving, on the one hand, nor the uses to which it was being put on the other, were straightforward. The result was to compound the existing mistrust between the emerging superpowers, the Americans believing that their generosity was unappreciated and the Soviets that scant credit was given for their having borne the brunt of the fighting.

The evolution of Anglo-American strategy in the western hemisphere is the subject of Correlli Barnett's chapter. He takes as his theme the problems facing the British and Americans in agreeing a strategy which would satisfy the predispositions of each, given the polarity created by the British horror at the spectre of re-enacting the Somme and American eagerness to abbreviate the conflict in the Mediterranean and cut straight to the heart of Germany through landings in north-west Europe. He stresses the significance for allied strategy of the battle of the Atlantic and the fact that the German challenge in this theatre was not beaten off decisively until the spring of 1943. This alone rendered an early second front, as demanded by the Russians and persistently proposed by the Americans, logistically impractical. Furthermore, he reminds us that the personal relationship between the allied leaders also played a role in the decision-making: by the Tehran conference in November 1943, when Churchill finally accepted a date for the landings in France, his relationship with Roosevelt had substantially cooled and the British voice in the Alliance was already much diminished. In his discussion of strategy in the Far East, Peter Lowe underlines the inevitability of Anglo-American friction in this region. Owing to the determination of the British to use the war to re-establish their colonial presence, British and American interests clearly conflicted. These differences manifested themselves variously in disputes about the strategic value of Singapore, the subsequent debates concerning the allocation of resources to defeating the Japanese in Burma, and the disagreements arising from the determination of the Americans to pursue their policy of unconditional surrender. This last stemmed in large part from the American moral indignation occasioned by Pearl Harbor. Lowe makes the point that Roosevelt's policy of putting Europe ahead of the Pacific in American strategic priorities has much to say about the quality of his political skills.

Soviet strategic planning was for the first two years concerned primarily with survival against German forces which enjoyed significant advantages in both equipment and training. John Erickson's chapter on Soviet strategy, which focuses particularly on the tactical aspect of the Soviet campaigns after the battle of Stalingrad, emphasises the growing professionalism of the Soviet armies which was complemented by an increased awareness of the connection between military and political objectives. This latter point is again raised in David Holloway's chapter on the impact of the atomic bomb on the Alliance. He draws on Soviet sources to explain that despite early knowledge of Anglo-American progress with atomic experiments it was not until the demonstration of the bomb's destructive power at Hiroshima that the potential connection between the bomb and foreign policy was understood by Stalin and Molotov. It is David Holloway's conclusion, therefore, that up to the summer of 1945, such covert knowledge as Moscow received regarding the Manhattan project did not contribute to the breakdown of the alliance.

However, its use against the Japanese effectively upset the balance of power created by the war; the Soviet Union was thenceforward committed to rapid acquisition of atomic weapons in order to regain parity as a superpower. Meanwhile, the Americans for their part were hopeful that they could use the interim to oblige the Russians to cooperate on American terms: the element of fear, which was an essential ingredient of Cold War mentality, only set in when this expectation was confounded by Soviet intransigence.

Christopher Andrew takes as his theme the seduction of the Americans into the British intelligence network. This was one area in which, owing to long experience, the British enjoyed primacy. It proved a strikingly successful collaboration. How effective Soviet intelligence was in the war against Germany, has yet to be determined, but there is no doubting its success in prising information out of Russia's partners in the alliance, a fact that was to cause much anger and embarrassment in the years to come. Against the failures of Western–Soviet intelligence relations, Andrew demonstrates the closeness of the Anglo-American relationship in the intelligence sphere, a collaboration which he assesses as having changed the course though not perhaps the outcome of the war.

The still perplexing question of Roosevelt's personality has been tackled here by John Charmley, who has placed his discussion in the context of the Churchillian view of Roosevelt as a friend and coadjutor, which is to ignore the fact that, as Charmley argues, the President's aims were inimical to those of the Prime Minister. Charmley assumes the validity of the thesis that Roosevelt, in seeking to internationalise the New Deal, aimed to replace the British empire with an informal American empire based on economic prowess. Provocatively, he raises the question of whether there ought to have been a Grand Alliance and, if so, whether Britain ought to have been a party to it. Perhaps Britain's interests would have been better served by not entering the war at all.

In the concluding chapter Norman Graebner traces the breakdown of the alliance through the 1945 inter-allied meetings concerning the postwar settlement. In so doing he demonstrates the incompatibility of the allies' aims in Germany and seeks to explain how these led inevitably to American–Soviet conflict as perceived Soviet ambitions became, in American eyes, challenges demanding a response. Graebner argues that, while the Truman administration initially perceived Britain as an aggravator of alliance relations with the Soviet Union, she became, after the Moscow conference in December 1945, a welcome partner in American efforts to hold the line against Soviet expansionism.

The Grand Alliance was characterised by, and ultimately foundered on, the absence of a shared postwar vision other than a nebulous commitment to establish a stable peace settlement. The means by which this might be accomplished were differently conceived by each of the protagonists. Britain sought in effect some containment of both US and Soviet influence in order to protect her own position as a Great Power with world-wide interests and situated at the centre of a vast empire, a position rendered increasingly tenuous by her own economic and military weakness. The Soviet Union meanwhile was seeking a new level of security through the crushing of German nationalism and the establishment of her own sphere of influence or *cordon sanitaire* on her traditionally unstable western frontier. In this she appears to have taken little cognisance of the concerns of her allies or the shared ideals for which they had supposedly been fighting. The United States also had an agenda, derived from an American belief in the virtues of economic liberalism and political self-determination combined with a nebulous but genuine loathing of empire. The circumstances which had led to political instability and the rise of the dictators, Americans believed, must never be allowed to occur again. In their view, the world would benefit most from an economic prosperity promoted under the aegis of American capitalism. Each of the three powers had sought to use the accidents of war to further its own ends. With the destruction of the one unifying bond these conflicting objectives now came to the fore.

Earlier versions of these papers were presented at a conference held in Norwich in September 1993. The event was sponsored by the Foreign and Commonwealth Office and the University of East Anglia with the assistance of the United States Information Service and UEA's de Freitas endowment. In particular, we would like to pay tribute to the late Richard Bone, whose idea it originally was and whose help with the planning of the conference and the preparation of this volume was invaluable. The conference was the latest in a series held at UEA, supported by the FCO and the de Freitas endowment, aimed at bringing together scholars, government officials, journalists and others concerned with European–American relations.

ANN LANE AND HOWARD TEMPERLEY

# 1 Anglo-American War–Aims, 1941–43, 'The First Review': Eden's Mission to Washington*
## Warren F. Kimball

As Hitler's armies advanced on Moscow (their brethren already occupying most of Europe), as Italo-German forces threatened Britain's hold over Egypt and the Suez Canal, as Japanese–American relations deteriorated over China and Tokyo's threats to European colonies in South and Southeast Asia – the President of the United States, Franklin D. Roosevelt, and Great Britain's Prime Minister, Winston S. Churchill, met aboard warships anchored in Placentia Bay, Newfoundland. On 14 August 1941, the two leaders authorised a press release following their secret four-day meeting. After brief references to supply talks came a vaguely foreboding mention of 'the dangers to world civilisation' posed by Hitler and his allies; the closest thing Churchill could get to what he wanted from a cautious Roosevelt – a promise to join the fray.

There then followed a 'joint declaration' that, to the pleasure of some and the dismay of others, served for the duration of the war as the fundamental public statement of Anglo-American war-aims (surely a curious action for a non-belligerent like the United States). Whatever the details of the drafting of the Atlantic Charter, as it quickly came to be called,[1] it was the kind of catch-phrase public statement that would not go away, even if Churchill and Roosevelt had so wished.

The Atlantic Charter, whatever the niceties of its phrasing, boiled down to four goals: first, popular self-determination for all peoples, which included denying any territorial gains for its sponsors. No exceptions were noted, although shortly afterwards both Britain and the Soviet Union exempted themselves – Britain, fearing the Charter would apply to its overseas Empire; the Russians fearing the same for its 'near abroad'. The second goal was protection of basic human freedoms. FDR had already identified

* My sincere thanks to the conferees and to Mark Stoler (University of Vermont), John A. Thompson (St Catherine's College, Cambridge), and Keith Sainsbury (University of Reading) for their most helpful comments, and to the Rutgers University Research Council for its support of my research.

what he called the Four Freedoms. 'Freedom from want' and 'from fear' were specifically mentioned in the Atlantic Charter in clauses that also spoke of social security and of people 'dwelling in safety within their own boundaries'; the other two, 'freedom of worship' plus 'freedom of speech' and information, were, according to Roosevelt, implied.[2] The third of the Charter's goals was economic liberalism – 'access, on equal terms, to the trade and the raw materials of the world', to use the words of the document; and the fourth, 'establishment of a wider and permanent system of general security' that rested primarily on disarmament. Self-determination, economic liberalism, the Four Freedoms, and an international organisation became shorthand for the four broad categories.[3]

In one sense the Charter was *sui generis* – begotten by specific historical events and designed to cope with a situation that existed in August 1941 and at no other time. The Charter was Roosevelt's suggestion and came as a surprise to Churchill, but the Prime Minister had no objections to the general idea.[4] After all, his purpose was to get the United States and Great Britain 'all mixed up together', and it was but a short step from a joint declaration of war-aims to a joint declaration of war.

Getting the United States into the war against Germany was Churchill's basic goal, for the survival of Great Britain as an independent state depended on such an alliance – given what we now *know* and what Churchill *sensed* about Hitler. The German attack on the Soviet Union had given the British some breathing-space, but Churchill and his generals had no faith in the ability of the Russians to withstand Hitler's onslaught. Their vague promises of aid to Stalin were made on the assumption that large-scale deliveries would never be necessary.[5]

Because Churchill and his aides were convinced that the collapse of Soviet resistance would be quickly followed by an invasion of Britain, the Government had only two possible responses – negotiate with Hitler, or bring in the Americans. Even the earlier pathetic schemes of the Duke of Windsor (one of which had him suggesting that if FDR called for peace the Duke would follow with a statement of support, a move Windsor claimed would 'start a revolution in England and force peace')[6] were based on the assumption that the United States would not enter the war – at least not in time to save Britain. Whatever the meandering thoughts of men like Halifax about the potential necessity of a new appeasement of Germany, their fears were based not on some exaggerated fear of an alliance with the United States but on Neville Chamberlain's long-held conviction that the Americans were all talk and no action. They will 'somehow fade out & leave us to carry all the blame & the odium', he once wrote his sister.[7]

Thus the Atlantic Conference, the first real Churchill–Roosevelt meeting, as well as the Charter it bred, served the mutual purpose of publicly allying the two leaders and, therefore, moving their nations closer together. For

Churchill and his colleagues at that juncture, that was *the* British war-aim.

In a crude broadbrush way, the Second World War consisted of three different struggles. Two were offensive – the Red Army against Hitler on the European continent, and the Americans against Japan in the Pacific. But those two campaigns depended, politically and militarily, on the first Allied victory of the war – Great Britain's fight to survive.

Survival seemed easier when war first began in September 1939. Hitler's attack on Poland did not directly threaten Britain, and Chamberlain and his Cabinet had high hopes of keeping the Italians at least neutral, if not making them an ally. Scandinavian and Low Country neutrality likewise provided what proved a deceptive sense of security, although neither Germany nor Great Britain had much respect for that status, as their opposing attacks on Norway illustrated. But Chamberlain, staunchly supported by then First Lord of the Admiralty Churchill, hoped for the collapse of Hitler's regime and rejected Hitler's proposals for negotiations. The Chamberlain Government's war-aims were straightforward – the restoration of the *status quo*, whatever the tactics and strategies.[8]

The stunning collapse of France in June 1940 along with the entry of Italy into the war on Germany's side changed all that. From then until the Pearl Harbor attack on 7 December 1941, Churchill, by then Prime Minister, and his government sought to replace their French ally with the United States. Given the military situation – with Germany and its allies in control of almost all of Europe and North Africa, and threatening the Suez Canal and the eastern Mediterranean – British war-aims leading up to the Atlantic Conference were starkly simple: survive, and bring in the Americans to create a glimmer of hope for victory. Considerations of empire, economics and political equality were luxuries that only survival and some degree of victory could provide. Some in Britain were less sanguine and muttered about negotiations with Germany, although fully comprehending the significance of that alternative will remain difficult for as long as the British Government refuses to open records that some have suggested may implicate prominent (even Royal?) persons and families.[9]

For Churchill, the process of creating an American alliance was painfully, even frighteningly, slow. When, in 1941 he heard of the President's desire to meet, the Prime Minister wishfully assumed deliverance was at hand, commenting that Roosevelt would not have called for the meeting unless he had an important move in mind.[10]

But for Roosevelt, the important move was to make haste slowly. Whatever his thoughts about the appropriate US military role in the war, he wanted firm and overwhelming American support, in Congress and the public, for any formal steps. He had taken that approach with the Lend-Lease Act six months earlier, and was determined to follow the same successful political strategy. In that sense, the Atlantic Charter was aimed at the US Congress and public. The long debate over aid to Britain had invariably boiled down to fears that the United States would end up fighting to protect the British Empire; and the conviction that American interests were not threatened by Germany. Typical of the rhetoric was a sarcastic proposal from one Member of Congress, a professional Irishman by the name of Michael Sweeney, for new words to the patriotic song, 'God Bless America':

> God save America from British rule:
> Stand beside her and guide her
> From the schemers who would make of her a fool.
> From Lexington to Yorktown,
> From blood-stained Valley Forge.
> God save America
> From a king named George.[11]

It was a delicate dance for FDR: too slow and Hitler would cut in and steal his partner. Too fast and the Congressional chaperons would stop the music and make him go home and stay there!

The Atlantic Charter neatly met Roosevelt's need for careful manoeuvring to create the image of Anglo-American accord without opening the Administration to charges of being manipulated by the British. Clauses calling for self-determination aimed clearly at the British Empire, regardless of Churchill's later denials. Calls for free trade promised access to the supposedly closed markets of the Empire and Commonwealth, thus genuflecting in the direction of traditional (if often inconsistent) American support for economic liberalism. Each was aimed at quieting American fears that the British had duped Roosevelt into protecting Britain and the Empire with American lives.

But the Charter was not just a limited response to the situation that existed in 1941. For the Americans, it was always much more than a mere short-term tactic in Roosevelt's campaign to help the British. The Atlantic Charter could not have surprised anyone familiar with American history and foreign policy. Economic liberalism, basic freedoms, and self-determination were causes and principles as old as the American Revolution. Some sort of international system to promote peace had gained increasing acceptance in the United States during the twentieth century, and popularity or at least notoriety with Woodrow Wilson's proposal for a League of Nations.[12] The Charter was mostly old wine in a new bottle, with just a taste of newer-vintage nationalism.

Whatever the lofty principles of the Atlantic Charter, FDR leavened them with practicality a week later. During a dinner at Hyde Park with guests who included the Duke of Kent, Eleanor Roosevelt, and Joseph Lash, the President called for 'disarmament by armament', meaning that the US and Britain would (according to Belle Willard Roosevelt's notes) 'have to police the entire world – not on sanction basis but in trust'. Overestimating Britain's strength, Roosevelt predicted: 'There will be complete economic and commercial and boundary liberty, but America and England will have to maintain the peace.'

The concept that security required only political control over 'boundaries', thus separating economic and cultural matters from what we now call geopolitics, would resurface consistently in Roosevelt's thinking, culminating in his unsuccessful efforts to broker a settlement in Eastern Europe that limited the Soviet sphere of influence to politics. It was a distinction that listeners and aides either failed to comprehend or refused to accept. Eleanor Roosevelt warned that the concept 'is fraught with danger. You have more faith in human nature than I have. Even Anglo-Saxon races will become drunk with power and will use this power to bring economic pressure on the smaller nations for the things they want.'[13] But FDR never abandoned his belief in the practical necessity for a trusteeship of international policemen – though the number grew to three and then four.

In fact, Roosevelt expanded the number of police even as he spoke to his dinner guests. In the weeks before the Atlantic Conference, Roosevelt had begun to recognise that the war would change the status of the Soviet Union. His belief that the USSR would hold out against the Germans, already clear from his reaction to Harry Hopkins' visit to Moscow two weeks before the Newfoundland meeting, surfaced during the same dinner when the President followed his prediction of an Anglo-American trusteeship with the caution that the Russians would also be a factor. This is the 'tenth week' [of Soviet resistance to the German attack] was FDR's comment to his guests at the start of the meal.[14]

Only four months after Churchill and Roosevelt met, the Japanese put the Atlantic Charter in a new perspective. Their attack on the American naval base at Pearl Harbor meant Roosevelt no longer had to do his delicate dance, while Churchill no longer had to worry about bringing the Americans into the war. Nor, for that matter, did either leader by then have to worry about the Russians holding out at least through the winter of 1941–42, though that is a different story.

Whatever the accompanying rhetoric, the Atlantic Charter was not handed by a god to a prophet, despite Roosevelt's likening it to the Ten Commandments.[15] It was an organic political document that represented the attitudes of the societies that put it together, not a set of immutable principles. Treating the Charter only in its 1941 incarnation ignores a truism – that war-aims evolve and often change as the war progresses. That is true of tangible geopolitical goals; witness the opportunistic shift in Stalin's ambitions as the Red Army shifted from fighting for survival to pursuing unconditional surrender. It is likewise true for the kind of broader, structural goals set out in the Atlantic Charter.

Bureaucrats in London and Washington had begun postwar planning studies early in the war (American State Department officials may not keep proper minutes, but contrary to European mythology, they did and do try to plan ahead).[16] But the public cornerstone for that planning – the Atlantic Charter – had evolved by mid-war. The starting-point for planning by Secretary of State Cordell Hull and Foreign Secretary Anthony Eden for their October 1943 meeting in Moscow with their Soviet counterpart V. M. Molotov and his master, Joseph Stalin, was not 1941, but where things stood after two years of war, of talks, and of rethinking. That development, often lost in histories busy recreating the crucial military events of 1942–43, illustrates both the tenacity and flexibility of the ideas that underlay the Atlantic Charter. The process could be traced step-by-step from the early Eden–Stalin negotiations in December 1941, through the ongoing Churchill–Roosevelt conferences and correspondence, in the Maisky–Eden discussions in London,[17] Molotov's visit to London and Washington in May–June 1942, Roosevelt's comments as sent to Churchill via Oliver Lyttelton in the summer of 1942, the Churchill–Stalin meeting in August 1942, the Churchill–Roosevelt confrontation over India early in 1942: the list is long, the book would be longer.[18]

Better to take a short-cut designed to lead to an understanding of just how British and American leaders retained, changed, and adjusted their thinking about the Atlantic Charter; even while the Charter remained through war's end a guiding star rather than a law, to use Churchill's figure of speech.[19] We hardly need reminding that a guiding star – an assumption, a principle – is far more important and long-lasting than legalistic phrases designed either to implement or evade the broad concept.

In March 1943, Anthony Eden travelled to Washington for meetings with President Roosevelt and senior American officials. Typically, Winston Churchill took credit for initiating the trip, although he then ignored the talks in his memoirs, mentioning them only in terms of ever-improving Anglo-American relations. Eden gave credit to FDR, but the invitation may well have been in response to hints from the Foreign Secretary himself.[20]

Whosoever the initiative and whatever the channel, Eden's visit to Washington was, as historian-participant Herbert Feis perceptively put it over thirty-five years ago, 'the first review of war aims'.[21] The talks neither changed nor announced anything. But the visit remains a convenient, even instructive, episode; a bit like stretching your legs on a long train-trip during a brief stop somewhere short of your destination. Looking beyond the platform you can get a sense of where you have come from and where you are going, and even something of what you may expect to find once you arrive.

From the outset both the Americans and the British worked to prevent undue speculation that the visit presaged a major agreement or new initiative. Roosevelt was particularly concerned that Stalin not interpret the mission as an Anglo-American attempt to make political decisions without consulting the Soviets, going so far as to remove any mention of 'politics' from the press announcement of the visit. But however crucial matters of economics and monetary policy were, Eden was there to talk politics, not banking.[22]

Eden, who developed his own agenda for the talks, focused on preparing to discuss the postwar settlement in Europe.[23] Well aware of Roosevelt's insistence on the great powers acting as postwar policemen – the number had reached four by 1943 – Eden planned to force the President to confront the practical difficulties they would face in chaotic postwar Europe. He still believed what he had written a year earlier, that Stalin was 'a political descendant of Peter the Great rather than of Lenin'. Eden did not think Soviet leaders actively planned for the spread of international Communism, but even if they did, 'if we are to win the war and to maintain the peace, we must work with Stalin and we cannot work with him unless we are successful in allaying some at least of his suspicion'.[24]

By early 1943 Roosevelt was involved in ongoing discussions of postwar problems – discussions that presaged the talks with Eden, sometimes almost word-for-word. The most striking assumption of the President and his advisers was their perception of Great-Britain-as-rival. Agreement on the primacy of the four major powers (the US, Great Britain, the USSR, China) on all international committees was, in large part, designed to prevent the British from dominating those groups by insisting on membership for Canada and Australia. Moreover, noted Hopkins, the fact that the US would displace Britain as the nation with the largest major merchant marine would prove 'a powerful weapon at the Peace Table'. Roosevelt repeatedly said he wanted to avoid the appearance of ganging-up on the Russians – but he also feared the British Empire would gang-up on the United States. That image of a powerful, London-led combine, however unrealistic it may seem in retrospect, suggests the distortion created by Cold War perspectives on Second World War events.[25]

That is not to say that Roosevelt failed to perceive the outlines of the problems posed by growing Soviet strength. The Soviet victory at Stalingrad in February 1943, a month before Eden's visit, drove home the reality that Stalin no longer needed the Anglo-Americans in order to survive. In fact, the British and Americans needed the Red Army to achieve the total victory they had just proclaimed at the Casablanca Conference as their goal.[26] During the President's regular meetings ('weekly' claimed one participant in March 1943) with State Department officials tasked with planning for the postwar world, he frequently worried that 'he didn't know what to do about Russia'. He disliked what he called Churchill's plan for rearming France in order to balance Soviet strength, yet contradictorily took notice of a strategy set forth in a letter from William C. Bullitt, an old adviser and troubleshooter who had fallen into disfavour in the White House.

The Bullitt proposal, in the words of one State Department planner, 'was based on distrust of the Soviet Union, to the effect that all of Europe west of Russia should be organised as a single state and heavily armed so as to actually oppose the westward march of Russia'. Although the President 'actually praised' the concept during talks with members of the State Department Subcommittee on Postwar Political Problems in late February 1943, he did so in the context of an ongoing attempt to weigh the effect of a disarmed France and Germany if the Soviet Union was armed and uncooperative. When Roosevelt indicated his belief that only the four Great Powers (thus excluding France) should have anything larger than rifles, the subcommittee minutes noted the inconsistency – praise for the Bullitt scheme while disarming France – but no one appears to have confronted the President with the contradiction.[27]

FDR saw his four policemen in part as trustees for countries not ready for full independence, and had some specific nominations. The Pacific islands held by the Japanese (usually League of Nations mandates), Korea, and Indo-China were his favourite examples – but the idea tended to be Roosevelt's catch-all answer for any difficult territorial problem, as in the case of the Croatians and Serbs.[28]

But the Great Powers were to be much more than just trustees for a few problem areas – their fundamental trust was the peace of the entire world. It made sense to have an international forum for 'full discussion, but for management there seems no reason why the principle of trusteeship in private affairs should not be extended to the international field', he had remarked shortly after the Atlantic conference. That perception of overarching responsibility inevitably translated into full authority for the world's trustees. There was no need for a vast peace conference, he informed State Department planners, because peace questions would be handled by the heads of the four great powers and technical experts.[29]

Along with the concept of Great Power authority came the question of how the Big Four would perform their role. Again, no one tried to pin the President down on the question so his colleagues and advisers had to guess at his meaning – just like the historians who followed. Those guesses fell between Cordell Hull's internationalist approach and the narrow spheres of influence that Churchill instinctively preferred. Under-Secretary of State Sumner Welles' emphasis on American leadership in the Western Hemisphere probably came closest to FDR's thinking, even though Hull thought he had talked Roosevelt out of his preference for regionalism. The issue would not be joined until the Moscow Foreign Minister's Conference in October 1943, but the vagueness of Roosevelt's position would leave Eden as puzzled as Roosevelt's aides.[30]

At that point, 12 March 1943 to be precise, Anthony Eden arrived in Washington for talks with Roosevelt, Hull and other presidential advisers.[31]

The usual ceremonials went along with the visit. During an early meeting between Roosevelt and Eden, General George Marshall (US Army Chief of Staff) suggested taking the Secretary to visit some Army training sites. The three-day trip brought Eden to various Gulf Coast facilities and then on to Fort Bragg in North Carolina, after which he was briefly shanghaied by the Navy. Each stop invariably included the playing of 'God Save the King', once prompting a *sotto voce* whisper behind Eden: 'Why the heck do we salute at "My Country 'Tis of Thee?"'[32]

Each of the parties sat down with a set of attitudes and ideas that changed little over the course of the formal and informal talks. Nonetheless, the discussions did exactly what both parties intended – set forth their areas of agreement and delineated where they disagreed: a convenient way-station in the evolution of war-aims, and the Atlantic Charter.

Two of the Charter's broad goals – economic liberalism and basic freedoms – made only cameo or indirect appearances during the talks. Discussions of refugee issues, certainly matters that fell under the rubric of Roosevelt's Four Freedoms, found politics prevailing. Eden said the British were prepared to allow 60 000 more Jews into Palestine, despite Arab objections, but doubted there was sufficient shipping and expressed fears that German agents would infiltrate the refugees. Hull and the Americans mumbled about a few thousand refugees – not all Jews – being resettled here and there. The Foreign Secretary claimed that the principal problem was Jews in the Axis-occupied countries, and then, with obvious relief, they all referred the matter to the upcoming Evian Conference. Freedom as a gift from the world's trustees, the Great Powers, had its limitations.[33]

The other 'freedom' issue related to remarks by both Roosevelt and Hull that implied a willingness, even eagerness, to suppress free speech. The Secretary of State spent a good deal of time explaining to Eden the importance of what would eventually become the Fulbright–Connally resolution which committed Congress to an internationalist tack after the war. But Hull's lecture ended on a note vaguely ominous for freedom of speech. Like Roosevelt, he viewed so-called isolationists as dangerous. Moreover, they both recognised that jealousy and criticism of Britain lay at the root of much of the opposition to internationalism. The United States should not be fighting to preserve Britain's Empire, the argument ran. Hull's suggestion, made on two occasions to Eden, was to work together at 'keeping down' such anti-British sentiments. Perhaps, Hull later wondered, the Big Three ought to 'tighten up their policies' to prevent their citizens, 'especially those coming under governmental attention and control' from criticising the allies. The Administration had done its best to prevent public discussion of the problem of India, said Hull, and perhaps Eden could think about some sort of statement on colonialism that would have a calming effect. Perhaps Hull's true purpose was decolonisation, but stifling debate was hardly in keeping with basic freedoms, even if managing the news fitted in neatly with Roosevelt's notion of some sort of international news broadcasting system.[34]

Even though Hull played a major role in the talks with Eden, economic liberalism made surprisingly few appearances. Occasional references to planned international conferences on postwar trade in food, agriculture and other raw materials never developed into substantive discussions. Postwar civil aviation and international shipping rights came in for somewhat lengthier treatment, but again nothing significant emerged – possibly because all understood how far apart the two parties were, possibly because they were scheduled for later talks, possibly because Eden's own interests focused on geo-politics.[35]

The other two Atlantic Charter principles – self-determination and international organisation for peace – held centre-stage. They were, as things turned out, joined at the hip. Roosevelt never dropped his commitment to eliminating colonialism, although practicality forced him to adjust his timetable.[36] When he spoke to Eden of trusteeships for Japan's Pacific islands, for French Indo-China, and Portuguese Timor, Eden knew the President meant all European empires. The Englishman listened, but said little. Hull outlined an American plan regarding decolonisation and trusteeships and concluded that Eden was 'favorably impressed by the proposal'. But one suspects that the Foreign Secretary merely drawled a very British, non-committal 'right', so as to avoid open disagreement. In any event, the matter was put off until the Foreign Office had time to study the American scheme.[37]

But the decolonisation of European empires was only one aspect of self-determination. With the tide stopped and about to turn on the Russian front, the issue of European frontiers could no longer be evaded. As Woodrow Wilson had found at Paris, Europe's boundary questions came burdened with irreconcilable pieces of historical baggage. At the same time, achieving Roosevelt's and Eden's dreams of persuading Stalin to be a cooperative participant in the postwar world required that the Soviet leader feel secure, satisfied, and convinced of Anglo-American reliability. In other words, self-determination for India was one thing – Britain's stake in postwar cooperation with the United States was too crucial to jeopardise. Moreover the colonial boundaries seemed clear (even if that too proved deceptive). But self-determination for Lithuanians, Latvians, and Estonians – not to mention large groups of Poles, Bulgarians, Finns and Romanians was quite a different story for Stalin had made clear from the outset that his minimal territorial demands encompassed many such peoples.

Yet, as Sumner Welles told Eden, 'the real decisions should be made by the United States, Great Britain, Russia and China, who would be the powers for many years to come that would have to police the world'. Obviously self-determination would be a gift from the Big Four, assuming they could agree on the details. Little surprise then, that Roosevelt calmly proposed the

Curzon Line as Poland's eastern boundary, relegated the Baltic states to Moscow's tender mercies (though with some uneasiness about the public reaction), and left Finland to work out its own territorial problems with the Soviet Union – knowing full well that the Russians would impose their will.[38]

One can hear echoes of Woodrow Wilson's sly suggestion to the Austro-Hungarian government in 1917 that, if it negotiated a separate peace, it might expect to keep some of the *older* portions of its empire. As Sir David Owen asserted in 1993, regarding what had been Yugoslavia, 'self-determination is a qualified right'. The tricky question is, and was, who defines the qualifications? Charles de Gaulle discerned FDR's scheme when he concluded that the President believed France 'a little child unable to look out and fend for itself and that, in such a case, a court would appoint a trustee to do the necessary'. Roosevelt's assurances that the Great Powers were 'trustees' for the rest of the world carried no weight with nationalists from Korea to Karelia.[39]

The President's approach to postwar frontiers seemed so cavalier as to resemble someone playing a board game in which boundaries were changed and moved at the whim of the player or a roll of the dice. Other times he seemed more prescient than his guest, a representative of the presumably experienced and sophisticated (and hence 'un'naive) British Foreign Office. Roosevelt's major excursion into promoting national self-determination was also his most accurate historical prediction. He had long been concerned about keeping 'the Croats away from the throats of the Serbs and vice versa',[40] and proposed to Eden that they and the Slovenes be set up as separate nations. As with the Baltic states, the sugar coating was plebiscites – as many as necessary to get the right answer, which was different in each case.

At the same time the President advocated creation of a many-humped camel like Wallonia (a mythical creation to be made up of the Walloon parts of France, Belgium, and Luxembourg plus even the Ruhr and perhaps Alsace-Lorraine). The scheme reflected FDR's disdain for France, but in a broader sense he and Hull, like most Americans not recent immigrants from Europe, considered European identity and boundary squabbles 'piddling issues', to use Hull's unfortunate description of the question of Polish frontiers.[41] Self-determination was, for the Americans, a matter of practicality, not principle.

If self-determination meant independence for the Balts and the establishment of an anti-Soviet government in Warsaw, then how to avoid the obvious? The Stalingrad battle had demonstrated the likelihood of Red Army occupation of the territory Stalin demanded. What recourse was left to London and Washington? Military confrontation was no option, at least not with Anglo-American forces still struggling in North Africa and fifteen months away from an invasion of Western Europe. More to the point, what hope for peace if the United States and Britain chose to confront the Russians in the pre-atom bomb age?[42] Then there was Japan waiting in the wings. What Roosevelt and Eden agreed, whatever their differences on tactics, was to make the best of the situation. Rather than play dog-in-the-manger toward the expansion of Soviet power in Eastern Europe, they opted to promote long-term cooperation.

Much of the story of Eden's talks with the Americans is the story of their attempts to wrestle with that dilemma of growing Soviet strength. Their discussions were tentative, and even their points of agreement were only sketched out – but in the process they illustrated the dimensions of the problems. Eden got to the heart of the matter at the outset, at another dinner with the President and Hopkins the night after their initial get-together. According to Hopkins' notes, the Foreign Secretary flatly stated that the Soviet Union was 'our most difficult problem', echoing FDR's earlier comments to State Department planners. From that starting-point a whole series of subjects popped up – at that dinner meeting and afterwards – but each invariably returned to the central question: what would the Russians do?[43]

Historically most intriguing was the issue of physical presence in Europe at war's end. Twice Roosevelt, and particularly Hopkins, expressed deep concern that Anglo-American forces might be no further than Italy when Hitler's resistance collapsed. Hopkins feared anarchy or communism in Germany unless Britain and the United States acted promptly.[44] In one sense that was caution, not some sort of nascent or closet-Cold Warriorism. Anarchy concerned Hopkins and Roosevelt as much as communism. Nor is there anything anti-Soviet or confrontational about wanting to prevent the imposition of a communist regime in the chaos following a German surrender. Roosevelt and Hopkins supported elections and were unafraid that such elections would bring in a communist government.* The model they had before them was the Russian Revolution where a small band of dedicated revolutionaries, taking advantage of the collapse of Tsarist authority, took control. The fear was not so much that the Russians would do that in Germany, but more that some Germans would use the same methods.

In another sense, their concern over the positioning of forces mirrors the Bullitt proposal for confronting the Soviet Union lest it expand into central Europe and beyond. That Roosevelt even brought it up with Eden only illustrated that he still 'didn't know what to do about Russia'. Eden, committed to working with the Russians, responded a bit wishfully that Stalin hoped for cooperation in Europe since the Soviet Union was not prepared to take

---

* The Cold War was a confrontation with the USSR in which ideology exacerbated suspicions and raised the stakes. Without that ideological component, the Cold War is inexplicable. But an equally essential element in the Cold War confrontation was Soviet and American power. Without that component, suppression by the western capitalist democracies of what Gabriel Kolko grandly calls 'The Left' would surely have occurred, but it would not have been in a war that left hundreds of thousands dead in its wake – as did the by-proxy confrontations of the Cold War, from Korea to Vietnam to Afghanistan; Kolko, *The Politics of War* (Vintage edn; New York, 1968).

responsibility for postwar Europe – a reference perhaps to the burdens of reconstruction.[45] Roosevelt was cautious – hence the military's HADRIAN/RANKIN plans for quick action in the contingency of a German collapse. But his instructions to Hull to discuss the matter with both the British and the Russians, followed by the mission of Joseph Davies to Moscow in May 1943 indicate that cooperation remained his priority. Caution is not confrontation.[46]

The issue of postwar France was both less and more than a matter of finding a partner for Britain so as to balance Soviet strength in the policing of Europe. For the fifty years since the Second World War, popular wisdom has been that Roosevelt and, to a lesser degree, Churchill based their wartime policy for postwar France on their personal antagonism to Charles de Gaulle. Certainly De Gaulle's memoirs encourage that view. But that is, to put it bluntly, nonsense. De Gaulle was, as far as Churchill and Roosevelt were concerned, an arrogant, uncoĢperative ingrate. But Anglo-American planning for postwar France was based on interests and realities, not personalities.[47] Roosevelt not only believed France was a second-class power, but remained convinced that Franco-German quarrels lay at the root of much of Europe's inability to maintain peace. Churchill tended to agree, but also had to face the firm conviction of people like Eden that an Anglo-French entente was necessary if Britain was to play its proper role in Europe as one of FDR's policemen. The matter of recognition of a French provisional regime (i.e. recognition of De Gaulle) was, in itself, minor. But the role of France as part of a power structure that would not only restrain Germany but also balance the Soviet Union was, for Eden, crucial.

The British reaction to Roosevelt's attitude towards France was succinctly and sensibly summed up in a British Foreign Office minute attached to Eden's report: 'The most unsatisfactory feature of a conversation of this sort is the impossibility of telling how far the President is throwing flies or thinking aloud and how far he is expressing a considered opinion of what the U.S.A. will in actual fact be ready to do.' Roosevelt's suggestions for France (the internationalisation of Dakar and Bizerte as well as what one British official labelled 'the rape of Indo-China') would, the argument went, permanently poison Anglo-French relations.[48]

One other major issue appeared and reappeared throughout the Eden mission and, while the matter had its own dynamics, it affected the question of the Soviet Union's attitude in the postwar world. By 1943, Roosevelt had decided that China should be one of the four policemen. His commitment to great-power leadership assumed, or hoped for, self-restraint – despite Eleanor Roosevelt's doubts. Nevertheless, in East Asia, FDR worried that the Russians might again take up their traditional efforts to expand into Manchuria, China and Korea. That concern helped shore up his commitment to have China be one of the four policemen.[49] The question the President faced was a variation on the one posed in his talks with State Department planners: what would happen if an unarmed France and Germany faced an armed and uncooperative Soviet Union? According to Eden, Roosevelt believed China had neither imperialist nor aggressive designs and could, in fact, act as a 'useful counterpoise' to the Russians.

Eden was, himself, less sanguine about Chinese intentions (perhaps with Hong Kong in mind), saying he 'did not much like the idea of the Chinese running up and down the Pacific'. More to the point, he invariably raised questions about whether Chiang Kai-shek would survive the civil war that would follow Japan's defeat.[50] Whatever Eden's scepticism, Roosevelt intended China eventually to be a player in the postwar world.

Two issues that later took on great significance – the structure of the United Nations Organisation and the disposition of Germany – engendered only brief discussion. Eden did not dispute Roosevelt's basic assumption that any international organisation would be only as good as the Great Power cooperation that went with it. The President occasionally rambled on about three levels of representation: a general forum for all nations to 'blow off steam' (Eden's phrase), and a council of a dozen or so to take action on certain (smaller?) issues. But Great-Power authority remained his bottom line. As for Germany, the Foreign Secretary agreed that it should be broken up, though he remarked on Hull's reluctance to agree with that and did not dispute Halifax's concern that forcing dismemberment on a reluctant German populace might create the same sense of grievance that had followed the First World War. That exchange was repeated a couple of times, but no substantive discussion took place.[51]

The mission ended with all parties agreed, privately and publicly, that they had conducted what diplomats call 'a useful exchange of views'. Churchill expressed delight after British officials reported that the mission and Eden's performance before American newspaper reporters had been very well received.[52] The President held a post-mission press conference in which he emphasised the 'exploratory' nature of the conversations, sliding quietly past the major areas of disagreement – trusteeships, decolonisation and French political reconstruction. As he spoke, economic liberalism, in the guise of various international conferences on food, agriculture and raw materials, made a vigorous reappearance despite playing so small a role in the actual talks. The purpose of the mission, said FDR, was 'to take time by the forelock' and be better prepared for future conferences. Planning ahead for the future would prevent another Versailles débâcle, when 'everybody was rushing around grabbing things . . . and throwing them into suitcases'. Some were not needed at all, and some needed things were left behind.[53]

The Eden mission talks demonstrate that Roosevelt understood well the effect of self-interest combined with power. His absolute insistence on the authority and leadership (he would have rejected the word 'rule') of the

Great Powers expressed that understanding. Does that then validate brushing off the Atlantic Charter as 'little more than a declaration . . . against sin'? Was the Charter nothing more than a fatuous exercise in overblown rhetoric? Such sarcastic dismissals can, of course, represent the sincere disillusion of the idealist, caused by the failure of the two leaders to implement the Charter in its pristine 1941 form. But for the most part the disparagement stems from the conviction that the Charter was both un-Realistic and unrealistic (that is, not in the Realist/*realpolitik* tradition and also impractical). But most despicable of all, it was 'Wilsonian nonsense'.[54] And 'Wilsonianism', that catch-all label for anything less than untrammelled power politics, was dangerous daydreaming.

The Eden trip to Washington suggests otherwise. For the Americans the Atlantic Charter was more than merely a sermon against sin. It was a call for reform, for the New World Order – something that has punctuated American foreign policy before and since. Every nation-state equates its interests with its ideals. For the United States to pursue economic liberalism may have promised tangible economic benefits. But Americans had believed in economic liberalism since their Revolution – was that merely two centuries of cynicism? The decolonisation of European empires could, and sometimes did, enhance American power and interests. Shall we then conclude that Franklin Roosevelt and all his predecessors plotted to 'succeed John Bull'? The United Nations Organisation became, for over a decade after the Second World War, an instrument of American foreign policy. Does that mean internationalism in the United States was just a ploy?[55] *Post hoc, ergo propter hoc*?

Nor did Eden and the British cynically dismiss the Charter. A Foreign Office memorandum, 'The United Nations Plan for Organising Peace', distributed a few months after the Eden mission, opened with a striking endorsement: 'The principles embodied in the Atlantic Charter will be the basis of any international world order after the war.' The paper went on to warn that 'stability' and 'world order' (i.e. peace) were possible only if 'the World Powers are prepared to accept the responsibilities of leadership *within* the United Nations'. That required great-power agreement and a willingness 'to take joint action to enforce it'. The alternative would be 'the World Powers, each with its circle of client States, facing each other in a rivalry which may merge imperceptibly into hostility'.[56] One can hear Franklin Roosevelt applauding from the wings.

Roosevelt's expressions of concern over both Soviet expansion and British imperialism have prompted some to suggest that he tried to balance the other major nations off against each other in order to create a world in which the United States was the *only* Great Power.[57] That assumes a degree of manipulative long-term planning so foreign to FDR's nature that it serves as a warning to historians against playing Sherlock Holmes and trying to deduce goals and means solely by assessing results. Eden's mission came at a time when British officials like Eden, Duff Cooper and Alexander Cadogan believed the United States would return to isolationism. FDR feared the same. They were all wrong, while, ironically, Winston Churchill was correct in presuming the United States would continue to play a role in Europe and the world – though no one even suspected how great a role that would turn out to be. Perhaps the gibe of William A. Williams, that Hitler caused the Cold War, is correct. But if so, does the Soviet Union then get credit for unleashing American globalism?[58]

Roosevelt, Churchill, and Stalin all worked to establish spheres of influence in Europe and elsewhere. But to argue simply that the postwar spheres of influence were already in place as of the Eden mission exaggerates to the point of distortion, making the only sensible choice for the Anglo-Americans to confront the USSR early and often. A sphere of influence meant something very different to each of the Big Three, both tactically (i.e. as to specific boundaries) and conceptually (i.e. how the scheme would operate). So different, in fact, that Roosevelt rejected the phrase 'spheres of influence', choosing instead 'the Four Policemen'.[59]

If FDR were the Cold Warrior some would make him out to be, why did he not take a tougher line? If the British, including Churchill, were so concerned about Soviet expansion, why did they continue to push the Italian campaign instead of getting Allied forces into western Europe at the earliest opportunity?[60] If, on the other hand, Roosevelt was so naive about Soviet intentions, how to account for his concern, oft-expressed to Eden, that the Russians posed the greatest problem for the peace? Perhaps the most naive notion of all is that confrontation with the Soviet Union in 1943 would have meant self-determination for Poles and Balts in 1945.[61]

It is more plausible to conjecture that such a confrontation would have prolonged the war and resulted in the Germans gaining the leverage needed to negotiate – first with the Russians, then with the Anglo-Americans. When Harry Truman quipped in 1941 that the United States should help Germany if the Russians were winning, and Russia if Germany was winning, he reversed reality – for one to lose, the other had to win. Truman quickly added he did not want Germany victorious under any circumstances, a coda that FDR took as gospel. What Truman failed to recognise was that survival (victory of a sort) for both Nazi Germany and the Soviet Union was also possible.

At that presidential press conference on 30 March, Roosevelt, obviously concerned lest the Russians think they were being bypassed, made a point of mentioning ongoing and future British and American talks with Soviet officials. He then closed with a comment directed at those who had begun to raise doubts about cooperating with the Soviet Union after the war. With militant optimism – a tactic in itself – FDR grandly proclaimed that, in the conferences to date, *all* the United Nations, not just the British, were 'about

95 percent together.' No one mentioned that the President had yet to meet Joseph Stalin.[62]

NOTES

1. According to Theodore A. Wilson, *The First Summit: Roosevelt and Churchill at Placentia Bay, 1941* (rev. edn; Lawrence, KS, 1991), p. 192, the *Daily Herald* (London) christened the declaration the Atlantic Charter. Some American newspapers pointed out the contradiction in the United States declaring war-aims while at peace; ibid., p. 199. Wilson's book is the standard treatment of the Atlantic Conference and Charter although additional details on the Charter's drafting can be found in the monographic literature. For example, see David Reynolds, *The Creation of the Anglo-American Alliance, 1937–1941: A Study in Competitive Co-operation* (Chapel Hill, 1982), pp. 257–60; and Douglas Brinkley and David Facey-Crowther (eds), *The Atlantic Charter* (New York, 1994).

2. Report to Congress, 21 August 1941, *The Public Papers and Addresses of Franklin Delano Roosevelt [PPA]*, Samuel I. Rosenman, ed. (13 vols; New York, 1938–50), 10, p. 334.

3. A convenient text of the Atlantic Charter is US Department of State, *Foreign Relations of the United States* (hereafter *FRUS*) (Washington, 1862– ), 1941, I, pp. 368–69; also Brinkley & Facey-Crowther (eds), *The Atlantic Charter*, pp. xvii–xviii.

4. There is no evidence in the Hopkins papers (Franklin D. Roosevelt Library [FDRL], Hyde Park, NY) or elsewhere to support Robert Sherwood's contention that presidential adviser Harry Hopkins had discussed the Atlantic Charter with Churchill during their trip together aboard the HMS *Prince of Wales* from Great Britain to Newfoundland *en route* to the Atlantic Conference; Sherwood, *Roosevelt and Hopkins* (rev. edn; Grosset & Dunlap–Universal Library edn, 1950), p. 350. FDR, apparently fearing a repeat of the secret treaties of the First World War, suggested to Churchill, a month before their meeting, that they make a broad public commitment to avoid postwar commitments relating to 'territories, populations or economics'. Warren F. Kimball (ed.), *Churchill & Roosevelt: The Complete Correspondence* (3 vols; Princeton, 1984), I, R-50x, p. 222.

5. See '"They Don't Come Out Where You Expect": Roosevelt Reacts to the German–Soviet War, 1941', in Warren F. Kimball, *The Juggler: Franklin Roosevelt as Wartime Statesman* (Princeton, 1991), pp. 21–41.

6. The Duke of Windsor's jejune plot is recounted in an Associated Press report of notes made by author Fulton Oursler of a December 1940 message he carried to Roosevelt from the Duke; *The Star-Ledger* (Newark, NJ), 15 November 1991.

7. As quoted in William R. Rock, *Chamberlain and Roosevelt* (Columbus, Ohio, 1988), p. 35.

8. Reynolds, *The Creation of the Anglo-American Alliance*, pp. 63–92, provides a succinct summary of British policy between September 1939 and May 1940. See also the evidence presented in John Charmley, *Churchill: The End of Glory* (London 1993), pp. 355–82.

9. See, for example, the speculations of John Costello in *Ten Days to Destiny:*

*The Secret Story of the Hess Peace Initiative and British Efforts to Strike a Deal with Hitler* (New York, 1991). The wisdom, nature, and importance of Churchill's motives for 'fighting on', are the subject of a continuing debate, although no one questions the vital importance of Britain's survival for the overall Allied war effort. The outline of the debate on Churchill's leadership and motives can be seen in John Charmley, *Churchill*, and in his essay in this collection; David Reynolds, 'Churchill and the British "Decision" to Fight On in 1940: Right Policy, Wrong Reasons', in R. Langhorne (ed.), *Diplomacy and Intelligence during the Second World War* (Cambridge, 1985), pp. 147–67; and Warren F. Kimball, 'Wheel Within a Wheel: Churchill, Roosevelt, and the Special Relationship', in Robert Blake and Wm Roger Louis (eds), *Churchill*, (Oxford, 1993), pp. 291–307.

10. Reynolds, *Creation of the Anglo-American Alliance*, p. 214.
11. As quoted in Warren F. Kimball, *'The Most Unsordid Act': Lend-Lease, 1939–1941* (Baltimore, 1969), p. 187.
12. I have elaborated on this in 'The Atlantic Charter: "With All Deliberate Speed,"' in Brinkley and Facey-Crowther, *The Atlantic Charter*. Leaders like ex-president William Howard Taft favoured creating an international organisation even while they opposed Wilson's League of Nations.
13. Belle Willard Roosevelt mss., Library of Congress (Washington, DC), 'Unfinished Notes', August 1941. Belle Roosevelt was the wife of Kermit Roosevelt, one of former President Theodore Roosevelt's sons.
14. Joseph P. Lash, *Roosevelt and Churchill, 1939–1941* (New York, 1976), p. 401.
15. FDR speech, Ottawa, Canada, 25 August 43, *PPA*, 12, pp. 368–9.
16. See US Department of State [Harley A. Notter], *Postwar Foreign Policy Preparation, 1939–1945* (Washington, 1950) [hereafter *PFPP*], and the archives of that planning process, 'Postwar Foreign Policy Preparation', available at the National Archives (Washington, DC), and on microform with a printed finding aid, a set of which is in the Rutgers University Library (New Brunswick, NJ): US Department of State, *Post World War II Foreign Policy Planning: State Department Records of Harley A. Notter* [microform] (Bethesda, MD, 1987) [hereafter Notter files], and US Department of State, *Post World War II Foreign Policy Planning: State Department Records of Harley A. Notter* [guide to the microfiche collection] (2 vols.; Bethesda, MD, 1987).
17. Roosevelt and Churchill met thirteen times during the war. Six of those meetings were before the autumn of 1943. Ivan Maisky was the Soviet Union's wartime Ambassador in the United Kingdom until his replacement in the summer of 1943.
18. Most of these meetings and conversations are covered in the standard literature. The exception is Roosevelt's conversation with Lyttelton which is mentioned in a memcon by Welles of a conversation with Halifax, 30 November 1942, *FRUS*, 1943, III, 1–2. The details of the talk summarised in David Dilks' commentary in *The Diaries of Sir Alexander Cadogan, 1938–1945* (New York, 1972), p. 506 [citing the Halifax diary for 28 August 1942]. According to Dilks, Roosevelt insisted on unconditional surrender, destruction of German military capabilities, international inspection to prevent Germany from rearming, and a US/USSR/UK international police force to which France and Poland could contribute, though they could not reconstitute their armies. Lyttelton's visit came after FDR had spoken to Molotov about the three or four policemen.
19. Winston S. Churchill, *Triumph and Tragedy* (Boston, 1953), p. 393.
20. Winston S. Churchill, *The Hinge of Fate* (Boston, 1950), p. 726; Anthony Eden, *The Reckoning* (Boston, 1965), p. 425. I have found nothing on the origins of

the mission in the Foreign Office archives or Eden's diaries and papers at the University of Birmingham Library.

21. Herbert Feis, *Churchill, Roosevelt, Stalin* (Princeton, 1957), p. 119.
22. These background details are taken from various documents in *FRUS*, 1943, III, pp. 1–9, and Llwellyn Woodward, *British Foreign Policy during the Second World War* (5 vols; London, 1970–76) V, pp. 21–31.
23. Churchill displayed surprisingly little interest in the visit; perhaps because he was ill, perhaps because of his reluctance to discuss postwar planning, perhaps because he considered Anglo-American relations his patch. On his illness and what little Churchill had to say about the mission, see Martin Gilbert, *Road to Victory* (Boston, 1986), pp. 340–63.
24. Eden to Edward Lord Halifax (British ambassador to the US), 22 January 1942, FO 954/29xc/100818, Public Record Office (PRO), Kew.
25. Sherwood, *Roosevelt and Hopkins*, pp. 707–8.
26. For a full discussion of this see Warren F. Kimball, 'Stalingrad und das Dilemma der amerikanisch–sowjetischen Beziehungen' in *Stalingrad. Ereignis-Wirkung-Symbol*/Im Auftrag des Militärgeschichtlichen Forschungsamtes, ed. Jürgen Förster (München & Zürich, 1992), pp. 327–49.
27. Roosevelt's meetings were usually with selected members of the Subcommittee on Political Problems – primarily Hull or Welles, Leo Pasvolsky, Norman Davis, Myron Taylor, and Isaiah Bowman; Notter, *PFPP*, pp. 92–3, 96–7; and the Notter files (microform), file 548-1 (a summary of contacts with the President).
28. Notter files (microform), 548-1, summary dated 18 March 1943 of a White House meeting on 22 February 1943.
29. Ibid. Roosevelt's remark was to Myron Taylor and is quoted in Robert C. Hilderbrand, *Dumbarton Oaks: The Origins of the United Nations and the Search for Postwar Security* (Chapel Hill and London, 1990), p. 16. Hilderbrand provides a cogent summary of postwar planning through 1943 on pp. 5–25.
30. My thinking on what Roosevelt meant is set forth in *The Juggler*. Lloyd Gardner's *Spheres of Influence: The Great Powers Partition Europe, from Munich to Yalta* (Chicago, 1993) argues that, despite Roosevelt's attempts to create something other than classic spheres of influence, that is exactly how things turned out.
31. The Foreign Secretary's usual adviser, Alexander Cadogan, had fallen ill, so William Strang came as an assistant – perhaps an unfortunate choice since Hull quickly made it clear that the Americans considered Strang 'more or less unfriendly', *FRUS*, 1943, III, p. 13.
32. Eden, *The Reckoning*, pp. 434–5. Eden also spoke at the Maryland statehouse in Annapolis. His ancestor, Sir Robert Eden, who had been the last colonial governor of Maryland, is buried in the graveyard of nearby St Anne's Church.
33. *FRUS*, 1943, III, pp. 28–34; Eden, *The Reckoning*, p. 436.
34. Ibid. The President's musings about 'Free Ports of Information' were more than an attempt to manage the news, although that was surely part of it. It also fit in with his desire to avoid closed, exclusive spheres of influence. See Kimball, *The Juggler*, pp. 102, 182, 198. For an interesting addition to that discussion see LCDR George H. Earle, USN to RADM Wilson Brown, USN (naval aide to the president), 22 July 1944, enclosing a 'free exchange of information' proposal that is remarkably similar to the Free Ports of Information concept; Map Room papers, box 163, Naval Aide's File A-8, FDRL.
35. Woodward, *British Foreign Policy*, V, pp. 33–4; *FRUS*, 1943, III, 36–8. Eden's first report to Churchill contained the heartening news that Roosevelt wanted to continue Lend-Lease type aid after the war, and shortly before the talks ended they discussed the wartime British import programme. But neither of those matters

related to postwar economic liberalism; Woodward, *British Foreign Policy*, V, 31; Eden, *The Reckoning*, p. 440. FDR did indicate that two groups of French islands in the Pacific, the Marquesas and Tuamotu, should be internationalised as they were needed for trans-Pacific air routes; *FRUS*, 19143, III, p. 39. See Alan P. Dobson, *Peaceful Air Warfare: The United States, Britain, and the Politics of International Aviation* (Oxford, 1991).

36.  See Kimball & Fred Pollock, 'In Search of Monsters to Destroy,' in *The Juggler*, pp. 127–57.
37.  *FRUS*, 1943, III, pp. 36–8. Hopkins concluded, correctly, that Eden opposed the trusteeship concept.
38.  A succinct discussion of Stalin's demands is in Steven M. Miner, 'Stalin's 'Minimum Conditions' and the Military Balance, 1941–1942,' in G. N. Sevost'ianov and Warren F. Kimball (eds), *Soviet–U.S. Relations, 1933–1942* (Moscow, 1989), pp. 72–87.
39.  *FRUS*, 1943, III, p. 39; *FRUS*, 1917, suppl. 1, p. 40; David Owen, 'The Future of the Balkans,' *Foreign Affairs* (spring 1993), p. 8 (courtesy of Elaine Keyahas). De Gaulle's comment is from *FRUS, Casablanca*, pp. 695–6.
40.  Roosevelt to Churchill, 14 July 1941 in Kimball, *Churchill & Roosevelt*, I, R-50x, p. 222.
41.  Hull is quoted in W. Averell Harriman and Elie Abel, *Special Envoy to Churchill and Stalin, 1941–1946* (New York, 1975), p. 244. Roosevelt's board-gaming came up regularly during the conference, but see especially Eden, *The Reckoning*, pp. 432–3; Sherwood, *Roosevelt and Hopkins*, p. 711; Eden to Churchill, 16 March 1943, FO 371/35365/1316, PRO.
42.  Whether or not 'atomic diplomacy' would have been practised in 1943 (or was practised in 1945) is not the point. Until the TRINITY demonstration of nuclear fission in July 1945, the Red Army was the key factor in any European geopolitical equation. For the discussions see Eden, *The Reckoning*, pp. 440, 657–8.
43.  *FRUS*, 1943, III, 13; Sherwood, *Roosevelt & Hopkins*, pp. 708–9.
44.  *FRUS*, 1943, III, 17, 26; Sherwood, *Roosevelt & Hopkins*, pp. 714–15.
45.  Notter files (microform), file 548–1; Eden to Churchill, 16 March 1943, FO 371/35365/1316 (PRO). Eden's ideas of limited Soviet desires were his own and not hinted at in his talks with Soviet Ambassador Maisky; see, Eden to the British Ambassador in Moscow, Sir Archibald Clark Kerr, 10 March 1943, FO 954 (PRO).
     Eden's surmise is one possible explanation for why Stalin continued to insist on a Second Front even after Stalingrad and Kursk proved the Red Army could defeat the Germans. See Kimball, 'Stalingrad und das Dilemma der amerikanisch-sowjetischen Beziehungen'.
46.  *FRUS*, 1943, III, 13, 17, 22. But caution can be misread. One wonders if the Soviets got wind of the Bullitt letter and the currency apparently given the proposal by the Administration. If so, that would only add to their already considerable distrust of the Anglo-Americans.
47.  See the very fine study by Julian G. Hurstfield, *America and the French Nation, 1939–1945* (Chapel Hill and London, 1986), which argues that Roosevelt believed France was and should be a second-rate power – something De Gaulle obviously sensed. The same point, greatly exaggerated into an American conspiracy, is made by Anthony Verrier, *Assassination in Algiers: Churchill, Roosevelt, de Gaulle, and the Murder of Admiral Darlan* (London, 1990).
48.  Minute by Nigel Ronald (Asst Under Secretary), FO371/35366/1360 (U1430/G) (PRO) on Eden's report of a conversation of 27 March 1943.
49.  FDR's commitment to China faded after his meeting with Chiang Kai-shek at

Cairo in December 1943, but never disappeared. This is a matter that needs further study.

50. Eden, *The Reckoning*, p. 437; Sherwood, *Roosevelt & Hopkins*, p. 716; Woodward, *British Foreign Policy*, V, p. 36. For additional discussions of China see *FRUS, 1943*, III, pp. 36–8; Eden, *The Reckoning*, p. 440.

51. *FRUS*, 1943, III, pp. 13–18, 19–24; Woodward, *British Foreign Policy*, pp. 31–3; Eden, *The Reckoning*, p. 437, 439. The discussions about Germany mirror Roosevelt's comments to State Department planners before Eden arrived; Notter files (microform), 548–1, summary dated 18 March 1943 of a White House meeting on 22 February 1943. Eden's support for dismemberment contradicted his comments to the British War Cabinet a few weeks earlier; Keith Sainsbury, *Churchill and Roosevelt at War* (New York, 1994), p. 145.

52. Prime Minister's Operational files (PREM 3) 476/9, pp. 387, 390 (PRO).

53. Roosevelt Press conference, 30 March 1943, *FRUS*, 1943, III, pp. 41–3.

54. Charmley, *Churchill*, 460–1. This is not to single out Charmley; he is only the latest such accuser in what is a very long line.

55. That is not, of course, the interpretation of historians like D. C. Watt whose title I have expropriated; *Succeeding John Bull: America in Britain's Place, 1900–1975* (Cambridge, 1984).

56. Memorandum of 7 July 1943, Woodward, *British Foreign Policy*, V, p. 51.

57. That was the implication decades ago of A. J. P. Taylor, *English History, 1914–1945* (New York & Oxford, 1965), pp. 469n., 513, 533 (note A).

58. For British fears of American postwar isolationism see Charmley, *Churchill*, p. 569. The comment by Williams is in *The Tragedy of American Diplomacy* (rev. edn.; New York, 1962), pp. 206–7.

59. The assertion that spheres of influence were in place as of the Eden mission is made by E. Aga-Rossi, 'Roosevelt's European Policy and the Origins of the Cold War: A Reevaluation', *Telos*, 96 (Summer 1993), pp. 65–85. Gardner, *Spheres of Influence*, is a persuasive study of the issue as it developed during the war.

60. The myth of a campaign through the so-called Ljubljana Gap is just that: a myth. The British Chiefs of Staff dismissed the idea at the time, while the latest refutation is Thomas M. Barker, 'The Ljubljana Gap Strategy: Alternative to Anvil/Dragoon or Fantasy?' *The Journal of Military History*, 56 (January 1992), pp. 57–85.

61. This is the implication, if not the accusation, of a long line of American politicians and historians, set out most recently and illogically by Robert Nisbet, *Roosevelt and Stalin: The Failed Courtship* (Washington, 1988). It is being augmented by a growing number of European historians for whom the Second World War was but a prelude to the real horror – the suppression of freedom, and particularly nationalism, in Europe. This is, in any event, the impression I get from my reading of, to give two examples, Remi Nadeau, *Stalin, Churchill, and Roosevelt Divide Europe* (Westport, CT, 1990), and Aga-Rossi, 'Reorganizing Postwar Europe'.

62. Roosevelt Press conference, 30 March 1943, *FRUS*, 1943, III, pp. 41–3.

# 2 Soviet War-Aims
## Jonathan Haslam

The archives that can give us the definitive answer as to the war-aims of the Soviet regime are still closed: that is to say, all the Politburo papers relating to foreign, defence and intelligence matters and the greater part of the relevant files in the Foreign Ministry.[1]

From the documents currently available, however, the bare outline of these aims can be reconstructed. The purpose of this chapter is also to explain the rationale behind them. The minimalist aims were certainly geo-political, dictated by the needs of state security and buttressed by precedent. And it is the contention of this chapter that these aims emerged not during the period of hostilities which, for Russia, meant 1941 to 1945, but during the diplomatic prelude from 1939 to 1941. In addition more far-reaching and potentially limitless aims appear to have gathered impetus as the war proceeded and undoubtedly reflected the additional influence of larger ideological forces. But an objective and comprehensive treatment of them will have to await direct access to the archives.

The sum total of aims encompassed three distinct regions: Europe, the Near East (including Turkey), and the Far East.

## GENERAL AIMS BEFORE AND AFTER 1941

Between August 1939 and June 1941 the overriding purpose was to remain out of the war. An additional interest lay in seeing that the West remained a house divided. From June 1941 to May 1945 that purpose was forcibly changed to the defeat of the German alliance and, from August to September, the defeat of Japan. Yet concern lest the inter-capitalist conflict draw prematurely to a close leaving Russia alone at war with Germany remained lodged firmly at the back of Stalin's mind. The general aim for the conclusion of hostilities was almost certainly to ensure that Russia would emerge as the dominant Power on the Eurasian land mass. A specific but overarching long-term aim for the postwar world was the prevention of the re-emergence of a German and a Japanese threat to Soviet security. Within that framework, however, certain minimalist aims may be summarised as follows: repossession of the Baltic states (Estonia, Latvia and Lithuania) lost during the civil war and war of intervention in 1918–19; annexation of Finnish territory required for the defence of Leningrad; the transformation of the Black Sea into a *mare clausum*; the maintenance of a Poland friendly to the

22

Soviet Union (a *de facto* protectorate); a protectorate over Bulgaria (which would require the domination of neighbouring Romania); reacquisition of South Sakhalin as part of the abrogation of the Portsmouth Treaty of 1905; and the cession of Königsberg and the East Prussian hinterland to Russia.

## CONDOMINIUM WITH GERMANY

There is still no consensus as to what constituted Soviet policy between 1933 and 1939. This writer takes the view that Germany's alienation of Russia on Hitler's accession to power drove Stalin towards the creation of an alliance system that would forestall a likely attack at some point, as yet undefined, in the future. During 1935 and 1937 secret approaches were made to Berlin to test the water and see whether German intentions were still unalterably hostile. There was, in fact, at this stage no reason to believe otherwise. Not until the late spring and early summer of 1939, when Hitler had decided upon the invasion of Poland, did clear signals emerge from Berlin that the critical obstacle to good relations might be breached. Combined with Britain's refusal to sanction Soviet hegemony over the Baltic states or conclude a full-scale alliance against Germany, Hitler's overtures eventually resulted in the Nazi-Soviet non-aggression pact of 23–24 August 1939, containing the notorious secret protocol.

Up to 1939 the Soviet government had steadfastly avoided war to secure its security objectives in Europe. This was largely because Moscow was initially too weak to contemplate confrontation with mightier military Powers but also because of the perception that any such action would likely as not unite the capitalist world in a final war of intervention to overthrow the Soviet regime. Thus, although there was a steady accretion of military capabilities from the early 1930s, following upon the largely successful re-industrialisation of Russia, Stalin favoured the pursuit of external goals through political and diplomatic means, with the exception of the Far East, where limited military action could scarcely be avoided and where Moscow could act with a free hand against Japan.

The Nazi–Soviet pact, by splitting the capitalist camp down the middle, saw to it that the use of raw military power could be exercised on a limited scale in Europe without bringing down the walls of the Soviet regime. The Germans desperately needed Soviet help to prosecute their military objectives. As Foreign Commissar Molotov pointed out to Hitler in November 1940, with his usual lack of guile: 'last year's Soviet–German agreement . . . really was in the interests of Germany (first, a strong rear in the East for the conduct of war in the West; second, gaining possession of Poland). . . '.[2] The secret complementary protocol of the Nazi–Soviet pact had defined 'the sphere of mutual interests in Eastern Europe' between the two Powers. This gave the Soviet Union Eastern Poland, Finland, Estonia and Latvia and Bessarabia (part of Romania).[3]

After the outbreak of war in September 1939 Moscow thought a speedy conclusion of peace unlikely, despite the 'phoney war'. Feared most was a German defeat. It may seem strange that Stalin chose Berlin rather than London. But Stalin had decided London offered no substantial alternative. As he told Churchill later, he had the impression that the negotiations with the French and the British delegations (July–August 1939) were 'insincere and only for the purpose of intimidating Hitler, with whom the Western Powers would later come to terms'.[4] He saw the Nazi regime as riddled with contradictions, inherently weak, and therefore unlikely to survive a sustained conflict with major Powers: hence the Comintern's vigorous peace campaign. Britain, on the other hand, was viewed as the more likely victor. And in his darker moments Stalin believed it to have been British policy to push Russia into war with Germany: a mirror image of Chamberlain's sentiments. The war in Poland may have momentarily strengthened Hitler's regime but, as with the annexation of Austria (1938) and Czechoslovakia (1939), by absorbing hostile populations it has ensured long-term weakness from within the new empire. Moreover, in Moscow's view, fear of revolution in Germany still existed, and was not confined to Germany alone. Likely as not echoing his master's voice, Stalin's adviser on international affairs, Eugene Varga, explained the situation to a committee of the Comintern secretariat. The war was peculiar, he pointed out, because there had been no fighting except at sea. This was because 'on the one hand Hitler cannot risk any defeat while he fears the domestic political consequences of the first major defeat and on the other hand both Chamberlain and Daladier are likewise themselves afraid of the possible domestic political consequences [inside Germany] of Hitler's defeat [*eine Niederlage Hitlers*] and that is why they have manoeuvred to and fro, without making up their minds, without engaging in a real war'.[5]

And how likely was a German defeat? In the view of Georgi Dimitrov, head of the Comintern, a German victory was as unlikely a prospect as a speedy peace.[6] Britain was, in Moscow's view, the leading capitalist power, the power where the bourgeoisie was at its strongest.[7] Perhaps because of the traumatic experience of the allied war of intervention in 1918–19, Stalin displayed a persistent tendency to exaggerate British capabilities. Having thrown in his lot conditionally with Germany, he became anxious lest Britain win. His overriding concern was to sustain a balance of power between the protagonists in the war. His overestimation of British power and his underestimation of German power combined to lead him to a conclusion that, in retrospect, showed the most appalling judgement about the true situation, not for the first or the last time. In conversation with Germans on 27 September, during the conclusion of the Friendship Pact, Stalin expressed his appreciation of German assertions that they were not expecting Soviet aid and understood that Russia did not wish to be drawn into the war. The fact was that Germany needed no external aid and it was possible it would need none in the future. 'However,' Stalin added, 'if, in spite of expectations, Germany falls into a serious condition, then it can be assured that the Soviet people will come to Germany's aid and will not allow Germany to be crushed. The Soviet Union is interested in a strong Germany and will not allow Germany to be wiped off the face of the earth.'[8] The important issue was to keep the balance, but a balance between weakened participants, so that Moscow might enhance its position relative to both sides. The Russians counted on both sides exhausting themselves in a long-drawn-out conflict. This was certainly the view reportedly expressed by the Soviet *chargé d'affaires* in Peking, Nikitin.[9] And this is what Stalin said at a meeting with Molotov, Zhdanov, and Dimitrov on 7 September 1939: 'There is war between the two groups of capitalist countries . . . for the division of the world, for the domination of the world! We have nothing against the fact that they come to blows . . . and weaken one another.'[10] The rapid fall of France in June 1940 and the imminent danger that Britain might sue for peace with Germany momentarily gave Stalin serious cause for doubt – Khrushchev recalls that he became 'extremely nervous, racing around, cursing like a cab driver'[11] – but this was rapidly swept away by Churchill's obdurate refusal to negotiate and Roosevelt's decision to provide munitions for Britain to fight on. Yet Stalin continued to underestimate Hitler or, at least, to impute to him a greater degree of rationality than he in fact possessed; hence the disaster of 22 June 1941.

POLAND

Soviet aims with regard to Poland had not been unchanging. The conclusion of peace with Poland after the war of 1920 reflected Lenin's belief in trading space for time, territory for peace. He deliberately gave the Poles more territory than was actually warranted in order to forestall any likely *causus belli* re-arising from festering Polish grievances. What he did not foresee was that after his death it was Russian grievances that would fester over the lands lost at the Riga treaty of 1921. The Leninist philosophy, which took the long view, was predicated upon a fundamental optimism – tempered by a ruthless realism in the short term – that the international revolutionary cause would sooner or later triumph anyway, so a piece of territory here or there was of no ultimate consequence. But to those for whom such revolutionary commitment was never anything more than skin-deep and to those for whom the failure of the revolution to spread across Europe prompted a return to traditional notions of strategic frontiers and the expansion of national power for its own sake, the treaty of Riga and its counterparts elsewhere represented uncompleted work. Relations with Poland through the 1920s were troubled by several factors, not least the Soviet–German military collaboration hidden beneath the panoply of the Rapallo treaty of 1922, the activities of the Soviet-backed Polish Communist Party in attempting to foment revolution, and the activities of the Byelorussian and West Ukrainian guerrilla bands operating across the Soviet frontier into Polish territory.

Moreover Poland had allied to France and Romania in opposition to Russia, then aligned itself with Britain during the Anglo-Soviet confrontation of 1926–27, and attempted to force Lithuania into diplomatic subjugation in 1927–28, thus threatening the delicate balance of power in the region. After Hitler's assumption of power, the Polish–German declaration on non-aggression in January 1934 was followed by a sustained campaign from Warsaw to wreck Soviet projects for an Eastern Locarno arrangement that would link a Franco-Soviet alliance against Germany with the existing French alliance structure in Eastern Europe. Even the more moderate and better informed Commissar for Foreign Affairs, Litvinov, believed in his darker moments that there existed a secret treaty of alliance between Warsaw and Berlin. Needless to say, if Litvinov could believe this (and there is no evidence that it was true), then one can only imagine what the ever-mistrustful Stalin believed. And when the Poles set about demanding territory from the beleaguered Czechoslovaks in 1938 Moscow issued an indelicate reminder: 'Berlin and Warsaw must understand that, in the eyes of European public opinion, the question of the oppression in Poland of six and a half million Ukrainians and of two million or so Byelorussians has much greater weight than the question of the fate of a small group of Poles in Czechoslovakia, who anyway enjoy all their rights.'[12] Moreover, with the unseemly transaction completed at Munich late that September dividing Czechoslovakia and throwing part to the wolves, Deputy Commissar Potemkin alerted French diplomats – and thus the Poles, their allies – to the fact that 'Poland is preparing its fourth partition.'[13] Warsaw was also reminded that 'In embarking upon the path of aggression and imperialist annexations, Poland is taking the risk of herself becoming a victim of this policy in the near future.'[14]

The Poles blindly ignored all warnings and, along with the British, dogmatically adhered to the mistaken view that Soviet–German differences were irreconcilable. The division of Poland and the destruction of the Polish state under the Nazi–Soviet pact thus simplified Stalin's foreign policy position – one more variable had been removed. As Stalin put it: 'Poland was a great country. Where is Poland now? Where is Mosicki, Rydz-Smigly and Beck?'[15] But once Germany and Russia were at war it was in Soviet interests to back some kind of Polish revival – thereafter the Russians needed all the allies they could get – and therefore postwar aims with regard to Poland had to differ markedly from the policy of vengeance enacted in 1939. But the rationale for domination remained. As Stalin put it at Yalta:

> The fact is not only that Poland is a country neighbouring our own. This, of course, is significant; but the essence of the problem lies much deeper. Throughout history Poland was always a corridor through which the enemy has come to attack Russia. It is sufficient to recall just the last thirty years: in the course of this period the Germans have twice come through Poland in order to attack our country. Why have enemies up to now so easily crossed Poland? Above all because Poland was weak.[16]

Poland had, of course, prior to the Nazi–Soviet pact, resisted Moscow's proposals to provide for joint defence against Germany. Thereafter Stalin was determined this would never happen again. How this would be done, once the extinction of the Polish state in 1939–41 was tacitly recognised in Moscow to have been in error, was the question that remained. The solution the Soviet government came up with was artlessly indicated by Molotov at the Moscow talks in October 1943.

> No one is as interested in good relations with Poland as we, its neighbours, are. We stand for an independent Poland and are ready to help it; but it is necessary that Poland has the kind of government that would have a friendly disposition towards the USSR.[17]

The only way the Russians could ensure that the Polish government would be friendly would be to deny the Polish people the right to choose their own government through democratic elections and to impose upon them a government of Moscow's own choice, which is precisely what they eventually did.

## THE BALTIC STATES

The Nazi–Soviet pact – as amended by the Friendship Pact of 28 September[18] – not only divided Poland, it also provided for domination of the Baltic states. Soviet interest in the Baltic states was longstanding: they had formed an integral part of the Romanov empire until lost during the allied war of intervention in 1918–19. During the revolution and civil war they became a battleground between Reds and Whites, the latter supported by the Royal Navy and, somewhat idiosyncratically, by German troops bent on creating a *Balticum* of their own. In the mid-1920s these fledgling states fell largely under British influence at a time when Britain resumed its role as the Soviet regime's leading adversary. Britain's role ended with the incoming Labour administration in 1929 and in its place France arose to challenge the resurgence of Soviet and international communist power during the Great Depression.[19] From 1933, however, the Baltic states fell increasingly under a more traditional influence, that of Germany which, under Hitler's leadership, replaced France as Moscow's main adversary in Europe.

Thus the repossession of the Baltic states was not only the consequence of an imperial legacy, but also geo-political calculation, a calculation confirmed by Lithuania's enforced retrocession of the Memel to Germany in 1938 and Germany's subsequent expansion from central into south-eastern Europe. The annual report compiled by the Soviet embassy in Berlin for the year 1939 noted, *inter alia*, that the non-aggression pacts concluded by Germany with Estonia and Latvia earlier that year had as their aim 'not only to undermine the Anglo-Franco-Soviet talks on a mutual assistance pact but also to subordinate these states politically to Germany'.[20] By the end of 1940 the Soviet Commissariat of War still had 'no documentary data' on the operational plans of the Germans.[21] But it anticipated that the main blow from Germany would come from East Prussia through Lithuania, with only supporting concentrations attacking Brest and through to Minsk.[22] The Baltic states were accordingly seen as a most critical avenue for the German advance. The Russians therefore followed their invasion of Poland on 17 September 1939 with negotiations to force the Baltic states to accept protectorate status.

When the Russians opened these negotiations, relations with Germany were still extremely delicate; so it was not to be expected that the calculations of the military leadership would be referred to in the course of discussion. The discussions were revealing in a different way: geostrategic calculation and historical resentment were intermingled in a manner that revealed itself time and again in negotiations with other neighbouring countries during the war and the early postwar years. The first talks took place with Estonia. Referring to the Gulf of Finland, Commissar for Foreign Affairs Molotov told Foreign Minister Selter:

> Twenty years ago you made us sit in this Finnish 'puddle.' You don't think that this can last ... forever. Then the Soviet Union was powerless, but in the meantime she has greatly grown economically and culturally and also militarily. The Soviet Union is now a great power whose interests need to be taken into consideration. I tell you – the Soviet Union needs enlargement of her security guarantee system; for this purpose she needs an exit to the Baltic Sea. If you do not want to conclude with us a mutual assistance pact, then we have to use ... other ways, perhaps more drastic; perhaps more complicated. I ask you, do not compel us to use force against Estonia.[23]

The Latvians and Lithuanians met a similar fate. They all caved in under pressure. It was to be expected that Finland would follow suit. But the Finns did not concede, not least because Russian demands went considerably further here than elsewhere: in addition to bases, they insisted upon the cession of territory overlooking the channels leading to the port of Leningrad and the translation of the Soviet–Finnish frontier north of Vyborg. Moreover the Finns thought Stalin was bluffing.[24] By the end of October, however, Stalin had in fact concluded that 'we will have to fight with Finland'.[25] The Red Army advanced before the end of November.

The Soviet–Finnish war undoubtedly further complicated the Soviet position *vis-à-vis* the other Baltic states, particularly Estonians, who from ethnic affinity identified closely with the Finns as victims. An additional factor intervened soon after the bitter peace concluded by Helsinki in the spring of 1940: Hitler's expansion into western Europe tipped the balance of power decisively to his advantage. Stalin decided that protectorate status for the strategically critical Baltic states was insufficient insurance in the event of the Germans turning East and in June the Baltic governments were toppled and the states they ruled were hastily absorbed into the USSR under the figleaf of rigged elections.

At war with Germany, Stalin urgently sought British and US recognition of the territorial gains of 1939–40. Even when he was prepared to leave the question of the Eastern frontier of Poland open, he was insistent on recognition of the absorption of the Baltic states: 'it is very important for us to know whether we shall have to fight at the Peace Conference in order to get our western frontiers', he told Foreign Secretary Eden in December 1942.[26] Molotov was equally emphatic when negotiating the Anglo-Soviet alliance in May 1942,[27] but not only did Labour Party leader Attlee threaten to resign if recognition was conceded,[28] US President Roosevelt also refused to sanction such a concession.[29] However, this issue was in danger of poisoning relations because Stalin placed such a high priority upon it. At Tehran in December 1943 Stalin insisted: 'Lithuania, Estonia and Latvia did not have autonomy until the revolution in Russia. The tsar was then in an alliance with the United States and with England, and no one raised the question about the removal of these countries from the body of Russia. Why raise this question now?'[30] Roosevelt essentially conceded, having pressed for a popular vote, and then agreeing that any plebiscite held to determine the future of the Baltic republics should not be under international supervision. The fate of the Baltic was in any case undermined from the western point of view by the tacit acceptance that the Russians could take the warmwater ports of Königsberg and the Memel and the corresponding section of East Prussia. Stalin claimed with no justification that this was legitimately Slav territory.[31] Moreover 'this', Stalin said, 'would put Russia on Germany's neck'.[32] There was realistically no way Lithuania, for one, could remain independent if the Russians held these lands. In retrospect Churchill acknowledged as much: 'at Teheran when Stalin talked about keeping East Prussia up to Königsberg, we did not say anything about the Baltic States, which clearly would be comprised in the Russian dominions in any such solution'.[33] And the allies had no difficulty in accepting that any Soviet peace with Finland would be based on the 1940 settlement, including the territory ceded to Moscow.[34]

## THE BALKANS AND THE NEAR EAST

The signature of the Nazi–Soviet pact opened up the prospect of resolving longstanding Russian grievances in other parts of the world as well. Turkey was in the process of negotiating a tripartite treaty of alliance with Britain and France. The Turks were also negotiating with the Russians for a pact that would complement an Anglo-Soviet alliance. When – after 23 August – that proved impossible, the Russians suggested a mutual assistance pact limited to defending the Balkans and the Dardanelles against external aggression. The Turks duly came forward with a counter-proposal limiting mutual assistance to the straits and the Black Sea, allowing merely for consultations with respect to the Balkans and containing a caveat ruling out any possibility of such a treaty leading to conflict with Britain or France. Given the complete reorientation of Soviet foreign policy and the greater likelihood as a result of a confrontation with Britain and France rather than Germany, it occasions no surprise to learn that when the Turks arrived in Moscow for negotiations on 25 September the Russians showed more interest in the draft for the tripartite pact than in negotiating the projected Soviet–Turkish pact. Furthermore, Molotov handed Foreign Minister Saracoğlu a note calling for modifications to the Montreux convention.[35]

Hitherto the Soviet regime had always backed the Turks in attempting to negate Britain's efforts to internationalise control over the straits leading into the Black Sea, and to encourage the Turks to take control over the straits themselves. This was the substance of the Soviet stance at Lausanne (1923) and Montreux (1936).[36] In so doing Moscow had consciously distanced itself from the rapacious demands of the tsarist regime that culminated in the notorious secret understandings of March–April 1915,[37] according to which the Russians would annex Constantinople on victory over the Central Powers and the Ottoman empire, thus giving them the key to the gates of the Black Sea. Subsequent policy had been based upon Lenin's stance of support for national liberation against western imperialism, which meant support for Kemalist nationalism in Turkey. Such self-restraint was now cautiously abandoned to give away increasingly to what looked like old-style tsarist ambitions in Soviet dress.

Significantly, Stalin's demand for the revision of the Montreux convention followed on the heels of the attempt not only to preclude all possible Turkish assistance to Britain and France in the event of their being at war with the Soviet Union but also all hope of Soviet assistance to Turkey in the event of the latter being at war with Germany. Stalin wanted removed from the convention the stipulation that warships could enter the Black Sea on a decision of the League of Nations Council even if Turkey were not a belligerent. Instead he proposed a Turco-Soviet condominium governing the straits, barring League authorisation if obtained without Soviet participation and providing for Turkish and Soviet prior agreement before any future negotiations concerning revision of the straits regime. These discussions not only further illustrate the reassertion of tsarist imperatives in Soviet foreign policy but also underline the extent to which Stalin saw the Soviet–German alignment as indefinite in duration and the resultant possibility of a clash with Britain.

No more was heard of the subject until the summer of 1940, when Molotov proposed terms to Italy for an understanding with respect to the Balkans. The suggestion was that Moscow would recognise Italian pre-eminence in the Mediterranean if Italy took into account 'the interests of the USSR as the principal Power in the Black Sea'.[38] It is noteworthy that the Italian ambassador also expected the Russians to reclaim territory taken from Georgia and Armenia in the First World War. Nothing came of these Soviet proposals. This was in large part why Molotov visited Berlin in November. By then the Russians had not only completed the occupation of the Baltic states – with the exception of Finland, which had finally conceded to Soviet demands in what amounted to a dictated peace in March 1940[39] but had also occupied Bessarabia and Northern Bukovina, constituent parts of Romania. The occupation of Bessarabia had been provided for under the Nazi–Soviet pact. It was also the logical sequel to the consistent refusal of the Soviet regime to recognise Bessarabia's annexation by Romania in 1918–19. However, the annexation of Northern Bukovina was in no way justified by precedent, or by the pact. The Russians now claimed to be a Danubian Power and attended as a member a meeting of the Danubian commission on 28 October. But it was Stalin's undoing. It showed Hitler that Russia had aspirations in the Balkans that went beyond his understanding of the terms of the condominium. And given the critical importance of the Danube basin as the grain-basket of Europe, and the oil-wells of Romania, it prompted vigorous German penetration of the area. This is turn provoked Soviet anxieties: hence Molotov's trip.

Molotov arrived on 12 November 1940 to clarify and extend the relationship with Germany.[40] Hitler emphasised that the British empire was on its knees and that as a consequence he wished to discuss with the Russians the division of new spheres of influence. He directed Soviet attention towards Turkey (the straits) and the Persian Gulf. But this only highlighted Soviet concern about the fate of the Balkans. Secure control over the straits would depend upon a secure hinterland and that meant Bulgaria. On 19 October the Comintern publication *World News and Views* had pointed out: 'Germany's plans for domination in the Near East and over the Balkans menace a vital interest of the USSR in the Black Sea, quite apart from the well-known aspirations of German imperialism for Ukrainian wheat and Caucasian oil.' On 13 November, the day after Molotov arrived in Berlin, Stalin telegraphed:

> Concerning the Black Sea you can give Hitler the following response: that it is not only a matter of egress from the Black Sea but mainly access to the Black Sea, that has always been used by England and other states for attack on the shores of the USSR. Every event from the Crimean war of the last century to the landing of foreign forces in the Crimea and Odessa in 1918 and 1919 demonstrates that the security of the Black Sea regions of the USSR can never be considered guaranteed without regulating the question of the straits. . . . The question of guaranteeing Bulgaria by the USSR is organically linked to this, for the maintenance of peace in the region of the straits is impossible without coming to terms with Bulgaria about allowing Soviet forces through for the defence of the entrances to the Black Sea.[41]

In other words Stalin sought a protectorate over Bulgaria as an extension of his goal with respect to the straits. He added: 'Concerning Turkey: keep this for the time being within the realm of a peaceful solution in the spirit of Ribbentrop; but say that a peaceful solution will not be realistic without our guarantee to Bulgaria and permission for our forces to enter Bulgaria as a means of exerting pressure on Turkey.'[42] Soviet interest in the security of Bulgaria had originally been awakened by the Bulgarian anxieties in September 1939. Sofia was nervous about Anglo-French plans for landings on Salonica and the subsequent extension of the war to their territory. Would the Russians offer aid if called upon? Molotov seized the opportunity to offer a mutual assistance pact; doubtless on the model of what was being concluded with the unfortunate Baltic states.[43] The Russians followed up on their initiative after the failure of the talks with Turkey, but still got nowhere.[44] They resumed pressure for a Bulgarian pact in June 1940, backing Bulgarian claims on Romanian and Greek territory.[45] At the same time Molotov also put in a claim for Southern Bukovina from Romania for good measure.[46] Now, with the Germans, they hoped to include both Bulgaria and Turkey within their sphere of influence and thus solve the entire problem once and for all. The Germans were thus informed that far-reaching agreements on 'joint activity' [*sovmestnuyu rabotu*] between the USSR, Germany, Italy and Japan in the matter of marking out basic spheres of influence between them, which Molotov considered 'possible and desirable', were contingent upon the settlement of this vital issue as well as the thorny issue of the growing German presence in Finland.[47]

Hitler never conceded; instead on 18 December he signed directive No. 21, 'Barbarossa', for the invasion of the Soviet Union.[48] But Stalin and Molotov persisted in the belief that Hitler was unlikely to risk attacking Russia for the foreseeable future while Britain remained undefeated. And here Stalin's exaggerated estimation of British power re-emerged into view. The secretary-general of the Swedish Foreign Ministry returned from a visit to Moscow early in November reporting that Molotov personally, along with other important figures in Moscow, had expressed one and the same view: namely that the war with Britain would be hard and long because London had at its disposal 'infinite wealth and means of resistance' (in Molotov's words).[49] Hostility to Britain nonetheless remained unchanged. For instance, when Molotov saw the Italian ambassador on 31 December and once more raised the issues discussed in Berlin, he also argued that 'The Power that presents a threat is always England.'[50]

The issue of the straits re-emerged in a very different context after the German invasion of 22 June 1941. Once Moscow was at war, the Russians pressed the British and Americans to secure Turkish participation. The Turks resisted. In an unguarded moment at the Teheran conference (28 November – 1 December 1943), Churchill casually mentioned that should Turkey not enter the war, then this would affect its rights in relation to the Bosphorus and the Dardanelles.[51] At that time Stalin was more anxious to secure the opening of a second front in northern France as the first priority. He nonetheless took note, later asked Churchill for clarification,[52] and subsequently raised the matter again on meeting Churchill in Moscow in October 1944[53] and at Yalta in February 1945. But the query met only with a vague response: the Montreux convention would have to be revised at some future date.[54] In fact Churchill was prepared to concede to the Russians on this issue but hoped to hold a solution hostage to the conclusion of a satisfactory general settlement.[55] But, doubtless suspicious that the Anglo-Saxon Powers were now reluctant to facilitate this process, Stalin decided to put pressure on Turkey directly. There had been desultory talks about improving relations but they had led to nothing. On 19 March Stalin fired a warning shot across the Turkish bow. Molotov told ambassador Sarper that the Soviet government denounced the joint neutrality treaty of September 1925.[56] Then on 7 June a surprised Turkish ambassador was informed by Molotov that Moscow would require new terms for a new treaty: (1) the cession of territory from eastern Turkey; (2) Soviet bases on the straits; and (3) bilateral agreement before multilateral revision of Montreux.[57] Apart from the issue of territory, the Russians had returned to their stance of 1939–40. And, as at that time, Soviet aims with regard to Bulgaria were subordinate to the Turkish question. While Soviet armies pushed on to Warsaw, they also pressed on through the Balkans. From Moscow on 26 August 1944 the exiled leader of the Bulgarian Communist Party, Georgi Dimitrov, issued an instruction to the party in the country to organise and launch an uprising in anticipation of the arrival of the Red Army.[58] A month later and the country was occupied, the Communist Party taking local control. And when Churchill met with Stalin in Moscow to divide the Balkans into spheres of influence, Churchill originally offered 75 per cent Russian to 25 per cent British for Bulgaria. When Molotov followed up on the matter with Eden, he sought 90 per cent Russian and 10 per cent British. For both Romania and Bulgaria, as against Hungary (50–50 per cent), Yugoslavia (50–50 per cent) and Greece (10–90 per cent), the Russians sought and obtained maximum domination for themselves.[59] The rationale became explicit a short time later. In June 1945 the British military mission in Bulgaria reported that Soviet armies 'were being concentrated [in Romania and Bulgaria] for the purpose of browbeating the Turks into accepting Russian proposals for the Straits'.[60]

What all this suggests is that Stalin's geostrategic priorities, largely inherited from the tsarist era along with the realities of geography, carried with them larger political and ideological consequences which were perhaps incidental to his main purpose; that said, those consequences had a life and dynamic of their own. The supreme irony was that the man who had done so much to suppress the true revolutionary spirit within Russian had done more than anyone else to export its substance abroad. To hold the territories he had conquered, Stalin had to sovietise them and, having sovietised them, he expanded the scope of the communist revolution; rather in the manner that Napoleon spread the republican and anti-feudal revolution over a century before. The net effect was the same regardless of the initial intention.

THE FAR EAST

Hitherto Soviet relations with Japan had been governed by the terms of the Portsmouth treaty that brought an end to the Russo-Japanese war of 1904–5. It transferred Southern Sakhalin and the southern half of the Russian railway network in Manchuria to Japan. This gave the latter an immense strategic advantage for expansion throughout the region and at Russian's expense. And the fledgling Soviet regime had to accept the jurisdiction of the treaty in order to gain Japanese diplomatic recognition under the Peking convention of January 1925.[61] This remained a sore point in relations that soon deteriorated further when the Japanese invasion of Manchuria forced the Russians into conceding the northern half of the railway in order to appease militarist sentiment in Tokyo. Until the Russians had built up and consolidated their military power in the Far East, and until they had settled their relations in Europe, there was no likelihood that they could revise the Portsmouth treaty through the threat of force. In the interim the Russians accepted many petty humiliations and the degree of resentment at the Japanese, longstanding since 1905 even among the Bolsheviks, grew remorselessly. However, once the Nazi–Soviet pact relieved Moscow of the immediate threat of war in Europe and once Russian armies under Zhukov's command had inflicted a severe blow at the Japanese regiments on the Outer Mongolian frontier in September 1939, Tokyo had to seek a new *modus vivendi*. Facing the prospect of conflict with the United States because of their war in China, the Japanese General Staff recommended coming to terms with Moscow in April 1940.[62] In July Japan proposed a neutrality pact, lasting five years. This was replaced by the offer of a non-aggression pact in October. The Soviet response was to raise the issue of the Portsmouth treaty. More than that, Japan would also have to return not only South Sakhalin but also the Kurile Islands which the Russians lost to the Japanese in 1875. Possession of South Sakhalin would give more secure egress from the Sea of Japan for the Pacific Fleet stationed at Vladivostok. Reacquisition of the Kuriles would in turn guarantee safe passage through from the Sea of Okhotsk into the Pacific.[63] But it was unlikely the Russians could obtain such significant concessions without war. A neutrality pact was finally concluded in April 1941 on terms more acceptable to the Japanese. The Russians shelved the territorial issues for later settlement.

Although the German invasion distracted Stalin from Far Eastern affairs, the Americans, in particular, after Pearl Harbor, were especially eager to draw the Russians in against the Japanese. The issue was raised at Tehran and in Moscow a year later. Russian terms were entirely consonant with their demands in 1940. On 14 December 1944 Stalin told Harriman: 'The Soviet Union would like to receive South Sakhalin, i.e. restitution of what was handed over to Japan in the Portsmouth treaty, and also receive the Kurile Islands.'[64] Stalin also raised the issue of warm-water ports. At Tehran he had complained that the only warm-water port the Soviet Union possessed, other than Murmansk, was Petropavlovsk on Kamchatka.[65] He now asked for rental of Port Arthur and Dairen (Dalny) from the Chinese, plus reacquisition of the Chinese Eastern and South Manchurian Railways that linked these ports to the Russian hinterland.[66] At Yalta Roosevelt (and therefore Churchill) agreed to these terms.[67] Stalin was delighted, not least because he had thereby avenged the humiliation wrought by defeat in the 1904–5 war.[68]

Stalin outlined the general rationale for these acquisitions in negotiations with the Chinese Government: 'We are closed up. We have no outlet. One should keep Japan vulnerable from all sides, north, west, south, east, then she will keep quiet . . . Japan will be crushed but she will restore her might in 20, 30 years.'[69]


GERMANY


Stalin's words about the future rise of Japan mirrored his statements on the subject of Germany. At a speech in Moscow on 6 November 1944, he argued: 'It would, however, be naive to think that it [Germany] will not try to rebuild its power and unleash new aggression. . . . History shows that a short period of time of 20–30 years is sufficient for Germany to recover from defeat and re-establish its power.'[70] After the war, at least as recalled by the Yugoslav Djilas, Stalin gave them merely 'twelve to fifteen years' to recover; though this was after Soviet occupation had doubtless revealed the true extent of German technological and organisational achievements and therefore boosted Stalin's assessment.[71] Moreover, Stalin expressed the belief that the Germans 'would always want to reunite and take their revenge. It would be necessary to keep ourselves strong enough to beat them if ever they let loose another war.'[72]

But what exactly were Soviet aims with regard to Germany? Germany was obviously the key issue of the war. Germany's position was critical to the future balance of economic as well as political power in Europe. Yet there is no sign that Stalin had a clearer idea of what to do with Germany than did his allies. During the adverse phases of the war, he clearly played with the idea of a separate peace.[73] This was not just because the Soviet strategic position was at times desperate, but also because he suspected Churchill of doing the very same thing. These fears are well illustrated by Soviet reactions to the Hess affair. When Hess flew unexpectedly to Britain in May 1941, the Russians suspected this was the prelude to peace talks between London and Berlin. Matters were not helped by the excessive degree of secrecy imposed over the whole affair. As one British official noted: 'Never has so much been withheld from so many by so few!'[74] From London, Soviet spy Kim Philby sent in a report, after gossiping with friends at the Foreign Office and elsewhere. The summary sent to Stalin read: 'Söhnchen [Philby] considers that now the time for peace negotiations has not yet come, but in the process of the future evolution of the war Hess will possibly become the centre of intrigues for the conclusion of a separate peace and will be useful for the peace party in England and for Hitler.'[75] When the Soviet front began to collapse from the early spring through to the autumn of 1942 and Stalin's desperate pleas for a second front fell on deaf ears, suspicions that Churchill was up to something with Hess rose high. A *Pravda* editorial on 19 October thundered: 'To recognise that Hess will not be brought to trial until the end of the war, that he will be spared trial by an international tribunal for the whole period of the war, means closing one's eyes to the crimes of one of the bloodiest Hitlerite criminals and looking upon Hess not as a criminal, but as the representative of another state, as Hitler's envoy. How else is it to be understood?' That same day Stalin sent a despatch to ambassador Maisky in London:

> All of us in Moscow have gained the impression that Churchill is aiming at the defeat of the USSR, in order then to come to terms with the Germany of Hitler or Brüning at the expense of our country. Without making

this assumption it is difficult to explain Churchill's conduct on the question of the second front in Europe, on the question of the supplies of armaments for the USSR, which have been progressively cut despite the growth of production in England; on the question of Hess, whom Churchill, it seems, is keeping in reserve; on the question of the systematic bombing of Berlin by the English during September, which Churchill proposed in Moscow and which he did not carry out one iota, despite the fact that he could unquestionably carry it out.[76]

The line of continuity with the period 1939–41 in his attitude towards Britain emerges with great clarity. In the summer of 1944 he is said to have told Djilas: 'Perhaps you think that just because we are the allies of the English we have forgotten who they are and who Churchill is. . . . Churchill is the kind of man who will pick your pocket of a kopeck if you don't watch him.'[77] And Stalin's excessive estimation of British power continued to the end of the war. The Yugoslav Kardelj recalls a meeting with Deputy Commissar for Foreign Affairs Lozovsky in November 1944. Lozovsky expressed great interest in Kardelj's ideas about the postwar world but cautioned him on one point: 'I don't know what the Old Man [Stalin] will say to it all. You see, he still thinks that England is the centre of world imperialism, the main enemy of the proletariat, and that America plays a secondary role.'[78] Trust was thus at a premium, particularly *vis-à-vis* the Power Stalin believed to play the decisive role in the West. And this mistrust was accentuated by the lack of concrete decisions reached on the most critical question of all: Germany.

Churchill had, more or less as an aside, raised the issue of dismemberment, and at times Stalin seemed to go along with the idea. At Tehran he talked of the need 'to break up and scatter the German tribes' – a frightening solution if one bore in mind Stalin's own treatment of the Crimean Tatars and other unfortunate national minorities who were suspected of disloyalty or potential disloyalty.[79] On the other hand he thought the Germans would always want to reunite. Moreover the Russians sought massive reparations payments after the war and these would be impracticable without some form of centralised authority to deal with after hostilities. Soviet interests with regard to Germany were thus mixed and contradictory, just as were western interests, quite apart from the pressure that always existed within the Soviet regime to unfurl the Communist banner in every capital attainable. As late as June 1945 Stalin gave contradictory prognoses to the German communists: on the one hand acknowledging the likelihood of a division of the country, on the other hand recommending to the communists a strategy of 'unity by a uniform KPD, a uniform ZK, a uniform party of the working people'.[80] At the same time he was – as already indicated – very insistent upon the allies accepting the secession of Königsberg and the

East Prussian hinterland to Russia in order to be able to sit on the neck of the Germans. Clearly before the Red Army had actually taken Berlin, he was unsure whether he would be in a position to dominate Germany and he and his allies had yet to agree to anything specific with regard to Germany as a whole; hence the importance of making the essential demands in advance.

## CONCLUSIONS

But certainly by the time Stalin's forces had reached the German capital, other options had opened up and other ideas had come to mind. It seemed entirely possible to provide for Soviet security against a future conflict with either Germany or Japan entirely unilaterally through the extension of communist power on the back of the Red Army. It was quite simple. The problem was straightforward. The Germans attacked across Eastern Europe. 'The Germans could carry out the invasion through these countries because governments then existed in these countries that were hostile to the Soviet Union.'[81] The solution was obviously to give these countries governments friendly to the Soviet Union and the only such governments could be communist regimes imposed from Moscow. Stalin said: 'This war is not as in the past; whoever occupies a territory also imposes on it his own social system. Everyone imposes his own system as far as his army has power to do so. It cannot be otherwise.'[82]

By the end of hostilities only the appearance of multilateralism existed. The United Nations was formed; the Russians were to attend its sessions. But the real decisions were to be made elsewhere. In substance Soviet policy was entirely unilateral in conception and brutal in implementation. The continuity with the period 1939–41 reasserted itself with a vengeance, reinforced as it was by suspicions reawakened in the depths of desperation in 1942. But, as in 1939–41, Stalin and Molotov had produced a policy that was fundamentally flawed. They had created a security policy through *cordons sanitaires* that seemingly banished the conduct of diplomacy to the margin. The West would have to accept accomplished fact and find a new way of co-existing with this new Power until the forces of revolution undermined their own existence. And the prospects for those forces in 1945 did not seem bad; on the contrary, the Left was everywhere sweeping to power, though the forces of revolution were not yet something Stalin or Molotov were prepared to count on for the short term. The spirit behind these aims was morbidly misanthropic, a matter of personality as much as, if not more than, a matter of ideology. 'They will never accept the idea that so great a space should be red, never, never!' Stalin insisted.[83] In this sense the solution eventually chosen – a defiantly unilateral one – matched the innermost needs of Stalin's own personality as well as the demands of communist expansion. And in the circumstances it is impossible to see how events could have turned out other than they did.

## NOTES

1. The Foreign Ministry files are currently being declassified in parallel from 1917 to 1945 and from 1945 to 1962. The bulk of the files for 1917–27 and 1945–55 have now been declassified. These files, however, still do not include the mass of ciphered telegrams. Those telegrams – from 1917 – remain classified, though there are moves to declassify those from 1917 to 1941. The Politburo material mentioned above remains at the highest level of classification – *osobaya papka* (special file) – and its release awaits Yeltsin's decision.
2. Molotov (Berlin) to Stalin (Moscow), 13 November 1940: AVP, RF, f. 059, op. 1, p. 338, d. 2314, ll. 11–18; reprinted in 'Perepiska V. M. Molotova s I. V. Stalinym. Noyabr' 1940 goda', *Voenno-istoricheskii zhurnal*, 9, 1992, p. 19.
3. 'Sekretnyi dopolnitel'nyi protokol', 23 August 1939: AVP RF, f. 06, op. 1, p. 8, d. 77, l. 1–2: reprinted in *Dokumenty vneshnei politiki 1939 god*, ed. V. G. Kompletktov *et al.* (Moscow, 1992), doc. 485.
4. From the notes of Major Birse on conversations between Stalin and Churchill, 15–16 August 1942, quoted in M. Gilbert, *Road to Victory: Winston S. Churchill 1941–1945* (London 1989), p. 202.
5. 'Kommission des Sekretariats zur Frage der KPD, KPOK und KPT sch. Sitzung am 27.xi.39': Comintern archive (*Rossiskii tsentr khraneniya i izucheniya dokumentov noveishei istorii*, Moscow), 1300, f. 495, op. 18.
6. 'Sitzung der Kommission des Sekretariats des EKKI am 29.xi.1939': ibid., 1298. f. 495, op. 18.
7. As note 2.
8. From German ambassador Schulenburg's personal archive and quoted *in extenso* in DVP, p. 610.
9. Smyth (Peking) to Hull (Washington), 20 June 1940: *US National Archives, Department of State*, 740.0011. European War 1939/4043.
10. Quoted from Dimitrov's notes in his diary: L. Bezymenskii, 'Pobeda i ee porazheniya', *Novoe vremya*, No. 20, 1990, p. 34.
11. *Khrushchev Remembers: The Glasnost Tapes* (Boston, 1990), p. 54.
12. 'Le problème des minorités nationales comme prétexte à l'agression', *Le Journal de Moscou*, 5 April 1938; J. Haslam, *The Soviet Union and the Struggle for Collective Security in Europe 1933–39* (London, 1984), p. 164.
13. Coulondre (Moscow) to Bonnet (Paris), 4 October 1938: *Documents diplomatiques français 1932–1939*, second series ed. M. Baumont *et al.*, vol. 12 (Paris 1978), doc. 17; Haslam, *The Soviet Union*, p. 197.
14. BALTICUS, 'Ce qui attend les agresseurs polonais', *Le Journal de Moscou*, 11 October 1938; Haslam, *The Soviet Union*, loc. cit.
15. A warning uttered in negotiations with the Estonians in September 1939 'Minutes of the Soviet–Estonian Negotiations for the Mutual Assistance Pact of 1939', *Lituanus*, 14, No. 2 (1968), p. 92; cited in Haslam, 'Soviet Foreign Policy 1939–41: Isolation and Expansion', *Soviet Union/Union Soviétique*, 18, Nos 1–3 (1991), p. 111.

16. 'Zapis' zasedaniya glav pravitel'stv', 6 February 1945: *Sovetskii Soyuz na mezhdunarodnykh konferentsiyakh perioda velikoi otechestvennoi voiny 1941– 1945 gg.* Vol. 4, *Krymskaya konferentsiya rukovoditelei trekh soyuznykh derzhav – SSSR, SShA i Velikobritanii (4–11 fevralya 1945 g.) – Sbornik dokumentov* ed. A. Gromyko *et al.* (Moscow, 1984), p. 92.

17. 'Zapis odinnadtsatogo zasedaniya konferentsii ministrov inostrannykh del SSSR, SShA i Velikobritanii', 29 October 1943: *Sovetskii Soyuz...*, Vol. 1: *Moskovskaya konferentsiya ministrov inostrannykh del SSSR, SShA i Velikobritanii (19–30 oktyabrya 1943 g.) – Sbornik dokumentov*, ed. A. Gromyko *et al.* (Moscow, 1984), p. 234.

18. 'Germano-sovetskii dogovor o druzhbe i granitse mezhdu SSSR i Germaniei', 28 September 1939: *Dokumenty vneshnei politiki 1939 god (DVP)*, ed. V. Komplektov *et al.* (Moscow, 1992), doc. 640; 'Sekretnyi dopolnitel'nyi protokol', ibid., doc. 642.

19. See Haslam, *Soviet Foreign Policy 1930–33: The Impact of the Depression* (London, 1983).

20. 'Iz politicheskogo otcheta polnomochnogo predstavitel'stva SSSR v Germanii za 1939 god', 3 May 1940: *DVP*, doc. 905.

21. A memorandum on strategic preparations by the Soviet armed forces, west and east, for 1940 and 1941 from the People's Commissar of Defence to Stalin and Molotov, 18 September 1940: *Voenn-istoricheskii zhurnal*, 1 (1992), p. 24.

22. Ibid., p. 25.

23. 'Minutes . . .', *Lituanus*; cited in Haslam, 'Soviet Foreign Policy . . .', *Soviet Union/ Union Soviétique*, p. 110. Unfortunately the latter mistakenly refers to the Gulf of Bothnia instead of the Gulf of Finland and should have been, but was not, corrected before it went to print.

24. This is what Findland's Foreign Minister Erkko told Mollerson, the Estonian minister in Helsinki: record of a conversation between Wiley from the US embassy in Tallinn and former Estonian Foreign Minister Selter, 3 March 1940: *US National Archives, Department of State*, 860i.00/421.

25. Quoted in G. Kumanev, 'Chto my znaem o "zimnoi voine"', *Sovetskaya Rossiya*, 10 March 1990.

26. 'Record of an interview between the Foreign Secretary and M. Stalin, December 16, 1941, at 7 pm', Avon Papers 420/25, SU/42/3; WAR CAB. WP (42)8; 'Iz zapisi besedy Predsedatelya Soveta Narodnykh Komissarov SSSR i Narodnogo komissara inostrannykh del SSSR s ministrom inostrannykh del Velikobritanii', 17 December 1941: *Sovetsko-angliiskie otnosheniya vo vremya velikoi otechestvennoi voiny 1941–1945*, ed. A. Gromyko, Vol. 1 (Moscow, 1983), doc. 76.

27. 'First Meeting with the Soviet Delegation at No. 10 Downing Street, at 11.30 am on May 21, 1942', Avon Papers 420/25, SU/42/109.

28. Avon Papers 420/25, SU/42/2.

29. H. Feis, *Churchill, Roosevelt, Stalin: The War They Waged and the Peace They Sought* (Princeton, 1966), pp. 58–9. This is a classic that has withstood the test of time.

30. 'Zapis besedy I. V. Stalina s F. Ruzvel'tom', 1 December 1943: *Sovetskii Soyuz... Tegeranskaya konferentsiya rukovoditel'ei trekh soyuznykh derzhav – SSSR, SShA i Velikobritanii, 28 noyabrya – 1 dekabrya 1943 g.: Sbornik dokumentov*, ed. A. Gromyko *et al.* (Moscow 1984), doc. 63.

31. Ibid., doc. 62.

32. This appears in Churchill's record of the discussion, though not in the published Soviet record: Gilbert, *Road*, p. 593.

33. Written 16 January 1944: ibid., p. 652.

Jonathan Haslam 41

34. 'Zapis chetvertogo zasedaniya glav pravitel'stv', 1 December 1943: *Sovetskii Soyuz . . . Tegeranskaya . . .*, doc. 62.

35. F. Erkin, *Les relations Turco-Soviétiques et la question des Detroits* (Ankara, 1968), pp. 160–1. In 1939 Erkin was the head of the political department of the Turkish Foreign Ministry.

36. For the text of the two treaties: J. Grenville (ed.), *The Major International Treaties 1914–1973* (London, 1974), pp. 80–7.

37. Ibid., pp. 27–9.

38. For the complete text – Rosso (Moscow) to Ciano (Rome), 25 June 1940: *I Documenti diplomatici italiani*, 9 serie, Vol. 5, ed. M. Toscano (Rome, 1965), doc..104, note 1.

39. For a good summary of the tragic story, in English: M. Jacobson, *Finland Survived: An Account of the Finnish-Soviet Winter War 1939–1940* (Second, enlarged edition, Helsinki 1984).

40. Although the record of Stalin's instructions to Molotov have not been declassified, this much is apparent from Molotov's telegram to Stalin of 13 November: 'Perepiska V. M. Molotova s I. V. Stalinym. Noyabr' 1940 goda', *Voenno-istoricheskii zhurnal*, 9, 1992, p. 19.

41. Stalin (Moscow) to Molotov (Berlin), 13 November 1940: ibid., p. 20.

42. Ibid.

43. Molotov's record of a conversation with Antonov, the minister from the Bulgarian embassy, 20 September 1939: *Sovetsko–bolgarskie otnosheniya i svyazi: Dokumenty i materialy*, Vol. 1, ed. L. Valev *et al.* (Moscow, 1976), doc. 506.

44. Record of a conversation with Prime Minister and Foreign Minister K'oseivanov by polpred Lavrent'ev, 3 November 1939: ibid., doc. 510.

45. *I Documenti diplomatici*, Vol. 5, doc. 104, note 1.

46. 'Zapis besedy mezhdu fyurerom i predsedatelem Soveta narodnykh komissarov Molotovym v prisutstvii reikhministra inostrannykh del i zamestitelya Narodnogo komissara inostrannykh del Dekanozov, a takzhe sovetnika Khil'gera i Pavlova (perevodchiki) v Berline 13 noyabrya 1940 goda', *Mezhdunarodnaya Zhizn'*, No. 8, August, 1991, p. 107.

47. Molotov (Berlin) to Stalin (Moscow), 14 November 1940: ibid., pp. 20–1.

48. *Das Deutsche Reich und Der Zweite Weltkrieg*, Vol. 4 (Stuttgart, 1983), p. 34.

49. Fransoni (Stockholm) to Ciano (Rome), 9 November 1940: *I Documenti diplomatici*, Vol. 5, doc. 210.

50. Rosso (Moscow) to Ciano (Rome), 31 December 1940: *I Documenti diplomatici*, Vol. 6, doc. 382.

51. 'Zapis vtorogo zasedaniya glav pravitel'stv', 29 November 1943: *Sovetskii Soyuz . . .* Vol. 2: *Tegeranskaya konferentsiya*, p. 113.

52. 'Zapis chetvertogo zasedaniya glav pravitel'stv', 1 December 1943: ibid., p. 141.

53. M. Gilbert, *Road to Victory*, p. 1003.

54. 'Zapis zasedaniya glav pravitel'stv', 10 February 1945: *Sovetskii Soyuz . . .* Vol. 4: *Krymskaya konferentsiya . . .*, p. 201.

55. ' . . . we may be able to please them [the Russians] about the exits from the Black Sea and the Baltic as part of a general settlement.' This is what he told Eden in May 1945: Gilbert, *Road*, p. 1330.

56. Erkin, *Les relations*, pp. 286–7.

57. B. Kuniholm, *The Origins of the Cold War in the Near East: Great Power Conflict and Diplomacy in Iran, Turkey and Greece* (Princeton, 1980), pp. 257–8.

58. *Ustanovyavane i ukrepvane na narodno demokratichnata vlast sentembri 1944–mai 1945: Sbornik dokumenti*, ed. V. Bozhinov *et al.* (Sofia, 1969), doc. 1. For Dimitrov as author: *Georgi Dimitrov 1882–1949*, ed. D. Elazar (Sofia, no date), p. 187.

59. Gilbert, *Road*, pp. 992–9.
60. The information was said to have come from a 'sure' source: quoted in P. Stavrakis, *Moscow and Greek Communism, 1944–1949* (Ithaca/London, 1989), pp. 61–2, footnote 33.
61. For the background: Haslam, *The Soviet Union and the Threat from the East, 1933–41* (London, 1992), Chapter 1.
62. Ibid., Chapter 6.
63. For Stalin's thinking on these questions: K. Simonov, 'Glazami cheloveka moego pokoleniya: iz materialov ko vtorio chasti – 'Stalin i voina': Besedy s admiralom flota Sovetskogo Soyuza I. S. Isakovym, 21 May 1962,' *Znamya*, 65, April 1988, pp. 71–2.
64. *Sovetsko-amerikanskie otnosheniya vo vremya velikoi otechestvennoi voiny 1941–1945*, Vol. 2, ed. A. Gromyko *et al.* (Moscow, 1984), doc. 164.
65. 'Zapis besedy glav pravitel'stv vo vremya zavtraka', *Sovetskii Soyuz... Tegeranskaya...*, doc. 59.
66. Ibid.
67. *Sovetskii Soyuz... Krymskaya...*, doc. 27.
68. See the eyewitness account by the young Gromyko: A. Gromyko, *Pamyatnoe*, Vol. 1 (Moscow 1988) p. 189. For the overall significance of this in the history of Soviet–Japanese relations: Haslam, 'The Pattern of Soviet–Japanese Relations since World War II', *Russia and Japan: An unresolved dilemma between distant neighbours*, ed. T. Hasegawa, J. Haslam and A. Kuchins (Berkeley, 1993), pp. 3–48.
69. Quoted in Haslam, 'The Boundaries of Rational Calculation in Soviet Policy towards Japan', *History the White House and the Kremlin: Statesmen as Historians*, ed. M. Fry (London, 1991) pp. 43–4.
70. *Sovetsko-angliiskie otnosheniya*, Vol. 2, doc. 164.
71. M. Djilas, *Conversations with Stalin* (London, 1963), pp. 90–1.
72. This was said at Teheran: quoted in Gilbert, *Road*, p. 592.
73. The circumstantial evidence for this is not bad concerning September 1943. See W. Leonhard, *Child of the Revolution* (London, 1957), p. 257; also, Mastny, *Russia's Road to the Cold War*, pp. 83–4. The evidence lies either in the KGB archive – the initiative was taken through the secret service – or the Kremlin or Presidential archive, neither of which is open. The Foreign Ministry archive appears to contain nothing incriminating. There is also hearsay evidence concerning 1941: my informant, V. Dashichev, learnt of this from Zhukov.
74. Told to Louis Fischer and quoted by him in a talk at Chatham House, 4 September 1941: *US National Archives, Department of State*, 761.00/353.
75. Quoted in O. Tsarev, "Iz arkhivov KGB SSSR: Poslednii polet 'chernoi berty'", *Trud*, 13 May 1990.
76. Stalin (Moscow) to Maisky (London), 19 October 1942: *Sovetsko-Angliiskie...*, Vol. 1, doc. 147.
77. Djilas, *Conversations*, p. 61.
78. E. Kardelj, *Reminiscences: The Struggle for Recognition and Independence: The New Yugoslavia, 1944–1957* (London, 1982), p. 66.
79. Ibid.
80. From the German communist archives: D. Staritz, 'The SED, Stalin, and the German Question: Interests and Decision-Making in the Light of New Sources', *German History*, Vol. 10, No. 3, p. 277.
81. Stalin's answers to questions from *Pravda*, 14 March 1946.
82. Djilas, *Conversations*, p. 90.
83. Ibid., p. 62.

# 3 American Foreign Economic Policy and Lend-Lease
## Kathleen Burk

Lend-lease was a weapon, but it was a sword whose purpose differed depending upon who held it. At its most basic, it was a set of procedures intended to facilitate the transfer of American goods and services to Britain and the Commonwealth to enable them to continue the fight against the Axis powers. Separate from the procedures was the financial underpinning; separate again was the 'Consideration' which Britain was to render in recompense. But inseparable was the context: Lend-lease carried as baggage a weight of history which determined its shape, the use made of it, and the results flowing from its use. There are immense resonances between Anglo-American financial relations in the First and Second World Wars, both in problems which arose and in solutions imposed. Furthermore, Wilsonian aspirations unfulfilled in the First were achieved in the Second, primarily by determining to use American financial leverage against Britain – again, an intention of Wilson which he had failed to fulfil.

Britain had turned to the United States for finance even before the First World War, having raised four Boer War loans partly in America.[1] The channel was the House of Morgan, and the British Government turned to Morgans again in 1914, when the decision to raise a mass army meant that the Government had to go beyond their usual suppliers. The main source of supply was clearly the US, and Britain (as well as the other belligerents) began placing massive orders for munitions, food and supplies. By 1915 J. P. Morgan & Co., at the request of the British Government, had set up its Export Department, run by E. R. Stettinius, whose remit was to act as Purchasing Agent for the Entente powers in the US (his son, E. R. Stettinius, Jr, would be the first Administrator of the Office of Lend-Lease Administration). Dollars had to be found to pay for the orders, and this was achieved before April 1917, when the US joined the war, by a combination of shipping gold, selling off British-owned American securities (stocks) and, in 1915 and 1916, borrowing money on the New York money market. By April 1917 the UK had the dollars to pay for only three weeks' worth of orders, and with relief threw themselves into the arms of the American Government.

Once the United States was a belligerent, the government took over responsibility both for placing orders and for providing most of the funds to pay for them. There was never any question on the American side of providing the goods for free: the cost, totalling some $4.8 billion, was to be repaid. These were the war debts,[2] and their existence dogged the British Government for the subsequent generation. The fact that Britain eventually reneged on these debts after December 1932 was a major drawback in trying to build Congressional support for aid during the Second World War.

Both the British and the Americans drew various lessons from their experiences with the US as an arsenal of democracy and banker for the Entente powers during the First World War. First of all, private bankers were not to be allowed to become publicly involved.[3] It was no longer considered either appropriate or politically wise for New York bankers in particular to become involved in placing orders or raising funds. The whole controversy over whether the US had been lured into war by bankers seeking to protect their loans – whether they had acted as 'merchants of death' – had culminated in the Nye Committee hearings, the conclusion of which was that they had.[4] Irrespective of the truth, voters – and particularly isolationist congressmen and senators – believed the charge, and it would have been politically suicidal had the Roosevelt Administration countenanced any such proposal. Fortunately, none was made.[5] The British had no desire to follow that path again, and besides, the amount likely to be required was far beyond their own resources or the resources likely to be raised on money markets. The British were fully as stretched in March 1941 as they had been in April 1917; indeed, given the decline in assets in the 24 years separating the two dates, they were in much worse shape in 1941. Therefore, for reasons of history, politics and economics, the British were to turn immediately to the American Government for help in the Second World War.

A second lesson drawn was the extent to which the cash nexus had soured future relations. US officials believed that by not repaying the war debts, the UK had taken advantage of the goodwill of the US. Many were determined that the US was not going to be taken advantage of a second time, and persistently believed that the UK had greater assets than she was admitting that she had. The conclusion was that the UK was much more able to pay for supplies than appeared on the face of it to be the case, and thus that American officials should be rough, canny and persistent in order to uncover the truth. President Roosevelt himself seemed to share this idea, and in particular appeared to believe that British assets were extensive. Roosevelt, however, took an imaginative leap and eventually decided to 'take out the dollar sign' entirely: the US would lend rather then sell, and would extract recompense in non-monetary coin, such as future British policies, rather than forcing Britain to build up another set of war debts.

The plight of Great Britain in the First World War had given rise at the time to various ideas and inchoate plans to use this opportunity to benefit the US at Britain's expense. The then Secretary of the Treasury, William Gibbs McAdoo, and others wanted to replace the pound with the dollar as the world standard of value; furthermore, they wanted to help New York City to replace London as the supreme international financial centre. Both were conceivable: by April 1917, only the financial support of the US kept the pound even nominally on the gold standard, and when that support was withdrawn in March 1919, the exchange rate of the pound against the dollar plummeted. Likewise, the fact that so much of the world's monetary wealth had moved to the United States meant that New York in the 1920s found it much easier to loan funds than did London; furthermore, banks were aided by governmental measures such as the 1919 Edge Act, whose whole purpose was to enable American banks to combine abroad (which was illegal within the US) in order that they could take on the might of the British banks overseas. These financial aims seemed even more attainable during the Second World War than they had in the First, and certainly Henry Morgenthau, Roosevelt's Secretary of the Treasury, was quoted in 1946 to the effect that his primary objective during his years at the Treasury had been to 'move the financial centre of the world from London and Wall Street to the United States Treasury and to create a new concept between the nations of international finance'.[6] (It is worth remembering that McAdoo, too, had wanted to take control of domestic and international finance from the bankers in Wall Street and lodge it in the US Treasury.)[7] Keeping Britain short of reserves was a very good way of preventing her following an undesirable path financially both during the war and afterwards. It is also worth noting that Morgenthau was a bureaucratic warrior, and there were occasions when Britain was little more than a pawn in his struggle with the State Department to control foreign economic policy.

Woodrow Wilson himself had had rather higher ends in view, but he still wished to use the financial weapon: as he remarked to his adviser Col E. M. House in 1918, 'England and France have not the same views with regard to peace that we have by any means. When the war is over we can force them to our way of thinking, because by that time they will, among other things, be financially in our hands; . . .'[8] A major goal was the establishment of the League of Nations, but generally he wished to convince the Powers to accept and act upon certain liberal internationalist ideas, in particular the rule of law in international affairs and the implementation of multilateral free trade and convertible currencies. Cordell Hull, Roosevelt's Secretary of State from 1933 to 1944 and, in the somewhat confused words of the Permanent Under-secretary of the Foreign Office, 'a dreadful old man – [vague and wordy] . . ., and rather pig-headed, but quite a nice old thing . . .',[9] fully shared Wilson's ideas about economic liberalisation; he believed that political conflict was largely caused by economic rivalry, and that Wilson's complete neglect of economic issues at the Versailles Peace Conference in favour of concentrating on the League of Nations was a major contributory factor to postwar instability. A main theme of Hull's tenure at the State Department, therefore, was his continuing attempts to force other powers, and particularly Britain, to change their policies towards economic liberalisation. Britain had, of course, been the main proponent of free trade for much of the previous century, but this was entirely changed in 1932 with the signing of the Ottawa Agreements. These established the system of Imperial Preference, by which members of the British Empire and Commonwealth agreed to give members tariff preferences over non-members. Hull had an exaggerated idea of Britain's power: he believed that the Empire was a tightly-integrated economic system controlled by London from which Britain reaped great benefits but which greatly harmed the prospects of American exporters. He therefore determined to force Britain to end the system, which in his eyes was no better than Germany's drive towards autarchy. The Anglo-American Trade Agreement of 1938 was meant to be a step in this process, but hope that Britain would '"join the United States in a policy of trade liberalization" was to be dashed cruelly to the ground'.[10] The Agreement embodied tariff reductions, going against the trend of substantial British tariff increases after 1932, and included broad provisions intended to maintain trade between the US and Britain on a liberal basis, but there was no fundamental change of policy on the British side: rather, only that 'the British thought it unwise to refuse the American request for an agreement'.[11] In short, the British refused to countenance equality of treatment in trade, particularly in view of the high US tariffs.

Important members of the State Department policy-making team at the outset of the Second World War were, therefore, acutely aware of Britain's unwillingness to fall in with their strongly-held policy preferences. According to David Reynolds, Adolf Berle, the Assistant Secretary of State, Sumner Welles, the Under-Secretary of State, and Jay Pierrepont Moffat, Assistant Secretary of State for European Affairs, were all 'realists' who were deeply suspicious of Britain: they repudiated the English cultural connection as unAmerican, thought that the US should pursue its traditionally independent foreign policy rather than acting as a cock-boat in the wake of the British man-of-war, and had a sharp sense of Anglo-American commercial rivalry.[12] In short, they were Anglophobes; but others who would not merit that description, such as Dean Acheson,[13] who became Assistant Secretary of State for Economic Affairs in 1941, could still share their intention of using Britain's agony to further America's plans. As Reynolds writes,

> Welles, Berle and Acheson agreed that the U.S.A. should concentrate on securing a firm British commitment to abandon Imperial Preference and financial controls after the war, in return for a promise of radical reductions in U.S. tariffs. Unlike another war debt, this would be a meaningful quid pro quo, beneficial to the U.S.A. *and* to the world economy. They saw the leverage provided by the Consideration, at a time when Britain's bargaining power was greatly diminished, as 'their only chance to do it' [Acheson].[14]

Acheson himself was probably more concerned with the balance of power in the postwar world than with international political economy.[15] Basically an Anglophile, but devoted to furthering the interests of the United States, he believed a strong United Kingdom was vital. Randall Bennett Woods has argued that Acheson feared that if the UK maintained trade discrimination, the US would be forced by Congress to respond in the same manner, and the ensuing trade war, exacerbated by a resurgent isolationism, would prevent political and strategic cooperation.[16] Charles Bohlen, a member of the State Department for forty years and Counsellor to Acheson when the latter was Secretary of State, characterised Acheson as 'the tall man with the bristling mustache and cold eyes';[17] this sums up his essentially hardheaded (if basically sympathetic) view of what was required of Britain if she was to play her proper postwar role.

The State Department was supported by the US Treasury, headed by a Secretary whose ambitions to foster a shift in financial power from Britain to the US have already been described. Multilateral trade was, however, necessary but not sufficient, and Treasury had its own additional agenda, focused on convertible currencies and the dominant role of the dollar in the present and postwar world. Nevertheless, although no sentimental friend of Britain, Morgenthau did not share the antipathy of those such as Berle, and fundamentally supported aid to Britain, if the concessions were right. What he did not support was any attempt by the State Department to take control of Lend-Lease: as will be seen, when Hull in 1944 made such a bid over the question of British reserves, Morgenthau pulverised him.

Finally there is the question of President Roosevelt. It is a rash historian who claims to fathom entirely the workings of the presidential mind. Certainly he did not want Britain to lose the war, but equally he did not want to lose the next election. He would prefer that the US not have to fight if there was an alternative short of war; equally, like Wilson, he was determined to dominate the peace. He was persuaded that the plans of the American Government, self-evidently more far-seeing and selfless than those of the allies, especially those of Great Britain, should triumph. His personality helped: pre-eminently a politician, he had no permanent friends or permanent enemies, only permanent interests. The survival of Britain was vital to postwar plans; therefore he would facilitate aid to Britain to the extent that he could carry Congress with him.[18] This latter point is a strong theme in the story: the fight between the Executive, as it strove to control the making and implementation of foreign policy, and the Congress, as it strove to curtail or even roll back this perceived extension of presidential powers. In 1943, for example, Lend-Lease would constitute one of the battlegrounds on which the two branches of government fought it out.

The main argument, then, is that Lend-Lease must be seen as part of a continuum of American foreign economic policy, and in particular of policies whose implementation would require profound policy changes on the part of Britain. The British need for the aid promised by Lend-Lease provided the opportunity to apply such pressure, pressure which would be continued through the negotiations over the Atlantic Charter in 1941, during the Bretton Woods conference in 1944 and for the American Loan in 1945.

It is convenient to consider lend-lease in its successive phases. The first phase covers the period from British entry into the war in August 1939 through the passing of the Lend-Lease Act on 11 March 1941. The second phase, during which a major concern was 'the Consideration' by means of which Britain would recompense the United States, covers the period from March 1941 to the acceptance on both sides of the Master Lend-Lease Agreement in February 1942. The third phase covers the application of the agreement up to the spring of 1945, while the final phase covers the run-up to Stage II (the period between VE Day and VJ Day), Stage II itself and the abrupt cancellation of lend-lease on 20 August 1945, five days after VJ Day. Throughout the period, British needs remained constant, although the urgency of each component varied: access to matériel, dollars to pay for it and safe transport to get it back across the Atlantic.

It had been clear to the UK Treasury for several years before the outbreak of the Second World War that, without American financial help, it was going to be very difficult for Britain to fight a war of any duration. American financial help, however, was problematic, to say the least: the Johnson Act of 1934 forbade loans, except renewals or refundings, to any government which had not repaid its First World War war debts. The Roosevelt Administration never attempted to challenge Congress on this, and thus governmental loans to the UK were never a possibility.[19] Other ways would have to be found, and lend-lease, in essence, was the other way.

It is worth noting, however, that finance was only one of the problems faced by a British Government anxious to expand its sources of supply. It was not clear on the outbreak of war that the UK would be allowed to purchase munitions and supplies in the US, even with ready money. A series of Neutrality Acts passed during the 1930s forbade the sale of arms to belligerents, allowed the President to withhold raw materials from them, forbade loans to belligerents, and forbade American ships from carrying munitions to belligerent states. President Roosevelt failed in an attempt to convince Congress to amend the neutrality regulations in the summer of 1939; it required a mutual Anglo-German declaration of war to change Congressional minds and tempers (some congressmen were apparently convinced that there would not be a war). A revised Neutrality Act was passed on 4 November 1939: it repealed the arms embargo, allowing belligerents to acquire arms in the US as long as they paid cash for them and carried them away in non-American ships.[20]

During the period of American neutrality, then, Britain's access to the American munitions markets was handicapped by her belligerent status. She would be handicapped again with regard to her access to goods in the months just before and after Pearl Harbor on 7 December 1941, because the US service departments began to place large and numerous orders, thereby threatening to deprive Britain of the goods she had ordered or hoped to order to equip her forces. It would take some months before all conflicts were resolved.

Two of the overriding British problems, then, were access to goods and the means to pay for them. The third problem was that of getting purchases back to Europe: how were the merchant ships to be protected from German submarines? There was the offensive means, going after the submarines and destroying them; or there was the defensive means, convoying merchant ships. On 15 May 1940, five days after he became Prime Minister, Churchill wrote to President Roosevelt asking for 'the loan of forty or fifty of your older destroyers to bridge the gap between what we have now and the large new construction we put in hand at the beginning of the war'.[21] They were required for anti-submarine escorts in the Western Approaches, as well as generally for patrols against invasion. The former was important in keeping open the supply lines to the Western Hemisphere: this was crucial now that the German drive to the sea had closed off European sources of supply, and the Mediterranean and Suez Canal were effectively closed to merchant shipping.

Roosevelt was not immediately encouraging, but after long and difficult negotiations an agreement was concluded on 2 September 1940. In exchange for granting the US leases of land on eight British possessions in the Caribbean, on which the US could build air and naval bases, the UK received fifty First World War destroyers. It is doubtful that this made a significant difference immediately to the safety of merchant shipping in the Atlantic – for one thing, only nine were in service with the Royal Navy by the end of the year – but for Churchill it was crucial because it publicly drew the US ever closer to the UK.[22] In this sense, it was crucial, too, in the gradual shift in the Washington mind towards helping the UK.

Whatever the conditions of safety of the Atlantic supply lines, however, once the 1939 Neutrality Act allowed Britain to purchase goods in the US, she did so, and took the chance that they would actually reach the UK. Therefore, the overriding concern from November 1939 on was how to pay for the goods. During the period of American neutrality during the First World War, Britain had paid for her purchases in the US by shipping gold, selling British-owned American securities for dollars in New York City, and raising loans on the American money market. The last-named of these was clearly not an option in 1939–41, thanks to the Johnson Act, and therefore Britain had to depend wholly on the first two options. At the outbreak of the war the UK had gold and dollar reserves totalling £503 million ($2028 million), and these were gradually run down, until by March 1941, when the

Lend-Lease Agreement was signed, the reserves stood at £70 million ($282 million).[23] The only ways in which the reserves could be maintained were by acquiring more gold from the South African gold-mines and by earning dollars from exports to North America. The former could be counted on, although neither the exact amount nor the certainty of its safe arrival in the UK could be guaranteed. At the same time, increasing dollar-earning exports would become more and more difficult, as industry and labour were progressively mobilised for war-related production.

The other method of raising dollars was to mobilise securities which might find a market in the US and sell them. In the First World War, this had been done only gradually and for the first year-and-a-half in a somewhat piecemeal fashion.[24] In the Second World War, conversely, the mobilisation and sale of securities were organised at the outset. Securities in private hands were brought under the control of the Treasury by means of Defence (Finance) Regulation No. 1, and even before the outbreak of war (on 26 August 1939) the Treasury had called for their registration. (This gave the Treasury the right to require owners of such securities to inform the Treasury of the identity and size of holdings; the Treasury could then require that owners hand them in to be sold in the US for dollars, the Treasury then reimbursing the owners in sterling.)

The Treasury estimated that the value of such securities if sold in the US was about $1000 million (£250 million), and arrangements for their sale rapidly became urgently necessary. Once Congress had amended the Neutrality Act on 4 November 1939 to allow Britain and other belligerents to purchase war supplies – as long as they paid cash for them – orders began to be placed. Shipping gold would be very risky, and the Treasury decided, for the time being, to concentrate on raising money by selling securities. However, too many sold openly and immediately would cause their sale price to drop; at the same time, there was the fear that the French would also try to sell securities, and the competition would add to the depression of prices. Therefore, speed and discretion were necessary, and early in November 1939 a partner in a noted City merchant bank went across to New York City to advise and organise.[25]

In the first months, sales on private account at the rate of £2 million a week were carried out, the owners then surrendering the dollars to the Treasury for sterling, and the belief was that the New York market could not absorb more. However, by mid-February 1940 the need for dollars was overwhelming, and the Treasury took over some £30 million worth of American securities. As it happened, the sales were carried out so quietly that the market was unaware of what the British Government were doing, and by the end of April about $34 million had been raised. The market soon became accustomed, and regular and moderate selling operations were carried out, until the collapse of the market in April after the German invasion of Denmark and Norway. Little could be done until after the Presidential election in November 1940, but American officials made it clear that Britain was expected to sell not only American securities, but also South American securities, as well as direct investment in the US, such as insurance companies and manufacturing plant.[26]

During the months of the phoney war, the British Treasury emphasised economy: the War Cabinet had ruled in September 1939 that preparations should be made on the basis of a three-year war. The Treasury took this seriously, but their own private estimate was that financial resources would only last two years at best, and the money, therefore, had to be doled out as economically as possible. Once the Germans began their *Blitzkrieg*, however, the danger to Britain became so great that three years, or even two, was beside the point. Britain would need supplies and munitions as soon as possible, and on 24 May 1940 the British Government decided to throw financial prudence to the winds: the government would buy all the munitions and supplies which the US could produce until the dollars and gold ran out. This un-Treasury-like behaviour, however, is put into perspective by R. S. Sayers, the official historian, who points out that 'it seems likely that Treasury officials reconciled themselves to such prodigality only by private expectations that sooner or later America would loosen the purse-strings'.[27]

Nevertheless, massive orders now had to be paid for, and, unfortunately, one outcome of the *Blitzkrieg* and then Dunkirk was a widespread belief in the States that Britain might well lose. Therefore, businessmen and manufacturers wanted money up front, refusing to sign contracts calling for payment upon delivery of the goods. Thus Britain's proportional costs accelerated, and the Treasury was forced to make hard decisions as to which orders were vital and which merely desirable. Naturally, the British Government wanted to turn to the US for financial help; naturally the American Government realised and wished to discourage this.

A turning-point came in June 1940 when Henry Stimson became Secretary of War and Frank Knox became Secretary of the Navy. Knox actually favoured US entry into the war; Stimson, while not going that far, supported American ships' escorting of merchant ships carrying goods to Britain. Reynolds argues that, by joining Harold Ickes, the Secretary of the Interior, and Morgenthau as Cabinet hawks, they tipped the balance of power in the Administration in favour of helping Britain and France.[28] For whatever reasons, and British successes in the Battle of Britain during August must have contributed, both the public and the governmental perception of Britain and her chances of survival grew vastly more favourable over the next few months, underlined by the Destroyers for Bases agreement on 2 September. Nevertheless, nothing more substantial could be done until after the presidential and Congressional elections scheduled for 5 November 1940, and the British had to continue to find the funds to pay for their orders. Somehow – and somewhat embarrassingly, considering their pleas of poverty – they always found the money: as Adam Smith once pointed out, 'Be assured . . . that there is a great deal of ruin in a country.'

December 1940 was the crucial month. The election was now over, and Roosevelt could once again turn his attention to public affairs, but only after some rest and relaxation. He departed on a cruise on 3 December, but two days before he had met with Morgenthau and two other members of the Treasury and gone over the whole situation. He refused to believe that British bankruptcy loomed – he is quoted as commenting, after a quick glance at a US Treasury estimate of her dollar resources 'Well, they aren't bust – there's lots of money there.'[29] Rather, he continued to believe that a lack of will to sell marketable assets in Latin America or the US was at the root of the pleas for help in paying for orders. In short, Roosevelt believed that Britain could continue to cope with a steady, moderate need for money; what he feared they could no longer provide was the capital investment which had financed the extension of American plant for use in war production during the previous year. Roosevelt's concern at this point was American preparations: if the American Government could provide the investment in new plant, the British could pay for their share of the resulting production.

The British Government's concern at this moment was more wide-ranging than just finance. Obviously the Treasury was worried, but Churchill apparently shared the approach of Lloyd George during the Great War, namely that Britain should order the goods and the money would come from somewhere. There were additional desiderata. Churchill himself believed that the most important need was for ships. Lord Lothian, the British Ambassador to the United States, was on the firing-line in Washington; he decided that Churchill, whose strength was his global view, had to appeal to Roosevelt personally once the election was over. He would both push the need for funds and be able to encloak the request in a wide-ranging vision. Indeed, Lothian believed that 'Americans did not properly understand Britain's needs and that it would take a long time to educate them into effective action.'[30] A more general appeal, then, would serve several purposes: it would, ideally, bring a wide-ranging, synoptic view before the President; it would both call for help with shipping, which concerned the Prime Minister and others, and with American finance, which concerned the Treasury and others; it would show the interdependence of British needs; and it would do so at a time when, it was hoped, the winning of the election would make the President more susceptible to such an appeal than he had been for some time. Therefore, when Lothian drafted a telegram for Churchill to send to Roosevelt, it 'stressed very frankly our need for American support in obtaining the Irish naval bases, in guarding Singapore, in getting more ships and above all in buying munitions and aircraft on credit. It is intended to make R. feel that if we go down, the responsibility will be America's.'[31]

The letter reached the president in the midst of the Caribbean on 9 December; according to Harry Hopkins, Roosevelt's aide and confidant, Roosevelt 'read and re-read the letter and for about two days seemed unsure of what to do.... Then the following day he came up with the Lend-Lease idea.'[32] Meanwhile, Morgenthau had met with Sir Frederick Phillips, the UK Treasury representative in Washington, on 6 and 9 December. Morgenthau and the British Embassy in Washington both repeatedly urged the British Government to put itself in America's hands: they should come clean both on needs *and* on assets, and trust the US to help. The Treasury, however, feared being so open: partly it was traditional secrecy, partly it was apprehension that the Americans would put pressure on them to give up assets if they knew what they were, partly it was a shrinking-back from appearing to give the American Government the opportunity to demand a financial review of the British effort and partly it was disinclination to let the Americans know for certain just how weak Britain was.[33] Phillips shared these doubts. However, on 12 December, according to Morgenthau, when he told Phillips that he favoured making Britain a gift of supplies rather than forcing her to raise another war loan, and that the only reason he was urging Britain to be more forthcoming with information about their assets was to show the US public and Congress that Britain was genuinely in need of help, Phillips gave in. 'From then on he became a consistent exponent of the Lothian argument, also favoured by most British officials in Washington, that the best way to get U.S. help was not to adopt the reserved, hard-bargaining attitude of the Treasury but to lay Britain's cards on the table and trust to the Administration's goodwill.'[34]

Therefore, when upon his return to Washington Roosevelt consulted Morgenthau about his ideas, the latter was enthusiastic. The President announced his own views to a press conference on 17 December, although 'announced' is probably too straightforward a word for the hints and suggestions which he employed. He used to good effect the so-called fire-hose analogy first suggested to him by Ickes the previous summer: the US could take over British orders for munitions and 'enter into some kind of arrangement for their use by the British on the grounds that it was the best thing for American defence, with the understanding that when the show was over, we would get repaid sometime in kind, thereby leaving out the dollar mark'.... If his neighbour's house was on fire, and the neighbour wanted to borrow his garden hose, he would not say that the hose had cost $15, and that he wanted $15 for it; rather, he would loan the hose and reclaim it after the fire.[35]

Treasury lawyers prepared a draft bill on 2 January 1941, Roosevelt approved the draft on 7 January and on 10 January the bill, entitled 'An Act to Promote the Defense of the United States', was introduced into both Houses. Basically, the Act authorised the President 'to sell, transfer, exchange, lease or lend or otherwise dispose of' defence articles to those countries whose defence he considered 'related' to that of the US. No limit was placed on the total sum involved. Warren Kimball has described the process in some detail: it was long and complicated, involving both the passing of the Act itself and then the passing of an appropriations bill. Because the Democrats had large majorities, there was theoretically no problem about the bill's passage; however, Roosevelt wanted consensus behind the bill, and therefore was quite amenable to various amendments. The Administration stuck to a single line: Hitler was bent on world domination, which would clearly threaten the US; Britain and especially her navy constituted the front line of defence; and therefore the US had to facilitate the acquisition of necessary war supplies by the UK.

Opponents of the bill fell into two main camps. There were the isolationists who believed that the US should stay out of any foreign entanglement, and who feared that these economic links would pull the US into war just as, they believed, had happened in the First World War. The other group of opponents were those who feared both an expansion of presidential power in general and an expansion of unfettered presidential power in the area of foreign affairs in particular. It was the combination of the two groups that caused some apprehension in the Administration, and the response was to make a number of promises to Congress during the hearings and passage of the bill which were to tie the hands of those responsible for lend-lease for the remainder of the war. The US would not pay for any past or current orders, the so-called 'Old Commitments', in spite of assurances to the contrary: Morgenthau told the Senate Foreign Relations Committee that Britain would pay for them by selling her American securities and direct investments (Morgenthau forced the sale of the American Viscose Corporation, a subsidiary of the British company Courtaulds, to a consortium of American bankers at a knock-down price in order to demonstrate British willingness to Congress). This assurance was repeated by Harold Smith, the Budget Director, to the House Appropriations Committee. With these assurances, the Lend-Lease Act was passed on 11 March 1941. With the passing of the Appropriations Act on 27 March, Congress authorised $7 billion for the production of munitions and agreed that the Administration could allocate a proportion (unspecified) to countries whose survival benefited the US. Congress, however, insisted on the right to review lend-lease every six months.[36]

There was understandable hope in Cabinet and Whitehall that problems with American finance would now cease; those closer to the fire were not so sanguine. The following year, or Phase II, saw two main problems for Britain: how to pay for orders already placed, and how to respond to American attempts to impose, as the 'Consideration' for lend-lease, the requirement that Britain promise to restructure her external economic arrangements after the war, primarily by promising to give up discriminatory tariffs in general and Imperial Preference in particular and by agreeing to give up exchange controls. The former problem caused the more immediate anguish, since bills were continually falling due. The Administration had promised Congress that the US would not pay for these orders, so Britain herself had to do so, but she did not possess the reserves to cover the bills. Granted, Britain did not want to sell off all her American securities and assets, but even if she had positively wished to do so, they would probably have only attracted fire-sale prices. Therefore, the money had to be found elsewhere, and the answer was a loan of $425 million arranged through the Reconstruction Finance Corporation and secured on American stocks valued at $700 million as collateral. After this, according to Sayers, 'American complaints that the British were clinging to realisable assets' – i.e. not getting rid of their American investments to pay their bills – entirely ceased.[37]

The point about lend-lease was that it was intended to remove the dollar sign as a consideration in Britain's acquisition of American supplies. However, some recompense, some consideration, there had to be. Each nation who received lend-lease aid was required to sign a master agreement, and although negotiations on this for Britain were begun even before the bill was passed, it still took almost a year before the Master Lend-Lease Agreement was signed in February 1942. The question was, what was to be the 'consideration'? And who was to control the negotiations? Morgenthau and the Treasury, naturally, attempted to do so, but Roosevelt put his confidant Harry Hopkins in charge of the interdepartmental committee which was to oversee the Lend-Lease Administration. He, therefore, held the ring as Treasury and State Department battled over the thrust of the Agreement.

Discussions took place and drafts were circulated over the subsequent months. In March and April 1941 the US Treasury draft circulated, suggesting that Britain return surviving goods after the end of the war, and that she recompense the US in goods or raw materials. This, however, would have shackled Britain with another set of war debts, even if in kind rather than in cash. In May the State Department made its bid: it suggested that matériel that was meant to be destroyed, such as bombs and bullets, be written off, that goods which survived the war, such as ships and guns, be returned, and that a commitment to abandon Imperial Preference and financial controls after the war, in exchange for sharp reductions in American tariffs, be deemed recompense for other supplies. The draft Agreement which was submitted to Britain on 28 July 1941 was essentially that of the State Department: its centrepiece, for State, was Article VII, which prohibited discrimination in either country against any product originating in the other country. In other words, Britain would be required to abandon Imperial Preference and the closed Sterling Area and embrace multilateralism.

The need for Britain to respond highlighted the fact of continuing debate in London. The burst of economic nationalism in Washington during and after the passage of the Act had made it clear that Britain would have to reassure Washington that the former did not mean to take advantage of

America's generosity to build up an exporting capacity on the basis of lend-lease goods. This reassurance was made explicit by the issuing on 13 September 1941 of the White Paper on Export Policy: articles received by Britain through the lend-lease mechanism were not and would not be re-exported, nor would goods similar to those supplied under lend-lease be used by British exporters 'to enter new markets or extend their export trade at the expense of United States exporters', nor would scarce materials of any kind be used to manufacture goods for export.[38] It was quite clear that the exports needed to raise dollars would now decline even further, and this would be increasingly worrying – the White Paper would be substantially modified and virtually (unilaterally) repudiated in 1945, although this was not publicly announced,[39] in the face of a continuing American run-down on provision through lend-lease and the resulting need to build up dollar export income. In 1941, however, the overwhelming need was to ensure the increasing flow of lend-lease goods. In this sense the postwar future was mortgaged.

Where London was more unwilling to mortgage the future was in the American request that Britain agree to the Article VII draft. A major problem for the Churchill coalition government was that agreement could have driven those devoted to Imperial Preference, which included a substantial section of Conservative Party politicians, out of the Government. They were supported by those who agreed with the Treasury and its ministers that continued import and exchange controls would be necessary for a period after the war.[40] London finally sent back a modified draft in October, which the United States again modified and resubmitted to the UK in early December.

Pearl Harbor on 7 December 1941, followed by the American entry into the war, led London to hope that the whole question would now fall into abeyance. But it did not, forming part of the discussions in Washington in late December and early January between Churchill and Roosevelt, although only with difficulty: Roosevelt kept bringing up the question of Article VII, Churchill kept postponing discussion.[41] He justified this to his own advisers, such as Lord Cherwell, by saying that he had to avoid political trouble at home; furthermore, he argued, 'it is only the State Department which is pressing'.[42]

This was not the case, however, and the matter came to a head in early February, just before Congressional hearings on appropriations for 1942 were due to begin. With Roosevelt's backing, Acheson warned Lord Halifax, now British Ambassador to the US (Lothian had died on 12 December 1940), that if the British did not agree to Article VII, the whole matter would be turned over to Congress to solve – and Congress, bastion of economic nationalism, would certainly attach a dollar sign to lend-lease.[43] On 4 February Roosevelt sent a personal message to Churchill: 'I understand your need of maintaining unity at home in the great task of winning the war. I know you also understand how essential it is that we maintain unity of purpose between our two governments and peoples in this and equally important in the unfinished tasks that will follow it. I am convinced that further delay in concluding this agreement will be harmful to your interests and ours.'[44]

The receipt of this cable caused a political crisis in London. After a Cabinet meeting on 6 February, Churchill replied to Roosevelt that the Cabinet was now 'even more resolved against trading the principle of imperial preference as consideration for lend-lease'. A majority of the Cabinet believed that acceptance of Article VII was tantamount to accepting 'intervention in the domestic affairs of the British Empire'.[45] Churchill himself agreed with this assessment. How would Washington react? Roosevelt agreed with the State Department, but he also did not want to push Britain too far: after all, they were now allies *de jure* rather than merely *de facto*, and they had a war to win; beyond this, politicians of stature tend to recognise and allow for true political crises when appealed to by each other. A path had to be found out of the imbroglio.

The State Department solution neither excluded Imperial Preference – they did not want to sell the pass – but nor did it emphasise it: the British were told that acceptance of Article VII did not imply specific commitments about Imperial Preference, and they were also reassured that the US recognised the right of the Dominions to have their say in the matter, that the UK could not necessarily speak for them. Furthermore, reductions in preferences would always be linked to reductions in tariffs. This made the Article considerably less one-sided. Roosevelt telegraphed these concessions to Churchill, and the Cabinet found it possible to accept them. So did the Dominions, and on 23 February 1942 the Mutual Aid Agreement was signed.[46] This brought to an end the use of lend-lease as the main battleground to compel the acceptance of postwar policies: the battle now shifted to the negotiations at Bretton Woods and especially over the 1946 Loan Agreement. Rather, during Phase III, the period from February 1942 to the spring of 1945, lend-lease would be used to keep Britain in the state of financial weakness required for the successful imposition of American policies.

Implicit within all these, and subsequent, discussions were differing Anglo-American views as to the nature of the supply relationship. From the British point of view, the approach should be that of 'pooling': each country would put into the common pool what it was able to supply and would take out what it needed. This was the idea behind 'mutual aid', to be implemented by reverse lend-lease, e.g. the supply of raw materials to the US from the British Empire. The total was not negligible: while US lend-lease aid to the UK would total about $27 billion, UK aid to the US would total about $6 billion.[47] Thus the UK approach, naturally, was that the two countries were allies together, without too much about senior and junior partners – and if the latter approach was to dominate, much credit should go to the UK for experience.

From the American point of view, however, in spite of Roosevelt sometimes seeing the strength of the pooling argument, the approach was that of 'deficit': that is, the US was making up a deficit in British supplies, and thus was not only entitled but required to keep a close eye on what the British wanted and why. This approach always dominated, because it served the purposes of three important groups: Congress, the armed services and the US Treasury.

Congress was the political forum of isolationists who believed that Britain had lured the US into war once again; of economic nationalists, supported by various industrial and commercial interest groups, who saw the UK as the great industrial and commercial rival and wished to tie her down; and of partisans of the power of Congress against that of the Executive, who saw lend-lease as a programme which served to enhance the power of the latter, and thus repeatedly inspected, investigated and condemned: 1943, for example, saw two congressional investigations of lend-lease. The first was that of the Senate Military Affairs Committee, who toured the battlefronts and reported widespread waste and mismanagement of lend-lease supplies on the part of the allies and of the British in particular. The second was that of the Senate Committee to Investigate the National Defense Program, chaired by Senator Harry S. Truman (Democrat from Missouri), which proposed that if the allies could not repay in dollars, they could transfer some of their international assets to the US after the war. The committee also insisted that the allies be required to use all of their own assets before turning to the US for aid.[48]

The opposition of the armed services was more straightforward: as far as many were concerned, goods provided to the allies meant that much less for the American forces. This however, was more of a problem in the early months of American rearmament than it was later. A more important problem was that the armed forces, too, cottoned on to the idea of using lend-lease for its leverage against, in particular, the British. In September 1944, for example, General Brehon Somerville, chief of supply services for the US military, suggested that it be used to force the British to turn over their bases in the Pacific, to convert the ninety-nine year leases in the Atlantic into permanent transfers, to secure unconditional landing rights for United States military and commercial aircraft at British bases around the world, and to prevent the UK from blocking American access to strategic materials in the Middle and Far East.[49] The pressure would dramatically increase as Germany moved towards defeat, when the military suggested that aid be ended after VE Day, except for items which the UK could not produce for itself. In this the military could count on allies in Congress and in trade associations such as the National Association of Manufacturers.[50]

The third important force interested in restricting British financial strength was the US Treasury, which intended to dominate the international financial system after the war and thus needed to eliminate the UK as a viable rival. Morgenthau and the Treasury, later joined by the Foreign Economic Administration, established by Roosevelt in 1943 under Leo Crowley to replace the Lend-Lease Administration, plotted to restrict lend-lease. The intention was to force the British to pay cash for whatever they required that was not a war-need narrowly defined, and the straightforward intention of the US Treasury was to limit the size of the British reserves, ideally to about $600 million to $1 billion (£150–£250 million), as against the British claim that the minimum they required in order to service the sterling area and to hope to finance their sterling liabilities after the war was $1.5–$2 billion.

In October 1942 Morgenthau visited London, and in discussions the Chancellor of the Exchequer pleaded that the UK be allowed to increase the level of the reserves. Morgenthau disagreed, and on 3 January 1943 he recommended to Roosevelt that the US use their control of lend-lease to keep the UK reserves down to between $600 million and $1 billion; the President agreed. Nevertheless, the British managed to rebuild them to about $1.2 billion by July 1943. At the first Quebec Conference in the autumn, Churchill repeated the argument to Roosevelt and Hopkins. Morgenthau, however, remained unmoved, and wrote to the President in late October calling for a readjustment downward in the reserves.[51] On 14 November he told Ambassador Halifax that the limit was $1 billion.

At this point the State Department reasserted itself. Hull had attended the foreign ministers' meeting in Moscow which served as a prelude to the Teheran Conference in November, and there he had won the assent of the Russians and the British to the Moscow Declaration on postwar security. It became clear to Hull that Britain would not be able to share in the work of what would become the UN nor would she be able to accept a multilateral economic order if she were not allowed to rebuild her reserves. After all, in a dollar-dominated system, if multilateralism is to work, other countries need dollars, and therefore the State Department became an ally of Britain against the Treasury in her fight to accumulate gold and dollar reserves.

This new energy on the part of Hull and his department led directly to a clash with Morgenthau and the Treasury in the first months of 1944. Morgenthau and Crowley were purposely running down British balances by increasing the so-called 'take-outs', i.e. specifying goods such as sugar, fish and paper for which lend-lease aid would not be available and for which the British would have to pay cash. Through devious manoeuvres the State Department provoked a crisis during which either the President would have to slap down the Treasury or the British would be alerted to what the Treasury were doing – that is, arbitrarily limiting the British reserves to $1 billion – and thus give Churchill a chance to protest to the President. The latter is what happened, and the Treasury had to agree that there would be no more 'take-outs'. Morgenthau then cowed Hull, and the State Department had to agree that Morgenthau and the Treasury were in charge of policy towards the British balances.[52]

At the Second Quebec Conference in September 1944, which was to be devoted to military matters – i.e. the last phase of the war against Germany and the strategy to be followed during Stage II, the war in the Pacific – the British aims were two-fold: they wanted the freedom to re-establish their export trade and they wanted a commitment from the US, preferably in writing, as to what they could expect through lend-lease in the now-foreseeable Stage II, the period between the defeat of Germany and that of Japan. US aims were mixed. Hull proposed that lend-lease aid be continued during Stage II, at two-thirds of its 1944 level, provided that Britain played a full part in the war against Japan; however, he emphasised that such aid should be made conditional upon discussion of and acceptance by Britain of the policy embodied in Article VII of the Mutual Aid Agreement. The military cared nothing about postwar economic policy, but had their own aims. Admiral William D. Leahy, the Chief of Staff, and General Somerville both opposed aid for anything other than direct use in the war against Japan. Beyond that, the military increasingly wanted to exclude Britain from America's war in the Pacific; this attitude would become progressively more important in the spring of 1945, as the final phase (Phase IV) of lend-lease began. However, Roosevelt's acceptance of Churchill's offer at the Quebec Conference of extensive military assistance against Japan meant that the requirement for Stage II lend-lease was now fulfilled.

The major shift in September 1944 came in the arguments of Morgenthau and the Treasury. There were two reasons for this. First of all, unlike Hull and the State Department, Morgenthau and the Treasury had achieved their postwar aims: the agreement at Bretton Woods in July 1944 set out the structure of an international monetary system in accordance with their plans. Therefore, they no longer needed the leverage over Britain provided by controls over lend-lease to the same extent. Indeed, successful working of the new International Monetary Fund would require a stronger Britain, who would be called upon to provide 16 per cent of the IMF's founding reserves. Secondly, Morgenthau had visited Britain in August 1944 and had concluded that Britain was indeed skint; she would have great difficulty with the reconversion of her economy. Therefore, he was now willing to consider the use of lend-lease aid to help Britain with her postwar economic problems – a use which he had heretofore adamantly refused to contemplate. His price would be British acceptance of his eponymous Plan to return Germany to an agricultural and pastoral economy. After some objection to this – Churchill apparently called the Plan 'un-Christian' – the British agreed. The Plan was doubtless made more palatable by Morgenthau's suggestion that the curtailing of Germany's industrial exports would provide an export opportunity for Britain.[53] At any rate, this smoothed the path; $5.5 billion for State II lend-lease was agreed, with some easement for civilian supply, as was the need to liberate Britain's export trade in some measure.[54]

Unfortunately for Britain, a storm of objections rained about Roosevelt's head. Hull objected violently that aid had not been used to extract commitments on postwar economic policy; the joint chiefs had wanted bases; others in the military still wanted Britain to play only a minor, if any, role in the Pacific; and they were all apparently angry at the Treasury for godfathering the Quebec Agreement. When, at the end of September, the Morgenthau Plan was leaked to the press, there was such an outcry against it that Roosevelt retreated. This had the effect of weakening Morgenthau's position and power. In mid-November 1944, while the British delegation were in Washington for talks on Stage II, Roosevelt abandoned the Agreement; as Morgenthau described it, Roosevelt 'doesn't want to give anything to the British, he doesn't want any publicity, he wants to be able to tell the newspapers that there was no agreement'.[55] This effectively left the status of the $5.5 billion agreed for Stage II lend-lease for Britain uncertain and subject to the political winds in Washington. In essence the British were now on their own.

The final phase in the story, Phase IV, can be said to have begun in the spring of 1945, when the British were subject to the first of a series of blows. In March, with the collapse of Germany clearly imminent, lend-lease was renewed only for war purposes, Congress inserting a special proviso that no lend-lease funds should be used for postwar relief, rehabilitation or reconstruction. This was a blow; but the death of President Roosevelt in April underlined that the British were now without a sympathetic higher authority to whom they could appeal. Granted there was a new President, but Truman knew very little of the background, and what he did know came from the Congressional side; the Truman Committee had, as noted above, issued a disapproving report on Britain and lend-lease in November 1943.

The effect of the Congressional decision was quickly felt. M. Duncan Hall notes that the decisions taken at the second Quebec Conference frequently did not percolate down to the middle reaches; furthermore, the political trends operating in Washington clearly did not favour generosity in lend-lease. Therefore, 'from April onwards British officials in Washington, watching events closely at these lower levels, could see the brakes coming on slowly at many different points. . . . For over a year lend-lease requirements had been subjected to more stringent tests as to eligibility.' This accelerated, and 'officials at the lower level of supply . . . [challenged] more and more freely the eligibility of particular requisitions. . . . In fact, as they watched developments in Washington on the working level of requisitions and assignments, the British missions . . . [began] to feel that the system of assignments, if not the whole basis of lend-lease itself, was crumbling.'[56]

Conditions rapidly worsened with the defeat of Germany in May. Roosevelt had promised that this would mark the beginning of American reconversion, and indeed had promised the same freedom to the UK.[57] This meant that there was, if possible, even less inclination to supply goods to Britain: according to Sayers, a 'wave of economy' swept through Congress and the Administration, and Truman directed on 5 July 1945 that military supplies under lend-lease should be confined to those required for operations against Japan; this meant that there were no lend-lease supplies for (for instance) Occupation Forces in Europe.[58]

The end of lend-lease came with brutal suddenness. On 11 August a British representative was warned by an official in the FEA that shipments were likely to end very quickly indeed, and the British should rapidly arrange for a loan to cover shipments in the pipeline. On 15 August the Japanese surrendered, on 19 August the UK Food Mission notified London that all loading of lend-lease foodstuffs had been stopped, and on 20 August the White House announced the termination of lend-lease forthwith: anything in the pipeline, as well as new contracts, would have to be paid for. Strictly speaking, the British Government should have been prepared: certainly they had been warned by all the announcements of the *terminus ad quem*, as well as by the reported 'crumbling' on the ground in Washington. Nevertheless, the British were profoundly shocked: as Sayers describes it, 'that the United States Government, after years of closer co-operation with the United Kingdom than had ever before been known between Great Powers, should have taken such drastic measures unilaterally, without any prior negotiation, left British Ministers and officials gasping for breath'.[59] The only path open to Britain was to apply for a loan: and it was during these negotiations over the 1946 Loan Agreement that both the State Department and the Treasury finally achieved the collapse of British external economic policy which had been so long desired.

The tale is not altogether a pretty one. Indeed, Sayers warns against the natural reactions of his British readers at the outset: 'It is a story, above all else, of unexampled generosity on the part of the American nation. Unless this all-important fact is remembered throughout, these chapters are bound to convey a false impression, an impression insulting alike to the Americans who gave and to the British who strove to justify acceptance of the colossal stream of munitions, of food, of aircraft and of materials to sustain both direct war production and civilian life in these islands.'[60] Certainly those historians who lived and worked during the war and who had close relations with the Americans present a view considerably more generous towards the American Government and its manipulation of lend-lease than a later generation of historians.[61] Disillusionment can have many causes. Partly it is a reaction against the sentimental hands-across-the-sea approach to the relationship, particularly as hymned by Churchill; partly it is a realistic appraisal of the fact that especially in international relations, public pronouncements and private actions frequently do not accord – and this works both ways; and partly it is the case that the documents are making what happened quite clear without the ameliorating gloss which human explanation often provides.

Hall attempts to set out the importance of lend-lease supplies to the war effort of Britain and the Commonwealth. About 70 per cent of the munitions used by them during the war was provided by the UK, while the US provided about 17 per cent under lend-lease and another 4 per cent for cash. Munitions were the largest element in lend-lease, about 65 per cent, while services (mostly shipping) came to 10 per cent and other supplies (about half of which was food) to 25 per cent. Other supplies also included machine tools, which were not available from any other source.[62] In other words, although the UK was by far the largest provider of munitions to British and Commonwealth forces, much of this depended on the orders placed in the early years of the war. The UK was in dire straits by the time of lend-lease, and certainly the shipping and food were vital.

What is at issue is American pressure and British response. The British should have been prepared for the pressure, and perhaps some were, but they were handicapped both by the American political system and by their lack of knowledge about its dynamics. Keynes tried to explain it:

To the outsider it looks almost incredibly inefficient. One wonders how decisions are ever reached at all. There is no clear hierarchy of authority. The different departments of the Government criticise one another in public and produce rival programmes. There is perpetual internecine warfare between prominent personalities. Individuals rise and fall in general esteem with bewildering rapidity. New groupings of administrative power and influence spring up every day. Members of the so-called Cabinet make public speeches containing urgent proposals which are not agreed as part of the Government policy. In the higher ranges of government no work ever seems to be done on paper; no decisions are recorded on paper; no-one seems to read a document and no-one ever answers a communication in writing. Nothing is ever settled in principle. There is just endless debate and sitting around. . . . Suddenly some drastic, clear-cut decision is reached, by what process one cannot understand, and all the talk seems to have gone for nothing, . . . the ultimate decision appearing to be largely independent of the immense parlez-vous, responsible and irresponsible, which has preceded it. Nothing is secret, nothing is confidential. The President laughed when I said that his method of deceiving the enemy was apparently to publish so much vital information that they would not have time to read it.[63]

The British did not understand that an apparent decision was not always a final decision; even more damagingly, many officials, particularly those in London, did not grasp the irrelevance of foreign concerns and foreigners in general to Washington politics, dominated as they were by Congress. They did not grasp that the President proposed but Congress disposed, and that Roosevelt had to manoeuvre like an eel to achieve what he did.[64]

Churchill has to bear a share of the blame for the state in which the UK found itself at the end of the war. Fertile in tactics, nevertheless he could have as fixed an ideé as anyone. In this case, his ideas that firstly, he and Roosevelt were linked by indissoluble ties of friendship, and secondly, that the United States looked upon Britain as forever a natural ally, prevented his taking steps which might have saved *angst* if not gold. Why did Britain never really consider calling the US's bluff, as Stalin did? Would the US really have taken the chance that Britain might pull out of the war? In this situation Britain's virtues and traditions worked against her.

Lend-lease was neither sordid nor unsordid. It was proposed by an Administration which saw it as a means by which the US could defend itself by proxy – perfectly in the British tradition – and agreed to by a Congress which in no way intended to give Britain and other recipients something for nothing. Lend-lease aid was always to be paid for in some sort of coin. It was necessary at the time for it to be wrapped in tinsel in order to reassure a people living under bombs and the threat of invasion that they had the support and aid of the great industrial power across the sea. A gift given in friendship is always more palatable to a proud people in time of peril than an item with the price tag prominently exposed. It was vital to Britain, and it is clear that British officials were not always behind time in those little arrangements which can bring advantage to ones own side.

Certainly many relationships forged during the wartime period helped smooth over the inevitable postwar conflict, but this does not mean that the conflicts in policies and personalities need be denied. The US was the rising power, and conscious of it, and Britain was the declining power, and conscious of it. In those circumstances it would have been miraculous if negotiations had gone as smoothly and the outcomes had been as satisfactory as Britain wished. As for the US, in the excitement of the fight and the euphoria of the victory, the disgruntlement of the British was easily dismissed. There was a world to police and to re-equip, and only when the utility of Britain in helping with the former was widely recognised would her pleas of poverty and need be fully accepted and something be done.

NOTES

1. For details see Kathleen Burk, *Morgan Grenfell 1838–1988: The Biography of a Merchant Bank* (Oxford: Oxford University Press, 1989), pp. 111–23.
2. Kathleen Burk, *Britain, America and the Sinews of War 1914–1918* (London and New Haven: Allen & Unwin, 1985), passim. For details on the war debts see Ibid., Appendix IV.
3. However, before the lend-lease arrangements were in place, Britain raised dollars partly by selling British-owned American securities in New York; British officials worked 'in very close touch' with J. P. Morgan & Co. in New York, 'whose co-operation made an important contribution to the efficiency of the British arrangements.' R. S. Sayers, *Financial Policy 1939–45* (London: HMSO and Longmans, Green and Co., 1956), p. 364.
4. United States Senate, 74th Congress, 2nd Session, Special Committee on Investigation of the Munitions Industry, *Munitions Industry*, Report No. 944, 7 vols (Washington, DC: United States Government Printing Office, 1936). For a discussion of the Nye Committee see Wayne S. Cole, *Gerald P. Nye and American Foreign Relations* (Minneapolis: University of Minnesota Press, 1962).
5. A suggestion made in 1939 that Morgans should again become Purchasing Agent for the British Government was immediately quashed. J. P. Morgan & Co. to Morgan Grenfell & Co. Ltd, 15 September 1939, Box II, file 84–19, Thomas Lamont Papers, Baker Library, Harvard Business School, Cambridge, Mass.
6. Letter from Morgenthau to President Truman in March 1946, quoted in David Rees, *Harry Dexter White: A Study in Paradox* (London: Macmillan, 1973), 138. For an analysis of the shift in financial power from Britain to the US over the twentieth century see the author's 'Money and Power: the Shift from Great Britain to the United States', in Youssef Cassis, ed., *Finance and Financiers in European History 1880–1960* (Cambridge: Cambridge University Press, 1992), pp. 359–69.
7. E. M. House to William Wiseman, 25 August 1917, File 90/26, William Wiseman Papers, Yale University Library; Lord Reading to the Chancellor of the Exchequer, 22 September 1917, T.172/433, fos. 57–8, Treasury Papers, Public Record Office, London.
8. Wilson to House, 21 July 1917, Box 121, E. M. House Papers, Yale University Library.
9. David Dilks (ed.), *The Diaries of Sir Alexander Cadogan 1938–1945* (New York: G. P. Putnam & Sons, 1972), p. 553, entry for 20 August 1943. According to Randall Bennett Woods, Hull 'appeared to believe that the articulation of a lofty principle was tantamount to its realization'. *A Changing of the Guard: Anglo-American Relations, 1941–1946* (Chapel Hill: The University of North Carolina Press, 1990), p. 13.
10. Carl Kreider, *The Anglo-American Trade Agreement: A Study of British and American Commercial Policies, 1934–1939* (Princeton: Princeton University Press, 1943), p. 81.
11. Ibid., p. 241.
12. David Reynolds, *The Creation of the Anglo-American Alliance 1937–41: A Study in Competitive Co-operation* (London: Europa Publications, 1981), p. 28. Moffat became US Minister to Canada in the summer of 1940 and thus, presumably, dropped out of the loop.
13. A lawyer, Acheson had worked to promote US aid to Britain and had collaborated with presidential aide Ben Cohen in drafting the constitutional justification for the Destroyers for Bases deal.

14. Reynolds, *Creation of the Anglo-American Alliance*, p. 274.
15. See his *Present at the Creation: My Years in the State Department* (New York: W. W. Norton), 1969, p. 7, for a paean to the nineteenth-century international order based on balance of power and empires, but balance-of-power assumptions dominate the book.
16. Woods, *Changing of the Guard*, p. 20.
17. Charles Bohlen, *Witness to History: 1929–1969* (New York: W. W. Norton, 1973), p. 283.
18. This is not to deny that he probably felt some affection for Britain, but there seems little evidence to demonstrate that this determined his policy-making, no matter what Churchill later claimed. Certainly any putative affection for Churchill played little part, although he may have occasionally been convinced by political arguments put forward by a masterful fellow politician.
19. Sayers states that 'There was at no stage any weakening of America's unwillingness to make ordinary loans, and this unwillingness to lend was matched by British unwillingness to assume responsibility for post-war debts.' He adds in a footnote that 'this method was so completely out of court that it went virtually unmentioned in the papers.' *Financial Policy*, p. 372.
20. Reynolds has noted, however, that 'until the act was passed US vessels were free to carry all but arms anywhere in the world, because the cash and carry provisions had lapsed in May 1939 and the summer fiasco in Congress had meant that they had not been renewed'. *Creation of the Anglo-American Alliance*, p. 313, n. 14.
21. Warren F. Kimball (ed.), *Churchill & Roosevelt: The Complete Correspondence*, 3 vols, *Volume I, Alliance Emerging: October 1933–November 1942* (Princeton: Princeton University Press, 1984), p. 37.
22. Reynolds, *Creation of the Anglo-American Alliance*, pp. 114–32.
23. Sayers, *Financial Policy*, p. 496 (Table 7: Gold and Dollar Reserves).
24. Burk, *Sinews of War*, pp. 64–91.
25. This was Walter Whigham, partner in Robert Fleming and Co. and a Director of the Bank of England. Sayers, *Financial Policy*, pp. 363–4.
26. Ibid., pp. 364–70.
27. Ibid., p. 366.
28. Reynolds, *Creation of the Anglo-American Alliance*, p. 110.
29. Quoted in Reynolds, *Creation of the Anglo-American Alliance*, p. 154, based on the Morgenthau manuscript diary, and in Warren F. Kimball, *The Most Unsordid Act: Lend-Lease, 1939–1941* (Baltimore: Johns Hopkins University Press, 1969), p. 103, based on Philip Young's files. Young and Harry Dexter White were also at the meeting.
30. Reynolds, *Creation of the Anglo-American Alliance*, p. 150. See also Reynolds, *Lord Lothian and Anglo-American Relations, 1939–40* (Philadelphia: American Philosophical Society, 1983), passim.
31. John Colville, *The Fringes of Power: Downing Street Diaries 1939–1955* (London: Hodder and Stoughton, 1985), pp. 291–2, entry for 12 November 1940.
32. As described by Kimball on the basis of Hopkins' comments to various contemporaries. *The Most Unsordid Act*, p. 119. Martin Gilbert, *Finest Hour: Winston S. Churchill 1939–1941* (London: Heinemann, 1983), pp. 936–7 for highlights. The letter may be found in the Churchill Papers, 23/4, as War Cabinet Paper No. 466 (Final Revise) of 1940, 8 December 1940, Churchill College, Cambridge.
33. See Sayers, *Financial Policy*, pp. 375–83. Sayers notes that in many cases the statistics required by Washington did not exist and the manpower required to

collect, collate and check them was not easily obtainable. Ibid., pp. 379–80. Sir Alec Cairncross has written that for most of the war the British 'were reluctant to expose the weaknesses of their position too nakedly to the United States and so undermine Britain's claim to be still a great power. To do this could have invited pressure "to go on our knees" (as Keynes put it) and beg like Roosevelt's dog Fala (as Churchill expressed the same thought).' Cairncross (ed.), Sir Richard Clarke, *Anglo-American Economic Collaboration in War and Peace 1942–1949* (Oxford: Clarendon Press, 1982), pp. xv–xvi.

34. Reynolds, *Creation of the Anglo-American Alliance*, p. 157.
35. Report of the press conference in *The Times*, 18 December 1940.
36. Reynolds, *Creation of the Anglo-American Alliance*, pp. 161–7. Kimball, *The Most Unsordid Act*, Chapters 5–6. The text of the Act is printed as an Appendix in Kimball.
37. This somewhat bland paragraph hides a deal of passion and despair on both sides: the British feared what would happen to their position if the money could not be found, while the Administration, and particularly Jesse Jones, head of the RFC, feared attack by Congress. See H. Duncan Hall, *North American Supply* (London: HMSO and Longman, Green and Co., 1955), p. 276 and especially Sayers, *Financial Policy*, pp. 392–6. Jones told Congress on 7 May 1941, during the hearings on the bill to increase the resources of the RFC and to permit loans to foreign governments on American securities as collateral 'for the purpose of achieving the maximum dollar exchange value' for the securities, that the new powers were 'to forestall liquidation of British assets at distress prices'. Ibid., p. 393. Jones insisted on interest at 3 per cent. Final quotation on ibid., p. 395.
38. 'Correspondence Respecting the Policy of His Majesty's Government in Connexion with the Use of Materials Received Under the Lend-Lease Act', Cmd 6311, September 1941. *Parliamentary Papers 1940–41, VIII: United States No. 2 (1941)*.
39. Sayers, *Financial Policy*, pp. 472–3.
40. This was vastly more complicated than indicated here. See Reynolds, *Creation of the Anglo-American Alliance*, pp. 271–2 and Woods, *Changing of the Guard*, pp. 34–48.
41. Acheson, *Present at the Creation*, p. 60.
42. Churchill to Halifax, 10 January 1941, PREM 4/17/3, ff. 363–4, Prime Minister's Records, PRO.
43. In a telegram to the Foreign Secretary, reporting on a meeting with Acheson and Feis, Halifax noted that he had seen Roosevelt's written comment that 'I strongly hope that the British will accept the first course [including Article VII in the Lend-Lease Agreement] because the second [striking it out] leaves them in a much more difficult future position.' Halifax emphasised that 'We might find congressional committees putting forward their own ideas of what the terms of settlement should be.' Halifax to Eden, no. 542, 30 January 1942, ff. 326–7, PREM 4/17/3.
44. Kimball (ed.), *Churchill and Roosevelt*, I, p. 345.
45. Ibid., 346. Eden sent Halifax a strictly personal telegram on 7 January 1942 in which he stated that the 'Principal difficulty appears to be imperial preference partly because this raises political issues of importance to us and the Dominions but principally because it raises domestic issues here which are peculiarly difficult for an all-party Government to deal with. As regards the domestic issue I personally feel too much weight is being given to this. Conservative Ministers are themselves divided.' f. 369, PREM 4/17/3.
46. Woods, *Changing of the Guard*, Chapters 1–2. Pressnell argues that the only

reason the Cabinet accepted the changes was because Churchill completely misunderstood the nature of the American response and thought that 'the President's exclusion of a specific commitment to abolish Imperial Preference covered also the exclusion of discussion of that issue'. L. S. Pressnell, *External Economic Policy since the War. Volume I: The Post-War Financial Settlement* (London: HMSO, 1986), p. 59. The before-and-after (July 1941 and February 1942) drafts of Article VII are printed in Pressnell and Appendices 1 and 2. Alan P. Dobson, *The Politics of the Anglo-American Economic Special Relationship* (Brighton: Wheatsheaf Books, 1988), Chapter 2.

47. Sayers, *Financial Policy*, Table 5: US Lend-Lease Aid to the British Empire to 31 August 1945, and Table 8: U.K. Reciprocal Aid to 1 September 1945.

48. Woods, *Changing of the Guard*, pp. 89–91. See also Richard E. Darilek, *A Loyal Opposition in Time of War: The Republican Party and the Politics of Foreign Policy from Pearl Harbor to Yalta* (Westport, CT: Greenwood Press, 1976), passim.

49. General B. Somerville, 'Lend-Lease Policy After the Defeat of Germany', 7 September 1944, Box 335, Harry Hopkins Papers, Roosevelt Presidential Library, Hyde Park, NY, as summarised in Woods, *Changing of the Guard*, p. 166.

50. Ibid., pp. 166–7.

51. At this point they stood at something over £400 million (over $1.6 billion). Sayers, *Financial Policy*, Table 7: Gold and Dollar Reserves.

52. Woods, *Changing of the Guard*, pp. 94–100; According to Woods, this was primarily a fight over bureaucratic power. Sayers, *Financial Policy*, pp. 427–37.

53. Anthony Eden, the Foreign Secretary, was shocked and appalled by the Plan. Woods, *Changing of the Guard*, p. 172.

54. Dobson, *Anglo-American Economic Special Relationship*, pp. 65–70; Woods, *Changing of the Guard*, pp. 168–73; John Morton Blum, *From the Morgenthau Diaries: Years of War 1941–1945* (Boston: Houghton Mifflin Company, 1967), pp. 306–16; Sayers, *Financial Policy*, p. 469.

55. Quoted in Dobson, *Anglo-American Special Economic Relationship*, p. 72. Woods, *Changing of the Guard*, pp. 173–6.

56. Hall, *North American Supply*, pp. 450–1.

57. The UK had wanted this freedom to export from 1 January 1945, and a partial remedy was to pay for raw materials and goods to be used for export. Sayers, *Financial Policy*, pp. 472–3.

58. *Financial Policy*, p. 477. Food supplies, however, were continued under lend-lease. Ibid., p. 478.

59. *Financial Policy*, p. 480.

60. Ibid., p. 375.

61. Among the latter see Dobson and Woods, British and American respectively.

62. *North American Supply*, pp. 429–31. Hall tends to refer to the combined effort as the Commonwealth effort, occasionally referring to the UK plus the Commonwealth as the British Commonwealth. This usage could cause confusion today.

63. J. M. Keynes to Sir Kingsley Wood [Chancellor of the Exchequer], 2 June 1941, in Donald Moggridge (ed.), *The Collected Writings of John Maynard Keynes. Volume XXIII. Activities 1940–1943: External War Finance* (London: Macmillan, 1979), p. 106.

64. There were, of course, exceptions to the above, especially among those who spent a long period in Washington.

# 4 The Soviet Economy and Relations with the United States and Britain, 1941–45
## Mark Harrison

There is a long history of studies of Allied economic relations with the USSR during the Second World War. Most of these were written from the viewpoint of diplomacy and strategy, and they were commonly influenced by a desire to search retrospectively for the historical roots of the Cold War which followed.[1]

Until quite recently, economic studies of wartime inter-allied relations were much fewer, and little special reference was made to aid to the USSR.[2] This is surprising since lend-lease was nothing if not a resource transfer, and it was the economic significance of the transfer to the USSR which fuelled controversy for so many years. Without independent economic analysis the controversy was unlikely ever to be resolved; it could never rise above the claim of the recipient that the scale of the transfer in cash and percentage terms was small, and of the donors that such overall totals were immaterial since it was the physical form of allied aid which represented the critical ingredient in Soviet victory.

Why is a distinctively economic analysis of inter-allied aid and trade necessary? The core of the problem is to understand what would have happened without these transfers of resources. Our ability to recast historical alternatives by the use of 'counterfactual hypotheses' is limited, and many historians rightly flinch from overt speculation. However, it is important to understand that, even after a certain amount of Cold War inflation of the American contribution in the late 1940s and early 1950s had been overcome, the western literature in this field remained dominated by very strong, usually unspoken, assumptions about economic alternatives which economists would often prefer to question or qualify.

A feature common to most western studies of aid to Russia has been an additive, 'building-block' approach. At its simplest, the Soviet war effort is seen as comprised of a number of building-blocks of military personnel and matériel, each of which was complementary to the effort as a whole at the given stage of the war; take away any one of these blocks, and the whole war effort was disabled. Some of these blocks were labelled as domestically sourced, some as originating in Great Britain and the United States. The main blocks of Red Army firepower and personnel, which sufficed to stave off defeat in 1941–42, were made at home. Added to these in 1943–45 were imported blocks of more technically sophisticated means of communication and mobility which made possible the great strategic offensives. This approach is additive in the further sense that it sees the allocation of domestic blocks to the war effort as predetermined independently of the availability of imported blocks, which were therefore simply added on to the war effort; if taken away, they could not have been replaced from domestic sources.

The timing and composition of aid are both seen as important to this analysis. The time factor was as follows. The inflow, slow at first, did not achieve its peak rate until the second half of 1943. By then the Germans had already suffered three huge defeats on the Eastern Front, at Moscow, Stalingrad, and Kursk-Orel. The strategic offensive capacity of the Wehrmacht had in practice been eliminated. With the turn in the war's tide, a new phase was under way which determined the character of allied victory and German defeat. But German troops were still deep inside Russia, and in the West allied forces had only just won their first toehold on the continent of Europe in Sicily. The Battle of the Atlantic was still intense. The German war economy was intact, despite allied bombing, and German war production was accelerating. Without a further rapid unravelling of the German position in the East it was easy to suppose that many years of fighting lay ahead. At the same time, the military feats of the Red Army had been purchased at huge cost in human life and equipment, while living and working conditions in the Russian interior were very poor and food supplies were even deteriorating.

The composition of allied aid to Russia has been seen in this context as having made a disproportionate contribution. The Soviet Union produced its own firepower in the Second World War, but relied extensively on imported means of mobility. The particular material form which aid took reinforces this view. Imported firepower (mainly aircraft and tanks) was prominent in the first trickle of aid in 1941–42, but from 1943 onwards it was motor vehicles, high-grade fuels, communications equipment, industrial machinery, naval vessels, and concentrated and processed foodstuffs which predominated, all essential to the manoeuvrability and logistical supply of modern armies.

Thus, the Red Army's destruction of Germany's offensive power in 1941–42 was accomplished largely on the basis of Soviet domestic supply; but its technical ability to pursue the retreating Wehrmacht, to project Soviet military power into the heart of Europe, to meet up with the Allied ground forces advancing from the west, and end the war in Europe in May 1945, was based significantly upon western resources.[3]

Why did the Soviet Union need this western aid? The explanation implicit in this approach stressed critical gaps and shortfalls in the technological and organisational assets available to Soviet industry, usually in high-technology processes or the capacity to finish products where qualitative attributes were crucial. On the whole, in this view, the technical form of each block was its defining characteristic; there was little or no substitutability between high-grade and low-grade building blocks, and similarly between blocks of domestic and foreign resources. A lack of high-technology, high-quality equipment could not be counterbalanced by increasing the availability of low-grade goods and human services; since Soviet industry could not match the quality of flow products of American electrical and mechanical engineering and petrochemicals, foreign resources could not be replaced by domestic resources.[4]

While reporting dollar and ruble totals of the aid inflow, and calculating them in varying percentages of Soviet industrial production or national income at the time, western studies tended to attach little importance to such figures; in more than one expert view, 'United States aid to Russia played a much more vital war role than it would appear from the cold statistics'.[5] What did the cash value or percentage ratio matter, if the simple truth was that without lend-lease it could not have been done? The literature emphasised the 'disproportionate effects' attributable to lend-lease supplies,[6] which filled 'critical gaps', made good 'painful shortages',[7] and permitted 'real additions' to the available assortment of supplies.[8] Western resources were simply indispensable to the Soviet war effort. In this spirit Khrushchev's reminiscences are often cited: 'Without Spam we wouldn't have been able to feed our army'; of American trucks, 'Just imagine how we would have advanced from Stalingrad to Berlin without them!'[9]

The additive, building-block approach, with its stress on the qualitative differences between Soviet and western products, captured an important aspect of reality – especially the way in which the military effectiveness of Soviet-produced defence assets was augmented as a result. However, the idea that there was no substitutability between domestic and imported means, or between products in military and civilian use, was excessively deterministic and led to unfortunate results. On one side the contribution of western aid to the Soviet war effort was exaggerated; the possibility that it released Soviet resources for non-war uses, while admitted in theory, was not identified in practice. On the other side, where identifiable lend-leased goods were diverted to non-war applications, this was judged illegitimate. Like some undeserving recipient of social security accused of going on holiday at the taxpayers' expense, the Russians were not supposed to have purposes of their own. Here the additive approach was very much in the spirit of the Lend-Lease Act, which intended aid commodities to be used only for the war, and to be additive to domestic resources already so committed. For the social scientist, however, it is behaviour which tests the law, not the law which tests behaviour.

In strictly converse fashion the official Soviet historiography remained dominated by a broad assumption that without lend-lease not much would have been different. Western analysts were accused of spreading the myth that the Red Army had won its victories only because of western means,[10] and that only American aid had 'saved Russia';[11] Lend-lease was described, in relative terms, as 'highly insignificant'.[12]

## INSTITUTIONAL ARRANGEMENTS

At first the British and the Americans offered aid based on loans – £10 million (16 August 1941) and $1 billion (30 October). Under the first supply protocol agreed among the three countries in Moscow (19 October), Britain and the United States took on a shared responsibility for supplying and shipping goods to the USSR. The American loan was shortly converted into a lend-lease credit (7 November), to which a further $1 billion was added (18 February 1942).

A few days after this (23 February 1942) the first Master Agreement governing lend-lease to the UK was signed by American and British representatives, and a similar master agreement was eventually concluded (11 June) with the USSR. The spirit of the master agreements (in Roosevelt's words) was to 'eliminate the silly, foolish, old dollar sign', that is, to get rid of the concept of the financial obligation of the recipient to the donor.[13] Instead of saddling her allies with postwar debts, the United States would instead require the sharing of information, and postwar cooperation in restoring a liberalised world economic order. This would apply not only to future shipments but also, retrospectively, to shipments already received under existing protocols. Thus, lend-lease ceased to involve either lending or leasing, and became instead a conditional gift.

The distinction between United States lend-lease and mutual aid originating elsewhere became thoroughly blurred. Under the first two protocols (October 1941–June 1942, and July 1942–June 1943), the British and the Americans organised aid to the USSR jointly, offering supplies from a common pool. For the third and fourth (1943/44 and 1944/45) they were joined by Canada, although Canadian aid to the Soviet Union remained small in quantity.

The logistical difficulties facing the aid programme were awesome. The land and maritime routes through which most prewar Soviet trade had passed were in German hands; indeed, a high proportion of this trade had been with Germany. Initially, supplies were concentrated on the north Atlantic route to Murmansk and Archangel, but eventually the dangerous northern convoys accounted for less than a quarter (23 per cent) of total tonnage supplied. A safer, but far more circuitous route was soon opened through the Persian Gulf and Iran into Soviet Central Asia, and this route too accounted for roughly a quarter (24 per cent) of total lend-lease tonnage. The Pacific route from American west coast ports, skirting Japanese waters to the Soviet Far East and across Siberia, was eventually most heavily used, carrying nearly one-half (47 per cent) in tonnage terms.[14]

The fulfilment of supply obligations was always patchy. The allies had their own strategic plans and priorities, and aid to the USSR inevitably detracted from these. Simply solving the logistical difficulties, which ranged from running the German submarine gauntlet in the north Atlantic to pioneering truck routes through the mountains of Central Asia, required substantial additional resources. From the Soviet standpoint, the allies used plans which they had no intention of carrying out (for example, to open a 'second front' in northern France, first in 1942, then in 1943) to justify the irregular arrival of incomplete consignments.[15]

The conditionality of lend-lease presented both sides with delicate problems never resolved. In the late summer of 1941 Soviet leaders were reluctant to consider an offer of lend-lease and preferred to think in terms of a loan, perhaps because they feared the conditions which might be attached to aid.[16] This reluctance was not overcome until September, when the severity of the German threat to Leningrad and Moscow had become all too clear to both sides.

Possible conditions for American aid ranged from the regulation of Soviet behaviour in Eastern Europe to the sharing of military and economic information. In the event, Roosevelt set his face against such conditions, believing that they would only get in the way of the main task, which was to enable the Russians to fight Germany.[17] Aid which was effectively unconditional would at least weaken Soviet mistrust and keep the Russians in the war. For their part the Russians, despite an initial preference for the prospect of postwar repayment over political ties, eventually made a variety of promises with regard to their future behaviour (for example, making a commitment to postwar trade liberalisation under the June 1942 master agreement). By the end of the war they had become unwilling to contemplate repayment on any significant scale, even for stocks of lend-leased civilian goods valued by the Americans at $2.6 billion, which no longer had any bearing on Soviet war needs.[18]

The disorderly character of the transition to peace in 1945 would beset Soviet–American economic relations for decades. In 1944–45 the combined dollar-value of industrial materials and products, motor vehicles and parts, and petroleum products accounted for 55 per cent ($2.8 billion) of lend-lease deliveries, compared with 41 per cent ($1.7 billion) of deliveries in 1941–43.[19] This implied a significant import of investment goods which were not going to be installed in Soviet establishments until after the war was over.[20] Both sides now failed to conclude an agreement under existing provisions of lend-lease legislation to allow for Soviet ordering and purchase of civilian equipment for postwar use on easy credit terms. This failure is attributable both to Soviet illusions and to American reluctance. In the changed conditions of 1943–44, American resistance to the policy of unconditional aid grew; this resistance had no immediate effect on policy, but ensured that when new initiatives appeared on the agenda congressional patience was already short. The Russians, on the other hand, believing that the war would be quickly followed by a new capitalist slump, saw the Americans in a weak position and overplayed their hand.[21]

Soviet representatives made three requests for a large, long-term, low-interest loan, the first (1 February 1944) for $1 billion, the second (3 January 1945) for $6 billion, the third and last (28 August) again for $1 billion; the latter request was said to have been lost in the transfer of files from the now-defunct State Department's Foreign Economic Administration, and failed to receive a reply. In the meantime, lend-lease to the USSR had been temporarily suspended (12 May) immediately following the German surrender, and was now terminated finally (20 September). The Americans requested payment of $1.3 billion for unused stocks of lend-leased civilian goods still on hand; final settlement in a considerably smaller sum awaited a new era in Soviet–American relations and a Nixon–Brezhnev summit in 1972.

## THE SCALE OF ECONOMIC ASSISTANCE

During the Second World War all the great powers except for the United States benefited from a significant net import of resources. Both aid and trade contributed to the Soviet economy, but aid was more important.

As far as trade is concerned, between 1941 and 1944 the total Soviet deficit on the external merchandise account reached four billion foreign-trade rubles. This was a sum equal to $765 million at the official exchange rate then current; alternatively, it represented roughly two prewar years' imports.[22] (Two years' imports may sound a lot, but by the late 1930s the Soviet economy had achieved a state of near total autarky, with trade ratios at an historic low – no more than one-half of 1 per cent of national income by 1937, according to one authority.)[23] Trade was particularly important in 1941–42, because the first agreements to ship munitions to Russia were essentially financed through barter, the Americans and British agreeing to accept Soviet raw materials in exchange.[24] The trade deficit was dwarfed by the far larger volume of resources imported into the USSR without charge from the United States and Great Britain under mutual aid. US lend-lease to the USSR alone accounted for $10.67 billion, and British aid for a further £312 million ($1.26 billion), making nearly $12 billion in total (see Figures 4.1 and 4.2).[25]

The timing and composition of aid can be further illustrated. According to

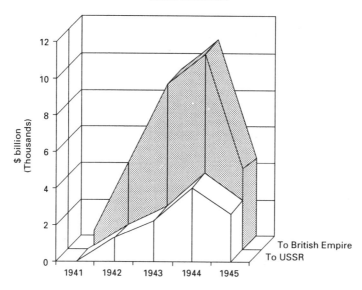

*Figure* 4.1   United States lend-lease to the British Empire and the USSR,
1941–45

*Source*: R. G. D. Allen, 'Mutual Aid between the US and the British Empire, 1941–
1945', Appendix 3 of R. S. Sayers, *Financial Policy, 1939–1945* (London: HMSO,
1956), p. 529.

incomplete monthly records, the bulk of lend-lease shipments – some 57 per
cent by dollar value – arrived in the second half of 1943 and in 1944.[26] A
commodity classification shows that, in the first phase, when the flow was
still restricted, weapons predominated, but from 1943 onwards the greater
part of lend-leased items by dollar value consisted of dual-purpose products
(industrial, transport, communications, and farm equipment, metals and metal
products, chemical, fuel and food products).[27]

   In terms of overall resources of the western allies these large-sounding
transfers amounted to less than one might suppose at first sight. Aid to
Russia was less than a quarter of the total of economic assistance rendered
by the British and Americans to each other and to others, as Soviet historians unfailingly pointed out (again, see Figures 4.1 and 4.2).[28] It was still
smaller as a fraction of the combined war expenditures of the United Kingdom and United States, which totalled approximately $295 billion from mid-
1942 through mid-1945; compared with this, aid to the USSR amounted to
no more than 4 per cent.[29]

   By coincidence, 4 per cent has more than one significance. At the end of
1947 the wartime planning chief N. A. Voznesensky published an account

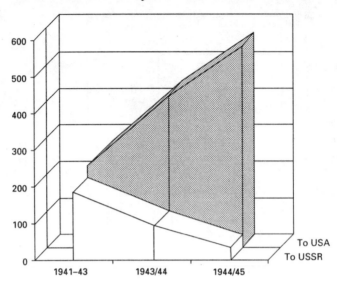

*Figure* 4.2.   United Kingdom reciprocal aid to the United States and USSR, 1941–45.

*Source*: R. G. D. Allen, 'Mutual Aid between the US and the British Empire, 1941–1945', Appendix 3 of R. S. Sayers, *Financial Policy, 1939–1945* (London: HMSO, 1956), p. 535 (figures for each period cover 1 July to 30 June).

of the Soviet wartime economic effort which included reference to the growth of Soviet imports in 1942–43, mainly from Britain and America, compared with the much lower level of 1940; 'a comparison between the amount of these allied deliveries of industrial goods to the U.S.S.R. and the volume of industrial production at the Soviet Socialist enterprises in the same period', he wrote, 'will show that these deliveries amounted to only about 4 per cent of the domestic production during the war economy period'.[30] But whether 'the same period' meant 1942–43, or 'the war economy period' as a whole, was left irritatingly vague. In later writing, east and west, this figure would be extensively misquoted, and was most commonly rendered as the proportion of all Allied deliveries to the total wartime product of the entire Soviet economy, described sometimes as 'highly insignificant',[31] or even as 'only 4 per cent'.[32]

Since 'only 4 per cent' did not sound like much at all (certainly much less than $10 670 000 000), American responses were angry. Alexander Gerschenkron pointed out, correctly, that in 1942–43 Allied deliveries had not yet reached their peak, and that any comparison of nominal values would understate the value of imports relative to Soviet domestic production

*Table 4.1.* The burden of defence on Soviet resources, 1940–44 (billion rubles and 1937 factor costs)

|  | 1940 | 1941 | 1942 | 1943 | 1944 |
|---|---|---|---|---|---|
| Total final demand | 253.9 | 219.0 | 174.5 | 204.4 | 243.2 |
| Gross domestic product | 253.9 | 218.7 | 166.8 | 185.4 | 220.3 |
| Net imports | 0 | 0.3 | 7.8 | 19.0 | 22.9 |
| % of TFD | 0 | 0 | 4 | 9 | 9 |
| % of GDP | 0 | 0 | 5 | 10 | 10 |
| Defence outlays | 43.9 | 61.8 | 101.4 | 113.2 | 117.2 |
| % of TFD | 17 | 28 | 58 | 55 | 48 |
| % of GDP | 17 | 28 | 61 | 61 | 53 |

*Sources*: Total final demand (TFD) is GDP plus net imports. Figures are from Mark Harrison, *Accounting for War: Soviet production, employment, and the defence burden, 1940–1945* (in preparation). The outline methodology of previous stages is described by Mark Harrison, 'Soviet Production and Employment in World War II: A 1993 Update', University of Birmingham, Centre for Russian and East European Studies, Soviet Industrialisation Project Series, no. 35.

because of wartime overvaluation of the ruble, and because of double-counting of domestic output in the Soviet production accounts; he also signposted the future course of western historiography by adding: 'the tremendous contribution to the Russian war economy made by scarce commodities delivered under lend-lease cannot be significantly measured in terms of a global percentage'.[33]

For the record, it is worth stating that 'only 4 per cent', although probably not an outright lie, certainly presented a misleading view of the real volume of allied aid to the USSR. Table 4.1 shows the present author's estimate, which compares volumes of allied aid with Soviet wartime GDP and defence outlays when all are calculated at peacetime factor costs in the prewar year 1937. It shows that by 1943, allied aid was contributing one-tenth of the total of resources available to ('absorbed' by) the Soviet economy, and represented 10 per cent of domestic output. This puts a very different complexion on the scale of assistance, of course, although the Soviet figure was no higher than the wartime import ratios of Britain and Germany.[34]

A final complication, to be mentioned only in passing, is Soviet reverse lend-lease. During the war the Soviet Union provided American transport ships and bomber aircraft with base and repair facilities and supplies, to a value officially reported at $2.2 billion.[35] Since there is no independent means of auditing this large sum, and since it was all spent on Soviet territory, I make no further allowance for it below.

## AID AND OVERALL SOVIET RESOURCES

The character of Allied credits to the USSR is an issue which, unresolved at the time, continues to haunt the writing of Second World War history. The issue has two aspects, one international, and one domestic. Aid affected the inter-allied allocation of resources. Was aid a unilateral subsidy from rich to poor; or was it, rather, one aspect of a broader wartime pooling of resources based on mutual specialisation and collaboration of equal partners? Aid also affected the domestic allocation of resources of the recipients. In the Soviet case, was aid essential to the Soviet war effort; to what extent did it support the civilian economy; how much was diverted to postwar economic objectives? Such domestic implications of aid are difficult to analyse, and mutual incomprehension often added to inevitable suspicions.

In terms of the Soviet domestic economy, aid had two aspects. It was an addition to overall resources, and it came in particular material forms. The material form of aid was often that of high-technology, high-grade products, which undoubtedly augmented the effectiveness of Soviet fighting power. It would have been very difficult and costly for the Soviet economy to have matched the military-technical qualities of American vehicles, fuels, communications equipment, and food rations. Nonetheless, if the Soviet armed forces had been denied these western resources, they would have procured replacements. The replacements might well have been inferior in quantity and quality. But military units still had to manoeuvre, communicate, and feed and clothe their troops on the march. For given total resources, they would have relied more on horses, despatch riders, dried fish, and stale bread. They would have moved more slowly, with less efficient coordination, and they would have fought more hungrily. The same applies to the American machine tools, generating equipment, and farm machinery imported to meet the needs of the productive economy. If aid had taken the form only of additional Soviet-technology, Soviet-grade products, the needs were still there, and would also have been met, but at higher cost and less well.

Aid was also an addition to overall resources. From this point of view its technical or military-technical form did not matter. What mattered was that aid gave the Soviet government the capacity to allocate additional resources of all kinds at the margin towards all of its objectives, whether military or civilian, immediate or postwar.

How did it, in fact, choose to do so? We do not have any very sophisticated means of answering this question. On one side we can speculate about official motivations. But no minuted decision tells us in what proportions Stalin's war cabinet proposed to allocate the incremental resources represented by aid, year by year. On the other side we can speculate about the uses of allied aid from observing the actual allocation of overall resources, but the picture is conditioned by many hypotheses, and the brush-strokes are very broad.

The choices made by Soviet leaders in allocating resources between war and non-war uses varied at different stages of the war. They were the outcome of a process of decision-making which operated at two levels of abstraction. Their starting-point was the extreme consequences of defeat for national and personal survival; defeat was to be avoided at all costs. At a higher level one may suppose, therefore, that Soviet leaders would have liked to maximise the resources for the war effort, subject to the maintenance of a minimum level of civilian and infrastructural economic activity. In practice, however, the location of the minimum was impossible to discover *ex ante*. This was for several reasons. For one thing, officials systematically repressed unofficial expression of civilian discontent, and mistrusted the signals of consumer and producer need officially transmitted upward through the administrative system from firms and households. For another, the degree of economic deprivation which could be tolerated by society depended on the period of time over which it had to be endured, and this could not be known in advance.

At a lower level of abstraction, therefore, in the first phase of the war, rather than risk immediate defeat for lack of sufficient mobilisation, they followed a course of taking everything available for the war effort – 'All for the front!' In the process the civilian economy collapsed, the minimum tolerance limits of society were breached, overworking and malnourishment became widespread, civilian mortality rose, and the infrastructure of war production was undermined. Postwar perspectives played no role in this first period, since the only priority was to stave off defeat and ensure the ability to continue fighting. During 1942 there took place a transition to a second phase in which the narrowly military mobilisation ceased to be all-important. The civilian economy rose in priority, and ceased to decline. From now on, defence outlays were allowed to rise only on the basis of newly-available resources. This was also a period in which, with the prospect of eventual victory, postwar perspectives reasserted themselves, and were expressed in a series of plans for reconstruction of industry and the capital stock.[36]

The actual allocation of resources in 1942–44, however, is shown in Table 4.2. Here are estimated series for total final demand (GDP, plus net imports), defence outlays, and gross investment at prewar constant factor costs. Real defence outlays rose rapidly from year to year, but less rapidly than the increase in the total of available resources. Of the 98.6 billion rubles of additional resources available ('absorption', at 1937 factor cost) in 1943 and 1944 over 1942, less than one-third was allocated to additional defence outlays, the remainder being available for civilian use. If allied aid was treated interchangeably with other resources, then only 30 or so cents in the dollar were reflected in increased defence outlays.

What about the remaining 70 cents, which were left available for civilian use? Civilian uses are shown in Table 4.2 as gross investment and non-defence

*Table* 4.2. The overall allocation of Soviet resources, 1940 and 1942–44

|  | 1940 | 1942 | 1943 | 1944 | Increment in 1943–44 over 1942 |
|---|---|---|---|---|---|
| *(A) Billion rubles and 1937 factor costs* | | | | | |
| Total final demand | 253.9 | 174.5 | 204.4 | 243.2 | 98.6 |
| Defence outlays | 43.9 | 101.4 | 113.2 | 117.2 | 27.5 |
| Gross investment | 50.1 | −0.6 | 17.5 | 20.3 | 39.0 |
| Nondefence consumption | 159.9 | 73.7 | 73.8 | 105.7 | 32.1 |
| *(B) Millions,* *working population* | 86.8 | 54.7 | 57.1 | 67.1 | .. |
| *(C) Rubles and 1937 factor costs* Nondefence consumption per head of working population | 1 842 | 1 348 | 1 291 | 1 575 | .. |

*Sources*: Total final demand and defence outlays are from Table 4.1. Gross investment for 1940 is from Abram Bergson, *The Real National Income of Soviet Russia since 1928* (Cambridge, Mass.: Harvard University Press, 1961), p. 128, and for other years from Raymond P. Powell, 'The Soviet Capital Stock and Related Series for the War Years', in *Two Supplements to Richard Moorsteen and Raymond P. Powell, The Soviet Capital Stock, 1928–1962* (New Haven, Conn.: Yale University, The Economic Growth Center, 1968), p. 21. Nondefence consumption (by both government and households) is the residual.

consumption. Gross investment collapsed with the outbreak of war, and was slightly negative in 1942, with small amounts of fixed capital formation more than offset by inventory disinvestment; to set these figures in context, nearly 12 billion rubles of fixed investment were necessary just to replace annual depreciation of the fixed capital stock in Soviet hands.[37] Investment recovery after 1942 was guided first by requirements of the defence industry, but as the chances of victory improved the Soviet government also began rapidly to restore its peacetime industries, raising the priority of housebuilding and civilian capital construction. The figures shown in Table 4.2 suggest that more than half the resources made available in additional aid over 1943–44, and not claimed by the requirements of defence, were used for investment purposes.

The idea of a 30:70 split in the uses of allied aid between defence and other uses is oversimplified, however, if we take into account trends in nondefence consumption, which includes consumption outlays both by government (on education, health care, administration, and so on), and by households. Here the critical variable is not aggregate consumption but consumption per head. The path of consumption per head is not easy to ascertain in the absence of good wartime population figures, but consumption per worker can be derived from figures for the working population. By 1942 consumption per worker had already fallen to 70 per cent of 1940. The further decline in 1943, despite stability in the total of resources available for civilian use, is attributable partly to recovery of numbers in employment, and partly to the renewed pressure of investment. (The composition of civilian consumption also varied, with consumer industries and services recovering, but per capita food supplies probably deteriorating through 1944.)

For the sake of argument, consider the level of consumption per worker registered in 1943 (when starvation deaths were already widespread), as an absolute minimum, below which standards could not be allowed to fall. Then the withdrawal of allied aid in 1943 would inevitably have been reflected in reduced defence and investment outlays, not consumption. On the other hand, in both 1942 and 1944 consumption standards were allowed to remain or rise above the floor, suggesting that additional civilian consumption did compete with defence and investment for claims on resources being made available at the margin.

Such speculations are undeniably crude, and serve only to illustrate the core proposition that the impact of western aid must be understood in light of the overall objectives and constraints of the Soviet economy; aid did not simply add additional blocks of imported resources to a predetermined domestic allocation, but also influenced this allocation. Aid freed resources for civilian use, both for investment and consumption; however, it seems likely that the effect of these civilian uses was no more than to mitigate undernourishment of the population and depreciation of the capital stock. This was necessary and inevitable given the high degree of domestic economic mobilisation, the extreme deprivation of the civilian sector, and the consequent blurring of the distinction between front and rear.

THE TECHNICAL FORM OF AID

The core proposition illustrated above makes no concession to the view that the material form of lend-leased commodities was significant for the outcome of the aid process. Western aid consisted of equipment in a broad sense (including weapons, machinery, vehicles, ships, means of communications, materials, and fuels), some for military and some for civilian use, and processed foodstuffs intended only for military use. To understand its impact, consider the Soviet workforce divided among soldiers, industrial workers and farmworkers. All of these were equipment users, but only industrial workers were equipment producers. Everyone was a food consumer, but only farmworkers produced food. Moreover, while in the long run the Soviet economy could theoretically be organised to produce any kind of food product or equipment, the innovation of some kinds of high-technology processes and high-grade products would certainly have been very expensive given the Soviet economy's skill, technology, and management deficits, and was not an option in the short run.

Probably, western *equipment for military use* unambiguously increased the Soviet capacity to devote resources to the war effort at all stages of the war, and was directly reflected in enlarged defence outlays. There was no immediately available domestic capacity for serial production of reliable motor vehicles, communications equipment, and so on. The replacement of high-grade imports would have required large quantities of domestically produced low-grade horsepower and equipment; this would always represent an inferior option. For example, railway transport could not solve the problem of dispersal of supplies across a front line of combat from the railhead. Domestic horse-drawn equipment and manpower could not create an offensive logistical capacity equivalent to motorised transport, partly because of slowness, partly because of the large supply multiplier attached to the requirements of horse and supply troops when advancing.[38] Imported American trucks, jeeps, field telephone systems, and portable radio sets were also complementary to Soviet equipment. Thus the import of western equipment for military use had a compound effect: it added to the quality of Soviet fighting power, made existing Soviet resources already committed to the war much more effective, and released at least some resources for civilian use.

It was important that aid resources arrived in a complementary package. High-quality imported vehicles without the high-grade imported fuels and fuel additives for their efficient operation, without the communication systems to enable coordination of highly mobile motorised infantry, without the ration packs to enable troops to subsist independently for days on the march, would have resulted in unused capacity and waste.

Other considerations probably applied also to imported western munitions, despite their poor reputation among Soviet fighting personnel. This poor reputation arose because western weapons were typically unsuited to combat conditions on the Eastern Front. British tanks were insufficiently rugged for climate, terrain, and the character of German opposition; British and American aircraft tended to be excessively, sophisticated for ill-educated and untrained Soviet operators. Such weapons added little to Soviet fighting power, and for that reason were no substitute for Soviet-produced weaponry. (Having no civilian use, they were also no substitute for Soviet-produced civilian equipment or consumer goods.) Probably imported weapons were reflected in increased ruble outlays on the war, but they did not release Soviet domestic resources from the war effort or make Soviet fighting power more effective.

A different range of effects can be attributed to imported equipment for use in the economy. Industrial, power, and farm machinery imports released Soviet workers from equipment-making, and allowed their transfer to other equipment-using activities. Equipment-using here has a broad sense – soldiers used military equipment, munitions workers used industrial equipment to make weapons, and agricultural workers used farm equipment to make food. In principle, therefore, imported equipment released resources in any of these directions. What decided the outcome was the policy context in which, from 1942 onwards, additional resources were shared out first to the equipment-users in the defence sector, then to food-producers whose task was to secure minimum consumption levels. To the extent that both military priorities and minimum food norms had been achieved (which may only have meant that no one of great significance was starving), however, Soviet workers could be retained in equipment-making to the benefit of civilian investment objectives, including for the postwar period.

In the first stages of the lend-lease operation, a relevant constraint was the rate at which resources could be released from equipment-making to equipment-using. Since overall labour resources were limited, it was possible in the short run to import too many machines. Western observers commented fretfully on the often neglectful attitude of Soviet handlers of western equipment, sometimes left to rot on sidings and in marshalling yards. But the underlying reason was probably not ungratefulness or careless indifference; rather, there was a lack of absorptive capacity. It was rational to allow imported machinery to rust if there was no factory accommodation available in which to install it, or workers to use it once installed. At this stage of the war, contrary to common perceptions, the Soviet economy needed overall resources more than it needed lend-lease matériel which could not be utilised effectively under the circumstances.[39]

Imported *processed foodstuffs*, largely in tinned or concentrated forms, were intended solely for military use. This increment to food resources clearly released domestic food supplies for civilian use, and prevented overall nutritional standards from falling further. To the extent that minimum standards had been achieved, however, then farmworkers could be released for other equipment-using employment – military service, or equipment-making for industry and the military. Moreover, since agricultural work was of very low productivity by 1943–44, in ruble terms far below that of industrial workers, especially in engineering and munitions, the transfer of workers from farm to factory could significantly affect total output.[40] To the extent that military needs were satisfied, capital investment gained.

## AID AND INTER-ALLIED SPECIALISATION

By comparison, the inter-allied dimension of wartime aid is easier to grasp. Was aid a subsidy from rich to poor, or an instance of resources shared among equal partners? Wartime governments naturally tended to emphasise the latter. It suited equally the Anglo-American desire to cement the USSR into a temporary union of strange bedfellows, and Soviet national feeling.

Nor were the ideas of pooled resources and effective collaboration merely rhetoric. There was a real, practical logic at work, expressed in the division of labour among the alliance partners. Within the alliance the wealthy, capital-abundant United States economy specialised relatively in the production of capital-intensive commodities such as weapons and machinery, high-grade materials and fuels, and high-grade concentrated and long-life processed foods. The Soviet Union continued to produce a broad range of military and civilian goods and services, but, relative to the other allies, specialised in the labour-intensive activity of fighting. The UK occupied an intermediate position, supplying weapons to Russia in the early stages of the war on the Eastern Front, but meanwhile receiving food, fuel, and machinery from the United States; eventually, American supply reached a scale sufficient to release significant British labour resources for the invasion of Europe from the west.

In principle, to the extent that the pattern of specialisation followed a common Grand Strategy of the wartime allies, each of the countries in receipt of American aid could have claimed a counterbalancing 'export' credit item based on the supply of military services to the alliance as a whole, matching the American contribution of machinery and matériel. Alan Milward has suggested that 'in those cases where British tank crews had used American tanks it would make at least as much sense to charge the United States for the crew as the United Kingdom for the tank'.[41]

In practice, of course, no such crediting took place. One suspects it was not just an accident of peacetime accounting conventions that the result appeared to show Britain and the USSR as in receipt of a large subsidy. For one thing, any alternative would have involved the distasteful business of costing the expenditure of British and Russian human effort (on current account) and lives (on capital account) in the same currency as machinery and fuel. It would have meant an explicit recognition that the Alliance had chosen 'rationally' to spend life most carelessly where it was cheapest; proportionally, the ranking of the three allies by income per head (America, then Britain, then the USSR) was the exact inverse of their ranking by the proportion of war deaths. Later, Soviet historians noted Truman's candid admission that lend-lease dollars were aimed at saving American lives: every Russian, British, or Australian soldier who went into battle equipped by means of American aid reduced the danger to young Americans.[42]

For another reason, despite the rhetoric of allied collaboration and the pooling of resources, there was never any doubt as to the national 'ownership' of national military personnel. If, even on the Western Front, the command structures of the British and American forces were merged only at the highest level, in the east the coordination of Soviet with allied military action was fragile in the extreme. It would have been no technicality or matter of indifference to leaders of the United Nations whether Soviet troops had operated with lend-leased American equipment, but under Soviet command, or had themselves been lend-leased to some multinational UN force.

In the end, therefore, it suited everyone to talk about mutual specialisation and the pooling of resources, but in practice to account for resource transfers as aid and trade favouring the poorer countries of the alliance. Both British and Soviet accountants dealt with the resulting ambiguity (aid as pooled resource, or as subsidy) by means of a common device; they accepted lend-lease, treated it as hidden revenue to the budget, and incorporated it in their own military spending totals.

Nonetheless, it seems that allied aid to the USSR made possible the division of labour which won the war. Without it, everyone on the side of the allies would have had a worse war. The Russians would have had to fight on their own resources, which were inadequate in quantity if not in quality as well, and would have fought less well, maybe only to a stalemate. The British and the Americans would have had to fight harder, because they would have had to take on a larger share of the killing of Germans and being killed by them; they would have had to choose either fighting with the same bitterness and intensity as the Russians, or accepting stalemate in the west. Perhaps, in 1942 and 1943, in place of surrogate combat for the few in the night skies over German cities, they would have had to choose combat for the many in the killing fields of Kent and Sussex; perhaps the required bitterness and intensity would have been supplied by an occupation regime on the south coast, with concentration camps in Kent, and corpses hanging from telegraph poles in Wiltshire villages.

## CONCLUSIONS

Even now when the archives are becoming more accessible, there is no 'true story' waiting to be uncovered among dusty documents, which will tell the world just how lend-lease was spent in the Soviet Union. Identification of the resources released by aid remains a matter for theoretical reasoning and scholarly conjecture, and will not be found in any auditor's report.

It is plausibly suggested that every lend-lease dollar raised about 40 cents of increased Soviet defence outlays. But to the extent that the technical form of lend-leased goods for military use increased the military effectiveness of Soviet defence outlays as a whole, 30 cents in the dollar understates the direct impact of lend-lease.

The other 70 cents went, under assumptions reviewed above, to underpinning the bare subsistence of the working population, and to investment in maintenance of inventories and the fixed capital stock. Whatever the true proportions of its utilisation, aid must certainly have freed some resources for civilian use, both for investment and consumption; this was necessary and inevitable given the high degree of domestic economic mobilisation, the extreme deprivation of the civilian sector, and the consequent blurring of the distinction between front and rear. In the last stages of the war, continued allied aid may have freed some resources for postwar reconstruction. But there is a strong possibility that civilian resources were already too constrained for aid to do much more than avert further deterioration in both the working population and the capital stock.

Aid to the USSR contributed to the mutual specialisation of the allies according to the comparative advantage of each. This specialisation made sense in so far as it allowed everyone to do what they were good at. The western powers could specialise in the serial production of sophisticated weapons, and in using them to fight at a distance, while the Russians could get on with combat at close quarters. This pattern was nonetheless perceived as burdensome on each side, since the qualitative differences of role were not felt to be mutually compensating. The British, and still more the Americans, resented the Russians' economic dependence, their official presumptions of moral superiority, and lack of official gratitude. The Russians resented the way their richer partners used their wealth to help the Russians to kill and be killed.

Here were the roots of mutual suspicion – the potential use and abuse of aid by both donors and recipients for purposes which had less to do with winning the war than with civilian and postwar objectives. Was lend-lease used in the allied interest, substituting young Russian lives for those of Britons and Americans? Was it exploited by the Russians for civilian as well as military purposes, to serve postwar as well as wartime objectives? The answer to both these questions is, realistically, yes. But allied aid was also, nonetheless, an effective 'Weapon for Victory', and there was no good alternative to it under the constraints of the time. Without it, everyone would have had a worse war. The western allies would have had to kill and be killed in greater numbers. The Russians would have done less killing and more being killed. The tensions were simply inherent in the aid relationship, as the history of postwar development aid will amply testify.

## NOTES

I am grateful to Stephen Broadberry for advice, Edwin Bacon, Hugh Rockoff, and Nikolai Simonov for assistance, Seth Axelrod, the late Alec Nove, and the conference participants for comments on previous drafts, and the Leverhulme Trust for financial support.

1. Raymond H. Dawson, *The Decision to Aid Russia, 1941: Foreign Policy and*

*Domestic Politics* (Chapel Hill, NC: University of North Carolina Press, 1959);
Robert Huhn Jones, *The Roads to Russia: United States Lend-Lease to the So-
viet Union* (Norman, Okla.: University of Oklahoma Press, 1969); George C.
Herring, *Aid to Russia, 1941–1946: Strategy, Diplomacy, the Origins of the Cold
War* (New York: Columbia University Press, 1973); Leon Martel, *Lend-Lease,
Loans, and the Coming of the Cold War* (Boulder, Colo.: Westview Press, 1979);
Joan Beaumont, *Comrades in Arms: British Aid to Russia, 1941–1945* (London:
Davis-Poynter, 1980); Peter J. Titley, 'Royal Air Force Assistance to the Soviet
Union, June 1941 to June 1942', unpub. MA dissertation, University of Kent
(1991); Seth J. Axelrod, 'The Soviet Union, the IMF, and the World Bank, 1941–
1947: from inclusion to abstention', unpub. PhD dissertation, University of Bir-
mingham (1994).

2. Thus R. G. D. Allen, 'Mutual Aid Between the US and the British Empire,
1941–1945', Appendix 3 of R. S. Sayers, *Financial Policy, 1939–1945*, (London: HMSO, 1956), pp. 518–56, made incidental reference to aid to the USSR
in a broader study of transatlantic transfers. For brief evaluations of the importance of lend-lease within studies of other topics in Soviet economic analysis,
see Abram Bergson, *The Real National Income of Soviet Russia Since 1928*
(Cambridge, Mass.: Harvard University Press, 1961), pp. 99–100n; G. Warren
Nutter, *The Growth of Industrial Production in the Soviet Union* (Princeton, NJ:
Princeton University Press, 1962), p. 214; Susan J. Linz, 'Economic Origins of
the Cold War? An Examination of the Carryover Costs of World War II to the
Soviet People', unpub. PhD thesis, University of Illinois at Urbana-Champaign
(1980), pp. 25–33; James R. Millar, 'Financing the Soviet Effort in World War
II', *Soviet Studies*, 32 (1980), p. 116; Mark Harrison, *Soviet Planning in Peace
and War, 1938–1945* (Cambridge: Cambridge University Press, 1985), pp. 149–
50; Susan J. Linz, 'World War II and Soviet Economic Growth, 1940–1953', in
Susan J. Linz (ed.), *The Impact of World War II on the Soviet Union* (Totowa,
NJ: Rowman & Allanheld, 1985), pp. 25–7; William Moskoff, *The Bread of
Affliction: the Food Supply in the USSR During World War II* (Cambridge: Cam-
bridge University Press, 1990), pp. 119–22; John Barber, Mark Harrison, *The
Soviet Home Front, 1941–1945: A Social and Economic History of the USSR in
World War II*, (London: Longman, 1991), pp. 33–4, 189–90; Mark Harrison,
'The Second World War', in R. W. Davies, Mark Harrison, S. G. Wheatcroft
(eds), *The Economic Transformation of the USSR, 1913–1945* (Cambridge: Cambridge University Press, 1994), p. 251. For special attention devoted to this
neglected field see only Robert Munting, 'Lend-Lease and the Soviet War Effort', *Journal of Contemporary History*, 19 (1984), pp. 495–510; Robert Munting,
'Soviet Food Supply and Allied Aid in the War, 1941–1945', *Soviet Studies*, 36
(1984), pp. 582–93; Hubert P. van Tuyll, *Feeding the Russian Bear: American
Aid to the Soviet Union, 1941–1945* (Westport, Conn.: Greenwood Press, 1989).

3. Munting, 'Lend-Lease', p. 495; Barber, Harrison, *The Soviet Home Front*, p. 190.
4. This hypothesis is supported by the suggestion that the wide range of goods
requested by the Soviet authorities for import under lend-lease arrangements
reflected a Soviet intention to copy across a wide range of western technology
(van Tuyll, *Feeding the Russian Bear*, p. 26).
5. Jones, *The Roads to Russia*, p. 238.
6. Herring, *Aid to Russia*, p. 286; Van Tuyll, *Feeding the Russian Bear*, pp. 72–3.
7. Herring, *Aid to Russia*, p. 286; Jones, *The Roads to Russia*, p. 224; Beaumont,
*Comrades in Arms*, pp. 212–3.
8. Van Tuyll, *Feeding the Russian Bear*, pp. 72–3; Moskoff, *The Bread of Affliction*, p. 122.

9. N. S. Khrushchev, *Khrushchev Remembers* (London: André Deutsch, 1971), p. 199.
10. *Istoriia Velikoi Otechestvennoi voiny Sovetskogo Soiuza 1941–1945 gg.*, 6 (Moscow: Voenizdat, 1965), p. 48.
11. *Istoriia sotsialisticheskoi ekonomiki SSSR*, 5 (Moscow: Nauka, 1978), p. 545.
12. *Istoriia Vtoroi Mirovoi voiny 1939–1945 gg.*, 12 (Moscow: Voenizdat, 1982), p. 187; in similar vein, Munting, 'Lend–Lease', p. 495; Millar, 'Financing the Soviet Effort', p. 123n.
13. Jones, *The Roads to Russia*, p. 95.
14. Jones, *The Roads to Russia*, p. 84. The remaining tonnage arrived via the Soviet ports of the eastern Arctic, and (in the last months of the war) across the Black Sea.
15. *Istoriia sotsialisticheskoi ekonomiki*, 5, pp. 542–3.
16. Jones, *The Roads to Russia*, p. 51.
17. Herring, *Aid to Russia*, pp. 38–9.
18. Jones, *The Roads to Russia*, p. 261.
19. United States President, *Reports to Congress on Lend-Lease Operations*, no. 14 (Washington, DC: US Govt Printing Office, 1944), p. 31; no. 19 (1945), p. 15; no. 21 (1945), p. 8. In fact this proportion rose steadily, period by period, from 34 per cent in 1941–42 to 44 per cent (1943), 54 per cent (1944), 58 per cent (the first half of 1945) and 60 per cent (the third quarter of 1945).
20. E.g. Jones, *The Roads to Russia*, pp. 223–4.
21. Herring, *Aid to Russia*, pp. 112–42.
22. Calculated from Ministerstvo Vneshnei Torgovli SSSR, *Vneshniaia torgovlia SSSR. Statisticheskii sbornik. 1918–1966* (Moscow: Mezhdunarodnye Otnosheniia, 1967), p. 60, applying the official exchange rate of 5.30 rubles per $1.
23. For estimated peacetime trade ratios in time series, see Paul R. Gregory, Robert C. Stuart, *Soviet Economic Structure and Performance*, 4th edn (New York: Harper & Row, 1990), p. 325.
24. Jones, *The Roads to Russia*, p. 52.
25. Figures are taken or calculated from Allen, 'Mutual Aid', pp. 529, 535, using current prices, and applying the official exchange rate of $4.03 per £1.
26. United States President, *Report to Congress on Lend-Lease Operations*, no. 14 (Washington, DC: US Govt Printing Office, 1944), p. 58; 1943–45 from no. 20 (1945), p. 49.
27. United States Department of Commerce, 'United States Trade with Russia (USSR) During the War Years', *International Reference Service*, 2, no. 41 (1945), p. 3.
28. *Istoriia sotsialisticheskoi ekonomiki*, 5, p. 586; *Istoriia Vtoroi Mirovoi voiny*, 12, p. 186.
29. See Allen, 'Mutual Aid', pp. 529, 535, and, for war expenditures of the US (in dollars) and UK (in sterling), ibid., p. 542 (I assume that US war spending in the first half of 1942 amounted to 40 per cent of the annual total; calculations are again based on current prices and exchange rates).
30. N. A. Voznesensky, *War Economy of the USSR in the Period of the Patriotic War* (Moscow: Foreign Languages Publishing House, 1948), p. 61.
31. *Istoriia Vtoroi Mirovoi voiny*, 12, p. 187.
32. M. L. Tamarchenko, *Sovetskie finansy v period Velikoi Otechestvennoi voiny* (Moscow: Finansy, 1967), p. 54; *Istoriia sotsialisticheskoi ekonomiki*, 5, p. 546 (emphasis added).
33. Alexander Gerschenkron, Review of *Voennaia ekonomika SSSR v period otechestvennoi voiny* (N. A. Voznesenskii), *American Economic Review*, 38 (1948), p. 656.

34. Mark Harrison, 'Resource Mobilization for World War II: The USA, UK, USSR, and Germany, 1938–1945', *Economic History Review*, 41 (1988), p. 189.
35. *Istoriia sotsialisticheskoi ekonomiki*, 5, p. 540.
36. Harrison, *Soviet Planning*, pp. 192–7.
37. Calculated from Richard Moorsteen, Raymond P. Powell, *The Soviet Capital Stock, 1928–1962* (Homewood, Ill.: Irwin, 1966), pp. 622–3.
38. On the increase in speed of movement with motorisation of the Red Army when advancing, see Jones, *The Roads to Russia*, pp. 233–4; on the railway burden of supplying the food and fodder requirements of horse troops, see Martin van Creveld, *Supplying War: Logistics from Wallenstein to Patton* (Cambridge: Cambridge University Press, 1977), pp. 111–13.
39. A classic treatment of this problem is the 'two-gap' model devised by H. B. Chenery, A. M. Strout, 'Foreign Assistance and Economic Development', *American Economic Review*, 50 (1966), pp. 679–733.
40. Mark Harrison, 'The Second World War', in R. W. Davies, Mark Harrison, S. G. Wheatcroft (eds), *The Economic Transformation of the USSR, 1913–1945* (Cambridge: Cambridge University Press, 1994), p. 323 (Table 61).
41. Alan S. Milward, *War, Economy and Society, 1939–1945* (London: Allen Lane, 1977), p. 351; see also Peter Howlett, 'The Wartime Economy, 1939–1945', in R. Floud, D. McCloskey (eds), *The Economic History of Britain Since 1700*, 3 (1993).
42. Cited in *Istoriia Vtoroi Mirovoi voiny*, 12, p. 186.

# 5 Churchill's Roosevelt
## John Charmley

Churchill's 'victory at all costs' strategy adopted in the high summer of 1940 broke all the conventions which had governed British foreign and imperial policy during the Baldwin/Chamberlain era. Instead of recognising the gap between Britain's commitments and her ability to meet them and covering it with skilful diplomacy, the new Prime Minister put forth the Empire's full strength. This was not simply a reaction to the special circumstances of war. Churchill had long argued that Britain's external policy was afflicted by the political equivalent of the palsy, excoriating the 'mood of unwarrantable self-abasement into which we have been cast by a powerful section of our intellectuals'.[1] For the whole of the previous decade he had preached against the 'defeatist doctrines' which saw 'Britain alone among modern States' casting away 'her rights, her interests and her strength'. He had prophesied that 'developments' would be 'swift and evil';[2] now he had the opportunity to stop the drift. If he was confident that he could do so it was because he had thrown overboard with the Baldwin/Chamberlain baggage their distrust of the United States. 'Westward Ho!' the land was bright, not simply for the war, but for the era that was to come. As his great but neglected speech at Harvard on 6 September 1943 made plain, Churchill's hopes for the future of the world lay in the formation of an Anglo-Saxon federation.[3] Assiduous in his cultivation of Roosevelt before Pearl Harbor, Churchill continued to align his foreign and imperial policies as closely as he could with those of the President. A firm believer in the 'Anglo-Saxonism' which had been intellectually fashionable in his youth, Churchill assumed a substantial identity of interest between Britain and the United States. This essay seeks to question that assumption.

American reaction to Churchill's speech at Harvard demonstrated that while there was admiration for Britain's wartime record, there was little desire to become involved in a permanent Anglo-American alliance. Those Americans who still remained attached to 'isolationism' would obviously scorn such a commitment, as did those who took the view of the Hearst–Patterson press and saw the speech as the opening move in a gambit to ensnare the United States in the British Empire and its concerns. But those newspapers which generally supported Roosevelt, the 'crusading liberals', also found the British Prime Minister's remarks little to their taste. They perceived that a man of Churchill's views on imperialism might seek to use an Anglo-American alliance for his own selfish ends, but they were more worried about the prospect that such a combination would militate against the reformation of the League of Nations which American internationalist opinion hankered after; collaboration, under the aegis of a new world organisation was one thing, old-fashioned power politics quite another.[4]

How realistic then were Churchill's hopes that the sedulous cultivation of Roosevelt would bring America not only out of isolation but into supporting Britain's position as a Great Power? Much of the answer to this question depends upon a reading of Franklin Roosevelt's aims and objectives.

Churchill's admiration for Roosevelt was not shared by his closest colleague, the Foreign Secretary, Anthony Eden. During his visit to Washington in March 1943 to discuss postwar planning he called the American capital a 'mad house', and told his private secretary that he preferred working with the Kremlin – at least there one could be sure who was in charge.[5] He thought that the Chief Executive was 'too like a conjuror, skilfully juggling with balls of dynamite, whose nature he failed to understand'[6] to have a firm grip on policy. FDR himself would not have disagreed with Eden's choice of phrase. He once told his old friend and Treasury Secretary, Henry Morgenthau, that he was 'a juggler' who 'never let my right hand know what my left hand does'.[7] FDR clearly thought he was juggling to some effect. Was he the 'feckless' patrician who relied upon his 'charm' to achieve unrealistic objectives which he defined in too diffuse a way; or was he a world statesman with a long-term strategy who was prepared to be flexible over tactics? There is ample evidence to suggest that FDR did indeed have aims which might be summed up as involving the internationalisation of the New Deal and the spreading of 'Americanism'. There was nothing in his policy which precluded tactical cooperation with Churchill in the short term; and if Churchill failed to recognise that his aims and Roosevelt's were incompatible at a long-term strategic level – well, that was his problem.

The notion of treating the Second World War as the war of 'the British Succession' is likely to shock those Americans who idolise Churchill as a way of celebrating (while not seeming so to do) their own country's victory in the Cold War.[8] One historian has stated in authentic Macaulayesque tones that the idea that 'Britain should have trusted Hitler and not the United States is morally sickening'.[9] Leaving aside the view that historians have some special qualification to pronounce *ex cathedra* on morality, the suggestion that the alternative to trusting in America was 'trusting' in Hitler is an interesting Freudian slip. It also sets up a straw man instead of confronting the reality that America's peace aims were incompatible with those of Winston Churchill.

Roosevelt was too controversial a character ever to have received the sort of uncritical adoration of which Churchill was for long the recipient, yet the image of him which emerges from Churchill's war memoirs fosters such a notion. Of course the picture is not unspotted, but then since Churchill needed someone to act as scapegoat for the failure of his own policies towards the Soviets, it could not have been so. Yet when it comes to the central theme of the Second World War, the Anglo-American alliance, there is nothing to disturb and much to nourish the banalities of future generations of historians that what was going on was 'competitive cooperation'. When Professor Kimball writes about the President's desire to spread the New Deal, he denies that it was any 'kind of crude imperialism'; there was, rather, what he calls, 'the normal, human impulse to convert the unenlightened in a practical, mutually beneficial way'.[10] Those who had no wish to be forcibly enlightened into the 'American way' of life might be forgiven for failing to distinguish properly between this and 'informal imperialism'. The fact that historians can still discuss the Second World War in terms of Britain and America having common ideals which outweighed the fact that America wanted to put an end not only to the British Empire, but to the whole social system which underlay prewar Europe, is evidence only of the success of the internationalising of the New Deal. So widespread are the ideas that 'democracy' is not only the best form of government, but the only legitimate one, and that there are such things as 'human rights' and 'international morality', that it is easy to forget how recently most European nations embraced them. They were acquired at the same time as other 'New Deal' ideas: belief in the efficacy of government intervention in society and the economy; the inherent virtue of 'big' government and the need for 'progressive' taxation. Although so-called Conservatives have successfully challenged the latter set of ideas, the former still pass almost unquestioned. Yet there were few sterner critics of many of the Wilsonian liberal ideas which are enshrined in what Professor Kimball has usefully called 'Americanism' than Churchill in the 1930s. The argument which will be pursued here is that Churchill's decision to carry on fighting in 1940 bound him to a dependence upon America which FDR exploited, if not to the full, then pretty fully. The defender of the old order became the unwitting fugleman of a new world order.

That these things are still obscured, and that historians can still write happily of 'competitive cooperation' is yet another example of a widely acknowledged phenomenon – the success of Churchill's *The Second World War* in shaping history's perception of what went on between 1939 and 1945. Although centre-stage in the memoirs is occupied by Churchill, there is one other character who achieves the status of a major role – Roosevelt. The image which several generations of Britons have of FDR is largely the one which Churchill painted. The lineaments of this picture, indeed perhaps even its genesis, are most easily found in the speech which Churchill delivered in the Commons on 17 April 1945. There, FDR was praised for his prescience in discerning the menace of Nazi Germany – the highest possible accolade in the Churchillian pantheon – and for never losing 'faith' in Britain. The litany went on in a way familiar to readers of *The Second World War*: lend-lease, that 'most unselfish and unsordid financial act of any country in all history'; the Atlantic Charter meeting; the wartime conferences and comradeship; the 'ailing' Roosevelt at Yalta (a notion to be used to great effect in Volume 6); and finally, the death 'in harness' and the apotheosis as 'the greatest American friend we have ever known, and the greatest champion of freedom who has ever brought help and comfort from the new world to the old'.

It is not being suggested that Churchill deliberately obscured a 'true' picture of FDR as harbinger of 'the American century', even if that is what happened; it is more complex. Roosevelt filled a place long vacant in Churchill's life. For all the conventional image of Churchill as a bull-dog figure of independence and gritty determination, there is a pattern in his career which contradicts this; Churchill stood in need of a father-figure, or some substitute therefor. In the early part of his career Asquith and then Lloyd George played this part, with the former treating Churchill as a gifted, if infuriating *enfant terrible*, and the latter establishing what Churchill himself described as a 'master and servant' relationship. Similarly, in what was certainly the closest friendship of Churchill's long life, his comradeship with F. E. Smith, later the first earl of Birkenhead, it was 'F. E.' who played the dominant role, his caustic tongue and ready wit easily reducing his less spontaneous friend to silence with comments such as: 'Oh do be quiet Winston, it's not as if you had a pretty voice!' It is not without significance that the one period of his life when he was without such a mentor, the 1930s, was the time when his political career appeared to go into eclipse; left to his own devices and desires, Churchill was no match for Baldwin and Chamberlain. However, with the advent of Franklin Roosevelt, another mentor was found, and Churchill's career once again appeared to enter a more fertile phase.

It is doubtful whether Churchill understood Roosevelt. For this he is hardly to be blamed – one of Roosevelt's main aims in life was to avoid any such possibility. It was hardly accidental that Roosevelt preferred the spoken word to its written counterpart. As Edward Halifax once put it to Eden, 'It is difficult to reproduce the kind of atmosphere and background against which these talks over luncheon on his table take place;'[11] what was difficult to reproduce could not be used in evidence against you. More than most politicians, FDR was adept at using words to camouflage thought. Listening to him, Eden was aghast at the 'cheerful fecklessness' with which he would redraw the boundaries of Europe and dispose of the fates of millions of people. What Churchill never recognised, and what Eden saw only too late, was that FDR was not so much the 'soldier of freedom', as the architect of the 'American century'; he was the personification of America's 'manifest destiny'.

If Churchill was the advocate of the 'indirect strategy' in warfare, FDR was surely its most deadly practitioner in the political field. It would have been a brave man during the period May 1940 to December 1941 who would have laid money on when, or even if, America would enter the war in Europe, yet FDR managed to give Churchill enough encouragement to commit the future of Britain and her Empire to the proposition that this would happen soon. Indeed, not only did FDR manage this, he did so without making himself too vulnerable to isolationist opinion at home; ambiguity had its uses, and FDR was master of all of them. Of course, FDR's procrastination was not all art, much of it was instinct; FDR disliked making decisions. More, perhaps, than any other democratic politician, FDR realised the fickleness of electorates and the fragility of the President's position; making decisions before they had to be made tied a President down, denied him the room to manoeuvre and the chance to take advantage of changes in circumstances. Like Lloyd George, Roosevelt could not see an obstacle without trying to find a way around it; but unlike the mercurial Welshman, he did care which direction he was travelling. FDR knew that the democratic process was too complex for the will of one man to shape policy, and he knew – none better – that it was necessary to carry Congress with him. Even if, as he went on, he arrogated more and more power in the field of foreign affairs to the chief executive, he did so gradually. A common theme among the various isolationists who opposed him, was that FDR was instituting what William E. Borah called 'executive domination over foreign affairs'.[12] Senator Vandenberg, watching the 'pressure and propaganda' which FDR utilised and invoked to override the Senate's opposition to arms sales to Britain and France in September 1939, correctly foresaw that the 'same emotions' would be used to drag America into war. This emotionalism was, he feared, a 'tribute to the American heart, but not to the American head'.[13] But neither he, nor Borah, nor anyone else for that matter, was able to stop the incremental drift of power in foreign affairs towards the President.

Trying to determine FDR's real aims during 1940–41 is probably a vain enterprise, but the simple verities of the Churchillian version, popularly accepted by a far wider audience than is ever reached by the odd scholarly sceptic, will not stand up to scrutiny. Whatever FDR was up to, it was not manoeuvring America into the war by the quickest route possible. This is not to substitute an infinitely indecisive Roosevelt for Churchill's Machiavelli or MacGregor Burns' 'fox', but rather to postulate a Roosevelt who knew what his goals were but was prepared to be infinitely plastic about the means by which they were to be achieved. Cromwell once said that it was the man who did not know where he was going who went the furthest, but his own career suggests that this resulted in such a man getting lost; FDR's method produced better results. FDR knew his goals, but if he could not take the main road to them, he would improvise another route. From his sailing days he knew it was often necessary to tack before the wind. Flexibility about means was not accompanied by flexibility about ends, even if the latter were often defined in ways which allowed for later fine-tuning. If Machiavelli had never written, the example of FDR's political career could have supplied posterity with a suitable substitute. Tactical concessions do not always imply the lack of a strategy, indeed they are more easily made by a man with a strategy. Such a political style demanded immense self-confidence, but no one ever accused Franklin Roosevelt of being deficient in that department; if he could not walk on water, he could wheel-chair upon thin ice. Behind, and underpinning Roosevelt's diplomacy was the boundless optimism which saw the war as the chance to realise the internationalisation of the New Deal.

Because their experience of the Second World War was one of great success achieved at little cost, Americans are apt to react incredulously to the notion that that war and the national interest were identical. The incredulity tends to take the form of invoking the horrors of Hitler and the holocaust to justify the war, but this is sheer hindsight. Clearly Americans did not feel that Hitler or the plight of the Jews was worth going to war for until their country was booted into things by the Japanese. But Americans have often confused international relations with personal ethics. As a former American ambassador to Kenya put it recently: 'America . . . is the place where freedom dwells . . . a beacon in the darkness, an ideal that illuminates the lives of millions . . . [who] believe in the ultimate goodness of America, its destiny of greatness.'[14] To the European, it might seem that having brought the benefits of American civilisation to the indigenous inhabitants of the North American continent and to the negro, the Americans were bent on extending it to the rest of the world – whether they wanted it or not. Such 'idealism' left itself open to Eden's jibe that American foreign policy 'is exaggeratedly moral, at least where non-American interests are concerned'.[15] But if, in politics, a majority is the best repartee, in international relations Power supplies its place. It was necessary for FDR to proceed carefully with the Soviets, who also possessed power; but with the British he could take advantage of Churchill's assumption of a commonality of interest and his ability to browbeat those who queried it.

Put thus, it is readily apparent why the Churchillian portrait of Roosevelt was necessary. If Roosevelt and the Americans were beneficent and had always intended to help the British, then it did not matter that Churchill had subordinated Britain to America – their interests were the same. Churchill's Roosevelt was a necessary part of the myth of the 'special relationship' – and as he had not existed in quite that form, it proved necessary to invent him.

There were plenty of unsent draft telegrams to bear witness to a version of the Anglo-American alliance which reflected a reality which had to be denied in retrospect. The famed bases for destroyers deal was a bad bargain entered into only because Churchill thought it would bring America a stage nearer to entering the war. Lend-lease was simply a way of ensuring that the British stayed in the war and did America's fighting for her at the same time as she was stripped of the financial assets which would have allowed her to have pursued postwar economic policies which did not accord with American wishes. These episodes were interpolated with incidents such as America sending destroyers to South Africa to distrain on the last gold assets of the Empire. Then there was the American pressure which in 1942 helped prevent the British from making a deal with Russia which would have recognised the June 1941 Soviet frontiers. This was thought to be 'immoral', yet it was no more so than Yalta, and if the British had satisfied Russian desires for security in this way, it would have gone far to improving relations between Britain and the Soviets. It was American pressure which produced the deal with Darlan in 1942, further inflaming Soviet suspicions. It was also American pressures which prevented the British from formulating a constructive European policy based on cooperation with de Gaulle and the French. If American policy had in its sights Axis power, it had, as part of its new world order, the end of European Empires. These were not objectives which were particularly compatible with British war-aims, and as they were achieved where Britain's were not, and as America was necessary to guard Britain from one of the consequences of his own folly – the growth of Soviet power, it was necessary for Churchill to tell the story which suited his political purposes in 1948, not the one he had experienced.

The contention that the British war effort was not particularly successful invites (apart from indignation) the question of what criteria can be used to reach such a verdict? Churchill's own concentration on the war at the front has naturally led most other historians down the same primrose-bestrewn path. Even if that criterion is used, it is far from clear that Churchill enjoyed any success except in a short-lived and localised sense. He certainly managed to persuade FDR to override General Marshall's objections to the North African landings, but the consequent failure to mount an effective 'second front' in Europe until 1944 (Stalin did not count the Italians), certainly helped to sour relations with the Soviets, and arguably prolonged the war by long enough to ensure that the British were totally bankrupt and entirely dependent upon the Americans. But was military success, narrowly defined, the only, or even the main criterion by which to judge British success or failure?

The argument is often heard that what was surprising about the 'Grand Alliance' was that it held together long enough to defeat the Nazis, but it is one tainted with the hindsight of the Cold War era. It ignores the expectations of many of the participants in the war, from the highest to the lowest levels, and by doing so misses one of the main criteria by which men such as Eden wanted to judge the war effort.

Eden found the absence of 'any guiding principle' of British foreign policy a 'grave weakness', and he spent a good deal of 1942 and 1943 trying to remedy this defect.[16] The need for some delineation was clear to Eden when the effects of its want were considered. He thought that 'an important element in our difficulties with the Russians' was 'the suspicions which they entertain of our ultimate intentions towards them'. Similarly, when it came to Anglo-American relations, a shadow was cast by American fears of British imperialism. While the two Great Powers harboured suspicions, the 'smaller allies' were 'puzzled by an apparent inability on our part to give them the kind of lead, to provide for them the kind of focus, which they have come to realise that they must have if they are to survive in a Europe which will continue to be overshadowed . . . by Germany'. At one level – the one which Churchill (and so many historians following him) concentrated upon, the main aim was to rid Europe of German domination and to 'continue to exercise the functions and to bear the responsibilities of World Power'. It was here, however, that there emerged a more important criterion, perhaps the most important, by which the success or failure to the British war effort could be judged. Eden was unequivocal (which is perhaps why he failed to quote extensively from this paper in his memoirs) on this score: 'We have to maintain our position as an Empire and a Commonwealth. If we fail to do so we cannot exist as a World Power. And we have to accept our full share of responsibility for the future of Europe.' 'If we fail to do that', Eden warned his colleagues, 'we shall have fought this war to no purpose, and the mastery of Europe which we have refused to Germany by force of arms will pass to her by natural succession as soon as the control of our arms is removed.' Churchill's admirers like to claim that their hero was something of a visionary, but it was Eden who saw most clearly what was to be the shape of Britain's future. Britain did, indeed, fail to remain a 'World Power', and the consequences which Eden had feared would follow, did so.

It is usual to greet such arguments with the question: 'was all of this not inevitable; was the Empire not doomed anyway?' The short answer is that nothing is inevitable until it has occurred, and that one of the main strands of the argument being pursued here is that it was, in part, the effects of the war which caused the foundations of the Empire to crumble;[17] in throwing aside the caution of the Baldwin/Chamberlain era, Churchill also threw away the only viable imperial policy on offer. Churchill looked upon the war and the American alliance as the solution to his problems when they were, in fact, the solvent of the Empire in whose defence he had fought so long.

Britain's dependence upon American aid precipitated conflict within the Roosevelt administration about the terms upon which it should be granted. Warren Kimball, elegantly erecting a straw man, has stated that 'no American official ever stood up and crassly proclaimed that a major goal of the nation's foreign policy should be the acquisition of Britain's Empire',[18] which ignores Dean Acheson's rather better-informed assertion that the American Treasury envisaged 'a victory where both enemies and allies were prostrate – enemies by military action, allies by bankruptcy'.[19] The latest study of the economic relationship between Britain and America has borne witness to the truth of Acheson's words. Indeed, it was not simply the Treasury which wanted to abolish imperial preference and to force Britain into a multilateral, American-dominated economic order.[20] Like the British a century before, America was possessed of the economic power to acquire an informal empire through economic influence. To this end, British economic policies which envisaged a sort of 'Schactian' solution to her postwar economic problems[21] were ruthlessly brushed aside and Britain was made, willy-nilly, to agree to join the free trade economic new order so beloved of Secretary Hull.

This was all, as the British Chancellor of the Exchequer, Sir Kingsley Wood, put it to Churchill in March 1941, very 'different from what we'd hoped';[22] it always would be. Believing in Roosevelt's rhetoric, the British had imagined that since they were the ones doing the fighting in 1941 they would get American finance on easy terms. After all, 'interventionists' like Secretary of War Stimson, held the view, so often expressed by Anglophiles, that Britain was fighting for common 'values', so what need was there for haggling over 'gold and securities'?[23] Yet, as usual, when it came to practicalities, the British were fobbed off with kind words and made to pay through the nose. The pious hope expressed by Churchill to FDR in December 1941, that 'you will agree that it would be wrong in principle and mutually disadvantageous in effect, if at the height of this struggle, Great Britain were to be divested of all saleable assets so that after victory was won with our blood . . . we should stand stripped to the bone', remained just a pious hope.[24] For Congress, blood was not enough. So deeply-rooted was the notion of the wily 'limey' taking advantage of naive cousin Jonathan, that the British were made to supply a complete list of their assets and to liquidate the Courtauld subsidiary, American Viscose in a 'fire sale' as evidence of good faith. Given the fate of the East End of London and of Coventry, it is no wonder that some Britons find American preaching on the morality of the Second World War a trifle nauseating: the war was a great moral cause, but not such a great one in 1941 that America wanted to pay the price for victory in the blood of her own sons. As Lord Cherwell put it when surveying the likely result of America's economic demands: 'the fruits of victory which Roosevelt offers seem to be safety for America and virtual starvation for us'.[25] Beaverbrook reminded Churchill that 'If we give everything away, we gain little or no advantage over our present situation', and exhorted him to 'Stand up to the Democrats!'[26]

Churchill was not very good at standing up to the Democrats, not least because he perceived them, through the medium of FDR, as 'interventionists', but what he failed to discern was the connection between American *innenpolitik* and *aussenpolitik*; nor did he understand the metamorphosis undergone by 'isolationists' and 'interventionists' alike, under the impact of America's entry into the war in December 1941.

One argument advanced by Churchill in defence of his policy towards America and the concessions which it involved, was that it was all worth it as part of the effort to bring the United States into the war. Yet, in the end, it was nothing that Churchill did which brought about the consummation he had so devoutly wished; it was Hitler's action in declaring war on America which brought Britain and America into the same war. To be more accurate, it was Hitler's decision which ensured that Britain and America could fight the 'Europe first' strategy upon which FDR and Churchill were both agreed; which was not the same thing. If the Atlantic Charter, for all its woolliness and high-sounding rhetoric, is taken as a characteristic expression of America's war-aims, then the differences between the British Empire and the Americans become apparent at once. The two articles which gave the British the most trouble were numbers III and IV. Article III proclaimed the 'right of all peoples to choose the form of government under which they live', while Article IV called for all nations to have 'access on equal terms, to the trade and to the raw materials of the world'; read literally, these two articles signalled the end of the British Empire. Churchill, of course, denied that Article III applied to the Empire, and he and other imperialists fought a tough, but unsuccessful rearguard action against Article IV, but in neither case was Churchill particularly successful in imposing his version of events;[27] that had to be left for his memoirs.

FDR's anti-imperialism is too well documented by historians to need dwelling on here;[28] what is relevant to our purpose is the contrast with Churchill's attitude. Except when it was a matter of implying that the Americans were to blame for stopping him from preventing the rise of the Soviet menace, the only time Churchill allowed himself to be critical of the President was over the latter's intervention in 1942 over India. Churchill's own views on India are perhaps best summed up in comments he made to one of India's representatives to the War Cabinet in September 1942, when he asked: 'Why should we be apologetic or say that we are prepared to go out at the instance of some jackanapes? Tell them what we have done for India. For eighty years we have given it peace and internal security and prosperity such as has never been known in the history of that country.' He was not, he declared, 'going to be a party to a policy of scuttle'. With an echo of his attitude towards the Government of India Act, he told Mudaliar that he would 'tell them that for the last 25 years the Conservative Party has gone on the wrong tracks, it has lost confidence in itself, and it has given way perpetually until the present state of affairs has come about. It is all wrong, thoroughly wrong. If we ever have to quit India, we shall quit it in a blaze of glory.'[29] Modern disdain for this view partakes of that ignorance of the realities of the Indian situation which was so marked a feature of American comment in the 1940s.[30]

In one sense it was unfortunate for the British that Churchill came to personify their war effort, for his attitudes on subjects like India were more reactionary than most. FDR saw Churchill as 'pretty much a nineteenth century colonialist',[31] and American policy-makers took their cue from this. In any event, the idea of the British as a race of colonialists was one which fitted easily into the American stereotype. FDR's vision of the future encompassed the notion that what might be called 'Americanism' was a 'third force' between the imperialism of the British and the Communism of the Soviets.[32] This idea informed American policy towards India, British protectionism and the shape of the postwar world, and in all three areas it operated against what many British Conservatives perceived to be imperial interests. The most vocal representative of this strain of American thought was the Vice President, Henry Wallace. Wallace believed in 'political internationalism' which 'could eventuate only with the end of European imperialism and with the abandonment of balance-of-power politics'. On that account he was 'especially critical of the British, particularly Winston Churchill. Continued British domination over India, in Wallace's understanding, violated the whole purpose of the war, as did Churchill's impulse for empire, his unabashed belief in Anglo-Saxon superiority, his disdain for China and distrust of Russia, his preference for secret negotiations, and his manifest intention to hold the reins of world leadership, whatever the semblance of world government, in British, American, and, unavoidably, Soviet hands.'[33] On 8 June 1942 the Vice-President delivered himself of an 'apocalyptic version of America as "the chosen of the Lord" in whom the culture of Palestine, Rome and Britain are to be brought to a final fruition'. It was the 'most unbridled expression to date of the view of the New Deal as the New Islam, divinely inspired to save the world.'[34]

This brave new world, as envisaged by FDR, Wallace, Berle, Welles and a host of publicists, publicity-seekers and self-proclaimed American messiahs, was the Democratic agenda, writ large, complete with, at least in FDR's view, a substantial increase in Presidential powers. Wallace's 'century of the common man' was little more than a veil for Government interference in the lives of individuals on an unprecedented scale, both through 'agencies' (a favourite Rooseveltian solution for problems), and through so-called 'progressive' taxation, which deprived individuals of the opportunity to pass on their wealth and with it a measure of independence of Government. Roosevelt's taxation policies would have deprived him of the leisure he needed to pursue his own career. In foreign affairs it meant an end to imperialism and protectionism, indeed to any barriers which stood in the way of the imposition of 'Americanism' on an unsuspecting world. This is not to say that FDR was simply after replacing the British Empire with an American one; his ideas were both more recondite and more naive than that. The President (like all liberals) genuinely believed that his ideals were those which ought to be shared by all sensible people, and he would have regarded as wounding (as liberals do) any allegation that his policy was self-serving. Of course, to many British officials, forced to listen to this sort of stuff with more respect than it deserved because of the quarter from whence it came, it seemed as though the 'American substitute for a colonial empire' was 'American big business'; nor was it without significance that rhetoric about the 'abolition of colonial empires' was usually accompanied by demands for 'equal access for all democracies to raw materials'.[35]

With the American entry into the war, something interesting had happened to the old 'isolationists' and 'interventionists'. British fears that America would retreat into isolationism faded, but they were replaced with new ones. The difficulty was now likely to be 'encountered from those who have gone over since Pearl Harbour, [*sic*] from isolationism and "America First" to a brand of interventionism which seeks to order the world purely in the selfish interest of the U.S.'.[36] The possibility of Roosevelt losing the next election, assuming that he chose to stand, was not one which the British could afford to ignore. Churchill may have tied himself firmly to the agenda of FDR and the internationalising of the New Deal, but there were those British politicians, such as Beaverbrook, who urged him not to ignore the Republicans. The possibility of a Republican administration did not necessarily imply a return to American isolationism. Many leading Republicans, Willkie being only the most vocal, recognised the need for America to play a role in the world that befitted her strength. Republicanism might mean an end to FDR's 'Hallelujah foreign policy',[37] but that was not a thing which many British Conservatives would mourn. Indeed, the possibility of a Republican administration, with someone like former President Herbert Hoover as Secretary of State suggested, at least if Hoover himself were to be believed, some intriguing possibilities. Where the 'interventionist' Democrats who had been all out to help Britain in 1940–41, now seemed to be chary of too close a connection with Britain, fearing that this might upset the Soviets and lead to America underwriting the British Empire,[38] the former isolationists seemed quite keen, as Hoover put it, 'that the closest cooperation between the British Commonwealth and the United States should be maintained now and after the war' to avoid Russian power coming to dominate the world.[39] This intriguing turnabout raised the possibility that a skilful use of '"the Bolshevist menace" would drive the isolationist Republicans to cooperate with us – even though we hold Stalin's right hand in our left', which might make it 'worth trying to stimulate further fear of the Russians by roundabout means'.[40] Such a *Realpolitik* approach aroused protests within the Foreign Office, and Eden minuted crossly that 'We must never try any tricks of this kind'. The British 'line' on Anglo-Soviet relations would remain: 'that the Anglo-Soviet treaty is a real and important thing to us, and that we intend to try all out to the full collaboration with Russia'.[41]

The British sought to find their future world role as mediator between the

Soviets and the Americans, but it was not until Tehran that Churchill began to realise that FDR saw no need for anyone to assume such a role. Shorn of this possibility, Churchill sought to make the best of a bad job by coming to his notorious 'spheres of influence' agreement with Stalin in October 1944 – only to withdraw from it under American disapproval. The fact was that Churchill's reliance upon FDR was not paying the dividends which the British Prime Minister had expected, but since it had been Churchill himself who had 'created' the FDR who might grant them, this was not surprising. Professor Kimball's speculation that Churchill's intention at 'Tolstoy' was to 'use the Soviet Union against the United States and vice-versa in order to maintain the form, if not the substance of the British Empire',[42] suffers from an excess of ingenuity. Without guarantees of a firm postwar Anglo-American alliance, Churchill was trying to save something from what Eden was to call the 'sad wreck' of British foreign policy. For all the later attempts by Churchill and his admirers to blame FDR and Yalta for what was to happen to postwar Europe, the fact was that neither at Tehran nor at 'Tolstoy' did Churchill show anything but willingness to concede Stalin's demands on Eastern Europe – provided only that they were put in a reasonable manner. Students of Chamberlain's reactions to Hitler's prewar demands in Middle Europe will be familiar with this refrain.

It was at Yalta that Churchill first began to realise that his hopes about America were about to be disappointed. FDR not only resisted attempts to have a special Anglo-American meeting in advance of the conference, he specifically said that American troops would be withdrawn from Europe within two years of the end of the war. This was where four years of wooing FDR had brought Churchill. For a short while, upon his return home, Churchill did a reasonable imitation of Chamberlain returning from Munich, declaring that Marshal Stalin was a man who could be trusted; even Churchill saw the resemblance and was troubled lest Stalin should prove as untrustworthy as Hitler.[43] Facing opposition in the Commons, ironically enough from some of those who had most thoroughly supported Chamberlain, Churchill disliked the experience of being assaulted by the sort of morally loaded arguments which he had been wont to use, and it was not long before he sought to enlist FDR's aid.

This was the last hurrah of the 'special relationship'. Throughout its course the British had consistently got less than they desired and FDR had secured British agreement to the creation of a peace along lines which America wanted. As far back as 1941, Eden had argued that it was worth paying a morally objectionable price to win Soviet goodwill. This, of course, assumed that Soviet goodwill was available and ignored the fact that the Nazi–Soviet pact had had one solid basis other than that of mutual convenience, and that was a mutual desire to upset the *status quo* and to benefit therefrom. American fears of 'another Munich' had prevented any accommodation with the Soviets, but they had not produced an answer to Eden's argument that if the Soviets were not given what they wanted voluntarily, they would seize it at the end of the war. As the end of the war approached the Soviets acted as they had since 1939, entirely consistently; they had stated their demands at the moment of their greatest peril and they did not change them (much) in the hour of their triumph. What changed was the British willingness to grant those demands. As the war appeared to be on the verge of being won, it was no longer necessary for Churchill to take a Chamberlainite attitude towards the Soviets; but if he wished to take a Churchillian stand (circa 1938) he needed to enlist American support. It might be said that if the Soviet menace had not existed, Churchill would have needed to invent it to frighten the Americans into providing support for British power in parts of the world like the Middle East and the Eastern Mediterranean where it faced a challenge from the Soviets.

Historians have given much attention to the notion of a 'consensus' being formed in British politics during the war, but they have usually confined their remarks to the domestic arena without commenting upon the existence of a cross-party consensus on external policy. Attlee's Government came to power determined to continue the more robust Churchillian line, and like their mentor they looked to America for assistance. Unlike say Eden, who suspected American ambitions in the Middle East and elsewhere boded ill for the Empire, Bevin was anxious to see 'America brought into the Mediterranean', and agreed to American plans concerning the future of the Italian colonies in North Africa.[44] Bevin was worried about Russian penetration in the region and realised that Britain could only resist it with American support.[45] But there was the rub. It was acknowledged that 'the process of inducing the United States to support a British challenge to Russia' would 'be a very tricky one'. If the Americans got hold of the idea that 'the motive behind our polices derived from the apprehension that we were being regarded as a second-class power', then there would be little hope of obtaining their help; it was hoped that the role of defender of liberal democracy against the Soviets might serve this purpose.[46] This 'Anglo-Saxon thesis' would, it was hoped, secure American support.[47]

Indeed in the months after Potsdam the Americans exhibited worrying signs of wishing to mediate between their two wartime partners.[48] Before the Conference of Foreign Ministers met in London in September, Bevin had told Byrnes that 'the time has come when we must face up to the question of whether or not we are prepared to acquiesce' in Czechoslovakia, Yugoslavia, Bulgaria, Hungary and Romania 'remaining definitely in the Russian sphere of influence', and what 'inducements, economic and cultural, we can offer these countries to look West rather than East'.[49] But Byrnes did not respond to this overture for a concerted Anglo-American line; indeed, since the Americans had already taken separate action in Bulgaria and

Romania, his assurances that he did not want to 'march out of step' with the British,[50] were little more than window-dressing. The conference itself was as barren of signs of any special relationship as other parts of the diplomatic spectrum: from Europe to Asia, from atomic diplomacy to aspects of the Eastern Question, British hopes of American support were proving illusory.

Churchill had left office convinced not only of the reality of Anglo-American collaboration, but of its firm foundation in atomic diplomacy.[51] It was, therefore, something of a shock when Truman seemed to imply in early October that if Britain wanted the bomb it would have to develop it.[52] Attlee and Bevin had been turning over the question of whether or not Britain and America should share their knowledge with the Soviets[53] – now they were not even sure whether the Americans would share it with them.[54] The failure to bring America along placed Bevin in a difficult position. Back in July the option of delimiting spheres of influence with the Soviets had been canvassed, only to be rejected partly on the grounds that this would 'represent the abdication of our right as a great Power to be concerned with the affairs of Europe', and partly because such 'cynical abandonment' would not get American support.[55] But the problem facing Bevin was that Truman and Byrnes did not seem to be interested in coming to the rescue of British power – which made the Churchillian foreign policy rather difficult to carry out. Much the same legacy awaited Bevin and Attlee elsewhere. One reason British negotiators went to Washington in late 1945 hoping for a 'grant' rather than a loan was the belief that America could give Britain the money because they wanted to see her continue as a Great Power. Here too disillusion was the result.[56]

When the Americans did enter the arena against the Soviets it was for their own reasons, and when they did so the British were to find themselves dragged along in an anti-communist crusade. They had sought American help as the means towards the end of preserving their position in the area between the Eastern Mediterranean and the Persian Gulf, but they were to end up sacrificing their position here to the dynamics of American policy – a most extravagant sacrifice of end to means.

But was it not the case, as has been constantly argued and recently reiterated, that what mattered was the 'shared ideals' of the Anglo-American partnership, even if Churchill's dreams of an exclusive relationship were in vain?[57] After all, the alliance destroyed Hitler, and no one whom anyone else takes seriously has been found to argue that that was not worth doing. It does matter, and it matters because of the nature of the Grand Alliance. As one prominent Soviet writer and later dissident, Victor Nekrasov put it some years ago: 'By fighting Hitlerism and defeating it we strengthened this earth's other form of dictatorship, a form in many ways even more conscienceless and cruel.'[58] This, as with Churchill's own appeasement of

Stalin, mocks the often-heard notion that the Second World War was some-how a 'moral' conflict with a 'morally' valuable result.[59] It was not. It was, in the final resort, about what international relations have always been about, power and who holds it. The Second World War saw Britain lose her power; the strain which Churchill's policy imposed upon the Empire and its complex economic and sociological underpinnings contributed profoundly to that result. Churchill, like his immediate successors, had thought this would not happen because they could rely upon America to uphold Britain's position. For perfectly good reasons of their own, this the Americans declined to do. Indeed, through the medium of the talking-shop that called itself (surely humorously?) the United Nations, and through her backing for Zionism in the strategically crucial area to the British of Palestine, the Americans were to make their own little contribution to further undermining the old imperial order.

It might be that this was worth doing – followers of intellectual fashion that they are, few historians have been found to agree with Lord Beloff's thesis that America materially assisted the passing of British power;[60] this essay does not share in that fashionable consensus. By ignoring the aims of Roosevelt's liberal foreign policy agenda, Churchill ensured that he had become the King's First Minister who would preside over the beginning of the liqui-dation of the British Empire.

## NOTES

1. M. Gilbert, *Winston S. Churchill, vol V.*, p. 486.
2. J. Charmley, *Lord Lloyd and the Decline of the British Empire* (London, 1987), p. 169.
3. Public Record Office, Kew, Foreign Office General Correspondence, FO 371 series, FO 371/34120/A 9559/32/45 for the speech and US reaction.
4. FO 371, loc. cit. BIS Report, no. 82, 12 September 1943.
5. J. Harvey (ed.), *The War Diaries of Oliver Harvey 1941–1945* (1978), 13 March 1943, p. 229.
6. The Earl of Avon, *The Eden Memoirs. The Reckoning* (1965), p. 374.
7. Warren F. Kimball, *The Juggler* (Princeton, 1991), p. 7.
8. C. Hitchens, *Blood, Class and Nostalgia* (London, 1990), Chapters 1–2, 7–8, for this in detail.
9. Gaddis Smith, 'Whose Finest Hour?', in *The New York Times Book Review*, 22 August 1993.
10. Kimball, p. 187.
11. PRO. Avon Papers, FO 954/29, US/42/227, Halifax to Eden, 29 October 1942.
12. R. J. Maddox, *William E. Borah and American Foreign Policy* (Baton Rouge, 1969) p. 59.
13. Arthur H. Vandenberg Jr (ed), *The Private Papers of Senator Vandenberg* (Boston, 1952), 15 September 1939, pp. 2–3.

14. Ambassador Smith Hempstone, delivering the 139th Commencement address at Westminster College, Fulton, Missouri, 9 May 1993.
15. Eden, p. 319.
16. PREM. 4/100/7, WP(42)516, 'The "Four Power" Plan', 8 November 1942. See also the discussion of this in my forthcoming book on this subject.
17. J. Darwin, *Britain and Decolonisation* (London, 1988), pp. 44–61.
18. Kimball, *Juggler*, p. 46.
19. Dean Acheson, *Present at the Creation* (New York, 1969), p. 28.
20. Randall Bennett Woods, *A Changing of the Guard* (Chapel Hill, 1990), Chapters 2–4, 6–7.
21. L. Pressnell, *External Economic Policy since the War, vol. 1* (1987), pp. 20–8.
22. PREM. 4/17/2, fos. 169–73, Wood to WSC, 15 March 1941.
23. J. M. Blum, *From the Morgenthau Diaries. Years of Urgency 1938–1941* (Boston, 1965), p. 162.
24. Warren F. Kimball, *Churchill and Roosevelt, the complete correspondence, Volume 1* (Princeton, 1984), p. 108.
25. PREM. 4/17/1, fos. 82–5, Cherwell to WSC, December 1940.
26. PREM. 4/17/1, fos. 49–50, Beaverbrook to WSC, 19 February 1941.
27. Randall Bennett Woods, *A Changing of the Guard: Anglo-American relations, 1941–1946* (N. Carolina, 1990), Chapters 2–4.
28. See Kimball and C. Thorne, *Allies of a Kind* (1978) in particular, but also W. R. Louis, *Imperialism at Bay* (1977).
29. Nicholas Mansergh (ed.), *The Transfer of Power 1942–1947, vol. III* (1971), Mudaliar to Sir G. Laithwaite, 21 September 1942, p. 3.
30. Ibid., Linlithgow to Amery, 3, 10 October 1942, pp. 82, 120, for examples. FO 371/30659, 30660 contain 122 files on British perceptions of American reactions to the Cripps mission; FO 371/30660/A7216/122/45 for FO attitudes to the US on India, August 1942.
31. Kimball, *Juggler*, p. 66.
32. Ibid., p. 64.
33. J. M. Blum (ed.), *The Price of Vision: The Diary of Henry A. Wallace 1942–1946* (Boston, 1973), p. 29.
34. FO 371/30653/A5948/31/45, tel. 3381, Halifax to FO, 22 June 1942.
35. FO 371/30653/A5574/31/45, Sir D. Scott, 17 June 1942.
36. FO 371/30654/A9668/31/45, FO minute, 22 October 1942.
37. FO 371/34114/A711/32/45, Mr. Price, reporting Alf Landon, 6 December 1942.
38. FO 954/29, US/42/225, 226, Halifax to AE, 30 October 1942.
39. FO 371/34114/A72/32/43, extract from WP(42)591, 16 December 1942.
40. FO 371/34114/A72/32/43, Mr Malcolm minute, 4 January 1943.
41. Loc. cit., marginalia by Eden, Mr Butler minute, 5 January 1943.
42. *Churchill & Roosevelt III*, p. 351.
43. B. Pimlott (ed.), *The War Diaries of Hugh Dalton* (1988), 23 February 1945, p. 836; J. Colville, *The Fringes of Power. Downing Street Diaries 1939–1955* (1984), 23 February 1945, pp. 562–3.
44. DBPO, series 1, vol. II, *Conferences in London, Washington and Moscow, 1945* (1985, no. 62, record of conversation, 16 September 1945, p. 191.
45. Ibid., no. 102, pp. 26–34.
46. Ibid. calendar to no. 102, i., minute by N. M. Butler, 30 July 1945.
47. DBPO 1/II, no. 193, FO memorandum, 11 September 1945, p. 533.
48. FO 371/44538/AN3159/4/45, minute by J. Donnelly, 17 October 1945.
49. DBPO 1/II, no. 9, Bevin to Balfour, 25 August 1945, p. 16.
50. Ibid., no. 10, Balfour to Bevin, 25 August 1945, pp. 18–19.

51. *DBPO 1/II*, no. 186, memorandum by Sir R. Campbell, 8 August 1945, pp. 516–20.
52. *Presidential Papers, Harry S. Truman, 1945*, pp. 381–8.
53. *DBPO 1/II*, no. 190, FO memorandum, 18 August 1945, pp. 524–6; no. 200, minute from Mr Butler to Bevin, 12 October 1945, pp. 559–62.
54. Alan Bullock, *Ernest Bevin*, (1983), pp. 184–5.
55. *Documents on British Policy Overseas, Series 1, volume I, Conference at Potsdam*, (1984), no. 102, Annexe II, p. 189; calendar to no. 102, minutes by Gladwyn Jebb, 20 July, by N. M. Butler, 30 July and Sir Orme Sargent, 31 July 1945.
56. *DBPO 1/II*, minute from Mr Butler to Sir E. Bridges, 2 November 1945, p. 579.
57. Gaddis Smith, 'Whose Finest Hour?', *New York Times Book Review*, 22 August 1993.
58. V. Nekrasov, 'The Shock of a Secret', *Encounter*, May 1978, p. 75.
59. Gaddis Smith, again, but I have heard that argument every time I have lectured anywhere on this subject.
60. See Max Beloff, 'The End of the British Empire and the Assumption of World-wide Commitments by the United States', in Wm Roger Louis & H. Bull (eds), *The Special Relationship* (1986), pp. 249–60.

# 6 Anglo-American–Soviet Intelligence Relations

## Christopher Andrew

No aspect of the Grand Alliance was more remarkable than the performance of, and the relationships between, its intelligence communities. Britain and the United States learned more about their enemies than any power had ever known before in any war. The Soviet Union was less well-informed about its enemies, but had better intelligence about Britain and the United States than any power had previously possessed about its wartime allies.

Despite the inevitable moments of tension common to all alliances, the British and American intelligence communities collaborated more closely and more successfully during the Second World War than the secret services of independent powers had ever done before. The prime mover of the intelligence alliance, as of the Special Relationship as a whole, was Winston Churchill. Churchill's passion for intelligence spanned over half a century. From his cloak-and-dagger adventures at the frontiers of the late Victorian Empire to his (still unresearched) fascination with covert operations and the work of GCHQ as peacetime prime minister in the early 1950s, he had a longer, more intense and more varied interest in intelligence than any other statesman in British history. Though his biographers usually fail to mention it, Churchill was a member of the Cabinet which in 1909 founded the forerunners of today's Security Service (MI5) and Secret Intelligence Service (SIS); he took a personal interest in both. As First Lord of the Admiralty in 1914, Churchill also presided over the rebirth of British codebreaking in the naval and diplomatic signals intelligence (sigint) agency, Room 40. Ten years later, he claimed to have read every decrypt so far sent to Whitehall by Room 40's interwar sigint successor, GC&CS:

> I have studied this information over a longer period and more attentively than probably any other minister has done.... I attach more importance to [the decrypts] as a means of forming a true judgement of public policy in these spheres, than to any other source of knowledge at the disposal of the state.[1]

In May 1940 Bletchley Park, the Second World War sigint agency, made the first major break in the hitherto unbreakable German Enigma machine cipher. By a remarkable coincidence, Churchill thus became prime minister just as the best intelligence in British history began to come on-stream. As war leader, his passion for intelligence and his desire for alliance with the United States converged. When 'Wild Bill' Donovan, the future head of OSS, arrived in London as President Roosevelt's special envoy in July 1940, Churchill ensured that he was shown the red carpet – indeed a whole series of red carpets. Donovan was received by Churchill, granted an audience with King George VI, and taken to secret meetings with most of Britain's intelligence chiefs. Once back in Washington, he urged FDR to begin 'full intelligence collaboration'.[2] When Donovan crossed the Atlantic again in December, Churchill again ordered that he be given 'every facility' both in London and on his tour of Middle Eastern command posts and intelligence stations. After the tour was over, Churchill telegraphed his thanks to FDR for the 'magnificent work' done by Donovan during his travels: 'He has carried with him throughout an animating, heart-warming flame.'[3]

Roosevelt was the first President since Washington to have shown a serious interest in intelligence during his early political career. As Assistant Secretary of the Navy from 1913 to 1920, he had direct responsibility for the Office of Naval Intelligence. In 1916, the Director of Naval Intelligence, Captain James Harrison Oliver, complained that Roosevelt was recruiting his own espionage network and interfering in the running of intelligence operations.[4] American naval intelligence, Roosevelt complained, did not compare with Britain's. 'Their Intelligence Department is far more developed than ours, and this is because it is a much more integral part of their Office of Operations', he wrote in 1918.[5] No existing study of Roosevelt's foreign policy grasps the importance of his admiration for British intelligence during the First World War in explaining his readiness to embark on a special relationship with it in the Second well before Pearl Harbor. During a visit to London in 1918, FDR had listened spellbound as Admiral Sir Reginald 'Blinker' Hall, DNI and the most powerful of Britain's First World War intelligence chiefs, explained how British spies crossed the German–Danish border each night, went by boat to Sylt and thence by flying-boat to Harwich. When Hall's Second World War successor, Admiral John Godfrey, visited Washington in the summer of 1941, he was amazed to be regaled by FDR's recollections of these and other amazing operations of Britain's 'wonderful intelligence service' in the First World War. Godfrey thought it prudent not to tell the President that the exploits which had so impressed him a quarter of a century earlier were in fact wholly fictitious. Hall had invented them to conceal from the young Assistant Secretary of the Navy that his best intelligence came from the codebreakers of Room 40 rather than from spies. Had Roosevelt realised how much sigint Room 40 produced, he might well have deduced – correctly – that Britain was tapping the American transatlantic cable, which for a period in the winter of 1916–17 also carried German diplomatic traffic. And had he deduced that, he might have suspected – also correctly – that the British had broken American as well as

German codes. The celebrated revelation of the Zimmermann telegram, which in April 1917 smoothed the United States' entry into the First World War by disclosing an absurd German plot to lure Mexico into the war, was at one level a successful British deception. To conceal the fact that the German telegram had been intercepted on an American cable, Hall pretended that he had first obtained it by espionage in Mexico City.[6]

Today's Anglo-American intelligence alliance is usually seen simply as a product of the Second World War. The precedents set during the First World War were, however, of crucial importance. SIS set out in 1940, with Churchill's blessing, to build on the achievements of its predecessor, MI1c, a quarter of a century earlier.[7] Operating under the cover of the Office of the British Military Attaché in New York, the MI1c station had reported to London in March 1918:

> There is complete cooperation between this office and
> 1. United States Military Intelligence
> 2. Naval Intelligence
> 3. U.S. Secret Service
> 4. New York Police Department
> 5. Police Intelligence
> 6. U.S. Customs House
> 7. The American Protective League and similar civic organisations
> 8. U.S. Department of Justice, Bureau of Investigation [the future FBI]
> Everyone of them is in the habit of calling us up or visiting the office daily.[8]

Most remarkable of all were the achievements of the MI1c head of station, Sir William Wiseman. By making himself the confidant of President Woodrow Wilson's confidant, Colonel Edward House, Wiseman won the confidence of the President himself. Wiseman found Wilson 'ready to discuss everything on the frankest terms'.[9] Lord Northcliffe concluded during his official missions to the United States in 1917, with only slight exaggeration, that Wiseman was 'the only person, English or American, who had access at any time to the President or Colonel House'.[10]

In 1940 the new SIS head of station in New York, Sir William Stephenson, later to pass into intelligence mythology as 'The Man Called Intrepid',[11] set out to emulate and surpass Wiseman's achievements during the First World War. Privately, Whitehall was dismissive of the fragmented United States intelligence community, which still lacked both a specialised foreign intelligence agency and a centralised system of assessment. After his visit to Washington in 1941, Admiral Godfrey delivered a scathing report on what he had found:

> Even the more senior U.S. Navy, Military and State Department officials

are credulous and prefer their intelligence to be highly coloured. For instance, the Navy Department's estimate of the size of the German U-boat fleet is higher than our own by approximately one third, while the War Department's estimates of the first line strength and first line reserves of the German Air Force are higher than ours by 250%.

This predilection for sensationalism hinders the reasoned evaluation of intelligence reports. For instance, in April, 1941, both War and Navy Departments accepted a report from the U.S. Embassy in Rome that there were more than 20 German Divisions in Libya. This report was believed for some time in spite of the known shortage of Axis shipping in the Mediterranean, and in spite of the inadequate port facilities at Tripoli and Benghazi, of which the U.S. authorities were fully informed.

There is no U.S. Secret Intelligence Service. Americans are inclined to refer to their 'S.I.S.', but by this they mean the small and uncoordinated force of 'Special Agents' who travel abroad on behalf of one or another of the Governmental Departments. These 'Agents' are, for the most part, amateurs without special qualifications and without training in Observation. They have no special means of communication or other facilities and they seldom have clearer brief than 'to go and have a look'.[12]

Stephenson's remarkably ambitious aim during 1941 was to create a United States intelligence community (excluding sigint) under his own tutelage without offending the Americans by making the tutelage too obvious. He began by cultivating Donovan as successfully as Wiseman had cultivated House. Donovan, he hoped, would have an even more important role as Roosevelt's intelligence supremo in the Second World War than House had played as Wilson's closest adviser in the First. Stephenson interpreted Roosevelt's appointment of Donovan as Coordinator of Information [Intelligence] on 18 June 1941 as a victory for his own lobbying on Donovan's behalf. He cabled triumphantly to SIS headquarters:

Donovan accuses me of having 'intrigued and driven' him into appointment. You can imagine how relieved I am after three months of battle and jockeying for position in Washington that our man is now in a position of such importance to our efforts.

A remarkable memorandum by Churchill's intelligence aide, Major Desmond Morton, vividly conveys both the prime minister's rejoicing at Donovan's appointment and his exaggerated expectations of Stephenson's future influence over Roosevelt:

[A] most secret fact of which the Prime Minister is aware but not all the other persons concerned, is that to all intents and purposes U.S. Security is being run for them at the President's request by the British. A British officer [Stephenson] sits in Washington with Mr. Edgar Hoover and

General [*sic*] Bill Donovan for this purpose and reports regularly to the President.[13]

Some years after the Second World War, Stephenson fantasised that he had become Roosevelt's trusted confidant, acted as Churchill's secret emissary to him, and that Roosevelt had told him, 'I'm your biggest undercover agent!' Though Stephenson vouched for the 'authenticity' of these and other fantasies on the publication of the best-selling biography of him, *A Man Called Intrepid*, in 1974, his mind later partially cleared. 'I never at any time claimed', he inaccurately declared in 1982, 'to provide a secret liaison between the British Prime Minister and the American President.'[14] Stripped of the myths that he later propagated about his wartime career, Stephenson's achievements remain remarkable. From his friendship with Donovan and his early contacts with Hoover and the FBI sprang a full-blown Anglo-American human intelligence (humint) alliance which eventually went far beyond the intelligence collaboration of the First World War. On the thirty-fifth and thirty-sixth floors of the International Building in the Rockefeller Center on Fifth Avenue, New York, Stephenson set up the offices of British Security Coordination (BSC) which, for much of the war, included liaison officers from MI5 and SOE as well as SIS. Stephenson also had a remarkable influence on both Donovan and Roosevelt. Though Donovan was not, of course, the compliant Anglophile tool suggested by Major Morton, he was strongly influenced by British advice both as Coordinator of Information and when setting up the Office of Strategic Services (OSS) in the summer of 1942. The postwar citation accompanying the award to Stephenson of the Medal for Merit eulogised his 'assistance and counsel of great value at every step' in the creation of American wartime intelligence and special operations. Never before had one power had so much influence on the development of the intelligence community of another independent state.

During 1941 and the early months of 1942, however, Stephenson took enormous risks which might well have ended in disaster. It was believed in the British intelligence community that 'Blinker' Hall's brilliantly stage-managed revelation of German intrigues in Mexico early in 1917 had played a critical role in bringing the United States into the First World War. Stephenson planned to use similar intelligence on Nazi conspiracies in Latin America to persuade Roosevelt to enter the Second. Since, however, there were no real Nazi conspiracies of sufficient importance, Stephenson decided to invent them. Among the BSC forgeries with which he deceived Roosevelt was a fabricated letter from Major Elias Belmonte, the Bolivian military attaché in Berlin, describing a plot to establish a Nazi dictatorship in Bolivia. Roosevelt used the letter on 11 September in his broadcast 'fireside chat', denouncing Hitler's designs on Latin America.[15] The attempt 'to subvert the government of Bolivia' was, claimed the President, evidence of Hitler's attempts to secure 'footholds and bridgeheads in the New World, to be used as soon as he has gained control of the oceans'.[16] The State Department and the FBI, if not the White House, were, however, less easily taken in by British intelligence than they had been during the First World War. Both privately complained to the British embassy that 'British intelligence had given us documents which they had forged'.[17]

Roosevelt, probably reassured by Donovan (who had also been taken in by Stephenson), seems to have remained convinced that the document was genuine. Despite the now evident risks involved, BSC continued to produce forgeries designed to inflame American opinion against imaginary Nazi conspiracies in Latin America. In October, Stephenson sent the President, probably via Donovan, a forged map which, he claimed, had been obtained by British agents from a German diplomatic courier in Argentina.[18] Roosevelt made the map the centrepiece of his 'Navy and Total Defense Day Address' on 27 October 1941:

> I have in my possession a secret map, made in Germany by Hitler's government – by planners of the New World Order. . . . the geographical experts of Berlin have ruthlessly obliterated all the existing boundary lines; they have divided South America into five vassal states, bringing the whole continent under their domination. . . . This map, my friends, makes clear the Nazi design not only against South America but against the United States as well.

Roosevelt also indignantly denounced another imaginary Nazi masterplan, almost certainly devised by BSC, 'to abolish all existing religions – Catholic, Protestant, Mohammedan, Hindu, Buddhist and Jewish alike'.[19] Roosevelt's most outspoken attack on Nazi Germany before Hitler's declaration of war on the United States thus relied on bogus intelligence foisted on him by Sir William Stephenson.

Even after the German declaration of war, Stephenson continued for several months to take enormous risks to promote Anglo-American intelligence collaboration on his own terms. Having decided that Adolf Berle, the mildly Anglophobe Assistant Secretary of State, was a threat to BSC, he set out to discredit him and force his resignation. This time, however, Stephenson came dangerously close to being sent home in disgrace. In February 1942, the FBI discovered that he was using a BSC official named Denis Paine to 'get the dirt' on Berle and publish it in the press. When confronted with the evidence, Stephenson feigned 'surprise and horror that any of his men would do such a thing', and hastily put Paine on a plane for Montreal. On 26 February, the Attorney-General, Francis Biddle, J. Edgar Hoover, Berle and the Directors of Military and Naval Intelligence met to consider what further action to take. It was decided that Biddle should inform the President of Stephenson's 'unscrupulous' and 'irresponsible' activities. On 5 March,

Biddle, Hoover and Berle met the British ambassador, Lord Halifax, and the British minister, Sir Ronald Campbell. Halifax was taken aback by what they told him:

> Specifically referring to the incident of Paine, he had understood that [Stephenson] had discovered Paine's activities and had promptly called him down and requested him to leave the country. He had not understood that the F.B.I. had intervened in the matter.

Biddle and his colleagues stopped just short of demanding Stephenson's recall, but said that both the President and his advisers felt that BSC 'probably . . . needed a different type of man to head it'.[20] Stephenson survived by the skin of his teeth, helped by his phenomenal personal charm. As even Berle later admitted, 'It was impossible not to like Bill Stephenson.'[21]

Parallel to the growth of Anglo-American humint collaboration was the construction of an even more important sigint alliance. At a meeting in London on 31 August 1940 between the British Chiefs of Staff and the American Military Observer Mission, the US Army representative, Brigadier General George V. Strong (later G-2), reported that 'it had recently been arranged in principle between the British and United States Governments that periodic exchange of information would be desirable', and said that 'the time had come for a free exchange of intelligence' – including sigint.[22] Roosevelt approved the beginning of sigint collaboration with the British in the autumn of 1940, but took no personal interest in it. He was content to leave the whole business to his Secretaries of State for War and the Navy, Henry L. Stimson and Frank Knox. Stimson noted on 24 October, 'the President was perfectly satisfied to rest upon the judgment of Knox and myself in the matter and approved of what we proposed to do'. Stimson's role was far more influential than that of Knox. The Army Signal Intelligence Service wished to collaborate with the British. The Navy Code and Signal Section initially did not. The military cryptanalysts, however, were the more successful and influential of the two. 'The Army has made wonderful progress', Stimson noted. 'I cannot even in my diary go into some of the things they have done.'[23] The most remarkable achievement of the Signal Intelligence Service had been to break the main Japanese diplomatic cipher, known to the Americans as PURPLE, in September 1940. In February 1941, military cryptanalysts delivered a copy of the Japanese PURPLE machine to Bletchley Park and demonstrated its working method.[24]

Bletchley Park was initially more guarded about what it told the Americans. The fact that Bletchley had broken the Luftwaffe variant of the Enigma machine cipher was one of the most closely-guarded secrets in British history, unknown even to a majority of Churchill's ministers. Both the Prime Minister and his leading cryptanalysts reasonably feared that the secret might be unsafe in the United States. But they also had one quite different reason for limiting the cryptanalytic exchange with the United States. The British continued, as they had done fairly regularly since the First World War, to decrypt American diplomatic cables. The selection of intercepts produced for Churchill each day occasionally included one from the United States – not a secret he was prepared to share with Roosevelt.[25] British willingness to share sigint with the United States was strengthened by growing Anglo-American naval cooperation in the North Atlantic during the summer of 1941. In June Bletchley Park broke German naval Enigma. Churchill pressed a reluctant Menzies to give Washington the contents of decrypts which referred to US naval units. After a U-boat attacked the US destroyer *Greer* on 4 September, American warships began escorting British and Canadian convoys three-quarters of the way across the Atlantic. The US Navy was by this time already routing convoys on the basis of ULTRA intelligence on U-boat positions supplied by the Admiralty.[26]

During 1941 MAGIC (decrypted Japanese diplomatic traffic) provided Roosevelt with the best foreign intelligence in United States history. Despite the President's fascination with secret agents, however, sigint failed to grip his imagination. Though he took a personal interest in the coordination of foreign humint through the establishment of the CoI and OSS, he tolerated an astonishing level of confusion in the production of sigint. To resolve interservice rivalry after the breaking of PURPLE in September 1940, he approved an absurd arrangement by which Japanese intercepts on odd dates were decrypted by military cryptanalysts and on even dates by their naval rivals.[27] Early in 1941 he sanctioned another eccentric interservice compromise which gave his naval aide the right to supply him with MAGIC during odd months and accorded the same privilege to his military aide in even months. But there was no provision for supplying the President with sigint either on Sundays or on weekday evenings. It is impossible to imagine Churchill tolerating such a system for a single day. The compromise began to break down in the summer after the military aide, General Edwin 'Pa' Watson absent-mindedly filed a MAGIC folder in his wastepaper basket.[28] The bizarre odd/even date cryptanalytic compromise continued to cause confusion until Pearl Harbor. In the early hours of Saturday 6 December, a naval listening station near Seattle picked up the first thirteen parts of the now celebrated 'fourteen-part message' containing the Japanese rejection of the final American terms for settling the crisis. The intercepts were forwarded by teleprinter to the Navy Office in Washington. As 6 December was an even date, the Navy, to its dismay, had to pass the intercepts on to the Army. Since the civilian staff of the Military Signal Intelligence Service stopped work for the weekend at midday on Saturdays, the Army, to its even greater chagrin, had to enlist naval assistance on an Army day while it tried desperately to salvage military honour by arranging a civilian night-shift until the next Navy day began at midnight. While the bureaucratic confusion continued in Washington, the Japanese fleet crept up, unnoticed, on Hawaii.[29]

The history of Pearl Harbor is bedevilled by endlessly recycled conspiracy theories which assert that Churchill or Roosevelt (or both) had advance warning from sigint of the impending Japanese attack but suppressed the information in order to ensure that the United States was forced into the war. Before Pearl Harbor, Churchill frequently telephoned Bletchley Park himself for the latest intelligence. One of the leading Japanese cryptanalysts, Captain Malcolm Kennedy, wrote in his diary on 6 December:

> The All Highest (Churchill) is all over himself at the moment for latest information and indications re Japan's intentions and rings up at all hours of day and night, except for the 4 hours in each 24 (2 to 6 a.m.) when he sleeps.

Kennedy, like Churchill, first learned of the attack on Pearl Harbor next day not from sigint but from the BBC:

> A message rec[eived] just before leaving the office this evening had indicated that the outbreak of war was probably only a matter of hours, but the news on the 9 p.m. wireless, that Japan had opened hostilities with an air raid on Pearl Harbor, more than 3000 miles out in the Pacific, came as a complete surprise.[30]

Roosevelt too was taken by surprise. Though he was not a part of any conspiracy to suppress evidence of an impending Japanese attack, he bears some personal responsibility for the intelligence failure which made it possible.

Not a single Japanese decrypt available in Washington provided a warning of the attack on Pearl Harbor. Since no Japanese mission abroad was given advance notice of the attack, MAGIC made no mention of it. In MAGIC intercepts reporting ship movements between 1 August and 6 December, there were only 20 references to Pearl Harbor as compared with 59 to the Philippines and 23 to the Panama Canal.[31] But if the diplomatic cables failed to point to an attack on Pearl Harbor, Japanese naval traffic did. Though thousands of naval signals were intercepted during the last six months of 1941, however, the great majority could not be decrypted. While the cryptanalysts had made progress in solving the basic Japanese naval code, known as JN25, the attack on the variant, JN25b, introduced in December 1940, had so far failed. A detailed study by the American postwar sigint agency, NSA, later concluded that the failure to break JN25b was due solely to a shortage of resources. For most of 1939, 1940 and 1941, usually two and never more than five cryptanalysts were assigned to work on all Japanese naval code and cipher systems. Not till late in 1941 was the number working on JN25 and JN25b raised to eight. 'If the Japanese navy messages had enjoyed a higher priority and [had been] assigned more analytic resources,' writes the NSA historian, Frederick D. Parker, 'could the U.S. Navy have predicted the Japanese attack on Pearl Harbor? Most emphatically yes!' When the unsolved intercepted messages of late 1941 were decrypted as part of a secret postwar study, they were found to reveal many of the preparations for Pearl Harbor. American successes in breaking Japanese naval ciphers after Pearl Harbour confirm the conclusion of the NSA study that, had their importance been recognised and an adequate number of cryptanalysts set to work on them, JN25b could have been broken in time to reveal preparations for the surprise attack on 7 December 1941. The low priority given to the attack on JN25b was due, in part, to the myopia of the Navy Department which had failed to grasp the importance of sigint in naval warfare. But it also reflected the shortsightedness of a President who, despite his passion for the navy, his longstanding enthusiasm for intelligence and his first-hand experience of the value of Japanese diplomatic intercepts, showed no interest in Japanese naval signals. It seems unlikely that he ever asked his naval aide what progress was being made in the attack on naval ciphers.[32] It is inconceivable that Churchill would have shown a similar indifference. When the leading cryptanalysts at Bletchley Park found themselves short of resources in October 1941, they appealed directly to the prime minister. Churchill wrote on their request, 'ACTION THIS DAY. Make sure they have all that they want on extreme priority and report to me that this has been done.'[33]

Pearl Harbor and the American entry into the war accelerated the creation of the world's first sigint alliance. On decrypts of particular importance, Churchill would henceforth sometimes add the minute: 'Make sure that President Roosevelt sees this at my desire.'[34] For the first time since the First World War, the British cryptanalytic attack on American communications seems to have ceased.[35] When Eisenhower arrived in Britain as commander-in-chief of American forces in June 1942, he was briefed personally on ULTRA by Churchill at Chequers. In July Roosevelt appears to have asked the Army Chief of Staff, General George C. Marshall, how sigint collaboration with the British was proceeding. Marshall sent a brief memorandum in reply which reported simply: 'We find that an interchange of cryptanalytic information has been in progress for over a year and appears to be satisfactory to both services.'[36] Marshall's memorandum was somewhat misleading. In June one Army Special Branch cryptanalyst and two from the naval sigint agency, OP-20-G, had begun work at Bletchley Park, but it took another nine months to establish full collaboration between Special Branch and Bletchley Park.[37]

The breaking of U-boat Enigma in December 1942 opened a new era in naval sigint collaboration. On 27 December, the Washington 'Secret Room', a submarine-tracking room on the British model able to exploit the newly available U-boat decrypts, began operating in the Main Navy Building.[38] The 23-year-old Harry Hinsley, recruited to Bletchley Park at the outbreak of war while still an undergraduate at Cambridge University, visited OP-20-G to settle details of its collaboration with the Naval Section at Bletchley. For the purposes of his visit he was given the title of Staff Officer Intelligence to the Head of the Naval Section. Bletchley and OP-2Q-G agreed to exchange all U-boat signals intercepted on either side of the Atlantic, and that whichever side broke the key for the day first would send it to the other. From early in 1943 British and American cryptanalysis of naval Enigma was carried out according to a single programme coordinated by Bletchley Park.[39] Communication via direct signal links between the U-boat tracking rooms in London, Washington and (from May 1943) Ottawa became so close that, according to the British official history, for the remainder of the war 'they operated virtually as a single organization'.[40] During the Battle of the Atlantic, the longest and most complex battle in the history of naval warfare which reached its climax in the spring of 1943, ULTRA made a major, possibly decisive, contribution to the allied victory.[41]

After the beginning of Operation TORCH in North Africa in November 1942, Eisenhower received ULTRA through his British chief intelligence officer, initially Brigadier Mockler-Ferryman, and later – and more successfully – Brigadier (subsequently General Sir) Kenneth Strong.[42] The G-2 in Washington, General George Strong (not to be confused with Kenneth), had been one of the earliest advocates of sigint collaboration with the British. He was outraged, however, not to be sent copies of the ULTRA supplied to Eisenhower and complained that he was being deliberately bypassed. A postwar American account concluded:

> As one examines the early records, the picture that emerges is of G-2 and British authorities walking around and eyeing each other like two mongrels who have just met. Presumably and quite naturally the ministries in London were reluctant to risk Source's [ULTRA's] neck by sharing his precious information with an unproved and shadowy group in Washington. G-2 was from Missouri and wished to be quite certain that he had access to all the material Source was turning up.[43]

The conflict was triumphantly resolved in the spring of 1943 by the signing of the BRUSA sigint agreement and by an exchange of missions between the Special Branch and Bletchley Park. The term BRUSA was devised by Hinsley, who had been sent to Washington to conduct the negotiations on the British side. The Americans, he had noticed, 'loved acronyms', but he initially worried – needlessly, as it turned out – that putting Britain ahead of the United States in the acronym he had devised might cause problems. His only major difficulty was in coping with continued interservice rivalries between the American military and naval sigint agencies. In order to avoid offending military susceptibilities, he travelled to Washington under a new title. Instead of being styled Staff Officer Intelligence to the Head of the Naval

Section, he was now designated Assistant to the Director of Bletchley Park, Edward (later Sir Edward) Travis. OP-20-G and the Special Branch were far more suspicious of each other than of the British. As Hinsley recalls, 'The Navy didn't like me talking to the Army. But I wasn't allowed to tell the Navy any details [of BRUSA] because the Army would have been furious.' Hinsley did, however, assure OP-20-G that the BRUSA agreement was not 'anything like as intimate' as its own less formal working arrangement with Bletchley. Whereas naval cryptanalysts on both sides of the Atlantic were decrypting the same German naval messages and exchanging keys daily, the basis of the agreement on military sigint was a division of labour.[44]

Over half a century later, parts of the BRUSA agreement still remain classified – one of a number of indications of its unusual importance. The essence of the accord, however, is summarised in its first three clauses:

(1) Both the U.S. and British agree to exchange completely all information concerning the detection, identification and interception of signals from, and the solution of codes and ciphers used by, the Military and Airforces of the Axis powers, including secret services (Abwehr).
(2) The U.S. will assume as a main responsibility the reading of Japanese Military and Air Codes and ciphers.
(3) The British will assume as a main responsibility the reading of German and Italian Military and Air Codes and ciphers.[45]

The still-classified sections of the BRUSA agreement are probably largely concerned with diplomatic sigint. In 1942, codebreakers at Bletchley Park's diplomatic section, based at Berkeley Street in London, broke the main German diplomatic code.[46] Anglo-American codebreakers also successfully decrypted the communications of a substantial number of neutral and allied powers.[47] Though the recently released diplomatic sigint archive has yet to be fully researched, there is no doubt about its importance. MIS WD posted a liaison officer to Berkeley Street with the primary task of cabling to Washington each night diplomatic intercepts 'which seemed to be of immediate intelligence value'. He also showed copies of important intercepts to the American ambassador every four or five days. Winant 'repeatedly expressed the opinion that the service was invaluable to him'.[48]

In April 1945, the head of Hut 3 (the section processing German military and airforce decrypts) at Bletchley Park, Group Captain Eric Jones (later head of GCHQ), praised 'the friendship and close cooperation that have throughout so clearly marked the integration of American and British personnel'. 'With not more than three exceptions,' writes Telford Taylor, the head of the Army Special Branch mission at Bletchley, 'the officers sent to BP fitted in personally and professionally with their British counterparts with ease and concord on all sides. . . . I take pride at the ease, goodwill and success with which the merging was accomplished by Britons and Americans alike.' The only substantial problem of sigint liaison which the BRUSA agreement and the working arrangement on naval cryptanalysis failed to resolve was not between Britain and the United States, but between the American military and naval sigint agencies. Taylor regretted that he had not been permitted to represent US naval as well as military interests at Bletchley Park. The problems of American interservice intelligence rivalry, he concluded, 'have not been solved by this war. A solution is not impossible and is greatly to be desired.'[49]

The relatively diffuse nature of the United States intelligence community caused some problems in London as well as Washington. By 1941 the British Joint Intelligence Committee (JIC), supported by the newly-founded Joint Intelligence Staff, was, with considerable success, coordinating, assessing and disseminating strategic intelligence. The United States JIC, founded early in 1942, largely in response to British pressure, never succeeded in playing the same role. When the British JIC visited Washington in September 1944, 'with a view to discussing the coordination of Far Eastern intelligence', they discovered that 'the U.S. Directors of Intelligence did not work so closely as a team as did our own Directors of Intelligence':

> The American J.I.C. . . . stated that while they were glad to discuss Far Eastern matters in individual talks for each Service, they were not prepared for a combined three Service discussion on this matter.[50]

The relative lack of coordination of the American intelligence community reflected, first and foremost, a lack of central direction from the White House. Behind the growing coordination both of the British intelligence community and of intelligence with the British war effort lay the powerful influence of the prime minister.[51] Quite simply, Roosevelt's grasp of the problems of wartime intelligence was not in the same league as Churchill's.

Despite the problems created by the lack of central direction within the American intelligence community, the closeness of transatlantic cooperation was remarkable. The Anglo-American sigint accords were simply the most important of a series of formal agreements and informal understandings between the various sections of the two intelligence communities which collectively made up an alliance unique in history. By D-Day there had been a complete merger of British and American strategic photo-reconnaissance from bases in the United Kingdom.[52] The founding of the OSS in the summer of 1942 was accompanied by an agreement with SIS and SOE on spheres of influence. SOE gained the major responsibility for most of Europe, but the OSS was given the leading role in North Africa, Finland, and, later, Bulgaria, Romania and Northern Norway.[53] The relations of the OSS with SOE and SIS, though not always smooth, were, in the words of Sir Harry Hinsley, 'always close and eventually harmonious'.[54] X-2, the counter-intelligence branch of the OSS, founded in 1943 partly in response to British pressure, rapidly developed a relationship with MI5 which compared in intimacy with that established by 3-US with Bletchley Park. An X-2 officer had a desk in the office of the head of MI5's Double Agents section and followed the entire Double Cross system in all its operational detail. X-2 itself concluded:

> For even an Ally to be admitted to a full access to all secret files and to a knowledge of their sources; to information on most secret methods and procedures; and to a knowledge of personnel and the system of organization and of operations – in short, to the innermost arcàna, in this case of perhaps the world's most experienced and efficient, and therefore most carefully guarded security systems – was beyond precedent or expectation. Yet the British did it. The implications of this fact are staggering – and completely inexplicable in terms of merely cheap exchange of mutual advantages. The advantages were enormously heavily on the American side.

X-2 did sometimes notice one false assumption behind British generosity – that the United States would be prepared to 'accept a pupil role' in intelligence even after the war was over:

> There is, however, no sign that this feeling went beyond the state of upset that oldsters usually fall into when the youngsters strike out for themselves. This fact does nothing to invalidate the other fact of their very real generosity to their erstwhile pupils.[55]

The many transatlantic friendships formed at Bletchley Park, and between OSS and British intelligence officers, were to be of fundamental importance in the postwar as well as the wartime development of the Special Relationship. It was because the sense of wartime comradeship was so close that former OSS officers later felt such a sense of personal betrayal when they discovered that some of those with whom they had shared their secrets – among them Kim Philby in SIS and Anthony Blunt in MI5 – had been working for Soviet intelligence.

The Great Patriotic War of 1941–45 marked a unique phase in relations between the Anglo-American intelligence communities and their Soviet counterpart. For the only time in the history of the Soviet Union there was a degree of official East–West intelligence liaison. Simultaneously, however, Soviet penetration of Western intelligence reached its peak. In August 1941 Colonel (later Brigadier) George A. Hill (transparently codenamed DALE) arrived in Moscow at the head of an SOE liaison team with the cover name 'SAM Mission'. Hill was a somewhat eccentric choice. After the October Revolution, he had worked as a British agent in Russia, initially trying to keep the Bolsheviks in the war against Germany, later plotting to overthrow them. Hill looked back on these exploits as 'a joyful adventure in the pages of my life'. His memoirs, published in 1932 and grandly entitled *Go Spy the Land*, relate with an engaging lack of modesty how he had won Trotsky's confidence, and allegedly helped to mastermind the development of both the Cheka and Soviet military intelligence. He was, however, no match for the NKVD in the Second World War. Kim Philby, briefly his colleague in SOE, relates that it was some time before Hill ordered a security check of the 'SAM Mission's' conference room in Moscow. When he did so, the inspection 'revealed a fearsome number of sources of leakage'.

In February and March 1942, Hill was allowed to accompany an NKVD unit behind German lines to study Soviet partisan tactics. For a time he became enthused by the idea of dropping NKVD agents behind enemy lines in Western Europe and the Middle East, and even proposed SOE/NKVD joint operations. After the problems he encountered in arranging to parachute an NKVD agent into Belgium, however, his enthusiasm began to cool. 'Oh dear', he told his diary, 'I'm not at all pleased about this.' According to SOE records, only 'a small number' of NKVD agents were dropped into Western Europe by the British, mostly in 1943. SOE headquarters in London and Cairo vetoed Hill's proposal for joint operations in the Middle East. In April 1944, however, SOE provided NKVD Major N. N. Krassovsky with wireless transmitter and smallarms, and parachuted him into Yugoslavia to visit Tito's headquarters. Two months later, the NKVD informed SOE that Krassovsky had been recalled to Moscow 'as efforts to establish liaison with SOE with a view to collaboration had failed'.[56]

The head of the NKVD wartime mission in London, Ivan Andreevich Chichayev, combined his liaison work for two years with an undeclared role as NKVD Resident, in charge of the running of the British agent network. The growing importance of the London residency, however, led to the appointment of a still more senior NKVD officer, Konstantin Mikhailovich Kukin, as Resident in 1943. While Kukin supervised the running of the British agents, Chichayev concentrated on the governments-in-exile. General František Moravec, the Czech intelligence chief in London, noted the change in Chichayev's manner as victory approached:

> After Stalingrad the Soviet smiles faded. As the Russian military situation improved, Chichayev's attitude changed completely. Whereas before he had come to me every day and thanked me for whatever he received, he now became critical, imperious and even threatening.[57]

Despite the limited success of SOE/NKVD liaison, General Donovan became attracted after the Teheran meeting of the Big Three in November 1943 by the possibilities of OSS collaboration with the Russians. At the end of the year, he proposed the establishment of an OSS mission in Moscow and an NKVD mission in Washington. General Pavel Mikhailovich Fitin, head of NKVD foreign intelligence, accepted with an alacrity rare in US–Soviet relations, avid for further information on OSS operations in Eastern Europe and the Balkans, as well as for access to OSS weapons and technology. Washington, however, had second thoughts about Donovan's proposal. Anxious to avoid controversy in election year, Roosevelt yielded to J. Edgar Hoover's insistence that no NKVD mission be allowed to set foot in the United States.[58]

The Anglo-American intelligence on Germany of most interest to Moscow was ULTRA. Stewart Menzies, the chief of SIS who also had overall responsibility for Bletchley Park, advised Churchill against passing on intelligence from Enigma decrypts in any form because of the insecurity of the Russians' own cipher systems. In the opinion of Bletchley Park, 'to tell the Russians that we were reading Enigma would be tantamount to telling the Germans too'. ULTRA revealed within a few weeks of the beginning of Operation Barbarossa on 22 June 1941 that the Germans were decrypting some Soviet naval and airforce signals. As early as 24 June, however, Churchill overrode Menzies's objections and instructed him to pass disguised ULTRA intelligence to the Russians via the British Military Mission in Moscow, 'provided no risks are run'. Thereafter the Prime Minister commonly noted on important intercepts dealing with the Eastern Front, 'Has any of this been passed to Joe?' The ULTRA origin of the intelligence passed to Moscow was disguised by formulae such as 'a well-placed source in Berlin' or 'an officer in the German War Office'. Unit identifications and other details which might identify the true source as sigint were routinely withheld. Whitehall became increasingly frustrated, however, by the one-sided nature of the Anglo-Soviet intelligence exchange. By the beginning of 1942, the Russians were usually unwilling to exchange even technical intelligence about captured enemy equipment. From the summer of 1942, the amount of disguised ULTRA officially supplied to Moscow was sharply reduced.[59]

Washington, too, occasionally sent disguised sigint to Moscow. In August 1942, at Marshall's suggestion, Roosevelt passed on to Stalin the contents of MAGIC intercepts which showed that Japan had no intention of attacking the Soviet Union. The President did not reveal the source of his information, but said that it was 'definitely authentic'.[60] Having received the same information from his own cryptanalysts, Stalin doubtless believed him. Unknown to its Western Allies, the NKVD had broken PURPLE, as well as the RED Japanese diplomatic cipher which preceded it. Moscow's most important Japanese intelligence came not, as usually supposed, from Richard Sorge but from sigint. After Sorge's arrest in October 1941, Japanese decrypts provided crucial reassurance that Japan would resist German attempts to persuade her to join in the attack on the Soviet Union. The head of the Japanese section of the NKVD Fifth (Cipher) Directorate, S. Tolstoy, later became the most decorated Soviet cryptanalyst of the war, receiving the Order of Lenin.[61]

Moscow's main sources of wartime intelligence from both London and Washington, however, were its own agent networks rather than official liaison. A generation later, students at the Andropov Institute, the KGB First Chief Directorate (Foreign Intelligence) Training School, were told that the ablest group of agents had been five young Cambridge graduates ('the Magnificent Five') recruited in the mid-1930s: Anthony Blunt, Guy Burgess, John Cairncross, Donald Maclean and Kim Philby, who between them had penetrated the three main British intelligence agencies and the Foreign Office.[62] Philby eventually established himself as the most important of the five, becoming head late in the war of the SIS Soviet counter-intelligence section. Until 1943, however, the most valuable British intelligence seems to have come from Cairncross. In 1940 Cairncross became private secretary to one of Churchill's ministers, Lord Hankey, then Chancellor of the Duchy of Lancaster and a man with longer and more varied experience of Whitehall committees than anyone else in British public life. His responsibilities included overseeing the intelligence services and chairing numerous secret committees. Besides receiving all War Cabinet papers and minutes, Hankey was also sent copies of top-secret diplomatic telegrams. When new War Cabinet regulations limited the circulation of diplomatic telegrams in June 1941, Hankey was temporarily taken off the circulation list. Cairncross as well as Hankey complained, and he was promptly reinstated. Among the committees chaired by Hankey which were of most interest to the NKVD was the Scientific Advisory Committee, which from October 1940 onwards discussed in detail both the scientific processes involved in the construction of the atomic bomb and cooperation with the Americans.[63] It is usually impossible to be certain which documents among the immense amount of classified documents which passed through Hankey's hands were also seen by Cairncross. In the case of the Scientific Advisory Committee, however, there is no such problem, since Cairncross was for a time joint secretary of it.[64] On the evidence available at present, it seems that Cairncross was probably the first of the 'atom spies'. Hankey also became a member of the better-known Tube Alloys Consultative Committee, formed in the autumn of 1941 to advise on atomic policy.[65] In NKVD documents of the period, Hankey is, perhaps significantly, given the codename BOSS.[66] (He was, of course, Cairncross's boss.)

The identities of the Soviet agents in the wartime United States remain far more controversial than those of their counterparts in Britain. None of the most important American agents ever confessed.[67] Two, Julius and Ethel Rosenberg, later went to the electric chair, bravely but dishonestly protesting their innocence. The monstrous, self-serving crusade against mostly imaginary communist conspiracies led by Joseph McCarthy in the early 1950s created a climate of opinion in which opponents of McCarthyism found it difficult to accept the reality of *any* Soviet penetration of wartime Washington. Some still do. A further problem was that the best evidence against many of the Soviet agents came from decrypted NKVD telegrams of 1944–45 (a source codenamed VENONA) and, like sigint in general, was considered too secret to reveal in court, even during *in camera* proceedings. It was VENONA, for example, which led to the detection of both the Rosenbergs and Donald Maclean, the first of the Magnificent Five to be tracked down. No VENONA decrypts have yet been declassified. The probability is, however, that the OSS was at least as penetrated as any British intelligence agency. After the war, the former NKVD courier, Elizabeth Bentley, identified seven officials in OSS headquarters who, she claimed, had worked for Soviet intelligence. There is little doubt that VENONA provided further evidence on the penetration of the OSS. By late 1944, the volume of intelligence supplied by Soviet agents in the United States was simply too large for NKVD communications systems to cope with it. As a result, some cipher clerks began reusing their 'one-time-pad' ciphers, thus committing the breaches of cipher security which later made possible the production of VENONA.[68]

The problem of Soviet wartime penetration attracted remarkably little attention either from the Roosevelt Administration or from the FBI. In September 1939 Adolf Berle sent the President a four-page memorandum entitled 'Underground Espionage Agent', based on information given him by the former Soviet agent and courier, Whittaker Chambers, and including the names of Alger Hiss and Harry Dexter White. Roosevelt was not interested. He seems simply to have dismissed the whole idea of espionage rings within his administration as absurd. Equally remarkably, Berle pigeonholed his own report. Chambers was eventually interviewed by the FBI in 1942 after an erstwhile associate in the communist underground had identified him as a former Soviet agent. Probably fearing prosecution after failing to gain immunity from legal proceedings, Chambers was less forthcoming than he had been to Berle three years earlier, stressing his role in the prewar communist underground rather than his involvement in espionage. Hoover airily dismissed an eight-page report on the interview as mostly 'history, hypothesis and deduction'. There was no follow-up interview with Chambers for the next three years.[69] When Donovan succeeded in purchasing an incomplete copy of the NKVD codebook from the Finns in 1944, Roosevelt ordered him to return it to the Russians. Donovan did so but, in defiance of his instructions, kept a copy which later helped in the production of VENONA.[70]

Possibly the most controversial aspect of Soviet penetration in wartime Washington concerns the contacts between the NKVD illegal, Iskhak Abdulovich Akhmerov (whose aliases included Bill Greinke, Michael Green and Michael Adamec), and Roosevelt's closest wartime adviser, Harry Hopkins. Akhmerov's claim twenty years later in lectures to the KGB Illegals Directorate that he had run Hopkins as a recruited agent is almost certainly false,[71] though some former KGB officers continue to believe it.[72] The most probable explanation, arrived at both by Oleg Gordievsky, who discussed the case while a member of the KGB Illegals Directorate, and by a 1992 CIA study, is that the NKVD regarded Hopkins as a 'confidential contact' but never as a conscious agent.[73] Akhmerov's technique was to tell Hopkins that he brought personal and confidential messages from Stalin, and to emphasise his unique role in the development of Soviet–American relations. Hopkins probably regarded Akhmerov simply as an unofficial intermediary chosen by Stalin because of their mutual distrust of the orthodox diplomatic establishment. What is certain is that Hopkins came to feel an extraordinary admiration for Stalin and to fear for the future of the postwar world 'if anything should happen' to him. Hopkins also seems to have responded to requests by Akhmerov for him to use his influence to remove 'anti-Soviet' officials who, Akhmerov claimed, were hindering Soviet–American cooperation: among them, the US ambassador in Moscow, Laurence A. Steinhardt, the military attaché Ivan D. Yeaton, and the head of the State Department Soviet desk, Loy W. Henderson. The techniques pioneered by Akhmerov were later used with equal success by another KGB officer, Georgi Nikitovich Bolshakov, during the Kennedy presidency. In May 1961, Robert Kennedy began fortnightly meetings with Bolshakov, who succeeded in persuading him, just as Akhmerov had persuaded Hopkins, that he could short-circuit the ponderous protocol of official diplomacy and gain direct access to the thinking of the Soviet leadership. According to Robert Kennedy: 'He was Khrushchev's representative. . . . I met with him about all kinds of things.'[74] Bolshakov, like Akhmerov, was used as a channel of deception. JFK's special counsel, Theodore Sorensen, later recalled the President's disillusion with Bolshakov after the Cuban Missile Crisis: 'President Kennedy had come to rely on the Bolshakov channel for direct private information from Khrushchev, and he felt personally deceived. He *was* personally deceived.'[75] Hopkins had died in 1946, probably unaware of the extent to which he, too, had been deceived.

Intelligence analysis about the West in wartime Moscow was of far lower quality than Soviet intelligence collection in Britain and the United States. The wartime intelligence eventually put to most productive use was probably that collected by the atom spies. The first Soviet atomic bomb was, concludes David Holloway, 'a copy of the first American bomb'.[76] Moscow showed a much poorer understanding of the political intelligence obtained by the NKVD in London and Washington. The paranoid tendency which Stalin had established as a virtually compulsory part of Soviet intelligence analysis during the 1930s did not suddenly disappear with the discovery on 22 June 1941 that the repeated warnings of an impending German invasion were not, after all, Western disinformation. Throughout the Great Patriotic War, Stalin's understanding of his western allies was clouded by variable, but usually impressive, quantities of conspiracy theory to which most intelligence analysis had to conform and which no amount of contrary intelligence could dispel. Conspiracy theory in any case came naturally to most NKVD analysts. Stalin remained convinced for the rest of his life that Rudolf Hess's flight to Britain in May 1941 was connected with secret Anglo-German negotiations for a joint attack on the Soviet Union. The same conspiracy theory was still being publicly peddled by the KGB in the final years of the Soviet Union.[77] Even after the formation of the Grand Alliance, Stalin continued to suspect his allies of planning a secret deal with Hitler at his expense. The NKVD was instructed to come up with evidence of this imaginary conspiracy. Shortly before his death Kim Philby finally admitted what he had concealed in his memoirs – that what most interested his main wartime controller, Anatoli Borisovich Gorsky, was intelligence on Britain's non-existent plans for a separate peace with Germany and schemes to join with Germany in attacking the Soviet Union.[78] In October 1942, Stalin cabled his ambassador in London, Ivan Maisky, 'All of us in Moscow have gained the impression that Churchill is aiming at the defeat of the USSR, in order then to come to terms with the Germany of Hitler or Bruning at the expense of our country.' Among the evidence which Stalin cited for this preposterous assertion were alleged British dealings with Hess 'whom Churchill, it seems, is keeping in reserve'.[79] What is also astonishing, once again, is the longevity of these conspiratorial fantasies. In an interview with the author in Moscow in December 1990, Valentin Mikhailovich Falin, head of the International Department of the Communist Party Central Committee, which played a major part in tasking KGB foreign operations, claimed to have documentary proof that:

> From 1943, no later, in both London and Washington, the idea was already being weighed up of the possibility of terminating the coalition with the Soviet Union and reaching an accord with Nazi Germany, or with the Nazi Generals, on the question of waging a joint war against the Soviet Union.[80]

The limitations of Soviet intelligence on Germany were vividly illustrated during the Battle of Stalingrad in the winter of 1942–43. When the Red Army encircled the Axis forces in November 1942, it believed that it had trapped 85 000 to 90 000 troops; in reality, it had surrounded three times as many. The Stavka was equally misinformed about plans for the German relief expedition. The first the Red Army learned of the despatch of six Panzer divisions from France was when Soviet cavalry ran into them. By the time of the next great battle on the Eastern Front, at Kursk in the summer of 1943, however, the quality of Soviet military intelligence on Germany had been transformed. On 8 April Marshal Zhukov sent Stalin a report correctly predicting a German pincer movement against the Kursk salient from both north and south, coupled with an attack from the west designed to separate the two Red Army groups defending the salient. The main reason for the transformation of Soviet military intelligence was the improvement in sigint – not, as sometimes alleged, the intelligence supplied by the Lucy spy ring in Switzerland. At Stalingrad, the Red Army captured intact an unknown number of Enigma cipher machines and key settings.[81] Far more valuable, however, was the capture of a larger number of German cipher and signals personnel, not all of whom can have resisted the pressing invitations of their captors to assist Soviet sigint. The odds are, however, that Soviet cryptanalysts were unable to decrypt Enigma or Geheimschreiber traffic on a regular basis. Despite their success in breaking PURPLE, NKVD and GRU codebreakers lacked the state-of-the-art technology which made possible the production of ULTRA at Bletchley Park. (By 1943, this technology included COLOSSUS, the world's first electronic computer.) The major advances in Soviet sigint on Germany during the spring of 1943 occurred among the foothills, rather than on the commanding heights, of cryptanalysis: in direction-finding, traffic analysis and the breaking of lower-grade ciphers rather than in the attack on Enigma and Geheimschreiber. Before the Battle of Kursk, however, the NKVD also obtained important quantities of ULTRA. The source was not its own cryptanalysts but John Cairncross, who had become the only member of the 'Magnificent Five' to succeed in finding employment at Bletchley Park. (Philby had tried and failed.) The most valuable sigint supplied by Cairncross seems to have been a series of Luftwaffe decrypts which helped to make possible the massive Soviet air-raids of 6–8 May which destroyed over 500 German planes. Cairncross's controller, Gorsky, told him that in recognition of his contribution to victory at Kursk he had been awarded the Order of the Red Banner.[82] Not until the Soviet sigint archive is opened, however, will it become possible to evaluate the real significance of Cairncross's intelligence. In the meantime, the role of sigint on the Eastern Front remains probably the least understood aspect of the history of the Second World War.

The relations between the intelligence communities of the Grand Alliance changed the course, though not the outcome, of both the Second World War and the Cold War. Neither the British nor the American intelligence communities could have achieved as much in relative isolation during the Second World War as they achieved as Allies. Their collaboration shortened the war. Operation OVERLORD, the high point of that collaboration, may well have used intelligence more successfully than any other great offensive in the history of land and amphibious warfare. The relationship during it between Eisenhower and his British G-2, Kenneth Strong, epitomises the unprecedented closeness of Anglo-American intelligence collaboration. 'The best time in a man's life', enthused Strong, 'is when he gets to like Americans.'[83] The official historian of British wartime intelligence, Sir Harry Hinsley, not a scholar given to rash speculation, argues controversially that, but for Anglo-American intelligence successes, OVERLORD would have had to be deferred from the summer of 1944 till 1946.[84] Had Hitler still been undefeated in the summer of 1945, the first atomic bomb would surely have been dropped on Germany rather than on Japan.

Ever since the Second World War, the Anglo-American intelligence alliance has remained the most special and most secret part of the Special Relationship. The War drew the United States into an intelligence network which, especially in sigint, covered much of the British Empire as well as Britain itself. When General Douglas MacArthur arrived in Australia in 1942, he set up a sigint agency, Central Bureau, with an American head and an Australian deputy.[85] The initiative in transforming the wartime collaboration into a postwar sigint alliance was taken by the British. The foundations were laid during a 'round-the-world tour' in the spring of 1945 by Sir Edward Travis, the head of Bletchley Park, Harry Hinsley, his assistant, Rear-Admiral E. G. N. Rushbrooke, the DNI, and Commander Clive Loehnis of the Admiralty Operational Intelligence Centre (later Director-General of the postwar British sigint agency, GCHQ, from 1960 to 1964).[86] The trip had two main objectives. The first was to transfer sigint personnel and resources from Europe, where the war was almost at an end, to the Pacific War against Japan. The second was to conduct negotiations on the future of Anglo-American sigint collaboration. In late April, while Rushbrooke travelled to Ottawa to brief the Canadians, Travis, Hinsley and Loehnis began negotiations in Washington. After separate talks with the Army, Navy and State Departments, they held a series of meetings attended by representatives of all three. By comparison with his last visit two years earlier, Hinsley felt that interservice tension 'wasn't so bad this time. They'd sunk some of their differences and they knew what each other was doing.'[87] On 10 March the US Army–Navy Communications Intelligence Board (ANCIB) had been founded to oversee and coordinate cryptanalysis by the armed services, although Admiral Ernest J. King, the Chief of Naval Operations, still refused to envisage an interservice American agency on the Bletchley Park model.[88]

The Anglo-American negotiations agreed on the principle of, and a broad framework for, postwar sigint collaboration.[89] Marshall and King were already persuaded of the need for an Anglo-American attack on Soviet codes and ciphers.[90] Though President Harry Truman, who succeeded Roosevelt in April 1945, was initially hostile to the idea of peacetime espionage, both his briefings on ULTRA (of which Roosevelt had kept him in ignorance) and his own experience of MAGIC during the final stages of the war against Japan persuaded him of the importance of sigint.[91] Truman's biographers fail to mention that a week before he closed down the OSS in September 1945, he signed a secret order authorising the Secretaries of War and the Navy 'to continue collaboration in the field of communications intelligence between the United States Army and Navy and the British, and to extend, modify or discontinue this collaboration, as determined to be in the best interests of the United States'.[92] That collaboration was to lead in June 1948 to the signing of the UKUSA sigint agreement by Britain, the United States, Canada, Australia and New Zealand. Though it ranks as the first global peacetime intelligence alliance, the UKUSA agreement is still as conspicuously absent from most histories of the Cold War as ULTRA was from histories of the Second World War published before the mid-1970s.[93]

In the short term, the Second World War left Soviet intelligence better prepared than its Western rivals for the beginning of the Cold War. The NKVD still retained numerous agents in the West. In Britain four of the Magnificent Five remained active after the war; only Blunt went into almost immediate semi-retirement. Neither the British nor the Americans, by contrast, yet possessed a single agent of any importance in Moscow. The CIA, founded in 1947, did not even set up a Moscow station until 1953.[94] Western cryptanalysts seem to have had little success against high-grade postwar Soviet ciphers. Soviet Russia was to prove a far more formidable adversary for the Anglo-American intelligence alliance during the early years of the Cold War than either Nazi Germany or Imperial Japan had been during the Second World War.

## NOTES

1. Christopher Andrew, 'Churchill and Intelligence', *Intelligence and National Security*, 3 (1988), no.2; reprinted in Michael Handel (ed.), *Leaders and Intelligence* (London: Frank Cass, 1988), pp. 181–93.
2. Christopher Andrew, *Secret Service: The Making of the British Intelligence Community*, Sceptre edn (London: Heinemann, 1986), ch. 14.
3. Anthony Cave Brown, *The Last Hero: Wild Bill Donovan*, Vintage Books edn (New York: Random House, 1984), pp. 153–5.
4. Jeffrey M. Dorwart, *The Office of Naval Intelligence* (Annapolis: Naval Institute Press, 1979), pp. 104–5.
5. Elliott Roosevelt (ed.), *The Roosevelt Letters*, vol. II (London: Harrap, 1950), p. 311.
6. A copy of the intercepted German telegram was indeed obtained in Mexico City in order to sustain the deception. Andrew, *Secret Service*, pp. 169–77, 652. Idem, *For the President's Eyes Only: Secret Intelligence and the American Presidency: From Washington to Bush* (New York and London: HarperCollins, 1995), ch. 2.
7. Christopher Andrew, 'Intelligence Collaboration between Britain, the United States and the Commonwealth during World War II', in Walter T. Hitchcock (ed.),

*The Intelligence Revolution: A Historical Perspective* (Washington, D.C.: US Government Printing Office, 1991).

8. MI1c (New York) report, 28 March 1918, Wiseman papers I/6, folder 173, Sterling Library, Yale University. On Anglo-American intelligence collaboration during the First World War, see Andrew, *For the President's Eyes Only*, ch. 2.

9. Wiseman to Northcliffe, 14 Feb. 1918, Wiseman papers, I/3, folder 63.

10. Northcliffe to Reading, 2 Sept. 1917, Wiseman papers, I/3, folder 59.

11. The codename INTREPID in fact referred not to Stephenson but to the SIS station.

12. Godfrey, 'Intelligence in the United States', 7 July 1941, CAB 122/1021, PRO: published, with an introduction by Bradley J. Smith, in *Intelligence and National Security*, I (1986), pp. 445–50.

13. Thomas F. Troy, 'The Coordinator of Intelligence and British Intelligence' [partially declassified CIA study: Declassified Documents Reference System, 1990, no.92], pp. 108–9. Morton, Memo to Colonel E. J. Jacob, 18 Sept. 1941, Churchill College Archives Centre, Cambridge.

14. William Stevenson, *A Man Called Intrepid*, paperback edn (London: Sphere Books, 1977), pp. 14, 107–8, 158, 161, 204. Sir William Stephenson, introduction to H. Montgomery Hyde, *Secret Intelligence Agent* (London: Constable, 1982), pp. xv–xvi. For critiques of some of the Intrepid myths, see: David Stafford, '"Intrepid": Myth and Reality', *Journal of Contemporary History*, **22** (1987); Nigel West, *A Thread of Deceit*, paperback edn (New York: Dell Books, 1986), ch. 10; Timothy J. Naftali, 'Intrepid's Last Deception: Documenting the Career of Sir William Stephenson', *Intelligence and National Security*, **8** (1993), no. 3.

15. Stephenson's assistant, the late H. Montgomery Hyde, who took a leading part in the Belmonte forgery, gave me permission to examine the papers on this and other episodes of his career which he had deposited in the Churchill College Archive Centre. Unhappily, Whitehall's historical censors beat me to it; by the time I was able to go through the Hyde papers, they had closed many items to historical research. For the time being, the most revealing account of the Belmonte forgery is in Hyde, *Secret Intelligence Agent*, pp. 150–60.

16. Samuel I. Rosenman (ed.), *The Public Papers and Addresses of Franklin D. Roosevelt, 1941* (New York: Harper, 1950), p. 387.

17. Adolf Berle, Memo to Sumner Welles, 27 Sept. 1941, Berle Diary, Franklin D. Roosevelt Library, Hyde Park, NY (FDRL).

18. Stephenson admitted obtaining the map but continued to maintain that it was genuine; Stevenson, *Man Called Intrepid*, p. 317. Among those studies which conclude that it was a BSC forgery is a recent CIA history, *The Intelligence War in 1941: A 50th Anniversary Perspective* (Washington, DC: CIA Center for the Study of Intelligence, 1992), p. 19.

19. Rosenman (ed.), *Public Papers . . . 1941*, pp. 439–40.

20. Adolf Berle Diary, 12, 26 Feb., 5 March 1942, FDRL. Andrew, *For the President's Eyes Only*, ch. 4.

21. Troy, 'Coordinator of Intelligence', p. 15.

22. COS(40)289, CAB 79/6, PRO. Smith, *The Ultra–Magic Deals*, pp. 38, 43–4. Sir F. H. Hinsley *et al.*, *British Intelligence in the Second World War* (London: HMSO, 1979–88), vol. I, pp. 312–13.

23. Henry L. Stimson Diary, 23, 24 Oct., 17 Dec. 1940, Sterling Library, Yale University. Andrew, *For the President's Eyes Only*, ch.3.

24. Thomas Parrish, *The Ultra Americans* (New York: Stein and Day, 1986), pp. 61–6. Bradley F. Smith, *The Ultra–Magic Deals* (Novato, Ca.: Presidio, 1993), pp. 53–8.

25. For examples of the occasional US decrypts included in Churchill's 'golden eggs', see decrypts no. 094864, 26 Aug. 1941, HW1/28; no. 095432, 13 Sept. 1941, HW1/64; no. 095510, 15 Sept. 1941, HW1/66; no. 096090, 2 Oct.1941, HW1/107; no. 097126, 30 Oct. 1941, HW1/179; no. 098061, 23 Nov. 1941, HW1/251, Public Record Office (PRO), Kew. On British interception of US diplomatic traffic, see the forthcoming (1995) article by Kathryn Brown in *Intelligence and National Security*.
26. Hinsley *et al.*, *British Intelligence in the Second World War*, vol.II, pp. 55, 174–5. Smith, *Ultra–Magic Deals*, p. 87.
27. 'Historical Background of the Signal Security Agency', part III, p. 308, RG 457-77-1, National Archives, Washington [hereafter NAW]. Christopher Andrew, 'Codebreakers and Foreign Offices', in Christopher Andrew and David Dilks (eds), *The Missing Dimension: Governments and Intelligence Communities in the Twentieth Century* (London: Macmillan, 1984), p. 52. Andrew, *Presidents and Secret Intelligence*, ch. 3.
28. David Kahn, 'Roosevelt, MAGIC and ULTRA', *Cryptologia*, **16** (1992), no. 4. Andrew, *Presidents and Secret Intelligence*, ch. 3.
29. The confusion is examined in detail in Andrew, *Presidents and Secret Intelligence*, ch. 3.
30. John Ferris, 'From Broadway House to Bletchley Park: The Diary of Captain Malcolm Kennedy, 1934–1946', *Intelligence and National Security*, **4** (1989), no. 3.
31. David Kahn, 'Pearl Harbor and the Inadequacy of Cryptanalysis', *Cryptologia*, **15** (1991), no. 4. Idem, 'The Intelligence Failure at Pearl Harbor', *Foreign Affairs*, winter 1991/92, pp. 138–52.
32. Andrew, *For The President's Eyes Only*, ch. 3.
33. Sir Stuart Milner-Barry, '"Action This Day": The Letter from the Bletchley Park Cryptanalysts to the Prime Minister, 21 October 1941', *Intelligence and National Security*, **1** (1986), no. 2.
34. See, e.g., Churchill's minute on decrypt no. 104768, 24 May 1942, HW1/592, PRO.
35. To judge from the decrypts so far released in the PRO, the supply of American decrypts to the Prime Minister ceased after Pearl Harbor. The argument from silence, or from lack of evidence, however, is never conclusive.
36. Marshall, Memorandum for the President, 11 July 1942, MR 162, Naval Aide's Files: A-6 Communications, Franklin D. Roosevelt Library, Hyde Park, New York. The phrasing of the memo suggests that it was a response to an enquiry from FDR.
37. Hinsley *et al.*, *British Intelligence in the Second World War*, vol. II, p. 56.
38. David Kahn, *Seizing the Enigma* (Boston, Mass.: Houghton Mifflin, 1991), pp. 242–3.
39. Interviews with Sir Harry Hinsley, March/April 1994.
40. Hinsley *et al.*, *British Intelligence in the Second World War*, vol. II, p. 48.
41. Ibid., chs 16, 19. Kahn, *Seizing the Enigma*, chs. 20–3.
42. Stephen Ambrose, *Ike's Spies* (Garden City, NY: Doubleday, 1981), part I.
43. 'Operations of the Military Intelligence Service War Department London (MIS WD London)', 11 June 1945, pp. 36–7, RG 457 SRH-110, National Archives, Washington, DC (NAW).
44. Interviews with Sir Harry Hinsley, March/April 1994.
45. 'Operations of the Military Intelligence Service War Department London (MIS WD London)', 11 June 1945, Tab A, RG 457 SRH-110, NAW.
46. A. G. Denniston, 'The Government Code and Cypher School between the Wars',

in Christopher Andrew (ed.), *Codebreaking and Signals Intelligence* (London: Frank Cass, 1986). P. William Filby, 'Bletchley Park and Berkeley Street', *Intelligence and National Security*, **3** (1988), no. 2.

47. Declassification of neutral and allied decrypts began on both sides of the Atlantic only in 1993. In August 1993, as the result of an FOIA application, substantial numbers of Belgian, Bolivian, Chilean, Colombian, Danish, Dutch, Ecuadorian, Egyptian, Finnish, French, Iranian, Liberian, Luxembourg, Mexican, Norwegian, Paraguayan, Peruvian, Polish, Portuguese, Saudi Arabian, Spanish, Swiss, Syrian, Turkish, Uruguayan, Venezuelan and Yugoslav decrypts dating back to the final year of the war were released to the Washington National Archives. 'U.S. Spied on its World War II Allies', *New York Times*, 11 Aug. 1993. Churchill's 'golden eggs' in the HW1 series at the PRO, declassified in 1993–94, contain an even larger sample of neutral and allied decrypts.

48. 'MIS War Department Liaison Activities in the United Kingdom 1943–1945', p. 12, RG 457, SRH-153, NAW.

49. 'Operations of the Miltary Intelligence Service War Department London (MIS WD London)', 11 June 1945, p. 38, RG 457, SRH-110, NAW. F. H. Hinsley and Alan Stripp (eds), *Codebreakers* (Oxford: Oxford University Press, 1993), p. 73.

50. 'Visit by the Directors of Intelligence', M.M.(S)(44)75, Sept. 1944, CAB 122/1417, PRO.

51. Andrew, *Secret Service*, ch. 14.

52. Hinsley *et al.*, *British Intelligence in the Second World War*, vol. 3, part 1, appendix I.

53. RG 218, box 370, file 385, NAW.

54. Hinsley *et al.*, *British Intelligence in the Second World War*, vol. 2, ch. 16; vol. 3, part 1, appendix I.

55. X-2 Unpublished History, RG 226, Entry 176, box 2, file 16, NAW.

56. Christopher Andrew and Oleg Gordievsky, *KGB: The Inside Story of its Foreign Operations from Lenin to Gorbachev*, Sceptre edn (London: Hodder and Stoughton, 1991), pp. 72–3, 79–80, 330–1, 333. Bradley F. Smith, *The Shadow Warriors* (London: André Deutsch, 1983), pp. 324, 335–6. Kim Philby, *My Silent War*, paperback edn (London: Panther Books, 1969), pp. 30, 32. George A. Hill, *Go Spy the Land* (London: Cassell, 1932).

57. Andrew and Gordievsky, *KGB*, p. 331. František Moravec, *Master of Spies* (London: Bodley Head, 1975), pp. 233–43.

58. Records of US Military Mission to Moscow, RG 334, box 18, NAW. Andrew and Gordievsky, *KGB*, pp. 331–3. Smith, *Shadow Warriors*, pp. 339–52.

59. Peter Calvocoressi, *Top Secret Ultra* (London: Cassell, 1980), p. 94. Hinsley *et al.*, *British Intelligence in the Second World War*, **2**, 58–66.

60. Kahn, 'Roosevelt, MAGIC, and ULTRA', p. 312.

61. Andrew and Gordievsky, *KGB*, pp. 192–5, 281–3, 316–17. In November 1987, I was able to interview in Washington Yuri Rastvorov, who had worked under Tolstoy in the Japanese section of the NKVD Fifth Directorate.

62. Burgess and Maclean were exposed in 1951, Philby in 1963, Blunt in 1979, Cairncross as the Fifth Man in 1990 (though he had been identified as a less important agent a decade earlier). Andropov Institute students were not told the identities of the Five until they had been publicly exposed.

63. Andrew and Gordievsky, *KGB*, pp. 272–3, 289–90, 313–14, 320–1. When we identified Cairncross as the Fifth Man in the first edition of *KGB* in 1990, he indignantly denied it. A year later, he admitted it in a front-page 'world exclusive' in *The Mail on Sunday* ('Yes, I'm the Fifth Man', 22 Sept. 1991); the story was

confirmed by Cairncross's former KGB controller, Yuri Ivanovich Modin. Cairncross's confession was a very partial one and made no reference to his period as private secretary to Hankey. The Russian Foreign Intelligence Service (successor to the KGB First Chief directorate) is unlikely to release any important material on Cairncross during his lifetime.

64. S.A.C.(D.P.)(41)4, CAB 90/8, PRO.
65. Andrew and Gordievsky, *KGB*, p. 321.
66. *Voprosi Istorii Estestvoznania i Tekhniki*, 1992, no. 3, pp. 107ff. Pavel Sudoplatov, *Special Tasks* (Boston: Little, Brown, 1994), pp. 437–8. David Holloway, *Stalin and the Bomb* (New Haven: Yale University Press, 1994), pp. 82–3.
67. Even in the case of the Cambridge Five, no evidence existed until their defections and/or confessions which would have been likely to secure conviction in a court of law. After the defection of Burgess and Maclean in 1951, Philby, Blunt and Cairncross successfully protested their innocence for some years. Philby was officially exonerated in 1955.
68. Andrew and Gordievsky, *KGB*, pp. 291–6, 380–2, 387–8. Hayden B. Peake, 'Soviet Espionage and the Office of Strategic Services', in Warren F. Kimball (ed.), *America Unbound: World War II and the Making of a Superpower* (New York: St Martin's Press, 1992), pp. 107–38.
69. Allen Weinstein, *Perjury: The Hiss–Chambers Case* (New York: Knopf, 1978), pp. 314–32, 340–2. The controversial, but much quoted, 'clearing' of Hiss by the Russian historian, Dmitri Volkogonov, does little to advance understanding of the Hiss case. Volkogonov was not given direct access to KGB and GRU foreign intelligence files. Yevgeni Primakov, head of the Russian Foreign Intelligence Service, has made clear that it does not release information on living former Soviet agents. The GRU follows the same policy. The best study of available material on the Hiss case remains that by Weinstein.
70. Andrew and Gordievsky, *KGB*, pp. 295–6.
71. Ibid., pp. 296–300.
72. Brian Crozier, *Free Agent* (London: HarperCollins, 1993), pp. 1–2.
73. CIA, *The Intelligence War in 1941*, pp. 20–2.
74. Andrew and Gordievsky, *KGB*, pp. 298–301, 346–7, 357–8, 473–5.
75. James G. Blight and David A. Welch (eds), *On the Brink: Americans and Soviets Re-assess the Cuban Missile Crisis* (New York: Hill & Wang, 1989), p. 248. Andrew, *For the President's Eyes Only*, ch.7.
76. Holloway, *Stalin and the Bomb*, p. 303.
77. Andrew and Gordievsky, *KGB*, pp. 273–4, 732n109. The BBC2 documentary, *Hess: An Edge of Conspiracy*, first broadcast 17 Jan. 1990 (Presenter: Christopher Andrew; Producer: Roy Davies), examined some of the Hess conspiracy theories.
78. Ibid., pp. 306–7. Phillip Knightley, *Philby: KGB Master Spy* (London: André Deutsch, 1988), pp. 105–10.
79. Jonathan Haslam, 'Stalin's Fears of a Separate Peace 1942', *Intelligence and National Security*, **8** (1993), pp. 97–9.
80. Christopher Andrew and Oleg Gordievsky, *Instructions from the Centre: Top Secret Files on KGB Foreign Operations* (London: Hodder & Stoughton, 1991; published in the USA as *Comrade Kryuchkov's Instructions*, Stanford University Press, 1993), p. 211. For evidence of the continuing addiction of the KGB to conspiracy theory, see ibid., passim.
81. Geoff Jukes, 'The Soviets and "Ultra"', *Intelligence and National Security*, **3** (1988), no. 2.
82. Andrew and Gordievsky, *KGB*, pp. 313–18. Granada TV documentary, *The Fifth Man: Secrets of the Ring of Five* (Presenter: Christopher Andrew; Producer:

Mike Beckham), Oct. 1990. Interview with Cairncross, *Mail on Sunday*, 22 Sept. 1991. Blunt, Leo Long (run by Blunt as a sub-agent), and Philby also provided smaller quantities of ULTRA-based intelligence.

83. Sir Kenneth Strong, *Intelligence at the Top* (London: Cassell, 1968), pp. 112ff.
84. Hinsley and Stripp (eds), *Codebreakers*, pp. 12–13.
85. Christopher Andrew, 'The Growth of the Australian Intelligence Community and the Anglo-American Connection', *Intelligence and National Security*, 4 (1989), no. 2. Idem, 'The Growth of Intelligence Collaboration in the English-Speaking World', Wilson Center (Washington, DC) Working Paper no. 87 (1987).
86. The route taken by this high-level British sigint delegation is recorded, together with precise times of arrival and departure at each stopping-point in a map entitled, 'Round the World Tour by Sir Edward Travis and Rear-Admiral Rushbrooke and Staffs, 14th March–27th April 1945', contained in the papers of Sir Harry Hinsley. My account of the 'World Tour' is based on this map and on interviews with Sir Harry Hinsley.
87. Interviews with Sir Harry Hinsley, March/April 1994.
88. Smith, *Ultra–Magic Deals*, pp. 195–6. ANCIB was the successor to the less influential Army–Navy Communications Coordination Committee founded in May 1944 as a purely advisory body.
89. Interviews with Sir Harry Hinsley, March/April 1994.
90. Smith, *Ultra–Magic Deals*, pp. 202–3.
91. Andrew, *For the President's Eyes Only*, ch. 4.
92. Smith, *Ultra–Magic Deals*, chs 8, 9.
93. The date of the UKUSA agreement is often wrongly given as 1947. Dr Louis Tordella, Deputy Director of NSA from 1958 to 1974, who was present at the signing, confirms that the date was 1948. Interviews with Dr Tordella, November 1987 and April 1992. Christopher Andrew, 'The Making of the Anglo-American Sigint Alliance', in Hayden B. Peake and Samuel Halpern (eds), *In the Name of Intelligence: Essays in Honor of Walter Pforzheimer* (Washington, DC: NIBC Press, 1994).
94. Andrew and Gordievsky, *KGB*, chs 10, 11.

# 7 Stalin, Soviet Strategy and the Grand Alliance
## John Erickson

The German invasion of the Soviet Union launched on 22 June 1941 found London and Moscow each after its own fashion catastrophically unprepared for such an eventuality. Double-vision afflicted both in equal measure. The Foreign Office, though aware of the scale of the German military build-up in the east, was convinced that this was but a prelude to further Soviet–German negotiation and possible Soviet capitulation to German demands. Stalin, in possession of mountains of intelligence data,[1] did not expect Hitler to embark on a two-front war; at worst, he anticipated that an ultimatum would precede war. His immediate preoccupation was to avoid a 'provocation', British-inspired, to involve him in war with Germany. Alternatively, he had to be on the lookout to thwart any devious Anglo-German 'compact' for a separate peace which would free Hitler's hands to strike in the east, a suspicion fuelled by the bizarre circumstances of the 'Hess affair'.

Stalin realised that to order full mobilisation was an act of war, triggering the very war he was anxious at all costs to avoid or at least to defer to a time of his own choosing. The two strategic war-games held in January, 1941, investigating the implications of a 'Blue' (German) attack and the 'Red' (Soviet) response, highlighted the importance of ensuring effective defence of the western borders of the Soviet Union.[2] The war-plan adopted in August 1940, had placed the main German thrust in the south-western sector, though General G. K. Zhukov, appointed Chief of the Soviet General Staff in January 1941, did not exclude the possibility of a major thrust developing along the Warsaw axis and engulfing the central sector.

Effectively deprived of any freedom of strategic choice, Zhukov was charged with producing a plan for the defence of the frontiers, *Plan oborony gosudarstvennoi granitsy 1941*, which was ready by the beginning of May. This document consisted of a general definition of assignments for the covering armies, plus an operational deployment plan delivered separately in 'Red packets' to the several army commands. But of *operational orders* there was neither hint nor sign. The two basic instructions required the prevention of hostile intrusion into Soviet territory and the implementation of a stubborn defence to cover the mobilisation, concentration and deployment of the Red Army. The destruction of enemy forces which broke through was assigned to second-echelon mechanised corps, anti-tank brigades and aviation. Only on receipt of *special instructions* from the High Command would operations be carried into enemy territory. The underlying assumption was that the Red Army would not be taken by surprise, that decisive offensive operations would be preceded by a declaration of war, or that enemy forces would be committed in only limited strength. Glaring deficiencies were the weakness of reserves meant to hold enemy penetrations and the absence of coordination between first and second echelons. As one Soviet Marshal ruefully observed, it was a case of preparing for the wrong war, 1914 not 1941.

The alarm bells rang on 5 May 1941 with Colonel-General Golikov's detailed intelligence report on German order of battle, making it unpalatably plain that the Soviet forces in the western districts were insufficient to repel a German attack. Zhukov pressed for reinforcement from armies deployed in the rear, to which Stalin grudgingly assented while demanding absolute secrecy. Four armies, the 16th, 19th, 21st and 22nd, trundled westwards 'for training' – some 800 000 men in various stages of dislocation, disarray and disorganisation, all of which precluded proper deployment.

Military nervousness increased. With the mobilisation plan for the covering armies in the west finalised, Zhukov followed this with a draft plan for a pre-emptive strike to 'forestall enemy deployment... to attack the German Army in the middle of its deployment' and before the 'full co-ordination of the movement of its various forces',[3] a plan modelled on Zhukov's success in the second January war-game. The plan to disrupt German deployment was based on the situation in mid-May, with 152 Soviet divisions facing 100 German divisions. But full Soviet deployment needed several more weeks to complete, by which time superiority would have passed to the Germans. The idea of disruption was discussed with Stalin (which Zhukov subsequently admitted was a huge mistake) and abandoned, leaving Stalin to berate his commanders for their 'fantasising' over things which could not be.

Stalin, while eschewing full mobilisation in June, also forbade bringing Soviet forces, deployed forward, up to full battle-readiness. Precautionary moves were imposed but surreptitiously, further confusing command and rank-and-file alike. The first warning order, issued on the eve of 22 June, demanded restraint in the face of any kind of provocative action which might bring about 'serious complications'. 'In the case of provocative action by the Germans, fire is *not* to be opened... [and] until such time as enemy aircraft undertake military operations *no fire* is to be opened on them', ran the orders in the Baltic Special Military District.[4] As the huge German attack unrolled, vague orders lost what utility they had since they failed to reach the numerous units struggling to survive. Not until noon 22 June 1941, did the Soviet government admit to a state of war. The Soviet Union was a warfare state without a war machine, its wartime operational high command hurriedly improvised, its mobilisation now having to be carried through under fire as the German Army ripped away the frontier defences and the Luftwaffe inflicted massive losses on Soviet aircraft neatly parked on their airfields. Stalin meanwhile remained strangely, mystifyingly, absent from the public scene.[5]

Though, a week before the German invasion, Foreign Secretary Eden had informed the Soviet Ambassador in London, Ivan Maisky, of the German concentrations in the east and had promised, in the event of war, to despatch a British military mission to Russia and to undertake 'urgent consideration of Russian economic needs', no machinery existed on either side to foster sustained collaboration. On the very eve of the German invasion, Stafford Cripps, on leave in London from Moscow, had approached Maisky on the subject of 'the close co-operation between England and the USSR' in the event of war. Cripps described British readiness to furnish 'maximum assistance' under these circumstances, but Maisky said nothing, for there was nothing he could say.[6]

Surveying the military cupboard, the British saw little possibility of rendering the Soviet Union real assistance. British strategic priorities centred on defending the British Isles against German invasion, on the Middle East and on India. The belief in the early collapse of the Soviet Union was widespread, offering the United Kingdom little more than a breathing space, possibly a fleeting opportunity with the enemy 'busy in Russia' to disrupt German preparations for invasion on the French coast. Nowhere was there interest or incentive to 'treat Russia as an ally'. Prime Minister Winston Churchill's famous broadcast on Sunday, 22 June signally failed to welcome an 'ally', though at Maisky's personal prompting the broadcast disavowed any move to conclude a separate peace and signalled support for Russia. 'We shall give whatever help we can to Russia and to the Russian people', curiously and carefully qualified Cripps' earlier assurance of 'maximum assistance'.[7]

The pledge not to pursue a separate peace nevertheless sufficed for the moment to allay one of Stalin's worst fears. What the speech did not do was to remove thick layers of suspicion on both sides or remedy the patent absence of mutual trust which was to plague the wartime relationship for many months to come and inhibit common action. Assistance for Russia in the event of war had not figured in any British contingency plans. Hopes of military collaboration were soon bogged down almost immovably in the crisis precipitated by the scale of the defeat inflicted on the Red Army in the initial stages of war, thereby seeming to bear out British predictions of imminent Soviet collapse.

It was this state of affairs which also disclosed fundamental Anglo-Soviet differences in strategic perspectives and priorities. The magnitude of these early disasters confirmed the British Chiefs of Staffs in their estimate of the faint chances of Soviet survival, at the same time hastening Stalin's personal crisis. Within a week the Soviet Western Front faced catastrophe, with the encirclement of four Soviet armies and German armour slicing through the North-western Front and threatening the Baltic states and Leningrad.[8] The Soviet General Staff, bereft of information, was overwhelmed, and General Zhukov reduced to a distressed state when faced with Stalin and Beria. On 29 June, Stalin finally grasping the vast scope of the calamity and the gravity of the situation, retired once more to his 'near *dacha*', listless and resigned.[9]

It was a state from which he was roused by a Politburo delegation desperate to organise effective command and a functioning government. By 3 July, 1941, Stalin was installed as head of the wartime government, the State Defence Committee (GKO), an all-powerful, highly-centralised machine with draconian powers. In his first radio broadcast of the war, on 3 July 1941, Stalin astoundingly addressed his 'brothers and sisters', promising all-out war, appealing to Russian nationalism and welcoming aid from the West.

The Soviet Military Mission, headed by Colonel-General F. I. Golkov, who had been personally briefed by Stalin,[10] arrived in London to a less than enthusiastic reception. They were a 'hard-looking lot', described by the Chief of the Imperial General Staff as resembling nothing so much as a 'bunch of pig-stickers', a reflection of an anti-Soviet disposition which pervaded the attitude of the British Chiefs of Staff for much of the war.[11] Stalin's priorities were formulated as the establishment of a 'common front' in the north of Europe' to secure sea communications between the Soviet Union, Great Britain and the United States, a British landing in the north of France – 'if not right away, then at least a month later' – and a secondary operation in the Balkans. Of these three requirements, the first, securing sea communications, was vital to protect a supply route to the north.

The instructions issued to the British Military Mission headed by Lieutenant-General Mason-Macfarlane could not have been more dispiriting, made aware, as the General and Rear-Admiral Miles were, that the Chiefs of Staff saw little more than 'an off-chance . . . a poor chance' of keeping the Soviet–German war going, possibly from afar in distant Siberia.[12] In the event of the expected collapse of the Soviet Union the demolition of the oilfields of the Caucasus would be critically important. The British Military Mission was given no authority to discuss matters relating to strategy or assistance. The prospect of, and provision for, Soviet defeat took precedence over any considerations of cooperation and collaboration.

Throughout July and into August, 1941, the Wehrmacht continued to advance at great speed, closing in on Leningrad in the north by 10 August, taking yet more prisoners in the battle for Smolensk at the centre and in the south encircling some 20 Soviet divisions in the 'Uman pocket' before driving into the bend of the Dnieper. In late August Hitler produced his decision for the further stage of the Russian campaign, aiming now at the flanks, seizing the Crimea and the Donbas, cutting off the Caucasian oilfields and investing Leningrad in the north before linking up with the Finns. Only with

Leningrad captured and the offensive in the south proceeding apace could the drive on Moscow be resumed.

In his message to Stalin on 7 July 1941, Churchill promised help but on a scale limited by the constraints of geography and the availability of British resources.[13] In Moscow, Molotov pressed Stafford Cripps for a specific Anglo-Soviet agreement, while Stalin himself expressed his disappointment at the 'incomprehensible position' [*neponyatnaya pozitsiya*] of the British Government, conveying as it did the impression that it did not wish to bind itself to any kind of agreement with the Soviet Union.[14] If this was the case, Stalin observed, it would be 'better to say so now without further ado'. The situation, in Stalin's view, demanded a clear statement about mutual Anglo-Soviet assistance 'without qualification and ulterior motives'. The present situation recalled the tardiness which had wrecked the Anglo-Soviet–French talks in 1939. The result of this first Stalinist onslaught was a stop-gap measure. The terse Anglo-Soviet declaration signed on 12 July 1941 committed both parties to render to each other 'assistance of all kinds' [*pomoshch' i podderzhka vsyakogo roda*] and to refrain from entering upon any negotiation or into any separate peace for the duration of the war.[15]

Pressure was now mounted on Britain from the Soviet side for a fundamental revision of its existing strategy with its emphasis on the Middle East and based as it was on the notion that the war in the east was only a short-term respite. Soviet pressure was also applied for a combined operation in the north, a plea for action reinforced by Cripps in Moscow, Eden, Beaverbrook and even General Macfarlane, now more readily convinced of the possibility of Soviet survival and the eventual failure of the *Blitzkrieg*. At this juncture, Stalin shifted his ground from seeking immediate military relief to the daunting question of war supplies and their delivery. Golikov, now assigned to Washington, the fount of war supplies, during his brief stop-over in London, pressed urgently for the establishment of a secure supply route to the north, a vital Soviet strategic priority, the significance of which had hitherto largely escaped the Chiefs of Staff, reluctant to spare ships, aircraft and men.

In his message to Churchill on 18 July, Stalin admitted the difficulties posed by a landing in France and stressed that 'a front in the North' would be easier, involving only British naval and air forces ... without landing troops or artillery'.[16] He was nevertheless at this stage fully seized by what he called British 'temporising' and the unalterable fixation with the Middle East which categorically ruled out the appearance of any 'second front' in the west. Maisky had already tackled Eden in a 'serious exchange', asking 'what strategy did the British government have for defeating Germany?' 'Was a Second Front totally ruled out or was this a temporary postponement?' Stalin much approved of this line, responding testily to Maisky on 30 August: 'The Hitlerites would like to pick off their enemies one by one – today the Russians, tomorrow the British'. ... What do they [the British] want? They want, it seems, to see us weakened. If that assumption is correct, we will have to be cautious in our dealings with the English.'[17]

On 25 August 1941, Soviet and British forces moved into Iran to force the removal of the German presence, hardly a model of joint operations since no coordination took place and the British Chiefs of Staff insisted on the 'right of independent action'. In any event, though momentarily mollified, Stalin remarked that it was not in Iran that the course of the war would be decided. Meantime the course of war seemed to be going badly for the Red Army, as from August to mid-September German forces carried out a giant encirclement in the Ukraine where armoured pincers met 150 miles east of Kiev, trapping seven Soviet armies. Here was the prelude to the resumption of the German advance on Moscow.

Stalin left Churchill in no doubt as to the magnitude of the setbacks: half the Ukraine lost, 'the enemy at the gates of Leningrad'. The 'way out of this unfavourable situation', the 'only way', must be the opening of a second front somewhere in the Balkans or in France designed to draw off 30–40 German divisions from the Eastern front.[18] In London, Maisky spelled out the apocalyptic consequences of a German triumph in Russia, catastrophe for both the Soviet Union and the British Empire, but learned that neither operations in France nor in the Balkans would be forthcoming.[19]

Desperately searching for 'active military aid' and fully aware of 'the impossibility of opening a second front at the moment', Stalin suggested to Churchill, in his message of 13 September, that a British expeditionary force of 25–30 divisions be landed at Archangel or moved through Iran 'for military co-operation with Soviet troops on Soviet soil'.[20] The Prime Minister returned a studied reply, emphasising the overriding need to 'clear our western flank in Libya', a development which might release forces 'to co-operate upon the southern flank of the Russian front'.

At the Supply conference, which convened in Moscow at the end of September,[21] on the Prime Minister's orders, General Ismay, who was to travel to Moscow, could discuss 'any plans for practical co-operation' on the spot. These promised 'strategic discussions' came to nought, resulting in only a brief exchange between General Ismay and Stalin, the latter bent largely on criticising British strategy. The official brief supplied to the two British generals sent to Moscow scoffed derisively at the idea of 20–30 British divisions being launched against the French coast or being 'sent round by sea for service in Russia'. The notion had 'no foundation in reality'.

Between 20 and 24 September 1941 Moscow was sent nine warnings, the data having been derived from the ENIGMA decrypts, of a German build-up at the centre of the front, signalling a possible resumption of the German thrust on the Soviet capital.[22] On 2 October the German Army Group Centre went over to the attack, carrying out three major encirclements, two near Bryansk and one to the west of Vyazma, bringing in a huge haul of prisoners thus denuding the forces covering Moscow. The threat to Moscow now appeared to be immediate. The capital was prepared for demolition and evacuated and there were scenes of panic flight , the *bol'shoi drap*,[23] the 'great skedaddle' on 16 October. But the flight was finally checked, and the city put on a defence footing. Stalin remained in the capital, assured by General Zhukov that Moscow could be and would be held.

Army Group South meanwhile moved north of Kharkov and to the upper Donets, advancing at the same time along the shore of the Sea of Azov towards Rostov-on-Don, which fell on 20 November. The German Eleventh Army had penetrated into the Crimea at the end of October, occupying most of the peninsula save for Sevastopol by mid-November. On 15 November 1941, Army Group Centre, under the command of Field-Marshal von Bock, jumped off in the final drive for Moscow as the ground held hard in the gathering frost. Two Panzer groups commanded by the generals Reinhardt and Höpner attacked north of Moscow; a third, under Guderian, advanced from the south of the Soviet capital. Amid fierce fighting, as the weather deteriorated, Stalin husbanded his reserves, drawing on crack Soviet divisions in Siberia and the Soviet Far East, assured for the moment of no Japanese attack developing in that theatre. (A Japanese carrier attack force was, in fact, already steaming to place aircraft within striking range of Pearl Harbor.)

The Red Army struck first at the flanks. On 9 November Marshal Timoshenko submitted a plan to attack Army Group South, striking at the flank and rear of First Panzer Army, an operation approved by Stalin but expressly denied any external reinforcement. The result was a striking success with Rostov recaptured and cleared on 29 November. At the other end of the Soviet–German front, where Leningrad was freezing and starving to death, General Meretskov fought to recapture Tikhvin and force German troops back to the river Volkhov, a key move in easing the precarious supply situation for Leningrad.

With German troops reaching the limits of their resources and resilience, General Zhukov on 30 November submitted plans for a Soviet counter-stroke at Moscow for the inspection of Stalin and the Stavka (GHQ). The aim was to bring about 'a swift and decisive transformation' of the operational scene. The movement of German siege-guns to within range of the Soviet capital added urgency to that action. The northerly German thrust was within 21 miles of the city, the southern advance as yet some 40 miles away. During these desperate encounters the German command had come to the view that the Red Army had fought to its last battalion, an estimate which proved to be fatally misplaced. At 0300 hours on the morning of 5 December, 1941, in temperatures of −25 and −30 degrees Centigrade, the Soviet counter-blow unrolled, the Kalinin Front in the north joining with the Western Front, Guderian to the south coming under heavy attack by the right wing of Timoshenko's South-western Front.[24]

It was Army Group Centre which had thrown its last battalions into the battle for Moscow. The Soviet counter-blows broke into the advance German units to the north and south of Moscow and expanded operations to engulf not only the whole of Army Group Centre but also its neighbour Army Group North. In this chaos Hitler forbade retreat, fearing a total rout. At the end of the month, deepening Soviet thrusts to the north and on the German southern flank disclosed that nothing short of the encirclement of Army Group Centre was now intended.

As the Red Army's counter-stroke at Moscow expanded rapidly into a counter-offensive, Foreign Secretary Eden met with Stalin in Moscow in mid-December. Stalin had ready and waiting his extensions of the wartime Anglo-Soviet agreement looking ahead to the postwar world and embracing the territorial reconstruction of postwar Europe, the burden of which was recognition of the Soviet Union's 1941 frontiers. Eden perforce could not agree to the addition of this 'small protocol', as Stalin termed it and further argument only produced deadlock.

Stalin professed himself to be neither hurt nor offended at the absence of a second front or at the failure to send British troops to Russia. 'I do not now insist on your sending troops to the USSR', he observed, a reflection of his growing confidence in the military situation. His strategy for survival, of which the demands for a military diversion and the security of supplies formed a key part, had worked though the Soviet Union had been brought to the very edge of destruction in early November.

Stalin hinted at the defeat of Germany within a year and that of Japan within a further six months, a war in the Far East and Pacific in which the Soviet Union could not immediately join but 'the situation might change by the spring [1942]'.[25] It would take some four months to replace the Soviet divisions withdrawn westwards but in the spring of 1942 Soviet forces would be up to full strength and the discussion might begin once more. In this new-found burst of confidence, fatal over-confidence as it proved, Stalin saw in the prospect of a second front not survival but an additive to victory and the lure of frontier lines which he might soon reach. For the next two months Soviet operations would proceed at full speed during which time Stalin did not anticipate fresh German divisions moving to the east.

On 5 January 1942 the Stavka, together with members of the State Defence Committee, assembled for a fateful meeting, setting the scope, timing and objectives for the transition to the Red Army's general counter-offensive. The main objective would be the destruction of German forces in the region of Leningrad, west of Moscow and in the south, with the main attack to be launched against Army Group Centre. Grandiose in scale, the plan was incommensurate not only with available resources but also with the present capabilities of the Red Army. General Zhukov argued for reinforcement of the Western Front and a powerful attack against Army Group Centre, threatened with encirclement. Stalin observed that Marshal Timoshenko was in favour of all-out, all-round attack: 'We must grind the Germans down with all speed, so that they cannot attack in the spring'. Marshal Shaposhnikov told Zhukov that he had argued to no purpose. The directives to Front commanders had already been issued.[26]

Hitler authorised a substantial withdrawal by Army Group Centre on 15 January, shortening the German front and releasing men for the flanks where a grave situation had built up in the north with a huge gap torn between Army Group Centre and the North. At Demyansk 100 000 men were encircled and were supplied by air. In mid-February fresh German divisions were closing the gap in the north as the Soviet offensive was losing momentum caused by stiffening German resistance, decimated Red Army formations, over-extended fronts, and a dangerous multiplicity of objectives.

In the middle of March 1942, Stalin, the Stavka, the General Staff and select Front commanders met to consider the coming summer campaign and a suitable strategy, offensive or defensive. Marshal Shaposhnikov and the General Staff came out unequivocally for the 'provisional strategic defensive', dictated by the absence of substantial trained reserves. The aim would be to wear down the enemy before going over to a general offensive. The 'main attention' of the Soviet command should be 'the central sector', namely Moscow. The build-up should proceed through May and June, assembling properly supplied reserves. Supplies were crucially important.[27] In April Major-General Belyaev, reporting to the Munitions Assignment Board, stated that 'the Russians intend to defeat the Germans in 1942 but they need all the help they could obtain with munitions'.[28]

Stalin proposed to 'attack and defend simultaneously', though Marshal Shaposhnikov referred to German superiority in manpower and the absence of a 'Second Front' which strongly suggested limited 'active defence'. General Zhukov did not care for 'partial offensives' which could only dissipate reserves. Stalin insisted on offensive operations to forestall the Germans: 'Don't let us sit down in defence, with our hands folded, while the Germans attack first!' Not surprisingly, Marshal Timoshenko's plans for an offensive with three fronts (Bryansk, South-western and Southern forming the 'South-western theatre' command) appealed to Stalin. The target was Army Group South. Timoshenko's 'Kharkov operation', timed for May, was designed to capture this key German base and even strike out for Dnepropetrovsk and Zaporozhe.

Hitler's directive of 5 April 1942, directed at regaining the initiative on the Eastern Front, assigned primacy to major offensive operations in the south aimed at the Don, Stalingrad and the oilfields of the Caucasus. Timoshenko attacked first. But early Soviet success met stiffer German resistance, leading to a crisis with an appeal to Stalin to abandon the offensive. Stalin refused, relenting only when encirclement faced the Soviet troops, a decision too late to save grievous Soviet losses in men and equipment at the end of May.[29]

The 'Second Front' once more took on its survival aspect and was hammered home by the Soviet Foreign Minister Molotov on his arrival in London on 20 May 1942. Molotov was authorised to negotiate the proposed Anglo-Soviet treaty and, of greater importance, the opening of a Second Front. What Molotov wanted was for the allies, primarily Great Britain, to engage at least 40 German divisions in Western Europe. The Prime Minister intimated in some detail and at some length that a cross-Channel attack was not feasible in 1942 but the availability of more landing-craft and American forces might be predicted for 1943.[30] The signing of the Anglo-Soviet treaty and the outcome of Molotov's talks in Washington were assumed to betoken the opening of a Second Front and even to be indications of its imminence, in spite of British disclaimers to the contrary.

The disasters at Kharkov, serious as they were, were but a part of the calamitous situation developing in the south. In the Crimea the incompetence of Lev Mekhlis, one of Stalin's intimates, brought on the loss of 21 Soviet divisions from three armies. On 28 June 1942 the German summer offensive opened, designed first to crush the Soviet southern wing and bring the German front to the Don, then proceeding to Stalingrad and striking into the flank of the Soviet forces holding the Caucasus. Rostov fell on 23 July, the day on which Hitler ordered Army Group A to strike deep into the Caucasus and Army Group B to make for Stalingrad. Though the Red Army escaped major encirclement Stalin decided to use the fall of Rostov to issue Order No. 227 of 28 July, 'Not a step back', prescribing the firing-squad and penal battalions for 'panic-mongers', 'cowards' and 'traitors'.

Not many days before, on 23 July, as the crisis in the south deepened, Stalin replied to Churchill's message of 17 July announcing the suspension of convoys to Russia. Both supplies *and* the Second Front were now key elements in a revived survival strategy. Most emphatically, the Soviet government could not acquiesce in the postponement of the Second Front to 1943 and the cessation of convoys was a breach of 'contracted obligations'.[31]

Stalin had already consented to a visit from the Prime Minister, now in possession of an agreement with President Roosevelt to give priority to a landing in North Africa, an operation to be launched as soon as possible. In a heavily charged atmosphere Churchill, at his first meeting with Stalin on 12 August, explained that no Second Front could be forthcoming in 1942 but large operations were in preparation for 1943. Little of this was to Stalin's liking though he brightened somewhat at the disclosure of a landing in North Africa, a response he subsequently qualified by pointing out that the North African landings did not directly concern the Soviet Union.

The dispute over the Second Front illustrated important differences over the significance of the Russian front; Stalin, for obvious reasons, regarded it as crucial, the British and American governments evidently accorded it lesser importance.[32] Meanwhile the military talks, in which the marshals Voroshilov and Shaposhnikov participated, were as dour as they were unproductive. Operation VELVET, the plan to base heavy bombers in the Caucasus, did not interest Stalin, even less Voroshilov, while General Alanbrooke and his associates parried discussions of a Second Front. Pressed for a date for a cross-Channel landing in 1943, General Alanbrooke declined to be specific.[33]

On 23 August, in a high-speed thrust, 16 Panzer Division reached the Volga at Rynok to the north of Stalingrad. The city was heavily bombed and left in flames, a fire-blackened ruin, to become the scene of close-quarter fighting which never ceased by night or day. By mid-September the old town, city centre and railway station were in German hands. This at a time when the generals Zhukov and Vasilevsky, assigned to the Stalingrad front, were reporting to Stalin the outlines of a massive Soviet blow designed to break into the German 'operational rear', an operation Zhukov said could be planned and prepared within 45 days.

Operation URANUS, the Soviet counter-offensive, involved a double encirclement with two armoured thrusts, one from the north from the Don bridgeheads moving south-east, the other from the south driving north-westwards, the two to link up at Kalach on the Don cutting off the huge salient occupied by the German Sixth Army and Fourth Panzer. On 19 November 1942, eleven days after the first Anglo-American landings in North Africa, the Red Army loosed its Stalingrad counter-offensive. Three days later, Soviet spearheads linked up at Kalach, five Soviet armies now hemming in 20 divisions of the German Sixth Army and elements of Fourth Panzer.[34]

Stalin could now sensibly anticipate growing, even grandiose gains. Operation URANUS, was but one phase of a whole constellation of operations designed to unhinge the entire southern wing of the German Army in the east. SATURN would follow URANUS, a huge outer sweep aimed at Rostov-on-Don, sealing off Army Group A fighting deep in the Caucasus. With the German southern wing smashed in, the prospect of decisive strategic success loomed up, with the road to the Dnieper opened and access to the coal and power-stations of the Donbas and the eastern Ukraine. Much, however, depended on the rapid reduction of the encircled Sixth Army to release fresh Soviet forces and, most immediately, German attempts to relieve the trapped Stalingrad garrison had to be fought off. Sixth Army was not relieved, freezing and starving to death until its final surrender on 31 January 1943. At the end of January, vastly overrating the capabilities of the Red Army and underrating the ability of the Wehrmacht to recover itself yet again, Stalin prepared to progress to a massive, multi-front counter-offensive along all axes: southern, western and north-western. This repeated the failed strategy of 1942, the absence of clearly defined objectives, either the destruction of enemy forces in the field or the recapture of territory and the recovery of vital resources. Stalin wanted both but obtained neither.

With the German lines ripped to pieces from Voronezh to the foothills of the Caucasus and confident that the strategic initiative rested with the Red Army, the Soviet command, at Stalin's behest, planned not only to eliminate the 75 German divisions in the Ukraine but also to break into the rear of Army Group Centre as a prelude to encirclement. In the north-west powerful mobile forces would break into the rear of German troops deployed against the Leningrad and Volkhov Fronts. The duel in the south, which lasted through the late winter, inflicted heavy loss on German forces, though the Germans successfully extricated themselves from the Caucasus. The prospect of amputating the entire southern wing of the German Army by closing off the Dnieper crossings was unbelievably dazzling but, at the height of the crisis, Field-Marshal Manstein acted to chop off the Soviet advance to the Dnieper, and so restore the situation between the Dnieper and the Donets and at Kharkov.

The Soviet command believed, mistakenly, that a German withdrawal behind the Dnieper was imminent, but the German movement involved was the prelude to a devastating counter-blow which saved Army Group South from destruction, breaking into Soviet armies, threatening encirclement and recapturing Kharkov.[35] In March came the thaw, the end of the Soviet winter offensive and a lull of some duration. The entire Soviet–German front from the Baltic to the Black Sea now appeared much foreshortened, its most prominent feature the massive Soviet salient jutting out westwards at Kursk.

Though declining to attend the Anglo-America Casablanca conference in January 1943, Stalin expressed his confidence that a Second Front would materialise in 1943. The Prime Minister intimated albeit somewhat delphicly that every effort was being made to implement a cross-Channel attack in August, but once again landing-craft were the problem. In his response on 16 February, Stalin expressed his disappointment at the delay in finishing the Tunisian campaign: 'instead of the Soviet Union being aided by diverting German forces from the Soviet–German front, what we get is relief for Hitler'. The Second Front should be opened before August or September. In no way relenting, Stalin repeated his view in his message to the Prime Minister on 15 March. Operation HUSKY, the invasion of Sicily, 'can by no means replace a second front in France ... the vagueness of your statements about the contemplated Anglo-American offensive across the Channel causes apprehension'.[36]

In the midst of these increasingly embittered exchanges, Stalin pored over plans which were to involve the Central and Voronezh Fronts in an attack towards Gomel and Kharkov respectively, to force the Dnieper and thus pave the way for the recapture of both the Donbas and Belorussia. But intelligence indicated formidable German concentrations on either side of the Kursk salient and in April the General Staff worked on new plans to deal with a potentially very dangerous situation.

Operation ZITADELLE, the German plan to eliminate the Kursk salient in a two-pronged attack, had been timed initially for March, with the ground hardening and Soviet forces disorganised after defeat at Kharkov. The Stavka was persuaded that the Red Army could strike first, indeed Stalin favoured a pre-emptive blow. But slowly, reluctantly, mindful of the disastrous outcome of the Red Army's defensive operations in 1941 and 1942, it nevertheless determined on a defensive battle at Kursk so as to absorb the German blow. Plans for the summer offensive envisaged a main thrust in a south-westerly direction to liberate the eastern Ukraine and the industrial regions of the Donbas, and a second attack to destroy Army Group Centre and liberate Belorussia. With offensive operations planned for the south-west there was an added incentive to concentrate in the Kursk region where ultimately 40 per cent of all Red Army rifle divisions and every existing Soviet tank army crammed into the salient.

In May the Prime Minister and President Roosevelt met in Washington to review military strategy with the conclusion of the Tunisian campaign. A cross-Channel attack was not ruled out but was contingent on a German collapse, which was deemed unlikely. A large-scale operation involving 29 divisions was agreed for 1944 and a provisional date of 1 May fixed. Stalin reacted predictably over the postponement, addressing himself now directly to President Roosevelt, stressing the 'exceptional difficulties' created by this decision (to which the Soviet Government was not a party). In his own message to Stalin on 24 June, Churchill stated bluntly that Stalin's reproaches upon his allies 'leave me unmoved'. The 'Mediterranean strategy' had fully vindicated itself, confusing the Germans and producing a delay in 'Hitler's third attack upon Russia'. The Prime Minister continued: 'It may even prove that you will not be heavily attacked this summer.'[37]

On 5 July 1943, massed Panzer forces opened the titanic battle of the Kursk salient, ZITADELLE, a huge armoured encounter with the salient under attack from the Ninth Army on the northern face and Fourth Panzer on the southern. After four days of heavy fighting Ninth Army was halted before yet another heavily fortified Soviet line. In the south on 12 July a highly dangerous situation developed at Prokhorovka, where 1800 Soviet and German tanks fought a stupendous battle, with heavy losses on both sides. The German attack from the west and the south had finally been held. Though Manstein sought more time to finish off Soviet armoured reserves, on 13 July Hitler decided to bring ZITADELLE to a halt, citing the threatening situation north of the salient, the threat to the Donets basin and the dangers to Italy and the Balkans presented by the Anglo-American landing in Sicily on 10 July.[38]

At a time of serious deterioration in the relationship between the Soviet Union and the western allies, in July and August 1943, defying German assumptions that Soviet forces in the south of the Kursk salient were too weakened to strike, a major Soviet attack unrolled against the Belgorod–Kharkov axis. The importance of Kharkov for the defence of the eastern Ukraine and the presence of strong armoured forces inevitably presaged a bitter struggle. In discussions for a proposed meeting between the three heads of state Stalin agreed on the necessity for such a meeting, but pleaded the impossibility of his 'leaving the front' (where, in fact, he never ever was throughout the war, save for one symbolic and heavily-guarded excursion).[39] He protested about the state of negotiations with Italy, demanding Soviet participation in a tripartite military-political commission. Most ominously, he broke off relations with the London-based Polish government-in-exile. And to add to his fury, convoy sailings to Russia had been suspended from March until further notice.

If Stalin's strategy was becoming militarily somewhat more realistic, it continued to be dangerously over-ambitious in its aims. His immediate objective was to hurl Soviet armies to the Dnieper on a broad front, part of a huge south-westerly sweep to destroy German forces in the Donbas and eastern Ukraine, as well as clearing the Taman peninsula and the northern Kuban. The relevant operational orders went out on the eve of the battle for Kharkov, which was liberated on the morning of 23 August 1943. Further north, the Western and Kalinin Fronts made final preparations for a further assault on Army Group Centre and the liberation of Smolensk. After hard and heavy fighting against powerful, well-organised German resistance, Smolensk fell on 25 September 1943, by which time more Soviet armies, driving over 150 miles westwards, had drawn up to the Dnieper and seized 23 bridgeheads ranging in depth from yards to miles on the western bank.

Early in October 1943, during the briefest lull, Stalin supervised plans to unleash an autumn storm designed to burst over both Kiev and Minsk, the regional capitals of the Ukraine and Belorussia. At the same time preparations went ahead for the meeting in Moscow of the Foreign Ministers of the three Allied governments, a precondition of the conference involving Stalin, Roosevelt and Churchill. The atmosphere was somewhat improved with the Prime Minister's message about the resumption of convoys, correcting what Stalin had called 'that catastrophic diminution in supplies'. He told Admiral Golovko commanding the Northern Fleet to be ready: 'No matter how the allies might delay – Churchill especially – they will have to resume the convoys.'

Molotov's letter of 29 September 1943, to the British Ambassador in Moscow concerning the agenda for the forthcoming Foreign Minister's conference, left no doubt about Stalin's strategic priorities, with 'measures for shortening the war against Germany and her allies in Europe' taking pride of place, amplified in the text as 'the decisive shortening of the war', with a cross-Channel attack in the west and Red Army offensives in the east. The Soviet autumn offensive was itself designed as a 'war-shortening' operation, as were

Soviet proposals for the entry of Turkey into the war on the Allied side and the use of Swedish air bases to intensify the air offensive against Germany. Neither of these suggestions aroused any great enthusiasm on the part of the British and Americans.[40]

Given the strained atmosphere, the Moscow conference of Foreign Ministers in the second half of October 1943 could be counted a success. Stalin and Molotov had an extensive exchange with Eden, General Ismay and the British Ambassador on 27 October,[41] at which Stalin asked whether the cross-Channel landing might have to be postponed. He took it that there would be a postponement of two months. Eden could give no authoritative reply and turned to General Ismay who also explained that he had no 'definite reply' lacking further information about the situation in Italy. Stalin expressed his satisfaction with the conference; Molotov still queried what had been done to accomplish 'war-shortening', to which Stalin retorted that 'we [the Russians] are not pedants. We will not demand what our allies are not in a position to do.'[42]

In oblique but unmistakable terms, Stalin had signalled that he intended to soldier on with the coalition. At the end of the conference he informed Cordell Hull that not only was the Soviet Union bent on the destruction of Nazi Germany but that there would be Soviet participation in the war against Japan. Stalin thus implanted himself into the heart of the coalition. He now had an undoubted commitment to OVERLORD even if the date hovered between spring or summer. Supply convoys were once more at sea. Red Army successes since Kursk had been on an impressive scale, this time recovering territory and also in cracking the structure of Germany's Eastern front. In October, Stalin had argued that the great dispersal of German forces was the core of his 'war-shortening' strategy. It was nonetheless a strategy which combined an almost reckless offensivism with costly attrition.

As the conference of the heads of government met in Teheran, the Soviet General Staff worked on operation schedules and attack timetables (*plan operatsii*) for the winter offensive which envisaged four main actions: the destruction of German forces in the Leningrad area, in Belorussia, the western Ukraine and the Crimea, with the Red Army's main striking forces deployed on the outer flanks aimed at Army Group North and Army Groups South and in the Ukraine. The decisive attack would unroll in the southwestern theatre to recover vital resources and to bring the Red Army most speedily to the 1941 frontiers of the Soviet Union.

At the beginning of December 1943, Stalin left the Tehran Conference well pleased. 'Operation OVERLORD is planned for May, 1944 and will be conducted with the support of a landing in southern France . . .'. Western strategic policy had been reshaped, shifted from a Mediterranean focus to one engaged principally with Western Europe, the former a British preoccupation, the latter the principal American concern. In a final, forlorn attempt to save his strategic vision, the Prime Minister attempted to emphasise the importance of the Italian campaign and what might be achieved eastward, in Yugoslavia and in the Aegean, but Stalin had ceased to show any real interest in eastern Mediterranean adventures.[43] Stalin could with some degree of certainty foresee, provided that the undertakings governing OVERLORD were finally met after so much equivocation, the Red Army playing a dominant role in both the Balkans and in Poland. Sensibly and shrewdly he put his full weight behind OVERLORD, promising his own contribution: the launch of a Red Army offensive 'by May' thus preventing the movement of German reserves westwards. A measure of Stalin's gratification over the assurance he had received at Tehran showed in the enthusiastic, even exuberant, orchestrated Soviet press reaction.

With the Tehran conference behind him, Stalin convened a council of war with the Stavka, at which the agenda was dominated by a wide-ranging review of the strategic position of the Soviet Union, with detailed reports on the fronts and possible operational developments prepared on Stalin's orders by the Chief of the General Staff, Marshal Vasilevsky and the First Deputy, Chief General A. I. Antonov. The main conclusion which emerged from these deliberations was that the Soviet Union now enjoyed military–economic superiority over the enemy and that this superiority would determine the further course of the war. Superiority in manpower and matériel, possession of the strategic initiative, the availability of powerful reserves of manpower and weaponry not only offered fresh operational possibilities but also a wholly different way of resolving strategic tasks.

Though no written record of this meeting was taken, after a review of where the Red Army should concentrate and where it should strike, ten areas were identified in which the enemy was marked down for destruction. Stalin ordered the General Staff to prepare further plans and calculations for these ten strategic operations.[44] The immediate political and strategic objective was to clear the remaining one-third of Soviet territory of German forces, which demanded that the German Army be deprived of any opportunity to shift to positional warfare. Unlike the previous pattern of simultaneous offensives, the General Staff now proposed a series of powerful consecutive operations, the 'ten decisive blows' of 1944, prescribed in the General Staff operational schedules dated 8 December 1943. The offensive in Belorussia occupied pride of place as *the* decisive operation.

The immediate operational situation disclosed four 'clearly definable concentrations' of German forces in the area of Leningrad, in the Ukraine west of the Dnieper, in the Crimea and in Belorussia. In pursuit of a strategy of 'dispersal', breaking up German forces, the Soviet General Staff proposed to rip open the German defence which the enemy could only seal by moving forces from other sectors, given the absence of operational formations as reserves, with the German command relying largely on corps and Panzer divisions. In order to 'disperse' German concentrations, the General Staff envisaged launching alternate blows at widely-separated points, requiring the enemy to shift forces from one sector to another, even to the outer flanks and thus eventually losing these assets. To succeed with this strategy it was necessary for the Red Army to build up superior forces with 'shock power' provided by yet more armour, artillery and aircraft supported by massive reserves. Rapid build-up of decisive superiority on selected sectors was also the key to maximising surprise.

The forthcoming strategic offensive was designed to unroll 'without pause' against the four main German concentrations. The main offensive would develop in the south-west, in the Ukraine west of the Dnieper, with the object of splitting and destroying the entire German southern wing where almost half the strength of the German Army on the Eastern Front was deployed with just under three-quarters of the available armour. Four Soviet Fronts (1st, 2nd, 3rd and 4th Ukrainian) were committed to operations designed to unfold in two stages: the first to eliminate German resistance on the Dnieper and advance the Red Army to the line of the southern Bug, the second to shatter the German 'strategic grouping' by destroying individual German armies and reaching the Dniester. The total effect would be the destruction of Army Group South between the rivers Dnieper and Dniester. Meanwhile General Tolbukhin's 4th Ukrainian Front would prepare to recapture the Crimea.[45]

The second great drive on the flanks was planned for the north-western theatre, involving three Fronts (2nd Baltic, Leningrad and Volkov) and designed to destroy Army Group North, completely lifting the inhumanly dreadful 900-day siege of Leningrad and clearing both the Leningrad and Kalinin *oblasts*. A further Soviet advance would bring the Red Army to the Pskov–Narva line and a favourable position for a thrust into the Baltic republics. Operations in this theatre had the definite purpose of meeting 'political requirements', namely, influencing the Finns towards withdrawing their allegiance to Germany.

The Western and 1st Baltic Fronts received orders to destroy German forces in the Orsha–Vitebsk area, with Bobruisk assigned to General Rokossovsky as his immediate objective, his terminal point being Minsk. But the Stavka had assigned this western theatre an enormous task, nothing less than an advance of some 100 miles to reach the Polotsk–Minsk line, all without substantial reinforcement. Throughout the spring only 20 per cent of infantry reinforcement, 25 per cent of artillery and a derisory 4 per cent of available armour went to these fronts, disastrously unbalancing objectives and actual capabilities. The bulk of the Red Army's available striking power went to the outer flanks. Formations already drawn into reserve, five rifle armies, two tank armies and nine tank corps, were earmarked for operations in the north or in the south.

The strategic plan took close account of political as well as military objectives. Success in the south offered enormous gains, the complete restoration of the Ukrainian political unit to Soviet power, the recovery of the metallurgical resources of Krivoi Rog, the grain lands, the Black Sea ports and even more dazzling, the reconquest of the western Ukraine, enabling the Red Army to strike through Romania, into the Balkans, and on to Poland, into the flank and rear of Army Group Centre.

The Red Army concentrated in the south no less than 169 rifle divisions and 90 cavalry divisions (with varying divisional strength, some as low as 2500) supported by 2000 tanks and 2360 aircraft. Soviet intelligence estimated German strength in the south, including both Army Groups, at 103 divisions, with 93 divisions including 18 Panzer and four motorised divisions in the western Ukraine. A major encirclement operation launched on 5 January 1944 was designed to trap First Panzer and Eighth Army and open the route to Romania. By the end of the month two German corps had been snared, though instead of sweeping westwards through the huge gap torn in the German lines Soviet forces fought to reduce this 'pocket' at Korsun. On the day of the final battle, on 18 February 1944, Stalin signed a directive for fresh offensive operations timed for early March, committing all six Soviet tank armies in the Ukraine. Gone at last were the days of flinging 'penny packets' of the Red Army against the whole length of the Soviet–German front. Now substantial Soviet superiority was aimed at completely destroying Army Group South.[46]

German military intelligence, Foreign Armies East (Fremde Heere Ost) accurately predicted the grand Soviet design, a pincer movement devised to encircle two Panzer armies, First and Fourth, with the 1st Ukrainian Front attacking in the direction of Poland and then striking south to the Dniester, the 2nd Ukrainian Front moving towards Romania, a huge blow intended to split the German southern front in two. The result would be to press one part of the German front into Galicia and southern Poland with the other rammed back into Moldavia and against the Danube. On 4 March 1944, Marshal Zhukov, in command of 1st Ukrainian Front, attacked, cutting Fourth Panzer in half and breaking through a 100-mile front. He planned to sweep south to the Dniester, striking deep into the German front to isolate First Panzer and cut the remaining German communications between their forces in Poland and those in southern Russia. The 2nd Ukrainian Front, already on the Dniester, swung northwards to encircle the 22 divisions of First Panzer. The German Sixth Army had already been sliced away from the Army Group and Fourth Panzer and Eighth Army were badly battered. The entire German front to the south of the Carpathians faced imminent collapse. Six Soviet armies were closing the trap on First Panzer, preparing to block the German break-out to the south, across the Dniester and into Romania. But First Panzer, though badly mauled, unexpectedly escaped to the west.[47]

With the Red Army closing on Poland, the 'Polish question' had already embittered the exchanges in March between Churchill and Stalin. Stalin made it plain that he would have no dealings with the 'Polish emigré government': 'men of that type are incapable of establishing normal relations with the USSR'. In his message of 24 March 1944, he lashed out at both the London Poles and the Prime Minister. He refused to consider that 'the problem of the Soviet–Polish frontier' be postponed until an armistice or the peace conferences. The implementation of the 'Curzon line' was nothing more than the re-establishment of the Soviet Union's 'legitimate right' to the territories in question. The Prime Minister's references to *'forcible* transferences of territory' which he opposed and would say as much in the House of Commons, was interpreted by Stalin as a 'gratuitous insult', 'an unjust and unfriendly act in relation to the Soviet Union'.[48]

The offensive on the northern flank opened on 14 January 1944, the final operational plan *NEVA-2* aiming the main attack against the Eighteenth Army, whose position Soviet intelligence considered to verge on the disastrous in the absence of operational reserves. The prize was Luga, the vital junction in the German rear. Once in Soviet hands the German escape route to the south-west would be sealed off. The planned encirclement, however, failed to materialise and by the end of January Eighteenth Army was fighting its way out of the trap. Stalin promised more men and more tanks but the price was the capture of Luga. Skilful German rearguard actions covered the German withdrawal to the south and south-west and with the help of 12th Panzer Division from Army Group Centre the Luga–Pskov road and the rail-link remained in German hands. Luga finally fell on 12 February by which time German units were falling back to Pskov and the south-west.

The Stavka now demanded the capture of Narva for 'military and political reasons' but this proved to be beyond Soviet capabilities. The Soviet winter offensive in the north had nevertheless achieved its immediate objectives, the elimination of the German Eighteenth Army south of Lake Ladoga and in the eastern sector of the Gulf of Finland. Leningrad was finally freed of blockade and the Red Army was across the Estonian frontier. The entire left flank of Army Group North had disintegrated and the German hold on the northern theatre was substantially, if not fatally, weakened. Finland saw the danger-signs, taking careful sounding of the Soviet attitude in Stockholm.[49]

At the end of March and the beginning of April 1944, the Stavka and the General Staff could look back with some satisfaction at the results of the winter offensive, in particular the damage inflicted on the German southern wing, though elsewhere expectations had been only partially fulfilled. There had been no breakthrough into the Baltic states. After a brief and promising start, operations in the 'western theatre' had dragged to a halt, cause for an investigation by the State Defence Committee into this 'organisational failure'.

Major-General Gehlen, head of Fremde Heere Ost, on 30 March 1944, submitted a gloomy appreciation of Soviet strategic intentions. The Red Army would press through the Balkans, into the *Generalgouvernement* (occupied Poland) and into the Baltic states, closing 'on the eastern frontiers of the Reich'. Now that the southern zone had virtually ceased to exist as a strategic entity, there could be 'no doubt' that Soviet armies would strike in great strength through the huge gap ripped in the German front between the Dnieper and the Pripet, an attack which would materialise before the Germans could build a defensive front.[50]

The General Staff embarked on its systematic survey of every Soviet Front, starting with Karelia in the north. The damage inflicted on the German southern wing amounted to some 1 000 000 casualties of the German and German-allied armies. Four German armies in the south, with a fifth in the Crimea, faced annihilation. Two Army Groups, North and South, had been shattered, three Panzer armies badly damaged, leaving only one (Third Panzer in Army Group Centre) so far largely unscathed. Ten German armies showed in the eastern order of battle as opposed to 13 at the end of 1943, with only one Panzer army standing ready and one being refitted in Galicia. A Hungarian army had reappeared but, with the unity of the southern theatre irreparably shattered, the German command faced virtually unmanageable problems. The Red Army's thrust into the Bukovina had meanwhile isolated Galicia from the 'Romanian zone', communication between them maintained only through Hungary.

The Soviet–German front still ran for some 2000 miles and was presently marked by two huge salients, one German and one Soviet. North of the Pripet marshes Army Group Centre was entrenched in Belorussia and anchored at Minsk, this salient jutting deep into the Soviet lines. Farther south of the Pripet, Soviet armies were jammed far into the German southern flank where the Red Army deployed 40 per cent of its infantry armies and 80 per cent of its available armour. Only one-third of Soviet strength was engaged on the 'central sector' to the north of the Pripet marshes. Most reluctantly Stalin agreed to move on to the defensive. Orders were deliberately delayed to the south-western and south-eastern commands as the winter offensive closed. A special briefing ordered by Stalin reviewed preparations for the final reduction of the German redoubt in the Crimea.

As General Tolbukhin began cutting through the Crimea, the main Soviet strategic plan for summer operations was finalised. Previous offensive plans had suffered from defective coordination of several fronts and from the failure to set specific objectives. The General Staff, therefore, carried out its own study of the Soviet–German front and Soviet strategic entities in particular. The north-western theatre looked unpromising, a 'main blow' here or even further north yielding little but knocking Finland out of the war, hardly a mortal blow for Germany. North of the Pripet marshes, in the great Belorussian salient, German forces not only covered the approaches to Warsaw but were also positioned to mount flank attacks against those Soviet armies closing for an assault on East Prussia as well as threatening the flank and the rear of Soviet armies operating along the 'south-western axis'. This could endanger a Soviet drive on Lvov or a thrust into Hungary.

After uninterrupted offensive operations the Soviet forces to the south were in urgent need of regrouping and reinforcement. The destruction of Army Group Centre clearly loomed up as the logical and desirable strategic objective. Whether it was feasible was another matter. The record of Soviet success in the 'western theatre' did not encourage optimism. Too often grim losses and utter failure had been the result of attempts to pull down the 'Belorussian balcony' and shatter Army Group Centre. On 12 April 1944, the all-powerful State Defence Committee ended its investigation of the Western Front, listing 'subjective and objective' failures. The long-established, war-weary Western Front should be split into two new Fronts, 2nd and 3rd Belorussian, a solution which had already been recommended by the General Staff, and given substantial reinforcement. Previous attacks aimed separately at Vitebsk, Orsha and Mogilev had simply dissipated the available offensive power.

By mid-April General Antonov at the Soviet General Staff had completed an outline plan for the Red Army's 1944 summer offensive, having already been informed of 'R' date, the cross-Channel attack. At the end of March General Deane, head of the United States Military Mission in Moscow, proposed informing the Russians of the 'target date' for OVERLORD in order to facilitate Soviet planning in line with the decisions taken at Teheran. An approach could be made to the Soviet General Staff to facilitate their own planning for coordination with the 'sea-crossing' in the west. To this end a Soviet officer could be attached to General Eisenhower's staff. On 3 April 1944, the British Chiefs of Staff, whose anti-Sovietism had become a matter of comment,[51] ruled out any direct approach to the Russians about their future plans on the grounds that the Soviet General Staff could not possibly know what the future would hold in two months' time, given a highly fluid situation. They also rejected that any Soviet officer be attached to the Supreme Allied Commander.

Both the American and British Military Missions were authorised to disclose 'R' date in Moscow, the timing subject to the variation of 'two or three days, one way or the other'.[52] On 10 April 1944, Marshal Vasilevsky, Chief of the Soviet General Staff, was duly informed of the 'sea-crossing' timed for 31 May, acknowledged by Stalin in his message of 22 April 1944, to the Prime Minister and President Roosevelt and confirming that 'the Red Army will launch a new offensive at the same time so as to give maximum support to the Anglo-American operations', as agreed at Tehran.[53]

To an unprecedented degree, deception (*maskirovka*) at all levels, strategic, operational and tactical, was built into Soviet planning, with the Soviet command intent on persuading the Germans that the summer offensive would unroll with even greater force on the flanks, in the Baltic and in the south. By way of strategic deception, to which plausibility was added by the far-reaching Soviet successes in the south-west, the impression was strengthened by conspicuous deployment and further limited attacks that the Red Army would strike into southern Poland and Romania. An attack across the river Prut aimed at Jassy in May by Marshal Koniev's 1st Ukrainian Front only confirmed German fears that Romania was a major Soviet objective, requiring the concentration of major reserves. Further 'confirmation' came with the weight of BODYGUARD rumours, the inter-Allied plan for deception and disinformation designed to protect OVERLORD, to the effect that Soviet and American naval planners were studying a landing operation on the Romanian coast.[54] In the event this proved to be a 'double feint' for while the 'build-up' in the south did not herald a major offensive, the additional Soviet strength, carefully rationed, reinforced the offensive which finally materialised in July.

The massive regrouping and giant redeployment to the north, involving five rifle armies, two tank armies, an air army and eleven corps, 3000 tanks and almost half a million men, demanded a vast concealment engineered by mixing simulated and genuine movement southwards as prescribed by General Staff Directive No. 220110 dated 29 May, signed by Zhukov and Antonov.[55] For the moment the tank armies, the constant object of German observation, remained in position in the south-west.

Timing also played a key role in the overall deception plan. The General Staff plan for the summer offensive involved five to six Fronts in operations extending from Idritsa in the north to Chernovtsy in the south. The Leningrad Front would open the offensive in June with an attack aimed at Vyborg, with Karelian Front operations designed to eliminate Finland from the war. The main attack, the Belorussian offensive, was designed to destroy Army Group Centre.

With the German command convinced that this was indeed the main blow, German reserves would almost certainly be moved from the south, whereupon the 1st Ukrainian Front would unleash a major offensive along the 'Lvov axis'. To restrain Army Group North from rendering any aid to its neighbour Army Group Centre, 2nd Baltic Front was poised to attack. If success attended all these operations Soviet offensive operations could be developed southwards into Romania, Bulgaria and Yugoslavia, even Hungary, Austria and Czechoslovakia.

Further deception was designed to persuade the German command that the Russians would be unable 'to launch their offensive before the end of June'. Russian 'reports' hinted at a joint Allied attack on northern Norway to open a supply route to Sweden and 'concentrations' indicated an attack on Petsamo. Absolute radio silence in the south was yet another indicator of an impending major assault.

Stalin held an intensive two-day battle conference between 22–23 May to review final preparations for Operation BAGRATION, the code-name for the Belorussian attack. The subsequent amendments to the operational plan were finally agreed and incorporated by 27 May, with operational directives (Nos 220112–220115) scrutinised on 31 May by Stalin, Zhukov, Vasilevsky and Antonov and transmitted to Front commands under the signatures of Stalin and Zhukov. The strategic objective was the elimination of the German salient in the area Vitebsk–Bobruisk–Minsk, crushing the German flanks and breaking the defensive front with concentric attacks aimed at Minsk. Simultaneous blows on the flanks to the rear of Vitebsk and Bobruisk plus the destruction of German forces at Mogilev would open the road to Minsk. West of Minsk, the Red Army would sever the German escape route, trapping Army Group Centre.[56] The 'Stavka coordinators' for BAGRATION, the marshals Zhukov and Vasilevsky, demanded that a 'significant element' of German strength must be destroyed in the actual breakthrough operation, requiring heavy-calibre guns and massed air-assault. The difficult terrain, with bogs and thick forest, could hamper the establishment of a firm encirclement front. Nor was the lie of the land ideal tank country but 5th Guards Tank Army was assigned to BAGRATION to furnish mobile forces operating independently as tank corps, brigades and regiments. The May conference finally determined on 15–20 June as the probable timing of the Belorussian attack.

Informed of the launch of the cross-Channel attack on 6 June 1944, Stalin responded by promising a Soviet offensive 'for mid-June on one of the vital sectors of the front', offensive operations developing in stages and turning into a general offensive 'between late June and the end of July'. Three days later he lifted the dense veil of secrecy enough to inform the Prime Minister that 'tomorrow June 10 we begin the first round on the Leningrad Front',[57] at a time when German intelligence clung grimly to the belief that the main Soviet attack must fall in Galicia against Army Group North Ukraine, to which German reserves were increasingly directed.

Army Group Centre, thought to be the target of mere diversionary attacks, held one division in reserve with Fourth Army and one with Third Panzer. A rapid build-up against Army Group Centre was admitted as a possibility, but Galicia seemed to be the most likely Soviet objective. The German High Command expected the Red Army's offensive to unroll in the south once American and British forces in France had driven to some depth from their coastal bridgeheads.

The Red Army's 'first round', the Svir–Petrozavodsk operation, was launched in the wake of the breakdown of the first serious Soviet–Finnish peace probe and the rejection of a Soviet 'peace offer'. Now almost half a million men, 41 rifle divisions with over 800 tanks poured over the Finns, fighting across the bloody battleground of the 'Winter War' of 1939–40. Far to the south Marshal Koniev, on Stalin's instructions, worked on plans to split Army

Group North Ukraine, to force one part back into Polesia, the other back to the Carpathians, bringing 1st Ukrainian Front up to the Vistula.[58] Simultaneously Front commanders for Operation BAGRATION had received final directives specifying lines of advance, objectives and forces to be committed, total Red Army strength amounting to 14 all-arms armies, 166 rifle divisions, eight tank or mechanised corps, 2715 tanks, 24 000 guns and four air armies with 5327 aircraft. Three years to the day after Operation BARBAROSSA launched the German invasion of the Soviet Union, on 22 June 1944 the 1st Baltic Front in the north opened the first phase of the staggered Soviet attack on Army Group Centre. Within 48 hours the three Belorussian Fronts (1st, 2nd and 3rd) launched their divisions, with a small time-differential but designed to mislead the German command over the actual scale of the attacks.

After one week of BAGRATION, Vitebsk, Orsha, Mogilev and Bobruisk had fallen, the situation of Third Panzer and Fourth Army and that of Ninth Army was catastrophic. The German defensive system was in ruins and the capture of Minsk on 3 July finally trapped Fourth Army.[59] The Red Army had torn a 250-mile gap in the German front; 25–28 German divisions had been obliterated, 350 000 men in all, leaving Army Group Centre with eight divisions.

The route to Lithuania and Poland lay wide-open. The ruination of Army Group Centre sent a shock wave across the entire Eastern Front. The Red Army could now ram the German centre back as far as the Vistula and the frontier with East Prussia. German forces in the Baltic states faced amputation from the main body, while the remaining German strongholds in the south-western theatre were about to face a new storm. This was the sequence in which the Soviet high command set about its strategic tasks in the summer of 1944. To 'disperse' more of the German fronts, Marshal Koniev launched 1st Ukrainian Front, the most powerful single entity in the Red Army, in a huge offensive aimed at Army Group North Ukraine holding a front running from the Pripet to the Carpathians, covering the approaches to southern Poland, Czechoslovakia and even Silesia with its industrial resources.

Koniev's attack split Army Group North Ukraine in two. Fourth Panzer fell back on the Vistula, First Panzer moved south-west to the Carpathians. At the end of July the Stavka placed Soviet armies in the foothills of the Carpathians under the independent command of 4th Ukrainian Front, with orders to seize the eastern Carpathians before debouching into the Hungarian plains. In the Baltic states Stavka orders demanded an offensive aimed at Kaunas to isolate Army Group North and to protect Soviet armies closing on Warsaw. A hasty Soviet drive on Riga was brought to a halt. Only half of Baltic territory had been taken from Army Group North but a German withdrawal from Estonia and Latvia could not be long delayed.

What Soviet strategy and Red Army exertions had achieved with the defeat of Army Group Centre facilitated the seizure of vital bridgeheads on the eastern bank of the Vistula and an advance to the outskirts of Warsaw, pushing the Red Army some 350 miles along 'the road to Berlin', only 400 miles by the shortest line of advance. Of the 70 German divisions facing the three Soviet Belorussian Fronts and 1st Baltic Front, 30 had been wiped off the order of battle, with 30 more trapped in the Soviet drive to the Vistula. However, the 47 divisions of Army Group North, covering East Prussia from the north-west, still remained to be reduced.

At the end of June, during an exchange with Ambassador Harriman, Stalin suggested in sudden and surprising fashion that a combined military staff be set up. Regarded by the Combined Chiefs of Staff as a 'tentative' suggestion on Stalin's part, the idea was examined throughout July and August. The Joint Planning Staff, on 10 August 1944, submitted that machinery was needed to coordinate the Allied war effort against Germany, the required coordination falling under three heads, 'broad political–military policies' (the province of heads of state), 'strategic direction' (handled by the Military Missions) and day-to-day coordination, as well as questions related to post-hostilities occupation policies.[60] Such a mechanism might also serve as a model in the event of Soviet entry into the war with Japan.

The British Chiefs of Staff at the end of August proposed a tripartite military committee, its functions consultative only and devoid of any power of decision. Its activity was not to impinge in any way on the European Advisory Commission. Late in September, Stalin was informed about this 'committee', a term he disliked with its implication of powers of decision, preferring rather 'commission'. The heads of the American and British Military Missions would be represented on this Commission, but Stalin refused to accept Lieutenant-General Burrows as the British representative. General Burrows was withdrawn from Moscow, Admiral Archer assigned as acting chief of the British Mission, but the idea of a 'consultative commission' dwindled and finally expired at Yalta in February 1945.[61] Even as Stalin was toying with the idea of such a Commission, he was also rumoured to have sounded out his senior commanders as to 'whether we [the Soviet Union] can now win this war by ourselves'.

Stalin and the General Staff were now studying the 'direct thrust', offensive operations aimed at Berlin through Warsaw, which had to be weighed against the need to destroy powerful German forces in the north-western and south-western theatres. Successive offensives had been aimed at three German Army Groups (North, Centre, North Ukraine). It was now the turn of the fourth, Army Group South Ukraine, to come under attack.

The Stavka issued orders for the attack on Romania on 2 August 1944. Two German armies, the Sixth and the Eighth, were sandwiched between the Russians waiting to attack them and the Romanians scrambling to betray them. The Jassy–Kishinev operation brought the rapid encirclement of German forces in Romania, Romania's defection from Germany and with it the dis-integration of Germany's southern flank resting on the Black Sea.[62] The Romanian defection pulled down the entire German defensive structure in south-eastern Europe. Ahead of General Malinovsky's 2nd Ukrainian Front lay Hungary, Soviet advances given a fresh military–political dimension through 'military cooperation with liberated countries'.[63]

But for political and national foes such as the 'London Poles', even in armed revolt against the Germans, no help was forthcoming. At the beginning of August Soviet lead armour on the eastern bank of the Vistula had suffered heavily from a strong German counter-attack. All Soviet units were ordered to go on to the defensive. Thus it was that the Warsaw rising, denounced by Stalin as a 'reckless and fearful gamble', found the Red Army immobile, though not from callous calculation as many suspected at the time. But while the Germans mercilessly bludgeoned the Polish rising, Stalin was as unmoved as he was unresponsive over the question of providing a measure of aid to the Polish insurgents.[64]

Belated signs of Soviet cooperation to furnish aid to Warsaw came too late to affect in any way a bloody and tragic outcome. The strain placed on Anglo-Soviet relations, embodied in the rasping exchanges between Churchill and Stalin, was exacerbated by the implications of the Red Army's closing on east-central Europe and the Balkans, prompting the Prime Minister within days of the gruesome surrender at Warsaw to make a second journey to Moscow for consultations with Stalin. The result, in so far as a scrap of paper counted, was an agreement covering Romania, Greece, Yugoslavia, Hungary and Bulgaria, concerning respective British and Soviet 'spheres of influence'.[65]

Stalin could make approving marks on bits of paper and have Molotov haggle with Eden over percentages, confident that the Red Army was, or soon would be, actually on the ground in question and the real arbiter of who controlled what. During the Moscow meeting, Stalin had evidently shown little reticence over what the Red Army had done and could do, in an atmosphere enlivened by the possibility of the war ending before the year was out. Already Anglo-American forces had crossed the frontier of the Reich in early September, though the failure of the Arnhem airborne operation as a 'war-shortening' measure signalled further German resistance. The hint was not lost on Stalin.

On 28 October 1944, the Soviet General Staff pored over maps and detailed calculations in planning a gigantic strategic operation. The strategic 'balance sheet' looked promising enough to give the Red Army a headstart in the 'race for Berlin'. All four German Army Groups had suffered drastic losses with 96 divisions and 24 brigades destroyed, 219 divisions severely mauled, all with the loss of one-and-a-half million men, 6700 tanks, 28 000 guns and over 12 000 aircraft. With the exception of Courland, the 1941

Soviet frontiers were everywhere restored.[66] The 'decisive zone of opera-tions', defined as the shortest direct route into Germany, lay between the river Niemen and the Carpathians but the present configuration of Soviet Fronts placed considerable strength to the north. The surrender of Finland and the reduction of the Baltic states released several armies to the 'Niemen–Carpathians concentration', but of the four Fronts deployed along the 'shortest route', two (3rd and 2nd Belorussian) faced the formidable barrier of East Prussia. Redeployment and reinforcement would provide only partial solu-tions. The whole strategic balance of the Eastern Front had now to be re-viewed by General Staff planners.

A thrust straight through East Prussia seemed the obvious solution, where 3rd Belorussian Front outnumbered the enemy, but this superiority was more apparent than real. Operations along the 'Warsaw–Poznan axis' and the 'Silesian axis' where the 'battle for Berlin' would be decided, meant encountering heavy German resistance, with the result that 1st Belorussian and 1st Ukrainian Fronts would advance 100 miles at the most. A radical alternative would be to select the 'southern solution' using the three Ukrainian Fronts in a deep penetration aimed at the Reich, sweeping through Budapest, Bratislava and Vienna. But in mid-October the German Army had imposed a tight grip on Hungary and the battle for Budapest had only just begun and promised to be both protracted and gruelling.[67]

In late October 1944, the Red Army in the east and Allied armies in the west stood roughly equidistant from Berlin. In the west, 74 German divi-sions, supported by 1600 tanks, faced 87 allied divisions and 6000 tanks; in the east, where the German Army was keeping the bulk of its strength, a defending force of some three million men and 4000 tanks sought to hold off a Soviet attacking force of more than double that size. If the Red Army was to win the race to Berlin, the Soviet General Staff concluded, it would need to take the most direct route, which meant attacking along the central sector where it would encounter the stiffest German resistance. In order to draw off some of this resistance and so hasten the process there would need to be maximum effort on the flanks involving Hungary, Austria and East Prussia, a powerful thrust into Budapest and on to Vienna, all designed to drain German strength. For the 'main task', smashing the German strategic front, 1st Belorussian and 1st Ukrainian Fronts were selected and provided with massive armoured reinforcement.

The General Staff plan, drafted in November 1944, submitted that the German war machine could be smashed within 45 days by offensives reach-ing to a depth of 373–440 miles in a two-stage operation without 'opera-tional pauses'.[68] The first stage would require 15 days, the second 30. In the final offensive the former 'southern axis' would take the initial shock, forc-ing the German command to move troops from the 'central sector'. Soviet planners were confident that Soviet armies on the lower reaches of the Vistula could reach Bromberg and capture Poznan, thus bringing them to a line running from Breslau to the Elbe. Further south the Red Army would be closing on Vienna. The Red Army would be thus advanced 220 miles from the positions held in October 1944. Once on these lines, the second stage would open leading to the capitulation of the Reich.[69]

The Soviet strategic plan involved simultaneous offensives by multiple Fronts along the 'Berlin axis' with the object of ripping apart the enemy front, destroying communications and breaking down coordination between German concentrations. The bulk of German strength was to be destroyed in the first phase and the main effort would be made along the 'Warsaw–Berlin axis', with the major role assigned to Marshal Zhukov's 1st Belorussian Front. Further south, Marshal Koniev's 1st Ukrainian Front was assigned Breslau as its immediate objective, since the Silesian industrial region lay astride its line of advance.

For this final massive irruption into Germany, Stalin appointed himself 'Stavka coordinator' for all Fronts. The strength of the Red Army had now risen to more than six-and-a-half million men, 100 000 guns and mortars, 13 000 tanks and over 15 000 aircraft, 55 'all-arms' armies, six tank armies and 13 air armies, and no less than 500 rifle divisions. No date had been fixed for the opening of the Soviet offensive but Stalin let it be known that it should be within the period 10–15 January 1945. During the first week in January the military situation in the western European theatre had an immediate effect on Soviet preparations to attack in the east. Amidst a sordid and increasingly intemperate wrangle over the Polish question, with Stalin lamenting that he had been unable to persuade the Prime Minister of the 'correctness of the Soviet Government's stand', Churchill on 6 January enquired as to 'whether we can count on a major Russian offensive on the Vistula front or elsewhere . . .' in order to relieve the pressure on the allied armies in the west presently bludgeoned by the German offensive launched from the Ardennes.[70] Stalin replied the following day promising that preparations would proceed 'at a rapid rate' for offensive operations timed for not later than the second half of January.

The German Army in the west had already shot its bolt by the time the Red Army attacked in the east. Koniev attacked on 12 January, Zhukov two days later. Within 100 hours a huge Soviet breakthrough had ripped across some 350 miles of the German front, staving in the German defensive system. At the beginning of February 1945, two of Zhukov's armies were on the Oder, with bridgeheads a mere 37 miles from Berlin. But there was no 'dash for Berlin'.[71] The Soviet timetable was derailed at this juncture by heavy fighting in East Prussia, the threat to Zhukov's right flank and severe logistical problems. The Red Army had outrun its resources. Here military realities and political circumstances played into Stalin's hands. A rapid occupation of Berlin could have prejudiced, if not wrecked, the political settlement taking shape at Yalta in which the Soviet Union came off handsomely in the proposed post-hostilities arrangement for Germany. Meanwhile the General Staff wrestled with the problem presented by Stalin's order that two Fronts, 1st Ukrainian and 1st Belorussian, should launch the assault on Berlin but that only Zhukov's 1st Belorussian Front would actually capture the German capital.

General Eisenhower's telegram to Stalin on 28 March 1945 intimated that after destroying German forces in the Ruhr, the main Allied thrust would be southwards in the direction of Erfurt–Leipzig–Dresden, thus splitting the German defence, once a junction with the Red Army had been effected. Stalin responded on 1 April, confirming his agreement for a junction in this area, to which the Red Army would not direct its major attack, Berlin having 'lost its former strategic importance'. That same day Stalin summoned a command conference to finalise plans for an all-out assault on Berlin to be launched *no later* than 16 April and to be concluded within 12–15 days. The race to Berlin was now all but run in the Red Army's favour. It remained but to forestall the Allies in Prague. Berlin surrendered on 2 May 1945. By 8 May three Soviet Fronts had closed on Prague, barring the way to the west and trapping what remained of Army Group Centre.[72]

At Tehran in 1943, Stalin had committed the Soviet Union to undertaking 'armed action against imperialist Japan' but only after the defeat of Germany. That time had now come. Since early in 1944 the Soviet General Staff had been engaged on preliminary operational planning, material Stalin used in his exchanges with the Prime Minister in Moscow in October. On that occasion a period of 'approximately three months' after the German surrender was mentioned, conditional upon allied deliveries of fuel, food and transport to Soviet Far Eastern ports.

At the Yalta conference in February 1945, the formal affirmation of Stalin's pledge was accompanied by the satisfaction of Stalin's principal war-aims, namely, the restoration of Russian rights 'violated' by the Japanese in 1904, the renewal of the lease on Port Arthur, the return of south Sakhalin and the transfer of the Kurile Islands to the Soviet Union.[73] With massive reinforcement already moving into the Soviet Far East, on 5 April 1945, the Soviet Union summarily denounced the Treaty of Neutrality and Non-aggression with Japan, much to the latter's consternation.

The Soviet General Staff operational plan involved the tightest timetable of no more than 20–23 days in which to accomplish the main strategic objective, the destruction of the Japanese Kwantung Army. At the time of the German surrender, Red Army strength in the Far East did not exceed 40 divisions. In little more than two months that strength stood at 11 'all-arms' armies, one tank army (6th), three air armies, and one air-defence (PVO) army, 1.5 million men, 26 000 guns, 5500 tanks and 3800 aircraft together with the Soviet Pacific Fleet.[74]

On 26–27 June 1945, by which time the General Staff operational plans were complete, Stalin, Molotov, Voznesensky together with Khrushchev, members of the Politburo and the Stavka with senior commanders of the Far Eastern Fronts, met in the Kremlin to review current preparations. Marshal Malinovsky, commander of the TransBaikal Front, presented his report after which Marshal Meretskov proposed Soviet occupation of the island of Hokkaido. In the discussion which followed, Khrushchev supported Meretskov, but Molotov pointed out that a Soviet invasion of the Japanese island of Hokkaido would be seen by the allies as an outright violation of the Yalta agreement.

Voznesensky, the economist who had masterminded the Soviet war economy, pointed to the cost of pitting the Red Army against the powerful Japanese defence of the islands. Marshal Zhukov dismissed the whole thing as 'an escapade'. On being asked by Stalin what forces would be required for such an operation he specified four full-strength armies fully supported by armour, artillery and much else, though it was apparent that the General Staff and the Main Naval Staff had already worked out the strengths and operational support required for an assault on Hokkaido.[75]

The Tripartite Military meeting at the Potsdam conference on 24 July 1945, concerned with coordinating strategy in the Far East, was given details of Soviet plans by General Antonov, mentioning the latter half of August as the date when the Red Army would begin military operations, though a precise date depended on the completion of negotiations for a Chinese treaty. That same day President Truman in 'unsensational' fashion informed Stalin of a 'new weapon of unusual destructive force', news which Stalin received with bland acceptance though he was fully aware of what a 'new weapon' meant. A second meeting on 26 July between the American and Soviet Chiefs of Staff agreed the demarcation lines for both Soviet and American naval operations in the sea areas around Japan and also for air operations, the subject of earlier American enquiries of the Soviet General Staff. Liaison officers from both sides would be attached to the respective American and Soviet headquarters once Soviet operations began.[76]

Upon Stalin's return from Potsdam Marshal Vasilevsky argued for Soviet operations to begin no later than 9–10 August if only to exploit weather which favoured the use of tanks and aircraft. On 8 August the Japanese Ambassador in Moscow was informed that 'as of 9 August the Soviet Union considered itself at war with Japan'. Rapid though the Soviet advance was, the political scene changed with even greater rapidity when the Japanese government on 14 August announced its acceptance of the surrender terms laid down at Potsdam. 'General Order No. 1' issued from Washington to

General MacArthur governing the Japanese capitulation met with Stalin's general approval on 15 August but in addition to the surrender of the Kuriles to Soviet forces he added 'the northern half of Hokkaido' with a demarcation line between north and south drawn from the city of Kushiro on the east shore of the island to the city of Rumoe on the west. 'Russian public opinion' would not be satisfied with anything less than possession of some part of Japanese territory.[77] President Truman agreed on the Kuriles but rejected out of hand any suggestion of a Soviet zone of occupation on Hokkaido. During the night of 15 August Vasilevsky ordered operations to occupy the northern Kurile Islands, using only Soviet forces to hand at Kamchatka. The immediate assault on Shumshu, an 'island fortress', brought heavy Soviet losses and protracted fighting.[78]

The Soviet command meanwhile prepared to implement the second part of its strategic plan, the assault landing on Hokkaido and the southern Kuriles, which demanded the expulsion of the Japanese from southern Sakhalin. The attack on Sakhalin began on 11 August but Japanese agreement to capitulate came only on 18 August. Though Stalin had learned on 18 August of American agreement to Soviet occupation of the Kuriles and of the exclusion of Soviet forces from Hokkaido at 0400 hours on 19 August, Vasilevsky issued orders to the 1st Far Eastern Front 'during the period from 19 August to 1 September to occupy one half of the island of Hokkaido in the north . . . and the islands of the southern part of the Kurile ridge'. Of the three divisions of 87th Rifle Corps, two would be landed on Hokkaido, one on the Kuriles.[79] A Soviet naval assault captured the port of Maoko in southern Sakhalin on 20 August, a 'favourable situation' Vasilevsky seized upon with his order of 21 August, issued at 1400 hours, to transfer 87th Rifle Corps to the south side of Sakhalin. Air Chief Marshal Novikov was instructed to have the 9th Air Army ready 'to take part in the capture of the northern part of the island of Hokkaido'. This also applied to the naval aviation of the Soviet Pacific Fleet. 'I will indicate the timing of the landing operation on the island of Hokkaido subsequently. Principal base for that operation . . . will be the island of Sakhalin. Readiness to be achieved by the end of 23 August 1945'.[80]

Stalin had already expressed his bitter disappointment to President Truman at being excluded from northern Hokkaido. At 1700 hours, no doubt after consultation with Stalin, in cipher telegram No. 677, Marshal Vasilevsky countermanded his orders issued only three hours earlier. 'Regarding the landing operation by our troops on the island of Hokkaido, it is necessary to refrain from proceeding, until special orders from the Stavka'. With news of Japanese readiness to capitulate on the Kuriles, a lead division of the 87th Rifle Corps would be transferred from south Sakhalin to the islands of Kunashir and Iturup, 'by-passing the island of Hokkaido'. The Stavka order categorically forbade 'sending any ships and aeroplanes to the mainland of Hokkaido'. Stalin's surrender was artfully phrased, a statesmanlike decision designed to avoid 'creating conflicts and misunderstandings in our relations with the Allies'.[81] 'Creating conflicts' had not discouraged him on previous occasions, not least over strategy, Poland and the Balkans. This time he ran the risk, too close to home, of military retaliation. Caution prevailed over cunning.

NOTES

1. For a recent publication of yet more intelligence material, see V. P. Pavlov, 'Moskve krichali o voine. Iz dokladnoi zapiski zamestitelya Narkoma vnutrennikh del SSSR L. P. Berii o sosredotochenii nemetskikh voisk vblizi sovetskoi granitsy' in *Voenno-istoricheskii Zhurnal* (cited as *ViZh*) 6 (1994) 21–26. A litany of intelligence reports and analysis of German plans was presented in *Izvestiya TsK KPSS* No. 4 (1990), pp. 198–223.

2. *The 1941 Soviet War Game: An Archival Record*, Moscow, Russian State Military Archive, Classification: Sovershenno sekretno, Documents No. 1–35, 1020 pp. (East View Publications, Minneapolis). The materials from these war-games were used operationally and erroneously by General Pavlov, commander of the Western Front during the first day of the war to mount a counter-attack. See V. A. Anfilov, *Nezabyvaemyi sorok pervyi* (Moscow, 1989), p. 134.

3. Sections of this document were reproduced by V. Karpov in 'Marshaly Velikoi Otechestvennoi Voiny. Zhukov', in *Kommunist vooruzhennykh sil*, No. 5 (1990) pp. 67–8. Karpov was bitterly attacked by A. Nikolaev, 'Marshal Zhukov protiv Zhukova?' in *Armiya* (successor to *Kommunist vooruzhennykh sil*), No. 15 (1991), pp. 64–9 for printing this material in the first place which only encouraged propagandists justifying preventive war against the Soviet Union and secondly the 'Zhukov plan' itself which, if activated, would have meant a Japanese response in the Soviet Far East, thus plunging the Soviet Union into a two-front war. Controversy over the significance of the 15 May 1941 document and Stalin's ultimate intentions continues unabated. See. G. A. Bordyugov and V. A. Nevezhin (eds), Gotovil li Stalin nastupatel'nuyu voinu protiv Gitlera (Moscow: AIRO-XX, 1995), 185 pp.

4. For intelligence reports on German concentrations and indications of a German attack, also photocopy of the hand-written draft of Directive No. 2 (signed by Malenkov and Zhukov with much scribbling and deletion) see Yu. A. Gor'kov, Colonel-General, 'Strategicheskie proschety verkhovnogo? . . .' *ViZh*, No. 8 (1992), pp. 19–32.

5. The supposition that Stalin was incapacitated or in a state of nervous collapse in the wake of the German attack in June 1941 is disproved according to the evidence of his visitors book, entries for 21–28 June, with name of visitor, time of arrival/departure, in V. P. Yampol'skii, 'Bezdeistvoval li Stalin v pervyi dni voiny?', *ViZh*, No. 6 (1994), pp. 27–30.

6. 'Conversation of I. Maisky with S. Cripps 21 June 1941. Top Secret. To Stalin, Molotov. From London. Received Moscow 1100 hours 22 VI.41.' In Russian. Reproduced from the archives in *Informatsionnyi byulleten*, No. 1 (Spring 1993), Natsional'nyi komitet istorikov Rossii, Moscow, pp. 39–40.

7. See G. Gorodetsky, 'An Alliance of Sorts. Allied Strategy in the Wake of Barbarossa' in J. Erickson and D. Dilks (eds), *BARBAROSSA: The Axis and the*

*Allies* (Edinburgh University Press, 1994) pp. 104–5; also *Stafford Cripps' Mission to Moscow* (Cambridge University Press, 1984), pp. 172–6.

8. Details and maps in D. M. Glantz (ed.), *The Initial Period of the War on the Eastern Front 22 June–August, 1941* (London, Frank Cass, 1993), 511 pp. In September, 1992 *The Journal of Soviet Military Studies* No. 3 (Vol. 4, 1991), began publication of translations of documents from *Sbornik boevykh dokumentov Velikoi Otechestvennoi voiny*, hitherto classified in the Soviet Union. This first collection is entitled 'Combat Documents of Soviet Western Front Armies 22–30 June 1941', with publication continued in subsequent numbers of this journal.

9. See A. I. Mikoyan, 'V pervye mesyatsy Velikoi Otechestvennoi voiny', in *Novaya i noveishaya istoriya*, No. 6 (1985), pp. 93–9.

10. F. I. Golikov, 'Sovetskaya voennaya missiya v Anglii i SShA v 1941 g.' *Novaya i noveishaya istoriya* No. 3 (1969), pp. 102–3.

11. *The Business of War, The war narrative of Major-General Sir John Kennedy* (London: Hutchinson, 1957), pp. 147–9.

12. Ibid., p. 148.

13. *Stalin's Correspondence with Churchill, Attlee, Roosevelt and Truman 1941–45* (London: Lawrence and Wishart, 1958), English edition of the Foreign Languages Publishing House, Moscow, 1957, two-volume edition, here No. 1, p. 11. This 'bibliographical rarity despite its large printing' according to the Soviet editors, has been republished in two volumes in English (Moscow: Progress Publishers). References here to the 1957 edition cited as *Stalin's Correspondence*.

14. *Sovetsko-angliiskie otnosheniya vo vremya Velikoi Otechestvennoi voiny 1941–1945*, Dokumenty i materialy v dvukh tomakh, (Moscow: Politizdat, 1983), here Vol. 1, Doc. 15, Stalin–Cripps, 8 July 1941, pp. 69–73. (Cited as *Sovetsko-angliiskie otnosheniya* with volume number).

15. Ibid., Doc. 21 'Soglashenie mezhdu pravitel'stvami SSSR i Velikobritanii o sovmestnykh deistviyakh v voine protiv Germanii', p. 82.

16. *Stalin's Correspondence*, No. 3, pp. 12–13. For a Soviet appraisal of the development of the 'Second Front' question, V. M. Kulish, *Istoriya vtorogo fronta* (Moscow, Nauka, 1971), Soviet and 'bourgeois' historiography, pp. 6–40 and Ch. 1, pp. 43–98.

17. *Sovetsko-angliiskie otnosheniya*, Vol. 1, Doc. No. 36, p. 109. See also previous Doc. No. 35, Eden–Maisky exchange, pp. 105–9.

18. *Stalin's Correspondence*, Stalin to Churchill, 3 September 1941, Doc. No. 10, pp. 20–2.

19. *Sovetsko-angliiskie otnosheniya*, Vol. 1, Maisky to Stalin, 5 September, 1941, here pp. 113–4.

20. *Stalin's Correspondence*, Stalin to Churchill, 13 September 1941, Doc. No. 12, pp. 24–5.

21. *Sovetsko-angliiskie otnosheniya*, Vol. 1, Docs No. 47–51 on the Moscow conference, pp. 132–40.

22. F. H. Hinsley *et al.*, *British Intelligence in the Second World War* (London: HMSO, 1981), Vol. 1., p. 73.

23. A. Werth, *Russia at War 1941–1945* (London: Barrie and Rockliff, 1964), pp. 235–41.

24. G. K. Zhukov, Marshal, *Vospominaniya i razmyshleniya* (Moscow: APN, 1990), 10th edn, Vol. 2, Ch. 14, on the 'battle for Moscow', pp. 202–70, here on the December counter-stroke, pp. 244–52. For a comprehensive Soviet study based on military archives V.D. Sokolovsky, Marshal (ed.), *Razgrom nemetsko-fashistskikh voisk pod Moskvoi* (Moscow: Voenizdat, 1964), 444 pp. with map supplement. Also M. Parrish (ed.), *Battle for Moscow: The 1942 General Staff Study* (Wash-

ington: London, Pergamon-Brassey's, 1989), 210 pp.; E. F. Ziemke and M. E. Bauer, *Moscow to Stalingrad: Decision in the East* (Washington: Center of Military History, US Army, 1992), Chs III–IV, pp. 47–87: K. Reinhardt, Lieutenant-General, 'Moscow 1941. The Turning Point' in *BARBAROSSA: The Axis and the Allies*, op. cit., pp. 207–26.

25. *Sovetsko-angliiskie otnosheniya*, Vol. 1, Doc. No. 76, Stalin–Molotov–Eden exchange, 17 December 1941, pp. 188–91 and Stalin–Eden, 18 December, Doc. No. 77, pp. 192–7.

26. Discussions summarised in G. K. Zhukov, *Vospominaniya i razmyshleniya*, op. cit,. Vol. 2, pp. 252–8; also 'Nekotorye voprosy rukovodstva vooruzhennoi bor'by letom 1942', discussion between Marshal Vasilevsky and the editorial staff of *ViZh*, No. 8 (1965), pp. 3–6.; see also V. L. Israelyan, *Diplomatiya v gody voiny (1941–1945)* (Moscow, Mezh. Otnoshen., 1985), Ch. III 'Dva pokhoda k vedeniyu voiny protiv fashistskoi bloka', pp. 71–84.

27. Details in J. Erickson, *The Road to Stalingrad* (London: Weidenfeld, 1975), pp. 335–9.

28. Conference, Russian Mission and Executives of Munitions Assignments Board, 19 April 1942.

29. This remains a highly controversial subject. See 'DOCUMENTS: The Khar'kov operation May, 1942: From the Archives Part I' also Part II, *The Journal of Soviet Military Studies* Vol. 5, Nos. 3–4 (1992), pp. 451–93 and pp. 611–86 respectively; for a revision of the role of Khrushchev, Timoshenko and Bagramyan see S. F. Begunov et al., 'Vot gde pravda, Nikita Sergeevich!' *ViZh*, No. 12 (1989), pp. 12–21 and No. 1 (1990), pp. 9–18.

30. Woodward, Sir Llewellyn, *British Foreign Policy in the Second World War* (London: HMSO, 1971), Vol. II, p. 252–4.

31. *Stalin's Correspondence*, Doc. No. 57, p. 56: 'In view of the situation on the Soviet–German front, I state most emphatically that the Soviet Government cannot tolerate the second front being postponed till 1943.'

32. *Sovetsko-angliskie otnosheniya*, Vol. 1, Doc. No. 130, Soviet archive record of Stalin–Churchill exchange, 12 August, 1942, pp. 265–71.

33. Soviet minutes in V. A. Lebedev, 'Kak marshal Tedder i general Bruk "otkryvali" vtoroi front', *ViZh*, No. 3 (1994), pp. 29–33, with footnote to the effect that the Second Front was only opened in 1944 when, thanks to the Red Army's victories, 'it became evident that the Soviet Army on its own could complete the destruction of fascist Germany'. Declassified from Top Secret.

34. For the defensive battle, planning of the Soviet counter-offensive see K. K. Rokossovsky, Marshal, (ed.) *Velikaya pobeda na Volge* (Moscow: Voenizdat, 1965), 327 pp.; also A. M. Samsonov, *Stalingradskaya bitva*, (Moscow: Nauka, 1989), 4th edn, 629 pp.; L. Rotundo (ed.), *Battle for Stalingrad: The 1943 Soviet General Staff Study* (London: Pergamon-Brassey's, 1989), 340 pp.; M. V. Zakharov, Marshal (ed.), *Stalingradskaya epopeya* (Moscow, Nauka, 1968), 719 pp., memoir material, Zhukov, Vasilevsky, Rokossovsky, Voronov, Moskalenko, Chuikov, Batov, Rotmistrov, commanders arms and services.

35. For a comprehensive narrative and analysis, see D. M. Glantz, *From the Don to the Dnepr: Soviet Offensive Operations December 1942–August 1943* (London: Frank Cass, 1991), Chs 1–4, pp. 10–214; also D. V. Sadarananda, *Beyond Stalingrad: Manstein and the Operations of Army Group Don* (New York: Praeger, 1990), 165 pp.; also E. Schwartz, *Die Stabilisierung der Ostfront nach Stalingrad. Mansteins Gegenschlag zwischen Donez und Dnjepr im Frühjahr 1943* (Göttingen, Munster-Schmidt Verlag, 1985).

36. *Stalin's Correspondence Stalin to Churchill*, Doc. No. 129, pp. 105–6.

37. Ibid., Doc. No. 167, p. 141.
38. The standard Soviet work is G. A. Koltunov and B. G. Solov'ev, *Kurskaya bitva* (Moscow: Voenizdat, 1970), 400 pp.; also B. G. Solov'ev, *Vermakht na puti k gibeli: Krushenie planov nemetsko-fashistskogo komandovaniya letom i osen'yu 1943 g.* (Moscow: Nauka, 1973), 311 pp.; also 'Documents: Collection of Materials for the Study of War Experience No. 11 – The Battle of Kursk July 1943' and 'Documents: The Defense Battle for the Kursk Bridgehead, 5–15 July 1943', *The Journal of Slavic Military Studies*, previously *Journal of Soviet Military Studies*), Vol. 6, No. 3 (1993) and Vol. 6, No. 4 (1993), pp. 450–512 and pp. 656–700 respectively.
39. Stalin never actually visited a front-line unit or got very near the front line. In August, 1943 he visited Yeremenko's headquarters at the Kalinin Front, travelling in a heavily escorted train. See A. I. Yeremenko, Marshal, 'Smolenskie vorota v Evropy, ili Tri chasa s I. V. Stalinym' *ViZh*, No. 12 (1993), pp. 6–12.
40. For details of exchanges, Woodward, *British Foreign Policy*, Vol. II, op. cit., pp. 581–3.
41. *Moskovskaya konferentsiya ministrov innostrannykh del SSSR, SShA i Velikobritanii 19–30 oktyabrya 1943 g.* in the multi-volume series *Sovetskii soyuz na mezhdunarodnykh konferentsiyakh perioda Velikoi Otechestvennoi voiny 1941–1945* (Moscow: Politizdat, 1978), Doc. No. 52, dated here 27 October, pp. 212–21.
42. Ibid., p. 219: 'Stalin govorit shto my nie bukvoedy'.
43. For two disparaging and polemical accounts of the 'Mediterranean strategy' and the Italian campaign see V. S. Strel'nikov and N. M. Cherepanov, *Voina bez riska* (Moscow: Voenizdat, 1965), 279 pp. and V. A. Sekistov, *Voina i politika* (Moscow: Voenizdat, 1970), 496 pp.; also V. M. Kulish, *Istoriya vtorogo fronta*, op. cit., Ch. 5, pp. 263–98.
44. See M.P. Kolesnikov, Colonel-General, Chief of the General Staff of the Russian Armed Forces, 'Osvobozhdenie Belorussii', *ViZh*, No. 6 (1994), p. 2; also A. M. Samsonov (ed.), *Osvobozhdenie Belorussii 1944* (Moscow: Nauka, 1974) 2nd edn, 799 pp. Memoir material, planning and operations, Zhukov, Vasilevsky, Bagramyan, Rokossovsky, arms and services commanders.
45. S. M. Shtemenko, *General, The Soviet General Staff at War 1941–1945*, trans. R. Daglish (Moscow: Progress, 1985), pp. 266–8. This highly tendentious work furnishes details of the planning but is misleading in discussing the political contexts, for example, 'The General Staff received no special instructions after the Teheran Conference.' General Kolesnikov makes it plain that it did.
46. See I. S. Koniev, Marshal, *Zapiski komanduyushchego frontom* (Moscow: Voenizdat, 1991), pp. 133–78, a revised edition of memoirs published under the rubric 'Biblioteka izbrannykh voennykh memuarov'.
47. For operational details, J. Erickson, *The Road to Berlin* (London: Weidenfeld, 1983), pp. 182–9.
48. *Stalin's Correspondence*, Doc. No. 257, pp. 212–13.
49. For a Soviet analysis, see N. I. Baryshnikov, V. N. Baryshnikov and V. G. Fedorov *Finlyandiya vo vtoroi mirovoi voiny* (Leningrad, Lenizdat, 1989), pp. 227–89.
50. Fremde Heere Ost (I) *Beurteilung im Grossen* 30.3.1944: 'Wichtige Abwehr-meldungen uber sow.–russ. Operationsabsichten'. German Military Documents (GMD) US National Archives Microfilm. Serial T-78/Roll 497 6485573-602.
51. See J. Lewis, *Changing Direction: British Military Planning for Post-war Strategic Defence, 1942–47* (London: Sherwood, 1988), pp. 138–9.
52. Records, Joint Chiefs of Staff. Red Army Action to facilitate OVERLORD. Joint Staff Planners. 27 March 1944. 9 pp.

53. *Stalin's Correspondence.* Stalin to the Prime Minister and President Roosevelt. 22 April 1944. Doc. No. 260, p. 215.
54. M. Howard, *British Intelligence in the Second World War*, Vol. 5, *Strategic Deception* (London: HMSO, 1990), Ch. 6, 'BODYGUARD and the Russians', pp. 110–12, also pp. 248–51.
55. M. P. Kolesnikov, loc. cit., 6/1994 *ViZh*, p. 5; see also D. M. Glantz, *Soviet Military Deception in the Second World War* (London: Frank Cass, 1989), on *maskirovka* and the Belorussian operation, pp. 360–71.
56. See under Zhukov and Vasilevsky in *Osvobozhdenie Belorussii*, op. cit., pp. 15–39 and pp. 40–69 respectively.
57. *Stalin's Correspondence* Doc. No. 276, p. 226.
58. See I. S. Koniev, *Zapiski*, op. cit., pp. 201 ff.; also M. A. Polushkin, *Na Sandomirskom napravlenii. L'vovsko-Sandomirskaya operatsiya (iyul'-avgust 1944 gg.)* (Moscow, Voenizdat, 1969), 176 pp., based on Soviet miliary archives.
59. See G. Niepold, *The Battle for White Russia: The Destruction of Army Group Centre*, trans. R. Simpkin (London, Brassey's, 1987), passim; also O. Heidkämper, *Vitebsk Kampf und Untergang der 3. Panzerarmee* (Heidelberg: K. Vowinckel, 1954), also passim; see also K. K. Rokossovsky in *Osvobozhdenie Belorussii*, op. cit., pp. 138–51.
60. Joint Chiefs of Staff Records. Machinery for Co-ordination of U.S.–Soviet–British Military Effort. Joint Staff Planners, 10 August, 1944, 8 pp.; also 17 August, 4 pp.
61. J. R. Deane, *The Strange Alliance* (London: J. Murray, 1947), pp. 153–4.
62. R. Ya. Malinovsky, Marshal (ed.), *Yassko-Kishinevskie Kanny* (Moscow: Nauka, 1964), 280 pp.; also M. M. Miniasyan, *Osvobozhdenie narodov Yugo-Vostochnoi Evropy* (Moscow: Voenizdat, 1967), Ch. 2, pp. 84–187 on operations in Romania; also S. M. Shtemenko, *Soviet General Staff*, Bk 2, op. cit., Ch. 4 on Romania, 117–61.
63. See the documentary collection, P. A. Zhilin (ed.), *Osvoboditel'naya missiya Sovetskikh Vooruzhennykh Sil v Evrope vo vtoroi mirovoi voiny. Dokumenty i materialy* (Moscow: Voenizdat, 1985), 640 pp., a mixture of military and political directives.
64. For the standard Soviet explanation of the failure to assist the Warsaw rising see S. M. Shtemenko, *Soviet General Staff*, Bk 2, op. cit., Ch. 3, pp. 83–93: 'The failure to break through to Warsaw without a pause, the inability of our exhausted troops to bring about a decisive turn in the battle and the need to provide much better rear services ... all this compelled the Soviet Supreme High Command to organise a new offensive for the liberation of Warsaw.'
65. Woodward, *British Foreign Policy*, op. cit., Vol. III, pp. 150–3; *Sovetsko-angliiskie otnosheniya*, Vol. 2, omits any record of the Stalin–Churchill exchange, confining itself only to Molotov–Eden talks and official documentation.
66. Details of the planning, J. Erickson, *The Road to Berlin*, op. cit., pp. 422–30.
67. R. Ya. Malinovsky (ed.), *Budapesht Vena Praga*, Istoriko-memuarnyi ocherk (Moscow: Nauka, 1965), Chs 1–3, pp. 8–169. For a detailed operational narrative, M. M. Minasyan, op. cit., Ch. 4, pp. 255–380.
68. S. M. Shtemenko, *Soviet General Staff*, op. cit., Bk 1, Ch. 14, pp. 372–84.
69. Ibid., p. 383 on rates of advance and objectives.
70. This has become the subject of a fierce controversy with V. N. Kiselev, 'Visla-Ardenny, 1944–1945', *ViZh* No. 6 (1993), pp. 29–34, claiming that this Soviet 'assistance' to the Allied armies in the Ardennes was a documentary fabrication designed to make Stalin 'look good' and that Churchill's 'request' was a thinly-disguised attempt to probe Soviet plans and intentions at a time when the real

threat had passed in the Ardennes, all hotly disputed by E. N. Kul'kov, 'Kto kogo spasal v Ardennakh?', *ViZh* No. 3 (1994), pp. 34–7.

71. The sudden stop to the 'non-stop' offensive on Berlin also generated famous controversy with the publication in *Oktyabr'* in 1964 and *Novaya i noveishaya istoriya* No. 2 (1965) of Marshal V. I. Chuikov's memoirs in which he argued that a rapid attack on Berlin from the Oder bridgeheads was possible. This was obviously a dire criticism aimed at Marshal Zhukov who on 16 April 1964 addressed a letter to Nikita Khrushchev asking for these 'denigrations' to be stopped. See *Istochnik. Dokumenty russkoi istorii. Prilozhenie k zhurnalu 'RODINA'* Nos. 5/6 (1993), pp. 154–8. The order for a 'non-stop' offensive was issued on 26 January 1945 but 'an unfavourable situation' developed, not least the exposed right flank of 1st Belorussian Front and the unprotected gap between 1st and 2nd Belorussian Fronts, a problem 'glossed over' in the November planning sessions. Strangely enough, in a very lengthy exchange with me in Moscow in 1963 Marshal Chuikov admitted that the 'non-stop' offensive could not have proceeded precisely because the Red Army, his 8th Guards Army in particular, had run out of supplies – ammunition, fuel, pontoons to force the Oder, to bridge the canals and waterways of Berlin. His signals to Zhukov reported lack of ammunition and the breakdown of the supply lines from the Vistula. If anything, Chuikov blamed Stalin for advancing the date of the Soviet 'Vistula–Oder operation' to ease the German pressure in the west and thus putting an intolerable strain on the Soviet rear. For Marshal Zhukov's final refutation of Chuikov's argument, see *Vospominaniya i razmyshleniya*, op. cit., Vol. 3, 10th edn, pp. 202–6. Chuikov's argument is not mentioned in the standard Soviet work on the Berlin operation, F. D. Vorob'ev *et al.*, *Poslednyi shturm (Berlinskaya operatsiya 1945 g.)*, (Moscow: Voenizdat, 1975), 2nd edn, 455 pp.

72. I. S. Koniev (ed.), *Za osvobozhdenie Chekhoslovakii* (Moscow: Voenizdat, 1965), Ch. 4 pp. 230–78; also I. S. Koniev '1-i Ukrainskii Front v Prazhskoi operatsii' in A. M. Samsonov (ed.), *9 maya 1945 goda* (Moscow: Nauka, 1970), pp. 122–60.

73. See *Krymskaya konferentsiya rukovoditelei trekh soyuznikh derzhav – SSSR, SShA i Velikobritanii 4-11 fevralya 1945. Sbornik dokumentov* (Moscow: Politizdat, 1979) in the series *Sovetskii Soyuz na mezhdunarodnykh konferentsiyakh*, here pp. 135–42 Stalin-Roosevelt exchange, 8 February 1945.

74. Figures in *Finale* (Moscow, Progress, 1972) translation of M. V. Zakharov (ed.) *Final. Istoriko-memuarnyi ocherk o razgrome imperialisticheskoi Yaponii v 1945 gody* (Moscow: Nauka, 1969) here p. 74.

75. See Boris N. Slavinsky, 'The Soviet Occupation of the Kurile Islands and the Plans for the Capture of Northern Hokkaido'. Orig. Russian, trans. L. Erickson. *Japan Forum* (Oxford University Press), Vol. 5, No. 1 (1993), here pp. 97–8.

76. H. Feis, *Japan Subdued. The Atomic Bomb and the End of the War in the Pacific* (Princeton: Princeton University Press, 1961), meeting of US and Soviet Chiefs of Staff, 26 July, p. 93.

77. *Stalin's Correspondence*. Stalin to President Truman, 16 August, Doc. No. 363, p. 266.

78. Boris Slavinsky, loc. cit., p. 102.

79. Ibid., p. 104. Vasilevsky on 'remaining tasks of the Soviet forces in the Far East'.

80. Ibid., p. 106. Similar documentation is presented in V. P. Galitsky and V. P. Zimonin, 'Desant na Khokkaido otmenit!', *ViZh*, No. 3 (1994), with the explanation that the cancellation of the assault on Hokkaido was to preserve Soviet lives since actual occupation was no longer a military necessity, to demonstrate

the 'compliant attitude' of the Soviet Union towards its allies and to avoid that 'bloody partition' of foreign territory for which 'certain Japanese and Western historians and official persons' tried to hold the Soviet Union responsible.

81. On the cancellation of the Hokkaido order, D. Volkogonov, General, *Stalin: Triumph and Tragedy*, ed. and trans. H. Shukman (London: Weidenfeld, 1991), p. 502. 'Stalin paused: what would he gain by a landing? It would probably spoil his already deteriorating relations with the Allies.'

# 8 Anglo-American Strategy in Europe
## Correlli Barnett

The outline of Anglo-American strategy against Germany in 1944–45 was sketched as early as December 1941 at the first Washington conference, held in the aftermath of the naval disaster at Pearl Harbor, which kicked the United States into the war. The conference took place during the fleeting moment when Britain's naval and military power, now nearing its apogee of expansion, broadly matched that of the United States, which had as yet hardly begun to muster its overwhelmingly greater human and industrial resources, and when the British could speak with the authority of hard-won expertise to Americans new to the game. Moreover, the British Chiefs of Staff [COS] and the Prime Minister came to the conference comprehensively prepared for debate; the American Chiefs of Staff and the President, their minds busy with the aftermath of Pearl Harbor, were not so. Thus the statement of global strategy finally agreed by the conference, 'WW1', was an amended version of a draft tabled by the British COS. In turn this professional staff paper owed much to the three papers on grand strategy written by Winston Churchill as minutes to the COS while crossing the Atlantic in HMS *Duke of York*. Since Churchill has come in for criticism by revisionist historians who have failed to think through the political and strategic realities of the predicament with which he, as British Prime Minister, had to cope,[1] it is worth noting that these three state papers still stand as a masterly overview of the war in all its complexities, coupled with a far-sighted vision of how the allies would eventually win it.[2]

'WW' confirmed a fundamental choice, first agreed at Anglo-American staff talks in February 1941 and later reaffirmed at the 'Arcadia' Conference that August (when the USA was still neutral), that Germany must be beaten first: 'notwithstanding the entry of Japan into the war, our view remains that Germany is the prime enemy and her defeat is the key to victory'. WW1 looked ahead to a return of the allied armies to the Continent of Europe in 1943 'across the Mediterranean, from Turkey into the Balkans, or by landings in Western Europe', such operations being only 'the prelude to the final assault on Germany itself'.[3] To avoid premature controversy the exact nature of this assault was left for the moment undefined.

Just as this first Washington Conference in December 1941 sketched the design of future allied grand strategy, so too did it begin to create an integrated allied command and control system, with grand strategy decided jointly by the President and Prime Ministers advised by the Combined [American and British] Chiefs of Staff, the precedent being provided by Churchill's relationship with the British Chiefs of Staff, an intimacy of sometimes stormy debate but eventual consensus. With the appointment in July 1942 of General Dwight D. Eisenhower as Allied Supreme Commander for Operation TORCH (the invasion of French North Africa) there followed the prototype of the integrated theatre command and staff structures which were to plan and carry out allied strategy in 1944–45, whereby the CCOS issued directives to supreme commanders who exercised (or were supposed to exercise) command as *allied* commanders rather than as national commanders given limited authority over other nations' forces (like Foch in the Great War). These commanders were to be served by integrated Anglo-American headquarters staffs – another innovation for which in this case Eisenhower was responsible. Moreover, since orders issued by allied supreme commanders carried the authority of the Combined Chiefs of Staff and ultimately of the President and Prime Minister, there existed no right of appeal from the national commander of an army to his own government (as Haig had enjoyed in the Great War) if he considered that orders from an allied general endangered his troops. Operations TORCH in 1942 and HUSKY and AVALANCHE in 1943 proved that this novelty of an integrated allied high-command structure could be operationally successful (given an incidental creak or two) even in large-scale amphibious landings, historically subject to ferocious quarrels between admirals and generals even of the same nationality.

It should never be forgotten that these structures marked a degree of integration surpassing any other alliance in the history of coalition warfare (such as between Britain and France in the Great War, or Germany and Italy in the Second World War) – far more intimate, indeed, than that existing between Britain and the British dominions. Much credit belongs to Churchill. It was he who had since the summer of 1940 so carefully cultivated the close personal relationship with President Roosevelt that provided the driving pinion to the whole machine; he who understood how vital it was to British interests that the war-making of the two countries should be bolted as closely together as possible; he who, a man in his late sixties, was willing to make long and hazardous sea or air journeys with his own Chiefs of Staff to hammer out strategy with Roosevelt and the American COS in the periodic summit conferences.

The global war jointly fought by Great Britain and the United States from December 1941 onwards, and which reached its victorious climax in 1944–45, was first and foremost a maritime war, for only by grace of sea communications could expeditionary forces open up land battlefronts against a continental enemy like Germany. There was no other way to victory, because Germany's territorial conquests gave her access to the food and raw materials she needed, and hence she could not be crippled by maritime blockade as in the Great War. Leaving aside the dream entertained by British and American airmen of defeating Germany by bombing alone, this meant that sooner or later the German Army in the West must be engaged in battle and defeated.

Landings in the strength needed to achieve this depended on having enough shipping-lift to move the expeditionary forces and all their equipment from their homelands, and enough landing-ships and landing-craft to put ashore the number of divisions necessary to effect an initial lodgement against a determined enemy defence. Success would thereafter depend on the capacity of shipping and of captured ports to reinforce and resupply the armies so that they could defeat the enemy in an extended campaign. The key to Anglo-American strategy throughout the war thus lay in availability of shipping and landing-craft. This was particularly true of 1944, when preparation of the largest amphibious operation of all time, Operation NEPTUNE/OVERLORD (the Normandy landings) had to compete for such resources with the American island-hopping offensives in the Pacific against the Japanese, in which Admiral Ernest J. King, Chief of Naval Operations, and 'owner' of the American-built main pool of landing-craft, usually took a much keener interest. In short, Anglo-American strategy in 1944–45 rested far more on the accountancy of maritime logistic resources and how best to deploy these resources than on the Schlieffen-Plan-like arrows on the map beloved of military historians. Nonetheless, historians of the land campaigns often give the impression that the Mediterranean or the English Channel were no more than a 'No Man's Land' over which the allied armies with one easy bound advanced to battle.[4]

The overall allied shortage of shipping from 1941 onwards was further complicated by the legacy of Victorian Free Trade, which had left Britain critically dependent for the national life itself on seaborne imports of foodstuffs and raw material. During the Second World War, such imports had been extended to American war equipment and industrial technology.[5] Thus Britain's estimated minimum (and that meant cut to the bone) import requirements in 1943 were estimated at 27 million tons.[6] Whereas the British needed shipping primarily for these economic reasons, the Americans needed it primarily for military reasons – transporting troops and supplies thousands of miles across the Atlantic and, above all, the Pacific. This discordance was to occasion not a little incidental grief between allies, especially as in 1942–43 America was building more dry-cargo ships than she was losing to the U-boats, while the reverse was true of Britain.[7]

It follows that whether there was even to be an Anglo-American strategy against Germany in 1944–45 depended absolutely on defeating the U-boats in the Battle of the Atlantic from 1941 onwards. If the U-boats won, no American expeditionary force with all its equipment could have been moved to Britain; and for that matter Britain herself would have been compelled to capitulate in any case. Therefore it can be said that the Battle of the Atlantic, so narrowly won by the allies in the spring of 1943, marked the turning-point battle of the Anglo-American war against Germany.[8]

Yet Churchill's own role in this battle was ambiguous. It was he who back in March 1941 had dubbed the struggle against the U-boats 'the Battle of the Atlantic'[9] and set up a Cabinet Committee chaired by himself as Minister of Defence to oversee it; he who thereafter took the closest interest in the fortunes of the struggle and the technical and tactical means employed to defeat the U-boats, and also in the linked questions of import tonnages, shipping capacity, shipping losses, and the statistics of shipbuilding and ship-repairing figures. However, in the prolonged and crucial debate in 1942 between the Admiralty (supported by RAF Coastal Command) and the Air Ministry in 1942 about the diversion of a fraction of Bomber Command's strength from the area bombing of German cities to the war against the U-boats, Churchill failed to come down decisively in favour of the Admiralty, even though no one better defined the question on which the whole argument turned, writing in July that year that 'it might be true to say that the issue of the war depends on whether Hitler's U-boat attack on Allied tonnage or the increase and application of Allied air-power reach their full fruition first'.[10] Yet the evidence available at the time went to show (except to pig-headed air-marshals and that fallacious scientist, Lindemann) that the U-boat was currently well ahead in that race.[11] That the Battle of the Atlantic was decisively won in the spring of 1943 by the slenderest of margins, and partly thanks to the very belated deployment of VLR [very long-range] aircraft, therefore owed nothing to Churchill's leadership.

As has been repeatedly chewed over in detail by historians,[12] Anglo-American strategy against Germany in 1944 represented the final outcome of a sometimes fierce debate between the British and American leaderships from spring 1942 onwards about the relative priority to be accorded to the Mediterranean campaign and a direct cross-Channel invasion. The debate reflected fundamental divergences of approach over which the generalities of 'WW1' had smoothly skated. The USA was a continental power in the process of raising mass armies, with a population of 120 millions and industrial resources which dwarfed Britain's (and for that matter even Germany's). The American Chief of Staff, General George C. Marshall, therefore conceived of strategy in classic Clausewitzian terms – the concentration of all forces at the decisive point for an offensive directed at the enemy's 'centre of gravity' (that is, his main army or one of his main armies), leading to a decisive victory and finally the occupation of the enemy's homeland, so destroying his military, industrial and moral power to resist. In essence, he wished to re-create as soon as possible the old Western Front, and was prepared to see all other (in his view, peripheral) operations closed down or reduced to a minimum in order to make this possible. However, Marshall's advocacy of a Western Front (which would have earned the plaudits of Field-Marshal Sir Douglas Haig and General Sir William Robertson) cut across the deepest instincts and prejudices of the British leadership, political and military.

For Churchill himself had been an 'Easterner' during the Great War, advocating fringe campaigns like the Dardanelles in 1915 as an easier way to victory than fighting great battles on the Western Front. Moreover, in the 1930s British politicians, public opinion and even the military themselves had all resolved that never again must Britain commit mass conscript armies in battle against the main body of the German Army on a Western Front. This aversion resulted in the first place from 'the Lost Generation' syndrome, an exaggerated subjective reaction to the British casualty figures on the Western Front in the Great War (512 564 killed, as against Italy's 460 000 on the Italian Front in only three years of war)[13] caused very largely by the harrowing best-selling novels and memoirs of literary veterans of the trenches.[14] To this has to be added the influence of Lloyd George's self-exculpatory slandering of Haig and his colleagues in his *Memoirs*,[15] and the preaching of Basil Liddell Hart, a noted strategic pundit of the 1930s, about a 'British way in warfare'.[16] This marvellously cheap route to victory entailed leaving the main brunt of the fighting to a Continental ally while Britain, thanks to seapower, engaged detached portions of the enemy's strength in peripheral theatres.

The collapse of France in 1940, who had been left to fight virtually alone thanks to Chamberlain's policy (bought from Liddell Hart in 1937 and reversed too late in 1939) of military isolationism, and the consequent extinction of the Western Front left Britain with no alternative but 'the British way in warfare', or, as General J. F. C. Fuller unkindly dubbed it, 'the strategy of evasion'. It was therefore out of sheer expediency, though certainly reinforced by Churchill's predilections, that Britain became entangled ever deeper in the Mediterranean theatre between 1940 and summer 1942, achieving little but disaster in return for an immense military, naval and logistic investment.[17]

Nevertheless, this investment existed as a fact (and to the British leadership, still a great opportunity) when Britain and America in the early months of 1942 sought to decide their joint strategy for 1942 and 1943.

There now emerged the basic differences between the two allies which were still to bedevil them through 1944 and 1945, and which may be looked upon as a continuation of the argument between 'Westerners' like Haig and Robertson and 'Easterners' like Lloyd George and Churchill in the Great War. Marshall in his clear-cut Clausewitzian way wished to concentrate all effort on preparing for a large-scale invasion of France in 1943 (Operation ROUNDUP) in order to reopen the Western Front and engage the main body of the enemy. His strategic reasoning remarkably echoes that of Haig in 1917, when Lloyd George wished to give priority to the Italian Front, and Haig wished to attack in Flanders. Wrote Haig to Lloyd George in June 1917:

> Comparing this operation with anything that we might do in other theatres its advantages are overwhelming.
>
> It directly and seriously threatens our main enemy, on whom the whole Coalition against us depends.
>
> It is within the easiest possible reach of our base [the UK] by sea and rail and can be developed infinitely more rapidly, and maintained infinitely more easily, than any other operation open to us.
>
> It admits to the closest possible combination of our naval and military strength.
>
> It covers all the points which we dare not uncover, and therefore admits of the utmost concentration of force; whereas, for the same reason, any force employed in any other theatre of war can never be more than a detachment. . . .[18]

And Marshall in 1942 to President Roosevelt:

> [France] is the only place in which a powerful offensive can be prepared and executed by the United Powers in the near future. Moreover in other localities the enemy is protected against invasion by natural obstacles and poor communications leading towards the seat of hostile power or by elaborately organised and distant outposts. Time would be required to reduce these and to make the attack effective.
>
> It is the only place where the vital air superiority over the hostile land areas preliminary to a major attack can be staged by the United Powers. This is due to the existence of the network of landing fields in England and the fact that at no other place could massed British airpower be employed for such an operation.
>
> It is the only place in which the bulk of the British ground forces can be committed to a general offensive in co-operation with United States forces. It is impossible, in view of the shipping situation, to transfer the bulk of the British forces to any distant region, and the protection of the British Isles would hold the bulk of the divisions in England.
>
> United States can concentrate and use larger forces in Western Europe than in any other place, due to sea distances and the existence in England of base facilities. . . .[19]

Here encapsulated was a strategic view from which Marshall was never to waver. However, whereas in 1917 the Western Front already existed and Haig had at his disposal alongside the French Army a British Army of some 50 divisions deployed ready for use, in 1942 the Western Front must first be re-created by a hazardous cross-Channel invasion. Marshall even hoped that a limited landing that year to establish a bridgehead (Operation SLEDGEHAMMER) might be possible. He certainly wanted the major offensive into France to take place in 1943 (Operation ROUNDUP).

The positions of Churchill and General Sir Alan Brooke, the Chief of the Imperial General Staff, were, and always remained, more ambiguous. Brooke, backed by his naval and air force colleagues, ruled out SLEDGEHAMMER as being quite beyond allied strength in 1942 (surely a correct judgement), and the project died. But Brooke seems to have wavered in spring and summer 1942 between supporting Marshall's view of the overriding importance of launching ROUNDUP in 1943, and believing that even in that year the balance of forces would still be too unfavourable to the allies, so dooming the landings to failure.[20] Partly because at that moment [June 1942] the Eighth Army was being routed by Rommel in the Western Desert, Brooke likewise had grave doubts about Churchill's own preferred option for an allied operation later in 1942, first put on paper by Churchill during the voyage to the December 1941 Washington Conference, namely an Anglo-American landing in French North Africa (GYMNAST, later codenamed TORCH) in conjunction with an offensive by the British Eighth Army in Egypt, with the objective of clearing the whole North African shore and reopening the Mediterranean to through merchant traffic. Only after Auchinleck had stopped Rommel and thrown him on to the defensive in the First Battle of Alamein (July 1942), did Brooke embrace TORCH.[21] But at the same time he acknowledged (gratefully?) that the diversion of Anglo-American forces to North Africa in 1942 ruled out ROUNDUP in 1943.

Churchill from the beginning of these arguments had remained the same lover of fringe theatres that he had been in the Great War. In 1942 he peddled – unsuccessfully – the idea of a landing in Northern Norway, and, by way of balance, GYMNAST/TORCH, which represented, of course, a development of the Mediterranean strategy he had been pursuing since 1940. And just as pressures of political and military expediency had first entangled Britain in that theatre, now the same factors, promoted by Churchill's powerful advocacy, entangled the United States as well. Roosevelt believed that it was essential for American forces to fight somewhere against Germany in 1942. With SLEDGEHAMMER ruled out, where else was there but North Africa? In any case, with the Soviet Union engaged in battle with 200 German divisions, the British argued that it was politically unthinkable for the Anglo-Americans to do nothing jointly in 1942 while they painstakingly prepared for ROUNDUP in 1943. Churchill first won over his own COS to TORCH, and finally President Roosevelt, who in July 1942 opted for the operation in the face of Marshall's strenuous objections that it would be a 'diversion' draining forces away from ROUNDUP, and imperilling the launch of that operation in spring 1943 (as in the event it did).

These arguments of 1942 are crucial because they set the scene for Anglo-American strategy and strategic debate from then on to the end of the war. That sheer pressure of expediency (and the subtle arguments of the byzantine British) had dragged the Americans too into 'the British way in warfare' in the Mediterranean only left Marshall resolved that he would be dragged no further. But already in Churchill's mind TORCH was no mere expedient to get the Americans into battle in 1942, no mere short-term sideshow; it had become the potential first stage in yet more distant, and characteristically opportunist, developments of his favourite 'blue-water strategy':

> If, however, we move from 'Gymnast' [TORCH] northward into Europe a new situation must be surveyed. The flank attack may become the main attack, and the main attack a holding operation in the early stages. Our second front [ie, second to the Eastern Front] will in fact comprise both the Atlantic and the Mediterranean coasts of Europe, and we can push either right-handed, left-handed or both-handed, as our resources and circumstances permit. . . .[22]

It should here be noted that from June 1941 Britain had once again enjoyed that essential ingredient of 'the British way in warfare', a Continental ally who was engaging the main body of the enemy in gigantic land battles: to wit, the Soviet Union. This fact was fundamental to British thinking in 1942–43 in regard to delaying a cross-Channel invasion while at the same time pursuing a Mediterranean strategy.

To telescope much complicated history, between 1942 and 1944 Marshall's worst fears of an ever-deeper entanglement in the Mediterranean, with a consequential major drain on allied resources, came true. After the conquest of North Africa in May 1943, expediency irresistibly led to the invasion of Sicily in July, and after the conquest of Sicily to the invasion of Italy in September (in the face of Marshall's stubborn but unsuccessful advocacy of closing down the Mediterranean theatre as a scene of active operations in favour of concentrating strength (including assault shipping) on preparations for the invasion of France. In the last three months of 1943 Italy therefore became that major theatre of British (and now, of course, American) effort which Lloyd George had so desired in 1917. However, by the end of December 1943 the Italian front, far from proving in Churchill's famous phrase, 'the soft underbelly' of the Axis, had become locked fast in a bloody stalemate reminiscent of such earlier essays in 'blue-water' strategy as Gallipoli in 1915 and the Allies' Salonika front in 1916–18.

It was Brooke's abiding conviction from 1942 onwards that the allied forces in the Mediterranean theatre were serving (relative to their own strength and casualties) to divert and destroy German forces which could otherwise oppose an allied landing in France.[23] This was a fallacy. According to two authorities on the Italian campaign, Dominick Graham and Shelford Bidwell, the allied commitment of manpower for land and air forces in the Mediterranean theatre was to rise by 1944 to a total of 1 677 000. This compares with 411 000 men under Field-Marshal Kesselring's command in Italy in July that year.[24] As for the high British hopes that the collapse of Italy (in September 1943) would force the Germans to drain away troops from other fronts to a possibly disastrous extent in order to hold the Balkans, the truth is that the German deployment in Yugoslavia increased by a net total of only seven divisions (mostly second-class and ill-equipped) between the time of the Italian surrender in September 1943 and February 1944, only one of which came originally from the Russian front.[25] Moreover, to supply the Allied forces in the whole Western Mediterranean area (including Italy) called for a commitment of over 1 million deadweight tons of British shipping alone. Kesselring by contrast drew his supplies direct from Germany, only some 600 miles distant along excellent road and rail links. As Graham and Bidwell acknowledge: 'It could be said, therefore, that it was not Alexander who was drawing in forces that would otherwise be employed against the Allies in north-west Europe, but Kesselring who was containing Alexander.'[26]

Thus it is one thing to accept at the time and in retrospect that irresistible political and strategic expediency compelled the Anglo-Americans step by step to entangle themselves deeper in the Mediterranean theatre; quite another to believe at the time and in retrospect (as did Churchill, Brooke and their admirers) that the allies were pursuing a brilliantly clever strategy.

How far did Churchill and Brooke come to regard the Mediterranean theatre (including the Balkans) as a potential *substitute* for the invasion of France as the final Anglo-American assault on Hitler's Europe, as Americans like Marshall deeply suspected? In late 1942 Churchill had favoured an each-way bet – an extension of the Mediterranean campaign beyond North Africa in 1943 *and* an invasion of France (ROUNDUP) late that year. He was finally persuaded by Brooke and his fellow Chiefs of Staff that ROUNDUP was militarily and logistically not 'on' for 1943, and that, to quote Brooke, 'there was no doubt' that 'the better strategy' was to 'force Italy out of the war and perhaps enter the Balkans . . .',[27] as a preliminary to ROUNDUP in 1944. Brooke and the Chiefs of Staff at this time and later flew large kites about occupying Crete and the Dodecanese, persuading Turkey to enter the war, thereby preparing the way for an entry into the Balkans.[28] In July 1943 Churchill himself, in a memorandum to the Chiefs of Staff, actually advocated in plain terms a combination of Mediterranean/Balkan offensives and a landing in Northern Norway as a substitute for an invasion of France.[29] In September 1943, in the aftermath of the Italian surrender, Churchill succumbed to a characteristic fit of opportunism and ordered hastily scratched together British forces to expel the Germans from the islands of Cos and Leros by way of a first step to Rhodes and eventually the Balkans. Eisenhower, as Allied Supreme Commander Mediterranean, stubbornly refused to divert forces (above all, air forces) to bail the operation out when it began to founder under intense German air attack, and it ended in a débâcle in the classic tradition of the Dardanelles in 1915 and Greece and Crete in 1941.[30] But while Brooke characterised this Churchillian exercise as 'another of those typical examples of dispersal of effort for very problematic gain',[31] he was nevertheless much of the same mind as Churchill on the larger issue of extending the Mediterranean campaign from Italy into the Balkans, confiding to his diary during the Cairo Conference (SEXTANT) in November 1943 that 'the drag' of the Americans

> has seriously affected our Mediterranean strategy and the whole conduct of the war. If they had come wholeheartedly into the Mediterranean with us we should now have Rome securely, the Balkans would be ablaze, the Dardanelles would be open, and we should be on the highway to get Rumania and Bulgaria out of the war.[32]

At the Cairo conference the British sought American consent for fresh attempts to exploit these opportunities, even if it meant postponing OVER-LORD [the cross-Channel invasion] from May 1944, as at present scheduled, to July. The British strategy was well expressed by Churchill himself: 'Rome in January, Rhodes in February, supplies to the Yugoslavs, a settlement of the Command arrangements and the opening of the Aegean, subject to an approach to Turkey; all preparations for "Overlord" to go forward *within the framework of the foregoing policy for the Mediterranean* [added emphasis]'.[33] The Americans (disingenuously?) accepted this – including a possible delay to OVERLORD – as a basis for discussion with the Soviet leadership at the forthcoming Teheran Conference (EUREKA), providing that the needs of eastern Mediterranean operations (above all, for landing-craft) 'would in no way interfere with the carrying-out of "Buccaneer". . . '. This was a proposed seaborne invasion of the Andaman Islands south of Burma, ultimately cancelled: a significant example of the interweaving of strategies against Germany and against Japan, which there is no room here to discuss.

At the Teheran Conference (November 1943), Churchill persisted in pushing this British 'broad-front' concept of Anglo-American grand strategy for 1944 against Germany: OVERLORD in late spring or summer with 35 strong divisions, of which 16 would be British; the capture of Rome and an advance to the Pisa–Rimini line, with the option of either advancing into southern France or north-eastwards towards the Danube; an attempt to bring Turkey into the war, followed by the capture of the Dodecanese. But Stalin and his soldier satellites, leaders of a Continental power engaged in a gigantic ground war with Germany, thought like Marshall in terms of concentrating all forces on a decisive front. As Stalin told the conference, according to the official record:

it would be a mistake to disperse forces by sending part to Turkey and elsewhere, and part to southern France. The best course would be to make 'Overlord' the basic operation for 1944 and, once Rome had been captured, to send all available forces in Italy to Southern France. These forces could then join hands with the 'Overlord' forces when the invasion was launched. France was the weakest spot on the German front. He himself did not expect Turkey to enter the war.[34]

Like Marshall, the Russians regarded the British proposals for wider involvement in the eastern Mediterranean and Balkans as at best mere wasteful diversions, and at worst a cunning means of ducking OVERLORD. Thus Stalin brutally cross-examined Churchill about the relative British commitment to OVERLORD and to action in the eastern Mediterranean and the Balkans. At the close of one session, according to the conference record,

> Marshal Stalin said . . . he wished to pose a very direct question to the Prime Minister about 'Overlord'. Did the Prime Minister and the British Staffs really believe in 'Overlord'?
> The Prime Minister replied that, providing the conditions for 'Overlord' were to obtain when the time came, he firmly believed it would be our stern duty to hurl across the Channel against the Germans every sinew of our strength.[35]

When Marshal Voroshilov put much the same question to Brooke, Brooke gave his well-worn answer that Mediterranean operations were designed to ensure the success of OVERLORD.

This cross-examination of the British by Stalin and Voroshilov, together with Stalin's insistence on the overriding priority to be given to OVERLORD, so mirrored the American position as to be consistent with collusion (although there is no evidence of this). Certainly the opportunity existed. For, as if to underline Churchill's and Britain's diminished importance, Roosevelt convened private meetings with Stalin early on in the conference while refusing one to Churchill.[36]

Did Brooke in his heart hanker for a Mediterranean/Balkan solution for beating Germany which – perhaps in conjunction with the allied bomber offensive against the German industrial machine – would avoid the necessity for a cross-Channel invasion and a slogging match with that formidable pugilist, the German Army, deployed in great strength? His biographer has to answer that this remains an enigma.[37] The same must be true of Churchill. Certainly at the second Cairo Conference (immediately following Tehran) Churchill did his vain best to persuade the visiting Turkish Prime Minister to agree to enter the war in conjunction with allied operations in the Aegean, even though the American Joint Chiefs made clear that these must not interfere with resources needed elsewhere.[38] In private negotiations with the Turks the British offered to send 17 RAF squadrons to Turkey at the time when Turkey should declare war on Germany. The Prime Minister and the Chiefs of Staff also formulated a plan for capturing the Dodecanese islands (including Rhodes) in March 1944, and the passing of war supplies through the Dardanelles.[39] In the event all this came to nought, for the canny Turks delayed declaring war on Germany until March 1945.

Churchill's fascination with the Aegean and the Balkans was by no means at the expense of his earlier preoccupation with the Italian campaign. The old question of the Mediterranean versus a campaign in north-west Europe came up afresh in 1944 after the capture of Rome at long last on 6 June (also of course D-day of OVERLORD) by General Alexander's 15th Army Group. Now, while the 15th Army Group pressed on after the retreating enemy, Churchill and Brooke tried for the last time to persuade the American leadership to make a further investment in their Mediterranean strategy. Brooke and Churchill wished the Americans to cancel the proposed seaborne invasion of the French Riviera (DRAGOON) so that Alexander could keep the two divisions and the landing-craft allotted to it for the sake of an extended advance to the north of Italy. Alexander even revived Churchill's vision of marching to Vienna (and getting there before the Red Army) from northern Italy via the so-called 'Ljubljana Gap' in Yugoslavia. Brooke himself, however, regarded this less as strategy than as mere 'dreams' or 'hopes', since the 'Ljubljana Gap' actually consisted of a long and tortuous route with bad road and rail communications through mountain country: ideal terrain for a German army on the defensive.[40] But the Americans would not hear of cancelling DRAGOON for the sake of the Italian campaign. Eisenhower (whose Allied Expeditionary Force was by now on the verge of final victory in Normandy), Marshall and Roosevelt all turned down the proposal flat, much to Churchill's chagrin.[41] In a final stroke of Churchillian opportunism the Prime Minister even urged that the DRAGOON forces should be switched to capture French Atlantic ports like St Nazaire, a proposal which his British naval and military advisers as well as the Americans killed stone-dead. DRAGOON duly took place on 15 August. Whereas Brooke had regarded the operation as both entirely redundant in itself and a wasteful diversion of forces from Italy, it in fact secured in Marseilles a major undamaged port which Eisenhower badly needed for the supply of his armies in northern France via the Rhone valley roads and railways.

To summarise briefly the conclusion of the Mediterranean strategy pursued by the British since 1940, the allied 15th Army Group in Italy became bogged down by December 1944 in stalemate before yet another stout German defence, where it remained until the final breakthrough into the valley of the Po in the closing weeks of the war. This left it still facing the encircling wall of the Alps. In regard to the Aegean and the Balkans, it was the Red Army's victories on the Eastern Front in 1944 which compelled the

Germans in September to thin-out garrisons in Greece, Crete and the Greek islands, and then to evacuate Greece altogether in October, opening the way for British landings.

Since this matter of an ever-deeper Mediterranean involvement constituted the fundamental strategic divide between the British and Americans *vis-à-vis* the German war, it is worth probing beneath the surface of the arguments in order to look at the two nations' contrasting circumstances and motivations. From 1942 through 1944 the United States was riding an economic boom that enabled her civilian standard of living to rise at the same time as her war production (including shipping and warships) grew to outstrip that of the United Kingdom by four times. She was subsidising not only the United Kingdom's war effort but also her very national life, for British exports had dropped by 1944 to a third of 1938, a level wholly insufficient to pay for necessary imports. Moreover, from a national population three times the size of Britain's, America had drafted, trained and equipped by June 1944 armed forces to a total of 11.5 millions, more than twice the size of the British armed forces.[42] In 1943–44 the United States therefore contemplated current and future campaigns from the enviable standpoint of abundant human and material resources. Not so the United Kingdom, at war for nearly two years longer, nationally bankrupt and dependent on foreign subsidies, existing on miserable rations, her manpower mobilised to the very limit and yet still proving not enough to meet all demands.[43] Whereas the United States was mass-producing new army divisions and had no anxiety about supplying the reinforcements needed in great battles, the British even by 1943 had already reached the point of being unable to meet the full manpower demands of the armed services as well as war production and minimum civilian needs.[44] By the beginning of 1944 the War Cabinet was having to gamble its manpower budgeting on the assumption that the German war would end that year, otherwise the armed forces would inevitably shrink.[45] In the event Britain already had to resort to breaking up divisions in the weeks that followed D-day.

The psychological distinctions are no less important. The Americans were buoyant with the confidence born of awareness of their surging power; the British were increasingly war-weary and conscious of waning strength. But in particular the two nations (and their leaderships) viewed the prospects of a major campaign in France against a main body of the German Army very differently – and because of contrasting historical experience. To put it bluntly, the United States and its armed forces had not fought a large-scale land war with consequent heavy casualties since 1865. Its limited battles in the Great War cannot be compared in scale or loss to the British experience on the Western Front. The American leadership therefore felt no profound qualms about engaging the German Army on a new Western Front. It was otherwise with the British, for reasons already discussed. There is no question but that

Churchill (who had commanded an infantry battalion on the Western Front) and Brooke alike wished above all to preserve the British Army from another Somme or Third Ypres: hence Brooke's obsessions with delaying an invasion until the German Army had been 'written down' elsewhere, above all by the Red Army on the Eastern Front. It may also be that the Americans, in their abounding confidence, took a more sanguine view of the combateffectiveness of allied troops (especially their own) compared with the enemy than did the British, who from 1940 to 1942 had been so often outfought by the Germans.

The shift in the balance of power – intellectual and psychological as well as material and military – is reflected by the fortunes of the Anglo-American arguments over grand strategy: whereas in 1941–42 the British generally prevailed, in 1943–45 they were almost brushed aside. The Tehran conference in November 1943 marked a turning-point. For by then the Americans had grown tired of the persistent British urging of a Mediterranean strategy even at the cost of delaying a cross-Channel invasion; more than that, deeply suspicious. Marshall in particular, a man now much grown in professional confidence and exercising great influence over his President and Commander-in-Chief, was resolved not to be outsmarted ever again by Brooke.[46] Moreover, Churchill's 'special relationship' with Roosevelt had faded into coolness and distance by Tehran. Harry Hopkins, once a vital link in the relationship had turned almost hostile.[47] Churchill himself, who celebrated his sixty-ninth birthday while at Tehran, was no longer the dominating personality of earlier war years, but a tired and worried man, telling his doctor one night during the conference: 'Do you think my strength will last out the war? I fancy sometimes that I am nearly spent.'[48] Much the same might have been said of his country, now dwarfed by its two great continental allies.

## NOTES

1. Cf. John Charmley, *Churchill: The End of Glory; a Political Biography* (London, Hodder and Stoughton, 1993); and Alan Clark, in his review article on Charmley's book in *The Times*, 2 January 1993.
2. Printed in full in J. M. A. Gwyer, *Grand Strategy*, Vol. III, *June 1941–August 1942*, Part I (London: HMSO, 1964), pp. 325–36.
3. Printed in full in J. R. M. Butler, *Grand Strategy*, Vol. II, *June 1941–August 1942*, Part II, Appendix I, pp. 669–74.
4. Cf. Dominick Graham and Shelford Bidwell, *Tug of War: The Battle for Italy, 1943–1945* (London: Hodder and Stoughton, 1986), Chapters 1 and 2, on the plans for invading Italy in 1943; Max Hastings, *Overlord: D-Day and the Battle for Normandy, 1944* (London: Michael Joseph, 1984), Chs 1 and 2. His section

'Commanders' (pp. 30–9), is devoted entirely to soldiers, and while he provides another section on 'Airmen' (pp. 39–45), he omits any mention of the sailors who actually got the allied forces to the Normandy shore. His account of D-Day essentially begins at the moment the landing forces hit the beaches. There is similar neglect of the essential maritime aspects of D-day in Carlo D'Este, *Decision in Normandy: The Unwritten Story of Montgomery and the Allied Campaign* (London: Collins, 1983), Part I, and John Keegan, *Six Armies in Normandy* (London: Jonathan Cape, 1982), Ch. I.

5. Correlli Barnett, *The Audit of War; The Illusion & Reality of Britain as a Great Nation* (London: Macmillan, 1986), p. 576. See this work passim, but especially Chs 7, 8 and 9, based on wartime records of the Cabinet and its committees, and of the Admiralty, Air Ministry and Ministries of Production and Aircraft Production.

6. C. B. A. Behrens, *Merchant Shipping and the Demands of War* (London: HMSO and Longmans, Green, 1955), p. 363. See also Correlli Barnett, *Engage the Enemy More Closely: The Royal Navy in the Second World War* (London: Hodder and Stoughton, 1991), pp. 436–40, 573–6.

7. See Behrens, op. cit., pp. 284–5.

8. See Barnett, *Engage the Enemy More Closely*, Ch. 19.

9. The Battle of the Atlantic: Directive by the Minister of Defence, 6 March 1941. Printed in full as Appendix O in S. W. Roskill, *The War at Sea 1939–1945*, Vol. I (London, HMSO, 1954), p. 609.

10. CAB 66/26, WP (42) 374, A Review of the War Situation. Note by the Prime Minister. See Barnett, *Engage the Enemy More Closely*, Chapter 15, for a full account of the 1942 'Battle of the Air' between the Admiralty and the Air Ministry.

11. Barnett, *Engage the Enemy More Closely*, Ch. 15.

12. Most exhaustively in Michael Howard, *Grand Strategy*, Vol. IV, *August 1942– September 1943*, Chs XI, XIV, XXII, XXIII, XXVI, XXIX; John Ehrman, *Grand Strategy*, Vol. V, *August 1943–September 1944*, Chs I, II, IV, V.

13. *Statistics of the Military Effort of the British Empire*, (London: HMSO 1922), Table (i) (9G), p. 238. The 'Lost Generation' of subalterns amounted to 37 452 killed, compared with the 55 888 lost by air crews of Bomber Command in the Second World War. Sir Charles Webster and Noble Frankland, *The Strategic Air Offensive Against Germany 1939–1945*, 4 vols (London: HMSO, 1961) Vol. III, pp. 286–7. For figures of Italians killed, see C. R. M. F. Cruttwell, *A History of the Great War* (Oxford: The Clarendon Press, 1934), p. 631.

14. See Barnett, *The Collapse of British Power* (London: Eyre and Spottiswoode, 1972; Stroud, Alan Sutton Paperbacks, 1984), pp. 424–36, for an analysis of the impact on 'educated opinion' of trench literature, c.1927.

15. *The War Memoirs of David Lloyd George*, 6 vols (London: Ivor Nicolson and Watson, 1933–36).

16. Cf. Brian Bond, *Liddell Hart: a Study of his Military Thought* (London: Cassell, 1977); John J. Mearsheimer, *Liddell Hart and the Weight of History* (London: Brassey's Defence Publishers, 1988).

17. See Barnett, *Engage the Enemy More Closely*, Chs 11, 12, 16, but especially pp. 368–9 and 516, on the cost-ineffectiveness of the Mediterranean theatre and the Desert campaign. Disasters: Rommel's first Desert offensive, March–April 1941; the abortive British BATTLEAXE offensive, June 1941; Greece and Crete, April– May 1941; cumulative virtual destruction of the Mediterranean Fleet, April– December 1941; rout of the Eighth Army in the Gazala battles May–June 1942. Successes: offensive in Western Desert against Italians, December 1940–January

1941; CRUSADER offensive in Western Desert against Germans and Italians, November–December 1941.
18. Cited in John Terraine, *Haig: the Educated Soldier* (London: Hutchinson, 1963), pp. 331–2.
19. Cited In Michael Howard, *Grand Strategy*, Vol. IV, *August 1942–September 1943* (London: HMSO, 1972), p. xiv.
20. See Fraser, op. cit., pp. 257–60.
21. Ibid., p. 262.
22. Howard, op. cit., Vol. IV, pp. xxiv–xxv.
23. Cf. David Fraser, *Alanbrooke* (London: Collins, 1982), pp. 358–60.
24. *Tug of War: The Battle for Italy 1943–1945* (London: Hodder and Stoughton, 1986), p. 401.
25. F. H. Hinsley, *British Intelligence in the Second World War; Its Influence on Strategy and Operations*, Vol. III, Part I (London: HMSO, 1984), p. 29.
26. Graham and Bidwell, op. cit., p. 399.
27. See Barnett, *Engage the Enemy More Closely*, pp. 617–22.
28. Howard, vol. cit., pp. 61, 198, 213, 227, 232–3, 252, 377, 381–3.
29. 19 July 1943, cited in Martin Gilbert, *Winston S. Churchill*, Vol. VII, *Road to Victory*, pp. 444–5.
30. Barnett, *Engage the Enemy More Closely*, pp. 681–5.
31. David Fraser, op. cit., p. 366.
32. Ibid.
33. John Ehrman, *Grand Strategy*, Vol. V, *August 1943–September 1944* (London: HMSO, 1956), p. 166.
34. Ibid., p. 175.
35. Ibid., p. 181.
36. Churchill, op.cit., Vol. 10, p. 33.
37. Fraser. op. cit., p.373.
38. Ehrman, op. cit., p. 194.
39. Ibid., p. 195.
40. Fraser, op. cit., p. 429.
41. Alfred D. Chandler (ed.), *The Papers of Dwight D. Eisenhower, The War Years*, Vol. IV (Baltimore and London: Johns Hopkins Press, 1970), letter from Eisenhower to Churchill, 11 August 1944; Gilbert, op. cit., Vol. VII, pp. 863–80.
42. W. K. Hancock and M. M. Gowing, *British War Economy* (London: HMSO and Longmans, Green, 1949), p. 366.
43. See ibid., pp. 369–78, for a general comparison of the two countries' war efforts.
44. Ibid., pp. 443–52.
45. Ibid., p. 450.
46. Ed Cray, *General of the Army: George C. Marshall, Soldier and Statesman* (New York, W. W. Norton & Co., 1990), Ch. XXIV.
47. Cf. Lord Moran, *Winston Churchill: The struggle for survival 1940–1965* (London: Heron Books, ND), pp. 133–44.
48. Moran, op. cit., p. 140.

# 9 The War against Japan and Allied Relations

## Peter Lowe

Allied strategy against Japan during the Pacific war was conditioned by the priorities and assessments determined by political and military leaders in 1941. It is essential to examine the formulation of British and American policies before Pearl Harbor in order to appreciate the approaches adopted during the bloody fighting in the Pacific and South-East Asia. Winston Churchill regarded the war in Europe as emphatically the top priority, followed by the Middle East; the Far East he relegated to third place. This was scarcely surprising given the situation facing him when he became prime minister in May 1940. The collapse of France and the sweeping German victories necessitated concentration upon the defence of Britain itself, the staving-off of invasion and a policy of encouraging indirect and then direct intervention by the United States.

Churchill's interest had focused largely on Europe during the 1930s and his understanding of Japan was flawed deeply by his failure to grasp the danger that that country's policies portended.[1] In a famous passage in his diaries Lord Moran described Churchill as 'a Victorian' in his attitudes towards Asian countries:[2] he viewed India and China as they had been in the 1890s and regarded Japan as it had been when he served as First Lord of the Admiralty before the Great War. Japan, he believed, was an eager, industrious society anxious to catch up with the West but with a long way still to go.[3] As Chancellor of the Exchequer in the 1920s he had brushed aside the need for Britain to devote substantial resources to containing Japan following the termination of the Anglo-Japanese alliance in 1923.[4] In June–July 1940, soon after he succeeded Chamberlain, Churchill was confronted with the crisis precipitated by Japan over the Burma Road. This resulted from Japanese pressure to prevent aid reaching the temporary Chinese capital of Chungking via Burma. At first he favoured a firm response but was then convinced by the chiefs of staff, supported by the ambassador in Tokyo, Sir Robert Craigie, that this would be most dangerous and the war cabinet agreed that the Road should be closed for a period of three months.[5] However, he strongly supported reopening the Road in October 1940 once they had survived the Battle of Britain and he resumed a more belligerent attitude.[6] This was based on a belief that the United States must accept primary responsibility for dealing with the Japanese challenge, Britain being too stretched in fighting Germany and Italy. This was logical and sensible but Churchill's policy was weakened by his erroneous assumption that a Japanese advance could be contained without excessive difficulty provided that the United States acted firmly.

Franklin Roosevelt agreed with Churchill that Nazi Germany represented the greatest menace and must be defeated first. He was constrained by his perception of American public opinion; it would be unwise, he believed, to move too far ahead of the American people or Congress.[7] He was far more perceptive than Churchill in appreciating the growing importance of nationalism in Asia; whereas Churchill expected colonial empires to endure for a long time to come, Roosevelt saw colonialism as expiring. But the president was no more accurate than was Churchill in discerning the menace of Japan. The American chiefs of staff were in the early stages of preparing for world war and favoured postponing conflict in the Pacific. Roosevelt authorised American officers to attend certain conferences convened by the British in 1940–41 in Singapore with the intention of fostering cooperation between the British Commonwealth and the Netherlands East Indies, but strict instructions were given that no commitments were to be entered into.[8] Roosevelt was particularly concerned that news of these contacts should not reach the ears of his critics.

The most important exchange of strategic thinking in the first half of 1941 occurred during high-level deliberations in Washington in January and February when a British delegation from the chiefs of staff met their American counterparts. Churchill told the British delegation to be diplomatic over the respective British and American roles:

> It was most important that the attitude to be adopted by our Delegation in the discussions on the naval strategy should be one of deference to the views of the United States in all matters concerning the Pacific theatre of war. It would be unwise to try and force our views on naval strategy in that theatre upon the United States Naval Authorities. . . . They would not be asking the Americans to come and protect Singapore, Australia and India against the Japanese, but would offer the use of Singapore to the Americans if they required it.[9]

The British delegation emphasised the significance of the Middle East, explaining that the fulfilment of a role there was vital to the defeat of Germany. The Far East and Pacific were also important because of the interests of the dominions and the territorial extent of the empire; the British underlined the strategic and economic contribution of Malaya[10] and reaffirmed their commitment to Singapore. While it was impossible to send a British fleet to Singapore in existing circumstances, it was essential to take all steps possible to avert its fall. The economic and strategic consequences of Singapore's surrender would be grave as would be the impact on morale.[11]

The American defence chiefs, in turn, underlined the extent to which they were hampered by the delicate political issues implicit in the American position. American and British forces should aim at defending the Malay barrier, at pursuing a limited offensive against Japan's eastern naval flank, and at implementing an economic blockade of Japan. The Americans diverged clearly from the British in their assessment of the importance of Singapore, since they were less obsessed with its symbolic significance. As they explained:

> Singapore has been built up in public opinion as a symbol of the power of the British Empire. The eastern Dominions, the Netherlands East Indies and China look upon its security as the guarantee of their safety. Its value as a symbol has become so great that its capture by Japan would be a serious blow. But many severe blows have been taken by these various nations and other severe blows can be absorbed without leading to final disaster.[12]

The Americans were, of course, correct in this statement, as events were to demonstrate, but the British, and Churchill in particular, continued to place heavy emphasis on the significance of Singapore which he saw as an indestructible fortress, an opinion he discarded only reluctantly when that proved not to be the case. The Washington defence talks improved mutual understanding and promoted personal contacts but they also reveal the problem of achieving sufficient coordination when the United States was not prepared to commit itself politically.

Nevertheless, the course of Anglo-American unity was furthered, even more than Roosevelt recognised at the time, by discussions held in Washington between the Secretary of State, Cordell Hull, and Japanese representatives. The ostensible aim of these talks, which began in April 1941, was to ascertain if sufficient agreement could be reached in informal exchanges to secure a settlement of American–Japanese differences. The discussions were marked by ineptitude and misunderstanding on both sides.[13] However, one consequence of these lengthy deliberations was that the United States henceforward accepted effective responsibility for the handling of Japan. The first part of Churchill's strategy was thereby accomplished; the second, a definite American commitment to fight Japan, proved more elusive. Controversy has raged since Pearl Harbor over how and why the United States became involved in the war. Isolationists have alleged that Roosevelt deliberately provoked the Japanese into attacking and this was reflected later in works by Charles A. Beard and Charles Tansill.[14] More recently, James Rusbridger and Eric Nave have alleged that Churchill knew from intelligence sources that the Japanese were going to attack Pearl Harbor and that he concealed this from Roosevelt so as to ensure full American involvement in the wars against Germany, Italy and Japan.[15] While producing interesting ideas, Rusbridger and Nave have not supplied the evidence to support their interpretation: it is possible but not probable that Churchill concealed vital information from Roosevelt – the risks would have been huge had deception been proved subsequently. Equally, however, it is clear that American and British intelligence possessed considerable information concerning Japanese intentions. The Americans had cracked the MAGIC code so that communications between the Japanese government and the embassy in Washington could be read; the information obtained therefrom revealed the Japanese aim to attack within the near future but it did not show where the attack would occur. Information had been obtained from the British via code-breaking and intercepts. Previously-closed files, now available in the Public Record Office, provide no tangible evidence to support the argument that Churchill was aware of the impending attack on Pearl Harbor. What these do reveal was his continuing anxiety that Chinese resistance should be sustained.[16]

Knowledge of the broad direction being taken by Japan was not accompanied by sufficient sensitivity and accurate analysis. Senior British officers in the Far East stressed the need for additional resources, particularly air and naval, but they underestimated, nevertheless, the Japanese capacity for inflicting grave damage. The joint planning staff and the chiefs of staff maintained that while air strength should be improved, the quality of Japanese aircraft and personnel should not be exaggerated – 'we have no reason to believe that Japanese standards are even comparable with those of the Italians'.[17] Churchill overruled advice from the Admiralty and dispatched the *Prince of Wales* and *Repulse* in a futile endeavour to bolster sagging faith in Britain in the southern dominions and with the hope of having a deterrent effect on the Japanese.[18] It is difficult to escape the conclusion that racial prejudice affected the judgement of politicians and defence chiefs. Japan had not succeeded in compelling the Chinese to surrender so the white race would surely succeed in blocking a Japanese advance.

Roosevelt and his advisers failed similarly to assess Japanese capability with precision. The imposition of drastic economic sanctions on Japan between July and September 1941 brought matters to a head. The sanctions were more comprehensive than Roosevelt intended originally, since the American bureaucracy, headed by Dean Acheson, had tightened them, but Roosevelt recognised that he was gambling when he imposed them and the gamble did not dissuade the Japanese from advancing further. On 1 December 1941 he at last gave the promise of support in the event of an attack on British territory which Churchill and his predecessors had sought, Roosevelt having indicated that it would take a little time to secure a declaration of war on Japan from Congress.[19] Thus as the Japanese moved into Malaya and attacked Pearl Harbor, Britain and the United States were involved in war together informally and, ironically for a very brief period, before they were united formally in war against both Japan and Germany in consequence of Hitler's declaration of war against the United States.

Allied strategy in the Pacific war was determined by the prior commitment to victory in Europe and by the underestimation of Japan which had characterised policy-making prior to 1941 and which continued to apply in the opening phase of the conflict in the Pacific and in South-East Asia. Churchill rejoiced at the news of Pearl Harbor for it solved some at least of the problems he had faced in the previous twelve months, but he was worried that Roosevelt might be pressurised by military, congressional, or public opinion into assigning greater resources to the war against Japan.

Had a president of different outlook or of less subtle political skills occupied the White House, Churchill's fears might have been borne out. The sense of outrage at the dastardly attack on Pearl Harbor, the political influence of General Douglas MacArthur, and a feeling on the part of Americans dwelling in the western states that war against Japan was more vital than war against Germany could have led the United States to concentrate more on its efforts in that theatre. Roosevelt agreed that the European war must take precedence when he met Churchill in Washington at the end of December 1941. He adhered consistently to this view but was forced, in consequence of the setbacks experienced in 1942, to devote substantial resources to the Pacific theatre; by the end of 1942 a total of 346 000 American troops were serving in the region.[20]

The failure of the allies to coordinate their policies more successfully earlier in 1941 compounded the difficulties of meeting Japanese aggression. The British refusal to prepare for the defence of the Netherlands East Indies until they had received a firm promise of support from the United States further handicapped the preparation of an effective strategy. In the event, the Japanese forces proved far more dangerous and efficient than had been anticipated, as was shown in Hong Kong, Malaya, the Philippines, and the Netherlands East Indies. The ABDA (American-British-Dutch-Australian) command was improvised at the Washington conference in December 1941 but proved unwieldy and was doomed from inception. It was not surprising that Roosevelt favoured a British commander for this role and that the unfortunate General Wavell was awarded the 'poisoned chalice'.[21] The command lasted two months during a period of unmitigated disaster in which the worst development for the British Commonwealth and Empire was the surrender of Singapore on 15 February 1942. This was a profound blow for Churchill, who had argued obstinately that the 'fortress' could survive, despite being told by the chiefs of staff in August 1940 that to defend Singapore would mean defending the whole Malayan peninsula.[22]

Friction within the Commonwealth, especially in Britain's relations with Australia and New Zealand, was thereby accentuated greatly. John Curtin, the Labour prime minister of Australia, spoke dramatically of Australia's reliance upon the United States rather than Britain for support in his immediate reaction to the outbreak of war in the Pacific. This was important in the longer term for marking a vital watershed in Anglo-Australian relations but, as David Day has shown, there was still considerable loyalty to the British connection within Australian political circles.[23] No British military hero was within sight and instead Australians welcomed MacArthur when he escaped from the Philippines to begin the task of re-establishing American power. In reality MacArthur was more critical of the Australians than they believed but this underlined MacArthur's dedication to ensuring that victory in the Pacific was an American achievement (and a MacArthur achievement).[24] The Australian minister for external affairs, Dr Herbert Evatt, was extremely ambitious but, unfortunately, possessed a capacity for antagonising people equivalent to his ambition. Evatt asserted Australian interest vehemently, believing that while Australia should maintain its historic links with Britain, it was essential that an independent Australian foreign policy should be pursued. Australian fear of Japanese expansion was profound in 1942 amid apprehension that Australia itself might be invaded. Curtin, Evatt and the Australian defence chiefs were worried at the exposure of Australian troops in the Middle East and this occasioned some bitter exchanges between Churchill and Curtin. In the middle and latter stages of the war Australian anxiety over invasion abated, to be replaced with growing suspicion of American economic ambition in the Pacific region. Curtin then retreated on the Labour party's commitment to appointing an Australian national as governor-general and instead proposed the appointment of the Duke of Gloucester who was indeed appointed.[25]

In military terms the allies were committed to a long haul in fighting Japan. The ferocity of the Japanese onslaught, the more urgent priorities in Europe and the Middle East, and the time required for the American war effort to develop fully meant that a process of marking time would have to be followed. Churchill hoped that tattered British prestige could be rescued in Burma. The Japanese took longer to triumph there than in Malaya and were manifestly overstretched, since their line of advance extended all the way to the borders of India. Louis Allen has written an outstanding and graphic account of the nature of the terrible struggle in Burma in which he participated as a youthful interpreter.[26] The depressing climate, jungle, and prevalence of disease contributed to the collapse of British confidence in 1942–43. Churchill described the failure of the Burma campaign in 1943 as 'one of the most disappointing and indeed discreditable which has occurred in this war'.[27] This encouraged American cynicism over the British role in a war which was seen increasingly as an American responsibility. General 'Vinegar Joe' Stilwell interspersed caustic remarks in his diary concerning the 'Peanut' (Chiang Kai-shek) with mordant comments on the 'Limeys' and their incompetent, indolent approach to war.[28]

This leads us into consideration of the Anglo-American relationship. Christopher Thorne captured the nature of this admirably in his excellent work, *Allies of a Kind*, which remains the best study of the subject.[29] On the positive side the two countries shared much in common: hatred of Nazi Germany and all it represented, a deep commitment to defeating Japanese aggression, a belief in liberal, civilised values notwithstanding the hypocrisy associated with the treatment of Black Americans and the analogous hypocrisy displayed by some British personnel towards non-white peoples (Admiral Somerville gave instructions that Indian patients were not to be treated by white nurses).[30] Despite developing strains in their relationship as the war continued, the cooperation between Churchill and Roosevelt was remarkable. But they were allies of a *kind*. They diverged fundamentally over the future of colonial empires, since Churchill was committed passionately to the restoration of the British Empire and Roosevelt to its dismantling. The unfolding of American might and the determination to assert American leadership was bound to lead to friction. Some American officers were highly critical of Britain, among them Admiral Ernest J. King and General Stilwell. Looking back, it is less surprising that differences developed between the allies than that they were not much worse. Initiatives came increasingly from the Americans in 1943, 1944 and 1945 until the war ended with the United States dictating the manner of its termination by dropping two atomic bombs.

The policy of unconditional surrender provides an example of differences in approach over time. The policy was announced by Roosevelt at the Casablanca conference in January 1943.[31] Churchill was more conversant with the president's intentions than he pretended later. Given the peculiar barbarity of the Second World War with atrocities of unprecedented scale committed by both Axis powers, a policy of unconditional surrender had much to commend it. It has taken the Japanese government nearly fifty years to make its clearest apology so far for the horrors of war including enforced prostitution for women in countries occupied by Japanese forces.[32] Yet there was more to be said for unconditional surrender in the case of Germany than Japan. The Nazi regime appeared more evil than did the imperial government in Japan. In addition, the dedication of the Japanese to the imperial system and their apprehension as to the repercussions of unconditional surrender encouraged leaders and people to pursue their struggle with a mixture of fanaticism and stoicism.

In the summer of 1945, after the European war ended, Churchill and the American joint chiefs contemplated dropping unconditional surrender and negotiating with Japan. Churchill was influenced by the war-weariness growing in Britain and the United States and by the view that Japan was different from Germany. The American joint chiefs suggested that he raise the issue with the president (now Harry Truman).[33] Churchill did so but discovered that Truman's attitude towards Japan had not softened. Truman commented that the Japanese forfeited military honour after Pearl Harbor to which Churchill responded that the Japanese forces were driven on by beliefs of a profound character.[34] Unconditional surrender was not abandoned but assurances were given regarding the future of the monarchy before the Showa emperor ordered his subjects to surrender.

But, going back to the situation in 1943, the only certainty then was that the struggle in the Pacific would be prolonged and there would be no shortcut to victory. The Americans pursued their campaigns in the Pacific vigorously against strong Japanese resistance. American and Australian forces slowly countered the Japanese advance in New Guinea. The British campaign in Burma failed but Churchill was captivated by the unorthodox personality and ideas of Brigadier Orde Wingate for undermining the Japanese via his theory of long-range penetration. Wingate's strategy was highly controversial, since it involved using forces in deeply unorthodox ways, disapproved of by conventional military minds. His death in an air accident precludes a definitive assessment of their chances of succeeding, for his successor lacked Wingate's originality and commitment.

The first Quebec conference in August 1943 saw the establishment of South-East Asia Command (SEAC), headed by an improbable combination (like an old-fashioned American presidential ticket) of Lord Louis Mountbatten and General Stilwell; the latter deputised occasionally for Mountbatten and was alienated by the pomp and luxury of Mountbatten's headquarters. SEAC was intended to improve coordination with the hope that a more positive contribution from China would complement the American drive in the Pacific. SEAC performed moderately well but played a crucial role only in 1945 and during the immediate aftermath of the war.[35] Developments in Burma in 1944 marked the decisive turning-point. The Japanese attempt to break through into India In the battles of Imphal and Kohima failed and General Slim's Fourteenth Army gradually, inexorably, and then rapidly inflicted the greatest defeat on land suffered by the Japanese army during the war. The British commitment to eventual success in Burma at last produced positive results, thus bringing about a partial restoration in British morale. Slim referred ruefully to his forces as 'the forgotten army', a not inaccurate description.[36]

Earlier in the war much faith had been placed in the potential Chinese military contribution to victory. Roosevelt was one of many affected by the popular image of the indomitable Chiang Kai-shek rallying his countrymen from the remoteness of Chungking. The impression of Kuomintang China conveyed by its influential American friends such as Walter Judd, Henry Luce and Claire Chennault was that China would soon contribute powerfully to the defeat of Japan provided enough economic and military aid was channelled in its direction.[37] If this were done, it was claimed, the war could be shortened appreciably, for American planes could operate from Chinese bases in bombing Japan. The British were more dubious or cynical but their relations with Chiang's regime had been poor for several years, since Chiang blamed the British for making excessive concessions to the Japanese and the

British criticised the incompetence and corruption of Chiang's government.[38] Roosevelt regarded the British as too negative and committed to obsolete attitudes. He was right in discerning that China was changing and would become more important but he was too sanguine in believing that Chiang would preside over a transformed China. Chiang was something of an absentee as far as allied meetings were concerned. He attended only one top conference during the war – Cairo in November–December 1943 – and this meeting was inevitably overshadowed by the Tehran conference which followed when Roosevelt and Churchill met Stalin, leaving Chiang behind, the Soviet Union not being involved in the war against Japan.[39]

Chiang promised that Chinese troops would participate in the Burma campaigns but pressed for a stronger allied commitment to fighting Japan. Churchill was alarmed for the familiar reason that launching a second front in Europe came first. Stalin's determination to ensure maximum allied support for Russia compelled Roosevelt to retreat in his undertaking to Chiang. Churchill was impressed mainly by Madame Chiang who demonstrated once more her ability to entrance. The British were sceptical as to what would be achieved by Chinese troops in Burma. The best Chinese soldiers were of good calibre, vindicating Stilwell's confidence in what could be accomplished if the necessary training and encouragement were provided. But only a small proportion of Kuomintang troops reached this level and Chiang was suspicious of commanders who became too ambitious or developed close links with the Americans. The mordant passages in Stilwell's diary convey starkly the extent of the irascible general's disillusionment with Chiang's regime as he became ever more obsessed with the malevolent effects of the 'Peanut's' rule.[40] Chiang was depicted as suspicious, vindictive, petty, intolerant, uninterested in the Chinese masses and dominated by reactionary and xenophobic opinions. Although exaggerated, the portrait is nevertheless largely convincing. By 1944 Roosevelt, too, was becoming disillusioned with Chiang. The provision of large-scale American aid had not regalvanised the Chinese effort; instead, the Japanese army had launched a successful offensive compelling Chinese troops to retreat. Stilwell advocated strong pressure from Washington to force Chiang to give him effective command of the Chinese Army. Roosevelt initially took a tough line but the proximity of the 1944 presidential election led him to reconsider and instead he removed Stilwell. The embittered 'Vinegar Joe' joined others in discovering that, whatever his numerous defects, Chiang could move swiftly when it came to protecting his vital interests.

By 1944–45 China had become irrelevant so far as allied efforts to defeat Japan were concerned (although she remained important in a practical sense by virtue of containing large numbers of Japanese troops). In particular, American successes in advancing rapidly in the Pacific ensured that Japan could be bombed intensively without using Chinese bases.

One key factor in ending the war lay in engaging the participation of an additional major combatant. The sole candidate for this role was the Soviet Union: the opening of a further front in Asia would be a huge drain on Japanese resources. The obvious and, in the short term insurmountable problem was that the Soviet Union could not be expected to enter into the Far Eastern conflict until Germany had been defeated. Another difficulty was that Stalin would demand concessions in return for Soviet action, a feature that loomed increasingly large in the course of the first half of 1945. When he visited Moscow in 1941, at the very beginning of the Pacific war, Anthony Eden urged Soviet entry.[41] At the Tehran conference in December 1943 Stalin indicated that he would be prepared to intervene three months after the close of the European conflict, a promise to which he adhered.[42]

The development of the atomic bomb could be seen as complementary to, or possibly replacing, the Soviet contribution. However, the uncertain nature of the project necessitated continued planning on the assumption that Soviet assistance would be essential. Roosevelt and Churchill agreed, at their Hyde Park meeting in September 1944, that TUBE ALLOYS (the atomic project) should be developed to the point where 'after mature consideration', the atomic weapon could be deployed.[43] American and Soviet representatives discussed the arrangements for Soviet intervention on various occasions between the Moscow conference in October 1944 and the exchanges in Yalta in February 1945. Soviet generals stressed the appreciable quantities of military aid required.[44] The Americans were keen to gain Soviet permission for using Soviet territory to bomb Japan by conventional means.[45] Stalin made it clear that he would require considerable concessions. Roosevelt's reaction was that these could not be avoided and that a significant price would have to be paid for Soviet action.

The Yalta conference has always been a source of profound controversy and it became highly contentious with the deterioration of American–Soviet relations and the onset of the Cold War.[46] Roosevelt was now a dying man and speculation continues concerning the extent to which his judgement was affected by his state of health. Nevertheless, his discussions with Stalin over the Japanese war were logical and balanced. He accepted that, in return for Soviet intervention three months after the end of the war in Europe, the Soviet Union would secure the southern half of the island of Sakhalin, the Kurile Islands, railway rights in Manchuria, and the leasing of Port Arthur and Dairen, thus fulfilling Stalin's aim of reversing the results of the Russo-Japanese war of 1904–5.[47] Keeping in mind that allied military planners envisaged the ferocious struggle against Japan extending well into 1946 if not beyond, Roosevelt's concessions were realistic. Allied losses, likely to mount appreciably in the concluding stages, could not be exacerbated for the sake of failing to provide enough inducements to Stalin.

What is harder to defend is Roosevelt's failure to consult Britain or China.

He emphasised his wish for a positive relationship with Stalin in the middle and latter stages of the Second World War and he showed an increasingly cavalier attitude towards Churchill. Eden was outraged when he heard of the Far Eastern provisions at Yalta and urged Churchill to protest.[48] The prime minister doubtless shared Eden's ire but was wise enough not to place added strain on his relations with Roosevelt. The failure to consult or inform China is remarkable given the origins of the Pacific war and is revealing of the degree to which American faith in China had declined by 1944–45. Chiang Kai-shek learned of the Yalta agreement only four months afterwards as American attitudes towards the Soviet Union began to change.[49] But the essential point is that the Yalta agreement was sensible and defensible when assessed in the light of the dilemmas confronting allied leaders and planners in February 1945.

The savage fighting for Iwo Jima and Okinawa stimulated fears of the magnitude of the losses which the allies could sustain, particularly if an invasion of the Japanese home islands had to be faced. In addition, the surrender of Germany in May 1945 accentuated a desire, if not determination, to conclude the war against Japan sooner rather than later. In June and July the American desire to see an early Soviet entry diminished with the growth of a serious divergence of opinion over Poland and Germany. The rapid development of the atomic bomb offered first the possibility and then the near-certainty of being able to drop at least one bomb on Japan. As we have seen already, Churchill and the American joint chiefs wished to amend the policy of unconditional surrender during the Potsdam conference but Truman demurred. He wanted to establish the credibility of his own leadership and the termination of the Pacific war could be viewed as, in part, his achievement in a way that the end of the European war could not. Truman made an oblique reference to the atomic weapon in a conversation with Stalin, not realising that the Soviet leader was already conversant with it through information supplied by his spies. The Potsdam ultimatum to Japan was blunt but open to the subsequent objection that it did not convey the full horror of the fate that awaited if she did not surrender promptly.[50] Truman was more suspicious of the Soviet Union than his predecessor and wished to minimise the extent of Soviet expansion in East Asia. For a combination of international and domestic reasons he was determined to end the Pacific war quickly and the atomic weapon was the most convenient method of bringing this about.

The first atomic bomb was dropped on Hiroshima on 6 August. In a public statement to the American people Truman defended his action vigorously and warned the Japanese that more bombs would be dropped unless they surrendered swiftly.[51] The Far Eastern department of the Foreign Office, which had not been consulted over the decision to use the bomb, protested at its deployment but in vain. The new Labour government of Clement Attlee continued Churchill's approach of accepting that the United States would preside over the termination of the Pacific war. The Soviet Union joined in the war on 8 August, dealing another grave blow to the already depleted Japanese forces in Manchuria and Korea. There was no doubt that Japan would surrender soon and the Showa emperor's intervention ensured that, given the rebellious inclinations in parts of the army, this occurred more smoothly than otherwise.[52]

By the summer of 1945 Japan clearly had lost the war but the difficulty lay in inducing Japanese leaders to accept the fact, together with the associated problem of preventing parts of the Japanese armed forces from continuing to fight in the numerous areas where their troops still operated. The war could have been ended without using the atomic bomb through relying on economic strangulation and Soviet intervention. But this would have entailed higher allied casualties among combatants and among prisoners-of-war and civilians held in Japanese camps. Truman's attitude towards Russia was negative but the purpose of his approving the use of the atomic bombs was to terminate the war rapidly and produce a solution to the problems facing him. The aim of warning the Soviet Union simultaneously to cooperate in Europe and in Asia was implicit in Truman's actions but only as a secondary factor – ending the war against Japan came first. Appropriately, the British role in the vital political decisions was essentially that of a bystander. In the military context Slim's victory in Burma was a great and underrated achievement. SEAC faced formidable tasks in re-establishing western authority in the reoccupied colonial territories. The principal success was that of the American-dominated campaigns in the Pacific headed by MacArthur and Nimitz. It was no surprise that Douglas MacArthur moved from vanquishing Japan to rebuilding it in his new responsibilities as Supreme Commander, Allied Powers. What was surprising was that he proved as liberal and flexible in his approach to governing Japan as he did.

Many of the challenges facing the allies resulted from the mistakes made in the prewar era. The same could no doubt be said of most wars but certain of the errors in formulating policies towards Japan before the autumn of 1941 were particularly striking and potent in their effects. Among these was the inability to coordinate allied responses during the 1930s. Much American moral indignation was expended on the alleged failure of the British government to support Henry L. Stimson's supposed desire to adopt a tough line with Japan during the Manchurian crisis. But there was no likelihood of Herbert Hoover's doomed administration using force to deter Japan in 1932. The events in Shanghai in January and February 1932, when serious fighting engulfed the great port, resulting from Japanese aggression, illuminated the dangers of Japanese expansion more sharply, from the viewpoint of British and American interests, than events in Manchuria. Sir Robert Vansittart was correct in his famous minute of 1 February 1932 in warning that Japan could only be dealt with properly by the use of force in which the United States would act, as she eventually did, in cooperation with Britain. Thus the United States would be 'kicked into war' by Japan just as Germany had kicked the United States into war in 1917.[53]

Given the character of the governments in Britain during the 1930s and Roosevelt's preoccupation with the economy and the prevalence of isolationist views, it is not surprising that British and American policies were so weak and uncoordinated. Sir Robert Craigie, the ambassador in Tokyo, played a poor hand with remarkable diplomatic skill in the four years preceding Pearl Harbor, recognising that limited concessions must be made to Japan until force could be used. His advice and recommendations over the Tientsin crisis in 1939 and over the Burma Road in 1940 were especially cogent. Craigie urged that he be empowered to negotiate the least humiliating solutions attainable to the grave confrontations with Japan provoked by these crises. His diplomacy was patient and shrewd, and still graver crises were pushed back into 1941.[54] Craigie wrote a lucid final report on his mission in Tokyo in which he criticised the ineptitude of British and American policies in 1941, thereby incurring the lasting wrath of Churchill.[55]

The two most serious mistakes made in the development of British and American policies in 1941 were the failure to secure fully-integrated defence planning and the underestimation of Japanese capabilities. The numerous Far Eastern defence conferences and exchanges in Washington in 1940–41 did not achieve a great deal as regards constructive cooperation between the British, the Commonwealth, the Dutch and the Americans. They were handicapped fatally by the absence of positive political will but due acknowledgement must also be made of the dilemmas confronting Roosevelt in manipulating American public opinion. The harsh fact was that for the Americans, British and Dutch to commit themselves fully to assisting each other in the first week of December 1941 came very late in the day.

A separate but related theme was the chronic misjudgement of Japanese efficiency and commitment. Ignorance and racial prejudice led to the arrogant assumption that war against Japan would be inconvenient but not profoundly dangerous because the Japanese could be contained. Had British and American leaders known how devastating the Japanese onslaught was to be they would have acted differently in a number of vital respects: Churchill might then have seen the wisdom of sending Hurricanes to Malaya rather than Russia and would have grasped the futility of dispatching the *Prince of Wales* and *Repulse* to Singapore; the defence of Singapore would have been viewed more realistically; British air chiefs would have appreciated the ability of Japanese pilots and the efficacy of the Zero fighter. American defences in Pearl Harbor would have been in a state of alert rather than somnolence. MacArthur's planes in the Philippines would not have been left sitting on the ground awaiting attack. It is unlikely that economic sanctions would have been imposed on Japan as clumsily as they were between July and September

1941; rather a slower tightening of the economic screw would have been applied, as the British had advocated.

However, all this would have amounted to no more than reducing the havoc Japan could wreak rather than averting it. The magnitude of the world crisis in 1939–41 meant that Japan would possess the initiative and that it would take considerable time to produce the resources for combating Japan. The blunders of 1941 compounded the challenges of 1942. Strategy in the Pacific area was largely determined by the United States and was broadly convincing. The landing in the Philippines in 1944 was most probably not necessary in military terms but arguably was important for American prestige (and certainly for the prestige of MacArthur). The British had to focus on the war in Burma as the only opportunity to inflict land defeat on the Japanese but it was bound to be a prolonged struggle. The original expectation of a Chinese contribution proved misplaced; here British cynicism turned out to be more accurate than American trust. Only the Soviet Union could affect the course of the war dramatically before the dropping of the first atomic bomb and neither of these eventualities could materialise earlier than 1945. While Japan experienced massive reverses, the will to continue remained and there was little likelihood of surrender in an unambiguous way before the use of the two atomic bombs.

Britain and the United States were 'allies of a kind' but this might be said of allied relationships in most wars. What was significant about the war in the Pacific and in South-East Asia was the potent message of ousting western colonialism permanently which was propagated sedulously by the Japanese in their bid to foster this 'Greater East Asia Co-Prosperity Sphere'.[56] It was a mendacious, hypocritical message since Japanese imperialism of a peculiarly brutal kind was replacing the western varieties but the stunning defeats inflicted on western forces in 1941–42 undermined fatally the moral credibility of the West. In this sense, as Thorne remarks, Japan won the war.[57] Ironically, the British, faced with daunting problems of decolonisation in the Indian sub-continent, Burma and, later, Malaya escaped relatively easily (except for the final problem of Hong Kong). The United States inherited the problems which overwhelmed the French in Indo-China and which led to an outcome that would have seemed incredible in 1945 – their ignominious departure from Vietnam in 1975. The final echoes of the Pacific war, from the western standpoint, were then heard. From the Japanese standpoint the final echoes can still, embarrassingly, be heard.

NOTES

1. See Peter Lowe, 'Winston Churchill and Japan, 1915–1942', in J. W. M. Chapman (ed.), *Proceedings of the British Association for Japanese Studies* 6, part 1 (1981), pp. 39–47, 236–7.
2. Lord Moran, *Churchill: the Struggle for Survival* (London: Constable, 1966), p. 131.
3. Between 1911 and 1914 Churchill regarded the Anglo-Japanese alliance as axiomatic to British naval strategy since the Royal Navy could be concentrated in or near home waters while the Japanese navy defended British interests in the Pacific and China Sea, Peter Lowe, *Great Britain and Japan, 1911–15: A study of British Far Eastern Policy* (London: Macmillan, 1969), pp. 178–9, 283–6.
4. See Martin Gilbert, *Winston S. Churchill*, vol. 5 (London: Heinemann, 1976), pp. 105, 250.
5. See Peter Lowe, *Great Britain and the Origins of the Pacific War: A study of British Policy in East Asia, 1937–1941* (Oxford: Clarendon Press, 1977), pp. 140–55.
6. Ibid., p. 174.
7. See J. Macgregor Burns, *Roosevelt: the Soldier of Freedom, 1940–1945* (London: Weidenfeld and Nicolson, 1971), R. A. Dallek, *Franklin D. Roosevelt and American Foreign Policy, 1932–45* (Oxford: Oxford University Press, 1979), W. F. Kimball, *The Juggler: Franklin Roosevelt as Wartime Statesman* (Princeton: Princeton University Press, 1991). For reference purposes, note W. F. Kimball (ed.), *Churchill and Roosevelt: the Complete Correspondence*, 3 vols (Princeton: Princeton University Press, 1984).
8. See Lowe, *Great Britain and Origins of Pacific War*, pp. 201–8.
9. Chiefs of Staff Committee, 'British–United States Technical Conversations', note by the secretary 19 Dec. 1940, C.O.S. (40) 1052, Cab. 80/24.
10. 'British–United States staff conversations, 'Relative Importance of the Middle East and Far East Theatres', 31 Jan. 1941, B.U.S. (J) (41), 6, Cab. 99/5.
11. Ibid., 'The Far East: Appreciation by the United Kingdom Delegation, 11 Feb. 1941, B.U.S. (J) (41) 13.
12. Ibid., 'Statement by the United States Staff Committee. "The United States Military Position in the Far East"', 19 Feb. 1941, B.U.S. (J) (41) 16.
13. For a thorough account of the background to, and character of, the Washington talks, see R. J. C. Butow, *The John Doe Associates: Backdoor Diplomacy for Peace, 1941* (Stanford: Stanford University Press, 1974).
14. See C. A. Beard, *President Roosevelt and the Coming of the War, 1941* (New Haven: Yale University Press, 1948) and C. C. Tansill, *Back Door to War* (Chicago: Henry Regnery, 1952).
15. See James Rusbridger and Eric Nave, *Betrayal at Pearl Harbor: How Churchill lured Roosevelt into War* (London: Michael O'Mara, 1991).
16. For the MAGIC intercepts, see *The 'Magic' Background of Pearl Harbor*, 5 vols (Washington, DC: Government Printing Office, 1978). I am very grateful to Dr Antony Best for giving me his impressions of the files released in the Public Record Office at the end of 1993. See also Chapter 6 by Christopher Andrew in this volume on American and British code-breaking.
17. Chiefs of Staff Committee, 'Visit of the Australian Prime Minister. Reply by Chiefs of Staff to Memorandum by the Prime Minister of Australia', 11 Apr. 1941, Cab. 80/27.
18. See A. J. Marder, *Old Friends, New Enemies: the Royal Navy and the Imperial Japanese Navy: Strategic Illusions, 1936–1941* (Oxford: Oxford University Press, 1981), pp. 365–521.

19. See Lowe, *Great Britain and the Origins of the Pacific War*, pp. 270–2.
20. Christopher Thorne, *Allies of a Kind: the United States, Britain and the War against Japan, 1941–1945* (London: Hamish Hamilton, 1978), p. 163.
21. Lowe, *Great Britain and Origins of Pacific War*, pp. 270–2.
22. Ibid., p. 163.
23. See David Day, *Reluctant Nation: Australia and the Defeat of Japan 1942–45* (Melbourne: Oxford University Press, 1992).
24. C. Thorne, 'MacArthur, Australia, and the British', *Australian Outlook* (April and August 1975), pp. 53–67, 197–210.
25. Day, pp. 163–4.
26. Louis Allen, *Burma: The Longest War* (London: Dent, 1984).
27. Day, p. 129.
28. See T. H. White (ed.), *The Stilwell Papers* (New York: Sloane, 1948), pp. 43–106 for Stilwell's comments on the retreat in Burma in 1942.
29. See Thorne, *Allies of a Kind*, and *The Issue of War: States, Societies, and the Far Eastern Conflict of 1941–1945* (New York: Oxford University Press, 1985). The latter provides more of a panoramic view of the war with less of the diplomatic detail and more on social developments than is to be found in *Allies of a Kind*.
30. Thorne, 'Britain and the Black GIs: Racial Issues and Anglo-American Relations in 1942', *New Community* 3 (1974). For Somerville's views, see Day, p. 179.
31. The apology was announced at the beginning of August 1993 following the defeat of the Miyazawa government in the general election. A more explicit condemnation of Japan's aggression between 1937 and 1945 was made by the new prime minister, Hosokawa Morihiro, heading a seven-party coalition government of disparate groups. Hosokawa stated, on 10 August 1993, 'It was a war of aggression, and it was a mistake', *The Economist*, 14 August 1993.
32. Thorne, *Allies of a Kind*, p. 166.
33. *Documents on British Policy Overseas*, series 1, vol. 1, *The Conference at Potsdam*, pp. 364–7, summarised note of conversation between Churchill and Truman, 18 July 1945.
34. Ibid.
35. Thorne, *Allies of a Kind*, pp. 297–300.
36. For Slim's lively memoirs but reticent on intelligence aspects, see W. Slim, *Defeat Into Victory* (London: Cassell, 1956). For the official history of the British war effort in the Far East, see S. Woodburn Kirby *et al.*, *The War Against Japan*, 5 vols (London: HMSO, 1957–69).
37. See Michael Schaller, *The US Crusade in China, 1938–45* (New York: Columbia University Press, 1978).
38. Lowe, *Great Britain and the Origins of Pacific War*, pp. 210–13, 295–7.
39. See Keith Sainsbury, *The Turning Point: Roosevelt, Stalin, Churchill, and Chiang Kai-shek, 1943: The Moscow, Cairo and Teheran Conferences* (Oxford: Oxford University Press, 1985).
40. See White (ed.), *The Stilwell Papers*, passim.
41. Lord Avon, *The Eden Memoirs: The Reckoning* (London: Cassell, 1965), pp. 294–5.
42. Sainsbury, pp. 241–2.
43. *Foreign Relations of the United States*, hereafter cited as *FRUS*, *The Conference of Berlin (Potsdam), 1945*, 2, pp. 1370–1, Churchill to Stimson, 18 July 1945, enclosing aide-memoire of conversation between Roosevelt and Churchill at Hyde Park, 18 September 1944. No record of the conversation could be located

in the American archives following Roosevelt's death and a copy was supplied by the British.

44. *FRUS, The Conference at Malta and Yalta, 1945*, pp. 370–4, Harriman to Roosevelt, 17 Oct. 1944 and Dean to Joint Chiefs of Staff, 17 October 1944.

45. *FRUS ... Yalta, 1945*, pp. 388–94, report by the joint staff planners, 18 Jan. 1945 and memorandum from Joint Chiefs to Roosevelt, 23 January 1945.

46. For comprehensive assessments of Yalta, see Paolo Brundu (ed.), *Yalta: Un Mito Che Resiste* (Rome: Edizioni Dell'Ateneo, 1989). See also D. S. Clemens, *Yalta* (New York: Oxford University Press, 1970).

47. *FRUS ... Yalta, 1945*, pp. 768–70, 894–7, record of meeting between Roosevelt and Stalin, 8 Feb. 1945, Stalin's political conditions for Soviet entry.

48. Clemens, pp. 310–11, Appendix A, and D. N. Dilks (ed.), *The Diaries of Sir Alexander Cadogan, 1938–1945* (London: Cassell, 1971), p. 715.

49. *DBPO, Potsdam*, 1, p. 573, minute from Churchill to Eden, 23 July 1945, reporting that the American Secretary of State, James F. Byrnes, was urging the Chinese to be firm in negotiating with the Russians.

50. Ibid., pp. 709–10, proclamation by the heads of government, the United States, Britain and China.

51. *FRUS ... Potsdam*, pp. 1376–8, statement by Truman, 6 Aug. 1945.

52. Far a lucid discussion of the complexities concerning the emperor's role in government, see S. S. Large, *Emperor Hirohito and Showa Japan* (London: Routledge, 1992).

53. *Documents on British Foreign Policy, 1919–1939*, 2 series, 9, pp. 282–3, minute by Vansittart, 1 Feb. 1932.

54. See Peter Lowe, 'The Dilemmas of an Ambassador: Sir Robert Craigie in Tokyo, 1937–41', in Gordon Daniels and Peter Lowe (eds), *Proceedings of the British Association for Japanese Studies* 2, part 1 (1977), 34–56 and Antony Best, 'Sir Robert Craigie as Ambassador to Japan, 1937–1941', in Ian Nish (ed.), *Britain and Japan: Biographical Portraits* (Folkestone: Japan Library, 1994), pp. 238–51.

55. Thorne, *Allies of a Kind*, pp. 74–5.

56. See Joyce Lebra (ed.), *Japan's Greater East Asia Co-Prosperity Sphere in World War II* (Kuala Lumpur: Oxford University Press, 1975).

57. Thorne, *Allies of a Kind*, pp. 728–9.

# 10 The Atomic Bomb and the End of the Wartime Alliance

David Holloway

The role of the atomic bomb in the breakdown of the wartime alliance has been the subject of extensive research and debate, on the basis of Western sources.[1] But the breakdown of the alliance involved the Soviet Union too, and the lack of Soviet sources has been a serious obstacle to research. It is only now becoming possible to examine the role of the atomic bomb with the help of Soviet sources. Those sources are fragmentary and problematic, and have to be treated carefully. Nevertheless they do throw light on the impact of the atomic bomb on Soviet policy. What effect did the Manhattan Project have on Soviet policy before Hiroshima? How did Stalin interpret the use of the atomic bomb against Hiroshima and Nagasaki? What view did he take of the military and political role of the bomb after August 1945? These are the questions this chapter addresses.[2]

## THE ATOMIC BOMB BEFORE POTSDAM

The first news of British and American work on the atomic bomb began to reach Moscow in the autumn of 1941. The most important information came originally from London, evidently from John Cairncross, private secretary to Lord Hankey, Minister without Portfolio in the War Cabinet and Chairman of the Cabinet Scientific Advisory Committee. In September 1941 a panel chaired by Hankey reviewed the report of the Maud Committee, which had concluded in July of that year that an atomic bomb could be built by the end of 1943. The Maud Committee had presented its case with great cogency, and put the possibility of the bomb in a new light. Its report persuaded Churchill to pursue the atomic bomb as a matter of urgency. When the findings of the Maud Committee were communicated to the United States in 1941, they played an important role in speeding up American nuclear research.[3]

The intelligence from London began to arrive in Moscow in late September 1941, less than a month before the great panic in the middle of October when most of the government was evacuated to Kuibyshev and thousands fled the capital. The Maud Committee's conclusion that an atomic bomb could be built within three years doubtless seemed irrelevant when the Red Army was trying to stop the Germans from seizing Moscow in the next few weeks. In March 1942, however, Lavrentii Beria, head of the NKVD, wrote a memorandum to Stalin and the State Defence Committee recommending that steps be taken to evaluate the intelligence about the atomic bomb. His memorandum reported that the British High Command believed that the problem of the atomic bomb was solved in principle, and that the efforts of the best scientists and the biggest companies in Britain were being directed to building the bomb. Beria recommended that a body be set up to coordinate and direct Soviet research on atomic energy and that leading scientists be shown the intelligence material.[4] Beria's memorandum shows how important the Maud Committee was in nuclear history. Besides providing the basis for the British decision to build an atomic bomb and helping to speed up American work, the Maud Report also set in motion the discussions that resulted in the initiation of the Soviet nuclear project.

Beria's memorandum led to consultations that lasted almost a year. The scientists who were consulted did not think that an atomic project should be set up, because they did not believe that a bomb could be built in time to affect the outcome of the war with Germany. (They were apparently not shown the intelligence material.) The one exception was the young physicist Georgii Flerov, who wrote to Stalin in April 1942 urging that the Soviet Union build the atomic bomb. It was only at the end of 1942 that Stalin decided to establish a small Soviet atomic project, and only in February 1943 that the State Defence Committee adopted a special resolution on the organisation of research into the utilisation of atomic energy.[5] A new laboratory was established under the direction of Igor Kurchatov. At the beginning of March Kurchatov was shown the intelligence material from Britain. It had, he said, 'huge, inestimable significance for our state and science'.[6]

The consultations about the atomic bomb took place at a very difficult time for the Soviet Union. The country was in mortal danger after the collapse of the Soviet offensive in the early months of 1942. The most intensive discussions took place during the battle of Stalingrad. The State Defence Committee's decision to set up a nuclear project was taken two weeks after the victory there. Stalin could not have expected that the small project he initiated would lead quickly to a bomb, or affect the outcome of the war with Germany. It is probable that he knew that Germany did not have a serious atomic project under way. The Soviet Union was receiving intelligence about German research, doubtless from sources in Germany, but also from its agents in Britain. In 1942 Klaus Fuchs became involved in making assessments of German progress in nuclear research. The information he transmitted to Moscow, before he left for the United States at the end of 1943, 'confirmed', in the words of the KGB officer who was his control in London after the war, 'that, first, the corresponding research in Hitler's Germany had reached a dead-end; second, that the USA and Britain were already building industrial facilities to make atomic bombs'.[7]

If Stalin did not think that an atomic bomb would affect the outcome of the war with Germany, what did he think during the war about the role of the atomic bomb in relations with his allies? What role did he think it might play in postwar international relations? There is no detailed account of discussions in the Soviet leadership about the atomic bomb before the Potsdam conference of July–August 1945. The progress of the Soviet project itself, however, does reveal something about the Soviet leaders' attitude. The project remained very small: by April 1944 Kurchatov had 74 people working in his laboratory, and of these only 25 were scientists. V. M. Molotov, the People's Commissar of Foreign Affairs, had been assigned general responsibility for the atomic project in 1943 (M. G. Pervukhin, the People's Commissar for the Chemical Industry, had more direct responsibility), but he did little to help Kurchatov.[8]

On 29 September 1944 Kurchatov wrote to Beria to complain about the slow progress of the project:

> During the past month I have been making a preliminary study of very extensive materials (3000 pages of text) dealing with the uranium problem [i.e. the atomic project].
>
> This study has shown once more that a concentration of scientific and engineering-technical forces on a scale unseen in the history of world science has been created around this problem abroad, and that it has already attained the most valuable results. With us, in spite of great progress in the development of research on uranium in 1943–1944, the state of affairs remains completely unsatisfactory. . . .
>
> Knowing that you are exceptionally busy, I nevertheless decided, in view of the historical significance of the uranium problem, to bother you and to ask you to give instructions for the work to be organised in such a way that it corresponds to the possibilities and significance of our great state in world culture.[9]

This letter did not have any effect. The project continued to develop slowly. A Soviet team went to Germany in May 1945 to recruit German scientists and to find uranium and laboratory equipment, but found that Germany had not made significant progress. The Soviet project was still not driven by a great sense of urgency. In May 1945 Pervukhin and Kurchatov wrote to Stalin urging that it be speeded up. Pervukhin later recalled that

> Matters connected with the solution of the atomic problem, for several reasons caused by the war, were going slowly. Therefore in May 1945 Igor Vasil'evich Kurchatov and I wrote a memorandum to the Politburo of the Central Committee and Comrade I. V. Stalin in which we briefly

elucidated the position with the atomic problem and expressed alarm at the slow development of the work.[10]

Pervukhin and Kurchatov proposed that extraordinary steps be taken and that the nuclear project be given the 'most favourable and advantageous conditions' in order to speed up the research and development work and the organisation of 'atomic industry enterprises'. The Soviet project was still basically a laboratory project, and could not proceed much further without the construction of isotope separation plants and reactors for plutonium production.

There is a striking disjunction between the relatively low priority that the Soviet leadership gave to the atomic project and the quantity and quality of the intelligence it was receiving about the Manhattan Project. Although Stalin, Beria, and Molotov were well-informed about the Manhattan Project, they did not take steps to speed up Soviet work. They apparently had no conception in the spring and summer of 1945 of the role that the atomic bomb would soon play in international relations. Evidently they did not believe in the reality of the bomb. They distrusted Soviet scientists: how could they be sure that Kurchatov was not deceiving them? Beria, according to the NKVD officer A. A. Iatskov, suspected that the intelligence information might be a trap, designed to lure the Soviet Union into large expenditures on an unrealistic project;[11] Stalin and Molotov may have shared this view. The discovery that Germany had not made much progress may have reinforced their suspicions. In any event, if Stalin, Beria, and Molotov had understood the potential connection between foreign policy and the atomic bomb, they would surely have provided Kurchatov with more support.

This conclusion is important because it suggests that there is no validity to the argument that the atomic bomb soured Soviet relations with the Western allies before the Potsdam meeting in July 1945. It was not the knowledge that the United States and Britain were building an atomic bomb that inspired distrust in the Soviet leaders. On the contrary, it was their existing suspicious attitude to the Western allies that prevented the Soviet leaders from appreciating the importance of the intelligence they were receiving.

## POTSDAM

The Soviet leaders may not have seen the connection between the atomic bomb and international relations, but others did. Niels Bohr, who feared a nuclear arms race but hoped that the nuclear danger might inspire a new approach to international relations, urged Churchill and Roosevelt in 1944 to inform Stalin about the bomb before it was tested. His advice was not taken. In May and June 1945 the Interim Committee, which Truman had set up to advise on the implications of the bomb, discussed the international control of atomic energy. The committee recommended that the President tell Stalin at Potsdam that the United States was working on the bomb and expected to use it against Japan; he should also say that he knew the Soviet Union was working on the bomb.

The Alamogordo test took place on 16 July, the day before the Potsdam conference opened. News of the successful test was sent to Potsdam on the same day. Five days later General Groves sent a detailed report conveying some of the tension and relief – but above all the awe – that those present at the test had felt.[12] Stimson, the Secretary of War, read the report that afternoon to Truman. Truman was 'tremendously pepped up by it', Stimson wrote in his diary, 'and spoke to me of it again and again when I saw him. He said it gave him an entirely new feeling of confidence.' The next morning Stimson took the report to Churchill, who exclaimed upon reading it that 'this is the Second Coming in Wrath'.[13] 'The bomb as a merely probable weapon had seemed a weak reed on which to rely,' Stimson realised, 'but the bomb as a colossal reality was very different.'[14]

Truman now decided to inform Stalin about the bomb. After the Plenary Session on 24 July he approached Stalin as the latter was about to leave the conference room. Truman casually mentioned to him 'that we had a new weapon of unusual destructive force'.[15] He did not say, however, that this was an atomic bomb, as the Interim Committee had recommended, nor did he refer to the possibility of international control. According to Truman's memoirs, Stalin said 'he was glad to hear it and hoped we would make "good use of it against the Japanese"'.[16] Truman's account may not be accurate, however. Anthony Eden, the British Foreign Secretary, who with Churchill was watching intently a few feet away, wrote in his memoirs that Stalin had merely nodded his head and said 'thank you', without further comment.[17] Stalin's interpreter, V. N. Pavlov, who translated Truman's remark, has confirmed Eden's account, but recalls that Stalin merely gave a slight nod of the head, without saying thank you.[18]

Truman and Churchill were convinced that Stalin had not understood that Truman was referring to the atomic bomb, but they were mistaken.[19] Stalin had received very detailed information about the Manhattan Project, and was also well-informed about the progress of the Soviet project.[20] Fuchs had told Soviet intelligence that the Alamogordo test would take place on or about 10 July.[21] 'On returning home from the session,' writes Marshal Zhukov, who was a member of the Soviet delegation,

'Stalin, in my presence, told Molotov about his conversation with Truman.
"They're raising the price", said Molotov.
Stalin gave a laugh, "Let them. We'll have to have a talk with Kurchatov today about speeding up our work."'

I realized that they were talking about the creation of the atomic bomb.'[22]

'It is hard to say what [Truman] thought, but it seemed to me that he wanted to dumbfound us', Molotov recalled many years later. "Atomic bomb" was not mentioned, but we guessed at once what he had in mind.'[23]

There is no reason to doubt that Stalin understood that Truman was referring to the atomic bomb. The interesting question is what he now understood the significance of the bomb to be. Some accounts say that he contacted Kurchatov at once to tell him to speed things up. This may be a legend, however, since speeding things up was not a matter of giving instructions to Kurchatov, but of creating new organisations that would make possible the transition from laboratory to industrial project. There are no good sources on Stalin's thinking about the atomic bomb in the period between his conversation with Truman and the bombing of Hiroshima two weeks later, but it may be doubted whether Truman's cryptic remark conveyed to Stalin a full understanding of the strategic significance of the atomic bomb.


HIROSHIMA

Whatever Stalin may or may not have understood at Potsdam, it was Hiroshima that brought the atomic bomb squarely into his strategic calculations. The connection between the bomb and foreign policy could no longer be ignored. The Soviet Union's entry into the war with Japan is analysed in other chapters in this volume, but some discussion is needed here too, because of the dramatic impact of Hiroshima on Soviet policy.

The Soviet Union had signed a Neutrality Pact with Japan in April 1941, and Stalin strove to keep that pact in force as long as the fate of the Soviet Union hung in the balance in the war with Germany. His policy changed, however, once the defeat of Germany was in sight. In October 1944 he told his allies that the Soviet Union would attack Japan about three months after the defeat of Germany, as long as the necessary arms and equipment had been stockpiled and the political terms clarified.[24] Agreement on the terms was reached at Yalta in February 1945. Some key provisions of the agreement – those affecting the status of Outer Mongolia and Soviet rights in Chinese ports and railways – required the consent of China, which did not take part in the Yalta conference. Stalin agreed to enter the war against Japan within two or three months of the defeat of Germany, and to conclude a treaty of friendship and alliance with China.[25]

As long as the Truman administration wanted the Soviet Union to enter the war with Japan, it had an incentive to press the Chinese to accept the Yalta agreement. By the summer of 1945, however, Soviet participation in the war against Japan appeared less attractive to some members of the

Administration, in light of Soviet policy in Europe. Averell Harriman, the ambassador in Moscow, urged T. V. Soong, who was leading the Chinese side in the negotiations on the treaty of friendship and alliance, to stand firm in his talks with Stalin and Molotov.[26] The Alamogordo test strengthened the belief that Soviet entry into the war was neither desirable nor necessary.[27] Believing that prolonged Sino-Soviet talks would delay Soviet entry, James Byrnes, Truman's new Secretary of State, cabled Soong from Potsdam to advise him not to give way to the Soviet Union on any point.[28] 'It is quite clear', noted Churchill on 23 July 'that the United States do not at the present time desire Russian participation in the war against Japan.'[29] In spite of the reservations among his advisers, however, Truman did not seek to withdraw from the Yalta Agreement.

Whether or not he knew of changing Western attitudes, Stalin feared that the war with Japan might be over before the Soviet Union was ready to enter. The secret *Bulletin of the Central Committee Information Bureau* reported in its issue of 1 July 1945 that reactionary circles in Britain wanted a compromise peace with Japan in order to prevent the Soviet Union from strengthening its influence in the Far East. The same question, it noted, was being raised in American newspapers and journals as well.[30] Stalin was afraid that if the war ended before the Soviet Union entered, the United States and Britain would renege on the Yalta Agreement, which was contingent upon Soviet participation in the war. 'Stalin was leaning on our officers to start military actions as soon as possible', Nikita Khrushchev later recalled. 'Stalin had his doubts about whether the Americans would keep their word. . . . What if Japan capitulated before we entered the war? The Americans might say, we don't owe you anything.'[31]

Stalin was aware that Japan was now in a hopeless position and that some elements in the Japanese government were seeking to end the war. Since February 1945 the Japanese government had been putting out very tentative feelers to the Soviet Union. In June the former Prime Minister Koki Hirota told Iakov Malik, the Soviet ambassador in Tokyo, that Japan wanted stable and friendly relations with the Soviet Union, and offered some specific concessions to Soviet interests in the Far East. Malik reported these exchanges to Moscow. On 8 July Molotov, on the basis of instructions approved by Stalin, told Malik to avoid giving the Japanese any pretext for presenting these talks as negotiations. 'Hirota's proposals', he wrote, 'testify to the fact that, as its military situation deteriorates, the Japanese government is willing to make ever greater concessions in the effort to prevent our intervention in the war in the Far East.'[32] The Soviet leaders showed no sign of being tempted by the Japanese overtures, however. There was more to be gained from participation in the war on the allied side than from a diplomatic *volte-face*.

The Japanese government made a new and more determined approach in

July when it decided to send another former Prime Minister, Prince Konoye, to Moscow with a letter from the Emperor seeking Soviet mediation in ending the war.[33] The Japanese overtures suggested that Japan was growing increasingly desperate, and might soon surrender. Stalin wanted Soviet forces to be ready as soon as possible. On 16 July, the day before the Potsdam conference opened, he telephoned Marshal A. M. Vasilevsky, the Commander-in-Chief of Soviet forces in the Far East, to ask whether the date of the attack could be brought forward ten days, but Vasilevsky had replied that more time was needed to make Soviet forces ready.[34] Stalin told Truman at Potsdam that Soviet forces would be ready to come into the war by the middle of August, and General Antonov, the Chief of the General Staff, made a similar statement to the allied Chiefs of Staff.[35] Stalin informed his allies of the Japanese approaches and of the Soviet response; his policy, he told Truman, was to lull the Japanese.[36] On 25 July and again on 30 July the Soviet Foreign Ministry told the Japanese ambassador that the Soviet government could not yet answer the Japanese request to send Konoye to Moscow.[37]

Soviet preparations for entry into the war continued during the Potsdam Conference. Stalin told General Antonov that the United States now possessed a new bomb of great destructive power, but neither Stalin nor Antonov gave the General Staff new instructions for the war against Japan.[38] On 3 August, after his return to Moscow, Stalin received a report from Vasilevsky informing him that preparations for the war were nearing completion, and asking him to launch the attack no later than 9–10 August, so that advantage could be taken of favourable weather.[39]

On 26 July Truman, Churchill and Chiang Kai-shek issued a joint declaration threatening prompt and utter destruction to Japan if the Japanese government did not proclaim 'the unconditional surrender of the Japanese armed forces'.[40] Stalin was not consulted about this declaration, and Molotov tried unsuccessfully to delay its publication, fearing no doubt that it might bring about a Japanese surrender before the Soviet Union entered the war.[41] But Japan did not surrender. Prime Minister Suzuki informed the press that his government intended to ignore the Potsdam Declaration.[42] 'In the face of this rejection', Stimson later recalled, 'we could only proceed to demonstrate that the ultimatum had meant exactly what it said.'[43]

On 6 August a United States B-29 bomber took off from Tinian Island and delivered an atomic bomb on Hiroshima at 8:15 a.m., local time. The initial reaction in Tokyo was confused; when Truman announced, on the day of the bombing, that it had been an atomic bomb, the Japanese military dismissed his claim as propaganda and played down the damage that had been done, as well as the destruction that might be expected in the future. Not until 10 August, the day after the bombing of Nagasaki, did Japanese government experts agree that the United States had indeed destroyed Hiroshima with an atomic bomb.[44]

On the day after Hiroshima, at 4:30 p.m. (Moscow time), Stalin and Antonov signed the order for the Red Army to attack the Japanese forces in Manchuria on the morning of 9 August (local time). The negotiations with the Chinese had not been completed, but it was urgent for the Soviet Union to enter the war, in case Japan surrendered soon. Although Stalin had informed the United States that the Soviet Union would not enter the war until the Treaty with China was signed, the timetable for Soviet entry was dictated more by the preparation of Soviet forces than by the talks with the Chinese. (The Sino-Soviet Treaty of Friendship and Alliance was signed on 14 August, five days after Soviet entry into the war.[45] The Treaty endorsed those elements of the Yalta Agreement that related to China.)

Molotov informed the Japanese ambassador at 5 p.m. on 8 August that the Soviet Union would consider itself to be in a state of war with Japan from 9 August.[46] A little more than an hour after this meeting, at 00:10 a.m. on 9 August (i.e. 6:10 p.m. on 8 August in Moscow) the Red Army moved into action. It seized control of Northern China in less than two weeks. The Kwantung Army, which had been stripped of its best troops and equipment for other theatres, was weaker than Soviet intelligence had anticipated and was no match for the Soviet forces.[47] The Soviet attack contributed to the defeat of Japan not only by destroying the Kwantung Army, but also by removing all hope that the Soviet Union might use its good offices to bring the war to an end.

On 9 August the United States bombed Nagasaki. A bitter debate now took place in the Japanese government about the terms on which Japan might sue for peace. The peace party was willing to surrender if the Emperor's prerogatives as a sovereign ruler were maintained; the militarists sought other conditions. Finally, on 14 August, the Emperor decided to accept the allied terms. On 16 August the Imperial General Headquarters ordered Japanese troops to stop fighting at once.[48]

In Manchuria the war continued for several days more. On 19 August General Yamada, Commander-in-Chief of the Kwantung Army, signed the act of surrender. The Red Army had made rapid progress, and had occupied Northern China as far south as the Liaotung Peninsula, as well as Northern Korea, southern Sakhalin and most of the Kurile Islands, by the time the formal act of unconditional surrender was signed by Japan on 2 September. The Soviet Union had strengthened its strategic position in the Far East but, as John Erickson points out in Chapter 7, Stalin had hoped for more. The prospect of occupying the northern half of Hokkaido was doubtless very tempting, but to have attempted to do so against American wishes would have created the risk of a clash with the United States. Stalin had to be satisfied with securing the concessions he had obtained at Yalta.

One of the central issues in the debate about Truman's decision to drop the atomic bomb is what his motives were: was his primary goal to bring the war with Japan to an end as quickly as possible, or was it to impress and intimidate the Soviet Union, in order to make it more tractable? From Stalin's point of view, however, the distinction between these two goals would have been meaningless. If the United States wanted to end the war quickly, that meant that it wanted to deprive the Soviet Union of the concessions won at Yalta, and also to prevent it from landing forces on Hokkaido and thereby gaining a voice in the postwar settlement in Japan. Stalin feared that the war might be over before the Soviet Union could enter, and realised that the bombing of Hiroshima would speed up the Japanese surrender. He told Averell Harriman on 8 August that 'he thought the Japanese were at present looking for a pretext to replace the present government with one which would be qualified to undertake a surrender. The bomb might give them this pretext.'[49] Although Stalin had intended to enter the war within a matter of days, the dropping of the atomic bomb appears to have precipitated his decision to attack on 9 August, before Japan surrendered.


THE POST-HIROSHIMA DECISION

Within two weeks of Hiroshima, Stalin put the Soviet nuclear project on a new footing. On 20 August the State Defence Committee issued a decree setting up a Special Committee to direct 'all work on the utilisation of the intraatomic energy of uranium'.[50] Beria was to chair this committee, which included two other powerful political figures: Georgii Malenkov, a Central Committee Secretary, and Nikolai Voznesensky, head of *Gosplan*, the State Planning Committee. The Special Committee included three industrial managers and two scientists (Igor Kurchatov and Peter Kapitsa) as well, but no military officers.[51] On the same day the State Defence Committee set up a new organisation, known as the First Chief Directorate of the Council of People's Commissars, to implement the decisions of the Special Committee. The atomic project had now become a matter of the highest priority for the state.

The decision to build a Soviet atomic bomb as quickly as possible was an automatic one on Stalin's part. There is no evidence of any discussion in the Soviet leadership about the wisdom of such a decision. It was assumed that if the United States had the atomic bomb, the Soviet Union should have it too. Hiroshima had demonstrated the immense power of the bomb, and had shown that the United States was willing to use it, and to do so in a way that thwarted Soviet strategic aims. Stalin clearly understood that a new element had now entered international relations. According to·one account, he told Kurchatov in the middle of August that 'Hiroshima has shaken the whole world. The balance has been destroyed. Give us the bomb – it will remove a great danger from us.'[52] The new balance of power that had been created by the war was upset by American possession of the atomic bomb. Stalin wanted to restore that balance by building a Soviet bomb as quickly as possible. That would take five years, the scientists informed him.[53]

Stalin believed at the end of the Second World War that postwar international relations would resemble those of the interwar period. Germany and Japan would rise from defeat. 'Japan will not be ruined even if she accepts unconditional surrender, like Germany,' he had told T. V. Soong in July. 'Both of these nations are very strong. After Versailles, all thought Germany would not raise (*sic*). 15–20 years, she recovered. Same would happen with Japan even if she is put on her knees.'[54] Stalin believed that world capitalism would run into crisis, and that rivalry would emerge between the leading capitalist powers. This would lead inevitably to war, for which the Soviet Union would have to be prepared.

Stalin wanted to prepare the Soviet Union for this future war, and to acquire the newest military technologies. But it is clear that he did not believe that a new war would take place soon, for he demobilised the Red Army in 1945–47 and converted industry from military to civilian production. He did not see an immediate military threat to the Soviet Union. He thought that the Soviet Union had emerged from the war stronger than before, and he believed that popular war-weariness would prevent even the most bellicose political leaders from starting a new war. Besides, he knew from Klaus Fuchs that the United States had very few atomic bombs.[55]

This did not mean that the bomb was unimportant. Andrei Gromyko writes in his memoirs of Stalin's fear that the United States and Britain would use the bomb to put pressure on the Soviet Union. Stalin, according to Gromyko, said that Washington and London doubtless hoped that the Soviet Union would need a long time to build its own bomb. During that time, he said, the Western allies would try to use their atomic monopoly to impose their plans for Europe, and for the rest of the world, on the Soviet Union. 'No, that will not be', said Stalin.[56] Stalin feared that the atomic bomb would be a potent political instrument in American hands, even though the United States could not yet use the bomb as a military weapon.

The atomic bomb was the 'scepter of state power', as the novelist Vasilii Grossman aptly put it.[57] It symbolised the economic and technological power of the United States, which the Soviet Union had been striving to 'catch up and overtake' through Stalin's policy of industrialisation. The bomb demonstrated more clearly than anything else that the United States was more advanced than the Soviet Union. Even if the United States did not make nuclear threats, its possession of the bomb was bound to be seen as a challenge by the Soviet Union. The power of the bomb in the immediate postwar period may have been symbolic, but it was none the less real for that. After Hiroshima the bomb cast a strong shadow over relations between the Soviet Union, Britain, and the United States.

## ATOMIC DIPLOMACY

The Truman Administration certainly expected to be able to use the bomb to influence Soviet policy. James Byrnes went to the London meeting of the Council of Foreign Ministers, which opened on 11 September, confident that the bomb would strengthen his hand. The Council had been established at Potsdam to prepare peace treaties with Germany and its allies. There were many issues in dispute between the three big powers, and Byrnes was sure that the atomic bomb would strengthen his hand in the negotiations.[58] 'His mind', wrote Henry L. Stimson, the Secretary for War, in his diary on 4 September, 'is full of his problems with the coming meeting of foreign ministers and he looks to have the presence of the bomb in his hip pocket, so to speak, as a great weapon to get through the thing.'[59] Byrnes did not want to use the bomb overtly, and instructed his delegation to avoid any mention of it, in the belief that the reality of the bomb would by itself make the Soviet Union more tractable.[60]

Molotov too came to the London meeting with the bomb on his mind. Atomic energy was not on the formal agenda, but he raised the issue himself, at a reception on the third day of the conference. When Byrnes approached him and asked when he was going to stop sightseeing and get down to business, Molotov enquired whether Byrnes had 'an atomic bomb in his side pocket'. 'You don't know southerners,' Byrnes replied; 'we carry our artillery in our pocket. If you don't cut out all this stalling and let us get down to work, I'm going to pull an atomic bomb out of my hip pocket and let you have it.' Molotov and his interpreter laughed at this remark which, though offered as banter, put into words what Stalin and Molotov feared the American attitude really was.[61] Molotov evidently wished to laugh off the American bomb and show that the Soviet Union would not be intimidated. Later that evening, at the Embassy, Molotov proposed a toast, 'Here's to the Atom Bomb! We've got it.'[62]

If the bomb made Byrnes stand firm, it also made Molotov stubborn. Molotov found Byrnes unyielding when he pushed for a control commission for Japan, with Soviet participation, and pressed the Soviet claim to trusteeship over Libya. He, in turn, resisted Western attempts to influence the complexion of the governments in Romania and Bulgaria. Moreover, although he accepted a British suggestion that the French and Chinese foreign ministers be allowed to take part in the discussions, he changed his mind ten days later and asked for them to be excluded. Appeals from Truman and Attlee to Stalin failed to change the Soviet position, and the conference ended on 2 October without agreement.[63]

At a formal dinner during the conference Molotov said that 'of course we all have to pay great attention to what Mr. Byrnes says, because the United States are the only people making the atomic bomb'.[64] But pay attention to

Byrnes was what Molotov conspicuously and pointedly declined to do. He behaved as though his overriding concern was to show that the Soviet Union would not be intimidated, or forced into concessions, by the American atomic monopoly. If this was indeed his goal, he succeeded brilliantly. Byrnes now realised that the Russians were, in his own words, 'stubborn, obstinate, and they don't scare'.[65]

Molotov's success in London was bought at a high price. The London meeting set the seal on his reputation as 'Mr. Nyet'. The *Manchester Guardian* wrote that 'during his stay in London Mr. Molotov has recklessly squandered the vast credit of good will towards Russia which accumulated in this country during the war'.[66] Lord Halifax, the British Ambassador in Washington, reported to the Foreign Office that, as a result of Soviet intransigence at the London meeting, 'thoughtful-minded Americans and especially those just right of Centre, felt themselves reluctantly drawn towards the conclusion that there were two great ideological *blocs* in the world'.[67]

In the Soviet Union, too, warnings were sounded about the breakdown of collaboration. An editorial in *Izvestya* on 5 October declared that collaboration would be shaken unless the United States and Britain changed their attitude to existing agreements.[68] Later in the same month, Stalin told Harriman that the Soviet Union might pursue a 'policy of isolation'. Harriman thought that the element of unilateralism in Soviet policy had already increased since the London conference.[69] Frank Roberts, Minister at the British Embassy in Moscow, reported in the same month that the atomic bomb had 'probably increased already existing Soviet suspicions of the outside world'.[70]

In a speech on 6 November, Molotov announced – to stormy applause – that the Soviet Union would have 'atomic energy, and much else'. He also warned against an arms race which, he said, some imperialists were advocating:

> In this connection it is necessary to speak about the discovery of atomic energy and about the atomic bomb, whose use in the war with Japan showed its huge destructive force.... *At the present time there can be no large-scale technological secrets that can remain the property of any one country or any one narrow group of countries. Therefore the discovery of atomic energy must not encourage... enthusiasm for using this discovery in a foreign-policy power game.*[71] [Emphasis added]

These last two sentences hint at the two major goals of Soviet atomic policy at the time: to break the American monopoly, and in the meantime to ensure that the United States did not derive political benefit from that monopoly.

In November Byrnes changed tack. Truman held talks with Clement Attlee and the Canadian Prime Minister, Mackenzie King, in Washington in the middle of the month on the international control of atomic energy.[72] They issued a statement that made no mention of the Soviet Union. A week later

Byrnes decided to raise the issue of atomic energy with Moscow. He was anxious to end the impasse caused by the London meeting, and wanted now to use the bomb as an inducement rather than an implied threat. On 23 November he proposed a meeting of the United States, British and Soviet foreign ministers in Moscow in December. He directed his staff to prepare a proposal on the international control of atomic energy. Molotov quickly agreed to the meeting.[73] Byrnes placed atomic energy at the top of the agenda, but Molotov moved it to the bottom. This, wrote Byrnes later, 'was just his way of informing me that he regarded the subject as one of little importance'.[74] In London Molotov had sought to defuse the bomb as a political threat; now he tried to devalue it as political inducement.

To Byrnes' surprise the question of atomic energy was settled in Moscow without much difficulty.[75] Molotov agreed to co-sponsor, at the first session of the General Assembly of the United Nations in January 1946, a resolution to establish a commission to make proposals on the international control of atomic energy. Molotov insisted that the commission be under the direction of the Security Council, in which the Soviet Union had a veto; Byrnes accepted this point.[76] The Soviet Union had nothing to lose by accepting Byrnes's proposal; rejection, on the other hand, might push the United States and Britain into closer cooperation, and indicate that the Soviet Union was really worried by the American monopoly. Stalin and Molotov can hardly have expected much benefit from the UN Commission. The Western allies had not informed them of the bomb when all three powers were fighting Germany: why expect them to reveal secrets now?

Stalin wrote to Truman to express his satisfaction with the results of the Moscow meeting.[77] Nikolai Novikov, who was chargé d'affaires in Washington at the time, has written in his memoirs that the 'principled and firm position of the Soviet government', demonstrated at the London meeting in September, had 'forced the Western powers to reject the tactic of head-on pressure and to seek mutually acceptable solutions on the most important questions of the postwar period'.[78] This new approach, he believed, was apparent in December at the Moscow meeting. Byrnes agreed to recognise the Bulgarian and Romanian governments in return for token changes in their cabinets; he also agreed to set up a toothless Allied Council for Japan, in which the Soviet Union would be represented. Byrnes failed to obtain assurances from the Soviet Union that it would withdraw its troops from Northern Iran, which it had occupied during the war, or to clarify Soviet intentions toward Turkey.

Truman did not share Stalin's satisfaction with the Moscow meeting. He was irritated by Byrnes' failure to keep him informed about the course of the negotiations, and unhappy with the results of the meeting. Byrnes, he wrote in his memoirs, 'had taken it upon himself to move the foreign policy of the United States in a direction to which I could not, and would not, agree'.[79] On 5 January 1946 he wrote a stiff letter reprimanding Byrnes and complaining about Soviet policy. He insisted that the governments in Romania and Bulgaria should not be recognised until radically changed; he regarded it as an outrage that the Soviet Union was keeping troops in Iran and stirring up rebellion there; and he was convinced that the Soviet Union intended to invade Turkey and seize the Black Sea Straits. 'Unless Russia is faced with an iron fist and strong language another war is in the making', he wrote. 'I'm tired of babying the Russians.'[80]

Truman's hardening attitude reflected a shift in American opinion about the Soviet Union. Washington was increasingly frustrated by its dealings with the Soviet Union, and puzzled by Soviet unwillingness to cooperate, especially in view of the American atomic monopoly.[81] In Moscow, too, attitudes were hard. In his speech on 9 February 1946 Stalin reasserted the Leninist thesis that imperialism inevitably generates wars, and portrayed the Second World War as the product of inter-imperialist contradictions. It was his prewar economic policies that had enabled the Soviet Union to defeat Germany, he claimed. The same policies must now be pursued once more: 'Only on that condition can we consider that our Motherland will be guaranteed against all contingencies. That will take, I dare say, three new Five Year Plans, if not more.' This speech reflected Stalin's view that postwar international relations would resemble those of the interwar period.

In February 1946, after Stalin's speech in the Bol'shoi Theatre, a long telegram arrived in Washington from George Kennan, Minister Counsellor at the US Embassy. The Soviet Union, by its very nature, wrote Kennan, was 'committed fanatically' to the belief that it could have no permanent *modus vivendi* with the United States, and that Soviet power could be secure only if the internal harmony of American society was disrupted and the international authority of the United States broken. This telegram had a sensational effect in Washington because it provided a coherent and eloquent answer to the question that preoccupied the Truman Administration: why was the Soviet Union so difficult to deal with?[82]

February and March 1946 marked a turning-point in US–Soviet relations. Soviet and American attitudes had hardened to the point where cooperation and agreement were now much more difficult. The atomic bomb did not cause the deterioration in relations. There were serious issues in dispute between the Soviet Union and the Western Allies before Hiroshima. Nevertheless, the failure of the London conference, which took place under the shadow of the bomb, marked an important stage in the breakdown of cooperation. Byrnes felt that the bomb allowed him to adopt a tough and demanding position in London; Molotov also evidently felt that the bomb required a tough and demanding position to show that the Soviet Union would not be intimidated. The agreements reached in Moscow in December did not repair the political damage that had been done. Atomic diplomacy – the hope on the one side, the fear on the other, that the bomb would prove to be a powerful political instrument – contributed to the failure of the London conference, and to the breakdown of the wartime alliance.

## NOTES

1. See, for example, Herbert Feis, *The Atomic Bomb and the End of World War II* (Princeton: Princeton University Press, 1971); Martin Sherwin, *A World Destroyed* (New York: Vintage Books, 1977); Gar Alperovitz, *Atomic Diplomacy: Hiroshima and Potsdam*, 2nd edn (New York: Penguin, 1985); Barton J. Bernstein, 'Roosevelt, Truman, and the Atomic Bomb, 1941–1945: A Reinterpretation', *Political Science Quarterly*, 1975, no. 1.
2. This chapter draws heavily on my *Stalin and the Bomb: The Soviet Union and Atomic Energy, 1939–1956* (New Haven and London: Yale University Press, 1994). The evidence on Soviet policy is set out more fully there. Here I focus particularly on the effect of the bomb on relations between the Soviet Union and the Western allies.
3. On the Maud Report, see Margaret Gowing, *Britain and Atomic Energy 1939–1945* (London: Macmillan, 1964); the Soviet documents referred to here can be found in 'U istokov sovetskogo atomnogo proekta: rol' razvedki', *Voprosy istorii estestvoznaniia i tekhniki*, 1992, no. 3.
4. 'U istokov . . .,' loc.cit., pp. 109–11.
5. Holloway, op.cit., pp. 84–8.
6. 'U istokov . . .,' loc.cit., p. 111.
7. A. S. Feklisov, 'Podvig Klausa Fuksa', *Voenno-istoricheskii zhurnal*, 1990, no. 12, pp. 24, 25.
8. Holloway, op.cit., pp. 96–115.
9. Reproduced in I. N. Golovin, 'Kurchatov – uchenyi, gosudarstvennyi deiatel', chelovek', in *Materialy iubeleinoi sessii uchenogo soveta tsentra 12 ianvaria 1993g.* (Moscow: Rossiiskii nauchnyi tsentr 'Kurchatovskii institut', 1993), pp. 24–5.
10. M. G. Pervukhin, 'Pervye gody atomnogo proekta', *Khimiia i zhizn'*, 1985, no. 5, p. 64.
11. A. A. Iatskov, 'Atom i razvedka', in 'U istokov . . .,' loc.cit., p. 105.
12. Sherwin, op.cit., contains the report, pp. 308–14.
13. Ibid., pp. 223–4.
14. Henry L. Stimson and McGeorge Bundy, *On Active Service in Peace and War* (New York: Harper and Brothers, 1948), p. 637.
15. Harry S. Truman, *Memoirs. Vol. 1: 1945, Year of Decisions* (New York: Signet Books, 1965), p. 458.
16. Ibid.
17. Anthony Eden, *The Reckoning* (Boston: Houghton Mifflin, 1965), p. 635.
18. V. G. Trukhanovsky, *Angliiskoe iadernoe oruzhie* (Moscow: Mezhdunarodnye otnosheniia, 1985), p. 23. Anatolii Gromyko, who was nearby when Truman made his remark to Stalin, writes in his memoirs that Truman said that the United States intended to use the new weapon against Japan, and that Stalin said 'Thank you for the information.' A. A. Gromyko, *Pamiatnoe*, Book I, 2nd

edn, (Moscow: Politizdat, 1990), p. 272. None of the American or British participants in the conference has suggested that Truman told Stalin about his intention to use the bomb in Japan.

19. Feis, op.cit., p. 102; John W. Wheeler-Bennett and Anthony Nicholls, *The Semblance of Peace* (London: Macmillan, 1972), p. 372.

20. M. G. Pervukhin, 'U istokov uranovoi epopei', *Tekhnika – molodezhi*, 1975), no. 7, p. 24.

21. 'U istokov . . .', loc.cit., p. 134.

22. G. K. Zhukov, *Vospominaniia i razmyshleniia, tom 2* (Moscow: Novosti, 2nd rev. edn, 1972), p. 418.

23. *Sto sorok besed s Molotovym: iz dnevnika F. Chueva* (Moscow: Terra, 1991), p. 81.

24. Wheeler-Bennett and Nicholls, op.cit., pp. 344–8.

25. Ibid., pp. 348–52.

26. W. A. Harriman and Elie Abel, *Special Envoy to Churchill and Stalin, 1941–1946* (New York: Random House, 1975), p. 483. For a Soviet analysis of the talks see A. M. Ledovsky, *Kitaiskaia politika SShA i sovetskaia diplomatiia, 1942–1954* (Moscow: Nauka, 1985, pp. 90–108).

27. Bernstein, loc.cit., pp. 44–6

28. James F. Byrnes, *Speaking Frankly* (New York: Harper and Brothers, 1947), p. 205.

29. John Ehrman, *Grand Strategy, vol. VI; History of the Second World War, UK Military Series* (London: HMSO, 1956), p. 292.

30. *Biulleten' Biuro informatsii TsK VKP(b): Voprosy vneshnei politiki* 1945, no. 13, 1 July, pp 1–6. RTsKhIDNI f. 17, op. 128, t. 1, d. 50.

31. N. S. Khrushchev, *Khrushchev Remembers: The Glasnost' Tapes* (Boston: Little, Brown, 1990), p. 81.

32. 'Za kulisami tikhookeanskoi bitvy (iapono–sovetskie kontakty v 1945g.)', *Vestnik Ministerstva Inostrannykh Del SSSR*, No. 19 (77), 15 October 1990, p. 53. This issue contains Soviet documents relating to the Japanese approaches to the Soviet Union.

33. Ibid., p. 54; Robert J. C. Butow, *Japan's Decision to Surrender* (Stanford: Stanford University Press, 1954), pp. 112–26.

34. A. M. Vasilevsky, *Delo vsei zhizni* (Moscow: Politizdat, 1974), p. 513. Vasilevsky writes that Stalin could not have known of the Alamogordo test when he telephoned, and that the call must have been prompted by general military-political considerations.

35. *Sovetskii Soiuz na mezhdunarodnykh konferentsiiakh perioda velikoi otechestvennoi voiny 1941–1945gg. Tom VI. Berlinskaia (Potsdamskaia) konferentsiia* (Moscow: Politizdat, 1980), p. 43. On 24 July General A. I. Antonov, the Chief of the General Staff, assured the allied Chiefs of Staff that the Soviet Union would be ready to start operations in the latter half of August, though the exact date would depend on completion of the negotiations with the Chinese. See Truman, op.cit., p. 422. This is slightly different from what Stalin had told Truman.

36. Feis, op.cit., p. 80.

37. Butow, op.cit., p. 128; Feis, op.cit., p. 104; 'Za kulisami . . .', loc.cit., pp. 54, 55.

38. S. M. Shtemenko, *The Soviet General Staff at War, 1941–1945* (Moscow: Progress Publishers, 1985), p. 431.

39. Ibid.

40. Feis, op.cit., pp. 105–7.

41. Feis, op.cit., p. 106; V. L. Israelian, *Diplomatiia v gody voiny, 1941–1945* (Moscow: Mezhdunarodnye otnosheniia, 1985), p. 439.

42. Butow, op.cit., p. 148.

43. Stimson and Bundy, op.cit., p. 625.
44. Butow, op.cit., p. 152.
45. J. A. S. Grenville, *The Major International Treaties 1914–1973* (London: Methuen, 1974), pp. 237–40.
46. 'Za kulisami . . .', loc.cit., p. 55.
47. In June 1945 the Soviet government apparently believed that the Kwantung Army was being strengthened. See 'Manchzhuriia–voenno-ekonomicheskaia baza Iaponii', in *Biulleten' Biuro informatsii TsK VKP(b) Voprosy vneshnei politiki*, 1945, no. 11, 1 June, pp. 11–12. RTsKhIDNI f. 17, op. 128, t.1, d.50.
48. Butow, op.cit., pp. 166–209.
49. Cable from George Kennan to Washington DC, 8 August 1945, Library of Congress, Harriman Papers, Box 181.
50. 'Delo Beriia . . .', *Izvestiia TsK KPSS*, 1991, no. 1, p. 145.
51. Ibid.
52. A. Lavrent'ieva, 'Stroiteli novogo mira', *V mire knig*, 1970, no. 9, p. 4. This article is a review of a biography of Vannikov by G. Ustinov, but, as far as I can discover, this biography was never published. The quotation is said to be taken from the biography.
53. I. N. Golovin, *I. V. Kurchatov*, 3rd edn (Moscow: Atomizdat, 1978), p. 71.
54. Hoover Institution Archive, Victor Hoo Papers, Box 2, File 'Sino-Soviet Relations, 1945–46', p. 2
55. For further discussion see Holloway, op.cit., pp. 150–3.
56. Andrei Gromyko, *Pamiatnoe*, 2nd edn, vol. 1 (Moscow: Politizdat, 1990), p. 277.
57. Vasilii Grossman, *Zhizn' i sud'ba* (Paris: L'Age d'Homme, 1980), p. 535.
58. John Lewis Gaddis, *The United States and the Origins of the Cold War 1941–1947* (New York: Columbia University Press, 1972), pp. 264–5.
59. Henry L. Stimson, *Diary*, 4 September 1945. Deposited at Yale University.
60. Gregg Herken, *The Winning Weapon* (New York: Vintage Books, 1982), pp. 45–9.
61. Herken, op.cit. p. 48.
62. Deborah Welch Larson, *Origins of Containment* (Princeton: Princeton University Press, 1985), p. 223.
63. *Perepiska Predsedatelia Soveta Ministrov SSSR s Prezidentami SShA i Prem'er-ministrami Velikobritanii vo vremia velikoi otechestvennoi voiny 1941–1945 gg.*, vol. 2 (Moscow: Politizdat, 1986), pp. 290–2.
64. Quoted by Daniel Yergin, *Shattered Peace* (Boston: Houghton Mifflin, 1978), p. 132. At another point Molotov jested, when the Western powers were reluctant to accede to the Soviet demand for the former Italian colony of Tripolitania, that 'if you won't give us one of the Italian colonies, we should be quite content to have the Belgian Congo', which was a major source of uranium. See Herken, op.cit., p. 50.
65. Herken, op.cit., p. 53.
66. Quoted in Alan Bullock, *Ernest Bevin. Foreign Secretary 1945–1951* (New York: W. W. Norton, 1983), p. 137.
67. DBPO, series I, vol. II, p. 496. This comment was contained in Halifax's quarterly report of 4 December 1945.
68. Series I, vol. II, p. 492; Roberts to Bevin, 5 October 1945.
69. Harriman and Abel, op. cit., pp. 514–15, 519.
70. DBPO, Series I, vol. II, p. 568; Roberts to Bevin, 26 October 1945.
71. 'Doklad V. M. Molotova na torzhestvennom zasedanii moskovskogo Soveta 6-go noiabria 1945g.', *Pravda*, 7 November 1945, p. 2.

72. Margaret Gowing, *Independence and Deterrence. Britain and Atomic Energy 1945–1952, vol. 1, Policy-Making* (London: Macmillan, 1974), pp. 73–7; Richard Hewlett and Oscar Anderson, Jr, *The New World: A History of the US Atomic Energy Commission Vol. 1, 1939–1946* (Berkeley: University of California Press, pp. 455–69).
73. Hewlett and Anderson, op.cit., pp. 469–72; Herken, op.cit., pp. 66–8.
74. James F. Byrnes, *Speaking Frankly* (New York: Harper and Brothers, 1947), p. 111.
75. Ibid., p. 122; James B. Conant, *My Several Lives* (New York: Harper and Row, 1970), p. 481.
76. DBPO series I, vol. II, p. 855; record of meeting of the three Foreign Secretaries on 24 December.
77. N. V. Novikov, *Vospominaniia diplomata: Zapiski 1938–1947gg.* (Moscow: Politizdat, 1989), p. 306.
78. Ibid.
79. Truman, op.cit., p. 604.
80. Ibid., pp. 604–6. Whether Truman ever communicated the contents of the letter to Byrnes is not clear. But the letter does reflect his attitude at the time. See Robert J. Donovan, *Conflict and Crisis. The Presidency of Harry S. Truman* (New York: W.W. Norton, 1977), pp. 160–1.
81. Gaddis, op.cit., pp. 282–90; Larson, op.cit., pp. 247–9.
82. George F. Kennan, *Memoirs 1925–1950* (New York: Pantheon Books, 1967), p. 295. The background to the telegram is described on pp. 290–5, and the text is given on pp. 547–59.

# 11 Yalta, Potsdam, and Beyond: The British and American Perspectives
## Norman A. Graebner

Despite the myriad of uncompromisable issues that confronted Franklin D. Roosevelt, Winston Churchill and Joseph Stalin at Yalta in February 1945, the three allied leaders succeeded in burying the accumulating disagreements in declarations that clouded their transparency, enabling the Grand Alliance to survive the conference apparently unscathed. The astonishingly effective ground and air war against both German and Japanese forces assured an ultimate victory. Still, as late as Yalta, Roosevelt continued to rely on the Soviet Union to carry the major burden of the war in Europe and to contribute significantly to the final defeat of Japan. That heavy contribution to the anticipated triumph of the Grand Alliance required a price and Roosevelt was willing to pay it in the form of superficial, non-enforceable agreements with the USSR. Roosevelt accepted a flawed Eastern European settlement, convinced that the Soviets would command the region's future, whatever the phraseology of the agreement.[1] Clearly the future of the Grand Alliance rested on the willingness of Britain and the United States to accept the Soviet definition of what the Yalta agreements permitted and not contest the burgeoning Soviet control of East-Central Europe and the Balkans.

Within days of Yalta, the Kremlin revealed its interpretation of the Yalta accords by confirming its established occupation policies in Romania, Hungary, Bulgaria and elsewhere. Throughout the war-zone of Eastern Europe, Soviet officials acted unilaterally, ignoring the Western members of the Allied Control Commissions as they tightened their hold. In late February Andrei Vyshinsky, Deputy Commissar of Foreign Affairs, arrived in Bucharest and ordered King Michael to form a new government. On 6 March the king dismissed General Radescu, the Romanian prime minister, and accepted a Communist-controlled regime under Petra Groza. The Soviets now signed a five-year treaty with the new government.[2] In Budapest, Soviet leaders, backed again by huge occupation forces, dismissed Hungary's Allied Control Commission and proceeded to exercise predominant political and economic power. Moscovite Hungarians – the hard core of the Communist Party – readily accepted Soviet political domination as well as economic measures that quickly undermined Hungary's market economy.[3] Similar procedures solidified Soviet domination of Bulgaria.

Ambassador Averell Harriman in Moscow warned Washington that such Soviet behaviour, unless countered effectively, would nullify the Yalta Declaration on Liberated Europe and with it the principle of self-determination. He pressed Roosevelt to challenge Moscow's flagrant defiance of the Yalta accords.[4] James F. Byrnes, who had returned from Yalta as Roosevelt's official interpreter of the Yalta agreements, assured the American press that the accords comprised a triumph for American democratic principles across Eastern Europe. Apparently the Declaration on Liberated Europe had lost its tentative quality; the United States, it seemed, could demand full and unquestioning Soviet compliance with its provisions.[5] Yet Roosevelt had no intention of contesting Soviet policy in the Balkans; he responded to King Michael's appeals for help with verbal protests, nothing more.

Churchill readily accepted Roosevelt's decision. For him the TOLSTOY accords of October 1944 still governed British–Soviet relations in the Balkans. The Soviets had not interfered in Greece. Therefore, Churchill reminded Foreign Secretary Anthony Eden on 5 March, Britain could not justify Western intervention in Romania. Again a week later Churchill informed Eden that the British government 'accepted in a special degree the predominance of Russia in this theatre [Romania]'.[6]

Poland was another matter. Britain had chosen war in September 1939 under the imperative of its special obligation to Poland. At Yalta Churchill sought above all to protect the interests of the exiled London Poles in the postwar reconstruction of their country. The Declaration on Poland, adopted at Yalta, provided for three-power involvement, operating under democratic procedures, in the creation of Poland's postwar provisional government. Unfortunately for London, the Soviet-backed Lublin Poles were firmly in control of the existing Warsaw government. After Yalta the Kremlin ignored Britain's known commitment to the London Poles and refused to expand the Provisional Government with members of either the Polish underground or the Polish government-in-exile. The Soviets jailed the chief leaders of the wartime Polish resistance and denied the London Poles the benefit of a Western presence in Poland.[7] With British elections approaching, Eden acknowledged to Lord Halifax that unless Britain could guarantee fair treatment for the London Poles, 'we and the Americans would be accused – rightly – of having subscribed at the Crimea Conference to a formula which we knew to be unworkable'. The Churchill cabinet wanted to avoid accusations of another Munich because it failed to defend a victim of aggression to which Britain was committed.[8]

Still, Britain remained powerless to mount an anti-Soviet offensive without Washington's strong support. When, as early as 20 February, New Zealand's prime minister chided the London government for its failure to honour its pledges to Poland, Churchill explained that Britain and the British Commonwealth possessed no power to enforce its point of view. 'We cannot', he wrote, 'go further in helping Poland than the United States is willing or can be persuaded to go.'⁹ As during the war, Churchill saw clearly that Britain's postwar standing in global politics required strong ties to the United States no less than the diminution of Soviet influence where it endangered Britain's historic interests. On 8 March Churchill approached Roosevelt on the necessity of Anglo-American unity in opposing Soviet domination of Poland. 'I have based myself in Parliament,' he warned, 'on the assumption that the words of the Yalta declaration will be carried out in the letter and spirit. ... [I]f we do not get things right now, it will soon be seen by the world that you and I by putting our signatures to the Crimea settlement have underwritten a fraudulent prospectus.' For Churchill, Poland had become Yalta's crucial test. To halt the Kremlin's defence of the Lublin regime, Churchill asked Roosevelt to join him in sending personal messages to Stalin; otherwise he would acknowledge the dishonesty of Yalta before Parliament.¹⁰

Roosevelt, too, was troubled by the Soviet impositions on Poland. He had demanded the Declaration on Poland in part to assuage the fears of his Polish constituents in the United States. Byrnes, moreover, had warned the nation that the Declaration on Poland comprised the foundation of postwar allied unity. At the same time he assured concerned Americans that the administration's desire to perpetuate the Grand Alliance did not include the acceptance of a Soviet sphere in Eastern Europe.¹¹ Roosevelt, like Churchill, presumed that the tripartite commission meeting in Moscow, consisting of Molotov, Harriman and British ambassador Sir Archibald Clark Kerr, would in time eliminate the clash of purpose within the alliance by designing an acceptable government for Poland. Indeed, the commissioners readily moved toward agreement until they faced the task of designating what Poles the commission would invite for consultation. Molotov argued that the Lublin Poles had the right to accept or reject whomever they wanted in the formation of the new Polish government. The British demanded free elections supervised by Western observers. On 3 March the State Department instructed Harriman to accept the British decision to postpone consultations with the Lublin Poles until the commission could name non-Lublin representatives.¹² Molotov continued to resist every effort to broaden the base of the Lublin regime while Harriman instructed Washington that Soviet support assured the perpetuation of Lublin control in Poland.¹³

Determined to preserve the Grand Alliance, Roosevelt was reluctant to press Stalin even on the question of Poland. During March he advised the departing diplomat, Robert Murphy, 'to bear in mind that our primary postwar objective was Soviet–American cooperation – without which world peace would be impossible'.¹⁴ On 12 March Roosevelt rejected Churchill's appeal for a strong message to Stalin. 'In my opinion,' he wrote, ' ... we should leave the first steps to our Ambassadors from which we hope to obtain good results.'[15] For the troubled Churchill and Eden the Grand Alliance had reached the point of collapse. Only the threatened loss of Anglo-American support, Eden concluded on 23 March, would compel the Soviets to mend their ways. But that solution required firm American cooperation in setting the limits to Soviet behaviour. On 24 March Eden caught Churchill's attention with the observation that Big Three disagreements over Poland endangered the San Francisco United Nations Conference, scheduled to open in late April. 'Nothing', Churchill responded, 'is more likely to bring [the Americans] into line with us than any idea of the San Francisco Conference being imperilled.' On 27 March Churchill asked Roosevelt whether a world peace organisation was possible without Great Power unity. He outlined for Roosevelt a case that he might present to Stalin. This message brought the response that Churchill had sought for almost a month. '[T]he time has come', Roosevelt agreed, 'to take up directly with Stalin the broad aspects of the Soviet attitude.' Even then Roosevelt reminded London that the Yalta agreement on Poland had placed greater emphasis on the Lublin Poles than on the other Polish factions.[16]

In his letter to Stalin, Roosevelt characterised the Polish Provisional Government as little more than a continuation of the former Lublin regime. 'I cannot', he wrote, 'reconcile this either with our agreement or our discussions [at Yalta]. While it is true that the Lublin Government is to . . . play a prominent role [in a reorganised government] it is to be done in such a fashion as to bring into being a new Government. . . . I must make it quite plain to you that any such solution which would result in a thinly disguised continuance of the present Warsaw regime would be unacceptable and would cause the people of the United States to regard the Yalta agreement as having failed.'[17] During subsequent days Roosevelt was torn between his acceptance of London's hardline stance and his refusal to face the consequences of a total break in US–Soviet relations. Conscious of the steady advance of Soviet forces across Europe, Churchill reminded the President on 5 April that the Western powers must establish a point beyond which they would accept no more Soviet repression. Roosevelt agreed.[18]

Roosevelt's reluctant message gave Stalin the opportunity to restate the Soviet case for Poland. In his reply of 7 April he reminded Roosevelt that the three powers at Yalta had accepted the existing Polish Provisional Government as the core of a new Provisional Government of National Unity. The US and British ambassadors in Moscow, he continued, had ignored the Warsaw regime entirely in their attempt to create a new government. 'Things have gone so far', Stalin complained, 'that Mr. Harriman declared in the Moscow Commission that it might be that not a single member of the Provisional Government would be included in the Polish Government of National Unity.' Harriman and Clark Kerr, he added, demanded the right to invite Polish leaders from London and Poland for consultation without regard to their attitudes toward Yalta and the USSR – all in direct violation of the Yalta Declaration on Poland. 'The Soviet Union', Stalin concluded, 'proceeds on the assumption that, by virtue of the Crimea decisions, those invited for consultation should be ... Polish leaders who recognize the decisions of the Crimea Conference ... [and] who actually want friendly relations between Poland and the Soviet Union.'[19] With war still raging across the heart of Europe, Roosevelt would not permit even such sharp disagreement over the meaning of Yalta to disrupt the Grand Alliance.

As the allied armies closed in on Germany during the early days of April, Roosevelt refused to confront the Kremlin with any active policy of opposition. Churchill challenged Roosevelt's mood of resignation when he advised the President that the advancing British and American forces might enable the Western powers to limit the extension of Soviet influence across Central Europe. Churchill hoped especially that Western forces would capture Berlin before the Soviets arrived. He warned Roosevelt on 1 April that, should the Soviets take Berlin, they would thereafter behave as if they had been the overwhelming contributors to the common victory. '[M]ay this not', Churchill added, 'lead them into a mood which will raise grave and formidable difficulties in the future?' It was essential, Churchill repeated on 5 April, 'that we should join hands with the Russian armies as far to the east as possible and if circumstances allow, enter Berlin'.[20] Churchill favoured the capture of Prague as well. But General Dwight D. Eisenhower, US commander in Europe, preferred to concentrate his forces rather than compete with the Soviets for Czech territory. He professed disbelief that the Prime Minister would intermingle political and military considerations in the advocacy of an anti-Soviet strategy. On 14 April he ordered General William H. Simpson, whose Ninth Army had crossed the Elbe, to withdraw to the west bank of the river.[21] Two days later Soviet forces numbering a million men launched their final assault on Berlin. Roosevelt no more than Eisenhower had any intention to contest the Kremlin's wish to crush German power within its designated zone.


Harry S. Truman entered the White House amid State Department efforts to assess the status of American–Soviet relations. On 3 April Stettinius had asked Harriman for a detailed report from Moscow. In his long response three days later Harriman declared that a full analysis required his return to Washington.[22] The Soviets, he wrote, would continue to act unilaterally in the border states to assure their domination. But no longer, he warned, did the Kremlin merely seek a security ring of totalitarian governments in Eastern Europe; it now sought to strengthen Soviet ties with Communist-controlled parties elsewhere to create a broader 'political atmosphere favorable to Soviet policies'. Harriman expressed his conviction that Stalin interpreted

Western generosity as a sign of weakness. The time had come to demonstrate to Soviet leaders 'that they cannot expect our continued cooperation on terms laid down by them'.[23] In Washington after mid-April because of Roosevelt's death, Harriman confessed to Truman that Soviet behaviour had become intolerable. When the Soviet Union had gained control of its bordering areas, he warned State Department officials, 'it would attempt to penetrate the next adjacent country'. This admonition suggested that the Kremlin's occupation policies were not only repressive but dangerous as well.[24] American security demanded that Washington make the Soviets understand 'that they cannot continue their present attitude except at great cost to themselves'. Unfortunately US and Soviet interests and strategic advantages in Eastern Europe and the Balkans were not sufficiently symmetrical to recommend policies that would levy the necessary costs.

By mid-April the Kremlin's unilateralism in the border states had created a crisis mood in Washington. On 13 April Stettinius briefed Truman on the situation in Eastern Europe. Nowhere in liberated Europe, ran his troubled summary, would the Soviets acknowledge that their actions justified any Western appeal to the Yalta agreements. Four days later Washington learned that the Soviets planned to sign a mutual assistance pact with the Lublin Poles. Vyshinsky argued that nothing in the Yalta accords precluded such a treaty; he refused to show the treaty, signed on 21 April, to British and American officials. Truman now resolved to lay it on the line when Molotov visited Washington *en route* to San Francisco. Admiral William D. Leahy, the President's Chief of Staff, predicted that Molotov 'would be in for some blunt talking from the American side'.[25]

On 20 April Truman conferred with Harriman, Stettinius, Under-Secretary Joseph C. Grew, and Soviet expert Charles E. Bohlen. Harriman dominated the meeting. He urged the President to frame an effective policy that would assure the inclusion of London Poles in the Warsaw government. Truman recorded his response: 'I declared that . . . we intended to be firm with the Russians and make no concessions from American principles or traditions in order to win their favor.'[26] Harriman urged the President to discard any illusion that the Kremlin would soon act in accordance with the principles to which the rest of the world held in international affairs. Any agreement should require concessions on both sides. 'I agreed', Truman recalled in his memoirs, 'saying I understood this and that I would not expect one hundred per cent of what we proposed. But I felt we should be able to get eighty-five per cent.' Before his departure for Moscow, Harriman met the President privately to acknowledge his relief that the new administration shared the Moscow legation's perception of the Soviet danger.[27]

Truman's meeting with Molotov on 22 April was cordial enough. The President reminded the Soviet leader that 'in its larger aspects the Polish question has become for our people the symbol of the future development of our international relations'. Molotov reassured the President that the two countries could reach the desired agreement on the Polish question. At the White House on 23 April Stettinius informed Truman that the subsequent conversations with Molotov had not gone well; in fact, they had ended in a complete deadlock on the future of Poland. Truman, conforming to the State Department's hard line, replied that 'our agreements with the Soviet Union had so far been a one-way street and that this could not continue'. Others present – especially Secretary of War Henry L. Stimson and General George C. Marshall – urged caution. The Soviets, they declared, had carried out their military obligations faithfully; therefore the United States should avoid an open break with the Kremlin over Poland.[28]

At their meeting that afternoon Truman informed Molotov that the American and British proposals on Poland were reasonable and embodied the maximum Western concessions. The US government would be no party to any political arrangements that did not represent the will of all the Polish people. At risk on the issue was the Grand Alliance itself. 'The Soviet Government must realize', Truman cautioned Molotov, 'that the failure to go forward at this time with the implementation of the Crimean decision on Poland would seriously shake confidence in the unity of the three governments and their determination to continue the collaboration in the future as they have in the past.' Molotov denied that the Yalta decisions demanded Soviet compliance with Western proposals. Truman informed Molotov that US friendship with the Soviet Union could continue 'only on the basis of mutual observation of agreements and not on the basis of a one-way street'. To Molotov's complaint, 'I have never been talked to like that in my life', the President retorted, 'Carry out your agreements and you won't get talked to like that.'[29] Truman boasted to the pro-Soviet Joseph E. Davies that he let Molotov have it straight. Stalin, unmoved, informed the President that the Warsaw regime had widespread public support and would remain the core of any new Polish Government of National Unity.[30]

In official Washington, Truman's anti-Soviet attitudes had become exceedingly pervasive. The President offered his advisers the assurance that 'the Russians need us more than we need them'.[31] Arthur H. Vandenberg, Republican leader in the Senate, found enough solace in Truman's words to Molotov to confide to his diary, 'FDR's appeasement of Russia is over.' The United States and the USSR could live together in the postwar world, he wrote, 'if Russia is made to understand that we can't be pushed around'. Admiral Leahy rejoiced at the President's new mood of confidence. 'Truman's attitude ... was more than pleasing to me', he noted in his memoirs. 'I believed it would have a beneficial effect on the Soviet outlook ...'.[32] Secretary of the Navy James V. Forrestal asserted at the White House meeting on 23 April that the United States might as well meet the Soviet challenge in Eastern Europe 'now as later on'. In May Forrestal informed a member of the Senate that Soviet communism was 'as incompatible with democracy as was Nazism and Fascism . . .'.[33]

In the State Department, Under-Secretary Joseph C. Grew had long harboured a deep distrust of the USSR. He found nothing reassuring in the elimination of German power on the Eastern Front. With its stranglehold on its western border states, the Soviet Union, he warned, 'will steadily increase and she will in the not distant future be in a favorable position to expand her control, step by step, through Europe. . . . A future war with Soviet Russia is as certain as anything in the world can be certain.'[34] Such top State Department officials as James C. Dunn, Assistant Secretary for European, Asian, Near Eastern, and African Affairs, and such regional office directors as H. Freeman Matthews and Loy Henderson shared Grew's deep anxiety towards the Soviet Union. For them any compromise with the Kremlin would merely encourage Soviet expansionism.

Berlin's fall in early May marked the end of Germany's long quest for world leadership. That event terminated as well five centuries of European dominance in world affairs. The joyous meeting of American and Soviet troops at Torgau on the Elbe symbolised Europe's decline. The burden of defeating Germany exhausted Europe beyond its capacity to sustain the global position it once commanded. More than ever, Britain's imperial greatness rested on the will of its more powerful allies. But British officials had long detected in Soviet expansionism a genuine danger to Britain's historic position in Europe and elsewhere. Europe's peace rendered Britain's plight even more acute by eliminating the wartime constraints on Soviet ambition. On 29 April Churchill warned Stalin not to misuse his narrowly-won command of vast stretches of the European continent with policies that would ultimately tear the world to pieces. '[D]o not, my friend Stalin,' he pleaded, 'underrate the divergences which are opening about matters which you may think are small to us but which are symbolic of the way the English-speaking democracies look at life.' Even as London celebrated VE Day – 8 May – Churchill concluded that his country's break with the USSR was almost complete. 'It is no longer desired by us', he acknowledged, 'to maintain detailed arguments with the Soviet Government about their views and actions.' Four days after the German surrender Churchill confided to his wife, 'I need scarcely tell you that beneath these triumphs lie poisonous politics and deadly international rivalries.'[35]

Churchill understood more clearly than ever that the support and approval of the United States alone could extend Britain's historic role as a European and world power into the postwar era. The British Chiefs of Staff observed accurately that the British Empire 'would by itself be unable to secure its world wide interests against Soviet aggression without the help of ... the U.S.A.'.[36] Yet British leaders had long detected the absence of a genuine American concern for the perpetuation of the British Empire or Britain's role in world affairs. That Churchill had failed to forge stronger ties with the United States during the war years reflected less a divergence of interests than Britain's marked decline in the global hierarchy of power. Richard Law of the Foreign Office advised Churchill in May 1945:

I see a great deal of evidence from the United States which suggests ... that the Americans ... are tending to regard us as a factor of little account in world affairs in the future. They are beginning to feel that it is Russia, not we, who are the only partners equal to them in strength. ...[37]

As the European war receded into history, American officials and writers resurrected the old American propensity to go it alone by denying that the USSR, any more than Britain, threatened vital American interests. General Marshall, no less than countless members of the armed forces, was not prepared to view the country that had carried the major burden of the recent war as a potential enemy. As late as November, General Dwight D. Eisenhower testified before the House Military Affairs Committee that 'Russia has not the slightest thing to gain by a struggle with the United States'. Stimson noted in his diary that the Soviet and American orbits need not 'clash geographically'. Bohlen agreed, observing in October that the United States and the USSR had no basic interests in conflict. 'The geographical location of the two countries', he wrote, 'do[es] not provide places where the friction arises automatically.'[38]

Such convictions warred against the close US–British ties that London desired. Finding no reason to confront the Soviets, many Americans resented Britain's open willingness to do so. For them, Britain, without legitimate cause, was making itself the Soviet Union's special antagonist and seeking to enlist the support of the United States. For Americans generally, Britain's imperial interests from Malta to Hong Kong had ceased to be matters of US concern. Noted columnist Walter Lippmann observed in June that the United States, facing no challenges to its vital interests from any of the world's major nations, could well play the role 'as mediator – that is, intercessor, reconciler, within the circle of the big powers'. An Anglo-American alliance against the USSR, he warned, would render any world organisation unworkable by aggravating the conflict of interests between Britain and the Soviet Union and dividing the organisation into blocs.[39] Whether London, in countering such convictions, would undermine American unilateralism in favour of an Anglo-American alliance depended on issues and events beyond its control.

Sharing the country's confidence, Truman refused to confront the Kremlin with active policies of opposition. He refused to publicise his private displeasure with Soviet behaviour and thereby suggest to the country that its wartime exertions had achieved a doubtful victory at best. The need to perpetuate the Grand Alliance in the interest of Europe's postwar reconstruction continued to override the ongoing disagreements over the meaning of Yalta. With Germany's defeat, however, Churchill addressed Truman on the need to confront the Soviets in their zone of occupation by refusing to withdraw US and British forces before the Kremlin accepted a satisfactory arrangement in Poland, the Balkans and Germany. Otherwise, he warned Truman on 11 May, 'the tide of Russian dominance [would sweep] forward 120 miles on a front of 300 to 400 miles, . . . an event which, if it occurred, would be one of the most melancholy in history'. Churchill wired the President again on the following day, urging a settlement with the Kremlin while Western forces still held their advanced positions:

> I have always worked for friendship with Russia, but like you, I feel deep anxiety because of their misinterpretation of the Yalta decisions. . . . Surely it is vital now to come to an understanding with Russia, to see where we are with her, before weakening our armies mortally or retire to the zones of occupation. . . . Of course we may take the view that Russia will behave impeccably, and no doubt that offers the most convenient solution. To sum up, this issue of a settlement with Russia before our strength has gone seems to me to dwarf all others.[40]

Truman accepted the advice of Joseph Davies, his special envoy to London, who argued that Churchill was too concerned with British interests on the continent.[41] With his advisers concurring, the President decided against the employment of the advanced positions for the purpose of bargaining. The deliberations over troop withdrawals did not include any formal Soviet guarantees on the question of Western access to Berlin. Following the allied occupation of the city, the massive requirements for adequate transportation facilities became obvious. On 28 June Eisenhower requested several roads and rail-lines, as well as unrestricted air travel, between the American and British zones and the Western sectors of Berlin. When one air-lane proved to be inadequate, the Soviets agreed to three Western air-corridors into West Berlin.

However limited the official American perceptions of danger in Europe, Washington assured London that it would not recognise any legitimacy in the Kremlin's Polish and Balkan policies. The record of Soviet repression, reported in detail by American diplomats, reinforced the conviction that any recognition of the existing Soviet hegemony, itself the creation of the repression, would be totally reprehensible. Unless the United States as well as Britain made the effort to establish self-determination for the peoples of Eastern

Europe, Harriman recalled, history would condemn them for wilfully selling out these countries. In May Truman accepted Harriman's advice to despatch Harry Hopkins on a special mission to confer with Stalin in Moscow on the Polish question. The President presumed that Stalin would have the good political judgement to assure the American public that he intended to keep his word.[42]

Hopkins, reaching Moscow in late May, confirmed the American wish to see no government in Poland unfriendly to the USSR, but he reminded the Soviet leader of the Polish question's importance to the American people. He pressed Stalin to broaden the base of the Warsaw government in accordance with the Declaration on Poland and to release the leaders of the Polish underground. Stalin recalled that Germany, in the course of one long generation, had invaded Russia twice through Poland. This had been possible, he continued, 'because Poland had been regarded as a part of the *cordon sanitaire* around the Soviet Union and that previous European policy had been that Polish Governments must be hostile to Russia'.[43] On the question of Poland's government Stalin remained adamant. Perhaps four or five London Poles, he said, could enter the Lublin cabinet. Harriman explained Hopkins's failure to move the Soviet leader:

> I am afraid that Stalin does not and never will fully understand our interest in a free Poland as a matter of principle. The Russian Premier is a realist in all of his actions, and it is hard for him to appreciate our faith in abstract principle. It is difficult for him to understand why we should want to interfere with Soviet policy in a country like Poland which he considers so important to Russia's security unless we have some ulterior motive.[44]

To Stalin, American opinion meant nothing; there would be no American solution to the Polish question.

If Stalin refused to alter his purposes in Warsaw, he agreed with Hopkins to name the Poles that the commission would consult in the reorganisation of the Polish government.[45] Stalin accepted several representatives of the London Poles, including Mikolajczyk. During June the Poles formed a Provisional Government of National Unity to fulfil the Yalta pledge. The new government included Boleslaw Bierut as Prime Minister, Mikolajczyk as Vice Prime Minister, and four members of the Peasant Party. Harriman assured Washington that the non-Lublin Poles had gained the best arrangement available.[46] London and Washington recognised the new Provisional Government on 5 July. Truman confirmed that its establishment was 'an important and positive step in fulfilling the decisions regarding Poland reached at Yalta . . .'.[47] Bierut had avoided any promises regarding free elections, but that mattered little. Soviet manoeuvring had enabled the Lublin-dominated government in Warsaw to gain complete control of Poland. Eventually some London Poles returned to Warsaw and received minor posts; their influence proved to be temporary and inconsequential.

Meeting at Potsdam near Berlin from 17 July to 2 August, Truman, Churchill and Stalin were no longer wartime leaders seeking victory over Germany; they were now political leaders burdened with the task of blocking out the territorial, economic and administrative arrangements for European reconstruction. Convinced that he and Byrnes, Secretary of State since 3 July, would possess little bargaining power at Potsdam, Truman had delayed the meeting as long as possible. Byrnes had established a reputation as 'a cautious mediator and conciliator in the most strained and tangled situations'. His career to 1945, however, had been limited almost exclusively to domestic politics; in foreign affairs he possessed little expertise.[48] Following the Labour Party's victory in Britain's general election, Clement Attlee replaced Churchill at the conference. The Big Three achieved quick agreement on the creation of a Council of Foreign Ministers to negotiate treaties for Italy and the former Axis states – Romania, Bulgaria, Hungary and Finland. In May, Stalin had urged Washington to recognise the governments of Romania, Bulgaria and Finland. Following State Department advice, Truman recognised the government of Finland, but not those of Romania, Bulgaria and Hungary.[49] On the concrete issues posed by the Soviet occupation of those three states Washington and Moscow had been unable to agree.

At Potsdam Stalin remained uncompromising. 'A freely elected government in any of these East European countries', he admitted, 'would be anti-Soviet, and that we cannot allow.' He denounced the US demand for changes in the governments of Romania, Bulgaria and Hungary, reminding Churchill that the Soviets had not meddled in Greek affairs. Molotov suggested that the Western allies simply recognise the Balkan states; allied supervision of elections was unnecessary. Byrnes assured the Soviet minister that the United States did not wish to become involved in the elections of Italy, Greece, Bulgaria and Romania; it merely wished to join others in observing them.[50] Eventually the conference made a major concession to the principles of Yalta by agreeing that only those states of Eastern Europe with 'recognized democratic governments' would be permitted to sign peace treaties or apply for membership in the United Nations. But no decision was made on the implementation of this agreement. The procedural gains at Potsdam left fundamental Eastern European issues substantially untouched. Admiral Leahy observed later that 'the only possibility of agreement would have been to accept the Russian point of view on every issue'. Stalin failed to win recognition of the Soviet Union's paramount position in Eastern Europe, but that failure in no way diminished the Kremlin's monopoly of power throughout the region.[51]

At Potsdam the Western allies faced the task of gaining Soviet collaboration in designing a fair and promising settlement for Germany. The Yalta accords anticipated the creation of a reformed and peaceful Germany but left unresolved the precise nature of that country's postwar role. Stalin demanded heavy reparations to limit Germany's industrial capacity and compensate the USSR for its wartime losses. Churchill, convinced that Germany's economic recovery was essential for Europe's reconstruction, opposed reparations that would cripple her economic revival. Roosevelt, committed to a united policy for Germany, agreed to large reparations provided that they were paid in capital goods and not from financial resources.[52] At the 13 July meeting of the Allied Reparations Commission in Moscow the US delegation, led by Edwin Pauley, insisted that reparations not infringe on Germany's capacity to maintain a minimum level of subsistance without continued external relief.[53]

Ignoring the American formula, the Soviets, during the weeks preceding the conference, inaugurated a programme of removing from their zone what the war's demolition had missed – machines, trolleys, trains, blueprints, drawings, and all useful information from the files of ravaged companies. At Potsdam Byrnes suggested that the Soviets take industrial material and equipment from the Western zones, provided that they paid for it with shipments of food and fuel from the Soviet zone. In addition, he offered the Soviets 10 per cent of all industrial capital equipment in the Western zones not required for Germany's peacetime economy. In accepting this arrangement the Soviets gave up their claim for $20 billion in reparations. The Big Three at Potsdam established the Allied Control Council, with headquarters in Berlin, to manage the occupation. Politically, the occupying powers were to denazify and democratise the country; unfortunately, they could never agree on the meaning of democracy. To the Soviets the Communist-controlled government in their zone was democratic. Economically the allies were to disarm and demilitarise Germany while treating it as an economic unit. Instead, the Soviets continued to dismantle factories for shipment to the USSR and appropriate much of the output of factories still in operation. Rather than attempt to influence Germany's total reconstruction, Stalin chose to convert the Soviet zone into an exclusive sphere, binding Poland to the USSR by assigning that country new western frontiers along the Oder–Neisse rivers at Germany's expense. This decision tied Poland's security to Soviet control of Germany's eastern zone. Such divergent political and economic purposes eliminated the possibility of any unified control system for Germany.[54]

Truman chose to bury the failures of Potsdam from public view. In his report to the American people he declared that the allies 'are now more closely than ever bound together. . . . From Tehran thin, and the Crimea, and San Francisco, and Berlin – we shall continue to march together to our objective'.[55] Privately the President and his advisers were not reassured by their recent experience. Stalin impressed Truman as smart, personally likeable, but scarcely trustworthy. Later Truman recalled the deep and unpromising divisions among the three wartime allies:

Potsdam brings to mind 'what might have been'. . . . Russia had no program except to take over the free part of Europe, kill as many Germans
as possible, and fool the Western Alliance. Britain only wanted to control
the Eastern Mediterranean, keep India, oil in Persia, the Suez Canal, and
whatever else was floating loose.

There was an innocent idealist at one corner [of] that Round Table who
wanted free waterways – Danube–Rhine–Kiel Canal, Suez, Black Sea Straits,
Panama – a restoration of Germany, France, Italy, Poland, Czechoslovakia, Rumania, and the Balkans, and a proper treatment of Latvia, Lithuania, Finland, free Philippines, Indonesia, Indo-China, a Chinese Republic,
and a free Japan.

What a show that was! But a large number of agreements were reached
in spite of the set up – only to be broken as soon as the unconscionable
Russian dictator returned to Moscow![56]

Shortly after Potsdam Truman made the fateful decision to terminate the
Pacific War abruptly with an atomic explosion over Hiroshima. He and Byrnes
hoped that they might still halt the Soviet advance into Manchuria, as well
as Soviet entry into the Pacific war, by forcing an immediate Japanese surrender. Thereafter the Kremlin would be in no position to press its claims
against China and Japan, especially to southern Sakhalin and the Kuriles,
promised secretly at Yalta. Beyond that the two American leaders hoped
that the United States, in sole possession of the atomic bomb, might eliminate the Soviet infringements on Yalta if not the unfortunate consequences
of the war itself. If the bomb worked, Truman remarked in July, 'I'll certainly have a hammer on those boys [the Russians].' The bomb was needed,
Byrnes observed, not to defeat Japan but to 'make Russia manageable in
Europe'. Byrnes added that 'in his belief the bomb might well put us in a
position to dictate our own terms at the end of the war'.[57] Stimson predicted
that the bomb would bestow enormous diplomatic advantage on the United
States. He noted in his diary on 4 September that Byrnes, in anticipation of
the London Foreign Ministers Conference, 'looks to have the presence of
the bomb in his pocket, so to speak, as a great weapon to get through the
things he has'.[58] Actually Truman employed the bomb to end the Pacific
war, not to make the Soviets more manageable in Europe. Indeed, the President revealed little subsequent interest in the bomb as a useful device for
either fighting a war or influencing US–Soviet relations. Not once did American
officials use the threat of atomic retaliation to achieve some national purpose. Such threats could affect Soviet behaviour only if the Kremlin chose
to take them seriously. Washington would never persuade the Soviets, at
London or later, that the United States had objectives in Eastern Europe
worth the price of war.

At London in September the Foreign Ministers tackled their first assignment of drafting peace treaties for Italy, Romania, Bulgaria, Hungary, and Finland. Byrnes repeated the American position that the Kremlin should establish governments in Eastern Europe that were both representative and friendly to the Soviet Union. Molotov was not impressed. He denied the possibility of forming governments both friendly and free. Moreover, he found gross inconsistencies in the American policy. The Radescu regime of Romania, he reminded Byrnes, was hostile to the USSR but had received American and British support. The United States then refused to recognise the new governments of Romania and Bulgaria although they were friendly to Moscow. The Romanian government, ran Byrnes's retort, was the product of Soviet interventionism. Molotov observed that the Kremlin faced the obligation to root out German fascism. When Byrnes insisted that the United States desired governments based on free elections, Molotov asked him why the United States had no trouble with governments in Italy and Greece that had never held free elections. Byrnes moved to break the deadlock by recognising the government of Hungary, one friendly to the USSR, on the promise that it would hold free elections. On Romania and Bulgaria, Byrnes and Molotov reached no agreement at all.[59]

At London, Germany again emerged as the central issue confronting the allies. To the Western powers a reconstructed German economy remained the necessary prelude to Germany's political independence. The Soviets' persistent removal of German assets from their zone in the name of security against Germany not only crippled German production but also created an enormous drain of resources from the Western zones. The issue in Soviet policy, Molotov argued, was the ease of the German advance across Poland, Hungary, Romania and Bulgaria in 1941. Byrnes countered Molotov's continuing security demands by offering a pact binding the United States to Germany's demilitarisation for 25 years. Molotov agreed only to report to Moscow. Soviet intransigence at London had the effect of driving the Western ministers into a solid, opposing bloc. When it became obvious that every disagreement produced a unified anti-Soviet reaction among the American, British, French and Chinese delegates, the Soviets demanded French and Chinese exclusion from the critical decisions. After staggering through a series of stormy sessions, marked by uncompromising Soviet manoeuvres, the conference adjourned without reaching a single substantive agreement.[60]

Following the London Conference, the western powers faced their immediate challenge in the burgeoning division of Europe into permanent spheres of influence. In early October the *London Observer* noted the accumulating cost of disagreement. '[A] line drawn north and south across Europe, perhaps somewhere in the region of Stettin to Trieste', it warned, 'is likely to become more and more of a barrier separating two very different conceptions of life.' Washington renewed its search for an Eastern European formula acceptable to all members of the Grand Alliance – one that would maintain the European continent's solidarity. Byrnes responded to the ongoing conflict over Romania and Bulgaria by despatching Mark Ethridge, editor of the Louisville *Courier-Journal*, to provide the State Department with an unbiased evaluation of the two Balkan states. Ethridge discovered that both countries had governments that defied the principles of the Yalta Declaration on Liberated Europe. In his December report Ethridge recommended the continuation of the established policy of non-recognition.[61]

In Washington the search for an acceptable Eastern European settlement was equally unproductive. In a long memorandum of 18 October, Bohlen suggested greater East–West economic and diplomatic cooperation as an antidote to Soviet exclusiveness in Eastern Europe. One week later, Cloyce K. Huston, Chief of the Division of Southern European Affairs, released a report that recognised the Soviet right to contest any anti-Soviet *cordon sanitaire* along its western periphery; like Bohlen, he rejected the exclusiveness of Kremlin policy. Huston recommended that the United States declare forthrightly, as had Byrnes at Potsdam and London, its desire to see governments in Eastern Europe friendly to the USSR.[62] In his noted Navy Day speech of 27 October the President again offered the Soviets the American principle of self-determination, nothing more. There would be no compromise. In his *New York Herald-Tribune* Forum address four days later, Byrnes again approved the Soviet Union's right to friendly relations with its western neighbours, but added the customary proviso: 'It is our belief that all peoples should be free to choose their own form of government . . . based on the consent of the governed.' Byrnes's prescription that the Soviets accept whatever border regimes the desired democratic processes might produce overlooked the fact that the region contained powerful anti-Soviet elements that Stalin and Molotov had repeatedly declared dangerous and unacceptable.[63]

What national interest was served by this uncompromising pursuit of the unachievable was not obvious. Lippmann noted in late October that generalities were inspiring but resolved nothing.[64] He, like countless Americans, saw little danger to US security in Romanian and Bulgarian political abuses. But for some Americans – among them top officials – the Soviet power-base in Eastern Europe and the Balkans had become a measure not only of Soviet repression but also of Soviet expansionism. Ethridge admonished the State Department in December that 'the strong position which the Soviet Government is establishing in Bulgaria and Romania will doubtless be used as a means of bringing pressure to bear on Greece, Turkey and the Straits, and could be converted without great effort into a springboard for aggression in the Eastern Mediterranean region'. Similarly John D. Hickerson, Deputy Director of the Office of European Affairs, warned Byrnes that the Soviet concern for friendly governments along its borders clouded a larger scheme to establish 'a security zone through the Balkans and the Eastern Mediterranean'. The Joint Chiefs of Staff observed that Eastern Europe was scarcely vital but that control of strategic points in the region would add significantly to Soviet military potential.[65] The notion that Soviet ambitions reached beyond the regions of occupation introduced a new, ultimately frightening and destructive element into US–Soviet relations.

The emerging conviction among Washington officials that Western civilisation faced new dangers exposed, to troubling scrutiny, the reality that the war had weakened or destroyed all the traditional sources of European and world stability. The historic international equilibrium had vanished. Western Europe was politically demoralised, economically prostrate, and militarily defenceless. Britain, historically the protector of the Ottoman Empire, the eastern Mediterranean, and the Indian Ocean, could no longer defend those strategic regions against external forces. Disease, famine and anarchy created a revolutionary international environment. Following the Soviet Union's heroic victory over Germany, Communist Party membership soared in Italy, France, Belgium, Holland, Czechoslovakia, Hungary and Finland. In France and Italy Communist parties, with suspected ties to Moscow, were members of coalition governments.[66] The opportunities that political ferment and economic upheaval offered to the Kremlin seemed limitless. The futile and humiliating US experience in Eastern Europe drove Washington to react resolutely to any apparent Soviet threat elsewhere, thus rendering an expanding conflict between the United States and the USSR inevitable.

Moscow's perceived ambitions in Iran, Turkey and Greece suddenly became challenges that demanded attention. Iran emerged in late 1945 as the Middle East's major point of confrontation. At the London Conference the allies had established 2 March 1946 as the final date for the evacuation of all foreign troops from Iran. Partially in retaliation for Tehran's refusal to negotiate mineral and oil rights, the Soviets supported a local communist attempt to take control of autonomous Azerbaijan. Finally in November 1945 a radical coup overthrew the Iranian regime. Soviet forces moved in, surrounded the Iranian army headquarters in Tabriz, and expelled officers who refused to join the Azerbaijani army. In December the rebels proclaimed their independence. In Washington the Iranian ambassador warned the State Department that Azerbaijan was only the initial move 'in a series which would include Turkey and other countries in the Near East'. If the Soviets succeeded in holding Azerbaijan, he added, 'the history of Manchuria, Abyssinia, and Munich would be repeated and Azerbaijan would prove to have been the first shot fired in [the] Third world war'.[67]

In Greece the British maintained some semblance of order against communist infiltration from Yugoslavia, Albania and Bulgaria. By late November 1945 the struggle for power had become so acute that London postponed elections until March 1946. Soviet ambitions in the Middle East appeared even more threatening when, in March 1945, the Kremlin announced that it would terminate its interwar treaty arrangements with Turkey. On 7 June the Soviets informed the Turkish ambassador in Moscow that they wanted the border districts in the Caucasus that the Russians had taken in 1878 but returned to the Turks after the First World War, a revision of the Montreux Convention governing the Straits, and a lease of strategic bases in the Straits for joint defence. Turkey rejected the demands outright. Washington regarded the Soviet pressures on Turkey as evidence of the Kremlin's insatiable ambitions in the Middle East. In December, Loy Henderson observed that the Soviets seemed determined to destroy Britain's historic position in the region 'so that Russian power can sweep unimpeded across Turkey through the Dardenelles into the Mediterranean, and across Iran and through the Persian Gulf into the Indian Ocean . . .'.[68] Soviet demands on Turkey and Iran suggested that the Kremlin intended to dominate the eastern Mediterranean as well as the waterways, pipelines and oilfields of the Middle East. With the danger of a communist coup in Greece, Truman recalled, 'this began to look like a giant pincers movement against the oil-rich areas of the Near East and the warm-water ports of the Mediterranean'.[69] Washington seemed prepared to meet the perceived Soviet dangers in the Middle East head-on.

Byrnes's decision to travel to Moscow in December without preparations or Republican advisers was his own. Diplomats and columnists warned him against venturing into a conference with Stalin without a precise agenda agreed on in advance. But Byrnes believed, as he wrote in his defence, 'that if we met in Moscow, where I could have a chance to talk to Stalin, we might remove the barriers to the peace treaties'.[70] Byrnes's advisers in Moscow, Harriman and Bohlen, agreed that continued non-recognition of Romania and Bulgaria would achieve nothing. When Byrnes raised the troublesome issue of these two countries, Stalin proposed that the allies urge the Bulgarian parliament to include some opposition members and the Romanian governmnent to add leaders from two opposition parties. Byrnes suddenly found the way open to recognise the two governments. He asked only that the conference's final communiqué include a statement of allied support for civil liberties and free elections. Unfortunately such phraseology was no guarantee of democracy.[71] Kennan revealed only contempt for Byrnes's effort to rescue the Yalta Declaration by accepting an arrangement that would hide the reality of Soviet-controlled dictatorships across Eastern Europe.[72] If Byrnes's agreements represented a retreat from previous US positions, they recognised that the United States had few choices remaining. Byrnes eventually gained Stalin's support for a peace conference in 1946, but accepted Stalin's demand that France and China be eliminated from the treaty-drafting process.[73]

Washington's exaggerated reactions to Soviet pressures in Iran and Turkey, regions of historic British concern, in no way improved Anglo-American relations. For London this was deeply troubling. Britain's long quest for some US commitment to its imperial interests had become critical as Britain faced the prospect of a direct Soviet challenge to the oil and sea lanes of the Middle East. State Department officials shared British concerns but preferred unilateral approaches to the USSR. Byrnes arranged the Moscow Conference with no effort to coordinate British and American action. At Moscow, British delegates accused the Secretary of ignoring them. Byrnes refused to include Foreign Secretary Ernest Bevin in many of his discussions with Stalin. When Bevin informed Byrnes that the Soviets were attempting to undermine the historic British position in the Middle East, the Secretary agreed only to discuss the matter with Molotov privately. Kennan noted Bevin's disgust at Byrnes's lack of concern for British interests. In Washington the British complained that Americans generally referred to the Moscow conference in terms of US–Soviet cooperation, blaming Britain for the persistence of international tension. At its conclusion the Moscow Conference marked the nadir of US–British relations.[74]

Washington's commitment to Britain's economic welfare was no greater than its concern for Britain's role in world affairs. Truman announced at Potsdam that lend-lease would be limited to munitions, not capital investment, and would end totally with Japan's defeat. Churchill believed the decision unnecessarily harsh; Chancellor of Exchequer Hugh Dalton complained that it came without warning or discussion. 'We had expected', he wrote, 'at least some tapering off of Lend-Lease over the first few months of peace.' Prime Minister Attlee reminded Truman that Britain's war effort had ruined its finances. In desperation the British, with little encouragement from Washington, pressed for a loan. Vandenberg argued that the United States should grant Britain a loan only if it was prepared to grant a similar one to the USSR; to do otherwise, he said, would terminate the Grand Alliance.[75] Likewise Secretary of the Treasury Fred M. Vinson expressed no sympathy for the British request. Finally in December 1945 a US–British loan agreement extended a $3.75 billion line of credit at 2 per cent interest, repayable in 50 years. The United States cancelled the $20 billion debt owed on lend-lease. What troubled the British was the provision that sterling would become freely convertible one year after the effective date of the loan. Churchill regarded that arrangement so perilous that in practice it would become self-defeating. *The Economist* (London) declared that 'our reward for losing a quarter of our total national wealth in the common cause is to pay tribute for half a century to those who have been enriched by the war'.[76] The loan agreement had yet to pass the congressional gauntlet.

Truman received the Moscow communiqué on 27 December. 'I did not like what I read', he recalled. 'There was not a word about Iran or any other place where the Soviets were on the march. We had gained only an empty promise of further talks.' The President's contentiousness reflected the country's changing mood, and that change reflected a gradual shift in the country's primary concerns to alleged Soviet ambitions outside the area of Soviet occupation, with their pervading power to instil fear rather than frustration. For some editors, Byrnes, in his determination to reach agreement, had given too much away.[77] When Byrnes returned to Washington the President accused him of making concessions without any evidence that the Soviets intended to change their policies. The Secretary, he recorded, had attempted 'to move the foreign policy of the United States in a direction to which I could not, and would not agree'. On 5 January he prepared his bill of particulars:

> There is no justification for [the Russian program in Iran]. It is a parallel to the program of Russia in Latvia, Estonia, and Lithuania. . . . There isn't a doubt in my mind that Russia intends an invasion of Turkey and the seizure of the Black Sea Straits to the Mediterranean. Unless Russia is faced with an iron fist and strong language another war is in the making. . . . I do not think we should play compromise any longer. We should refuse to recognize Rumania and Bulgaria until they comply with our requirements; we should let our position in Iran be known in no uncertain terms and we should continue to insist on the internationalization of the Kiel Canal, the Rhine–Danube waterway and the Black Sea Straits.

Truman later designated his memorandum to Byrnes as the point of departure in American policy.[78] Whether Truman's confrontation with Byrnes actually occurred is doubtful. At their first meeting Byrnes briefed the President on the Moscow agreements. He termed the Romanian formula satisfactory, the Bulgarian not. On all other agreements, Byrnes declared, he had simply followed established policies. Iran's future remained in doubt, but Byrnes had reminded Stalin of the Soviet promise to evacuate by 2 March. Stalin replied simply that he would not embarrass the United States. Leahy recorded Truman's satisfaction with Byrnes's account and arranged for the Secretary to address the nation on CBS radio.[79]

After January 1946, US relations with the Soviet Union began to unravel while those with Britain began to improve. Stalin inaugurated the process in his Moscow address of 9 February. He raised again the old Bolshevik concept of 'capitalist encirclement' and the continuing hostility between the communist and capitalist worlds. Stalin attributed the recent war to the dialectical imperatives of capitalism; those same forces, he warned, would again endanger the peace. His words were not reassuring: 'Our Marxists declare that the capitalist system of world economy conceals elements of crisis and war. . . . [W]orld capitalism does not follow a steady and even course forward, but proceeds through crises and catastrophes.' Stalin concluded by explaining the need of a new five-year plan to prepare the country for any eventuality.[80] Stalin did not intimate that the Soviet Union required a communist world order to prevent war; nor did he threaten open conflict with the capitalist enemy. To Soviet expert Elbridge Dubrow, the speech was designed to gird a reluctant Soviet populace for a programme of industrial expansion that would further cripple its standard of living. But for many Americans Stalin's references to capitalist iniquities seemed to inaugurate ideological warfare against the non-communist world. *Time* viewed the speech as the most ominous statement of any world leader since the end of the war. Justice William O. Douglas termed it 'The Declaration of World War III'. At the suggestion of H. Freeman Matthews, Byrnes requested George Kennan in Moscow to produce an analysis of the possible implications of Stalin's speech.[81]

Kennan's 'Long Telegram' of 22 February offered Washington's officialdom a frightening, yet totally welcome, definition of the Soviet problem. By attributing Soviet behaviour to internal rather than external causes, Kennan absolved the United States of all responsibility for the breakdown of US–Soviet relations. Soviet paranoia, demanding endless struggle against external enemies, explained why the United States could anticipate no satisfactory negotiations with the Kremlin. This presumption established the foundation of a new foreign policy consensus that recognised the USSR as a hostile power whose irreconcilable differences with the West, not the perpetuation of the wartime alliance, should govern US policy. By insisting that the United States could meet the Soviet threat successfully without war, Kennan rendered an attitude of 'getting tough' with the Soviets reasonable and scarcely even dangerous.[82]

Republican pressures for a tougher US response to Soviet actions, complemented by editorials in leading Catholic journals such as *The Commonweal* and *The Catholic World*, reinforced the new consensus.[83] Vandenberg took up the Soviet challenge with a telling speech in the Senate on 27 February. On the following day Byrnes continued the assault before the Overseas Press Club in New York (one wit termed it the Second Vandenberg Concerto). Still in the realm of action the new 'get tough' rhetoric, condemning Soviet policies as reprehensible and dangerous, offered no genuine response. Its effectiveness required the capacity and will to make the consequences of Soviet non-compliance with American demands unacceptably expensive. But nowhere did the Soviets endanger American interests sufficiently to require additional government expenditures. This was true not only in Eastern Europe but in Iran and Turkey as well. Columnist Edwin L. James observed in *The New York Times* of 3 March that it remained 'too early to say that this country has worked out an all-embracing policy vis-a-vis the . . . USSR'.[84]

The American public had no interest in any direct US confrontation with the Soviet Union; nor was Congress concerned with stronger defences or checking the speed of demobilisation. Byrnes ignored the question of means completely.

Winston Churchill, on 5 March, fought this national unconcern with preparedness by raising the issue of Soviet expansionism and the responsibility of the United States in meeting it. 'With primacy in power', he asserted at Fulton, Missouri, 'is also joined an awe-inspiring accountability for the future.' He drew a dark picture of the strength and outreach of the USSR and the need for another alliance of the English-speaking peoples to meet the danger. London responded with unstinting approval, Moscow with a burst of hysteria. For Stalin, as Nikita Khrushchev later reported, Churchill's Fulton speech signalled the end of the alliance: 'Our relations with England, France, [and] the USA . . . were, for all intents and purposes, ruined.'[85]

Despite the mixed US response to Churchill's plea, successive events were forming ever-closer Anglo-American cooperation. The first was the Iranian crisis of March 1946. The 2 March deadline for Soviet withdrawal from Azerbaijan passed without any Soviet response. Byrnes sent a protest to Moscow on 5 March and prepared for a showdown. On 17 March Iran appealed to the United Nations Security Council; Byrnes, joined by Britain's Bevin, called for an early meeting of the Council. When it met on 25 March the Kremlin announced an agreement with Iran that included oil concessions and a Soviet withdrawal in five or six weeks. On 15 April the Iranian government withdrew its complaint as Soviet troops began their withdrawal. The Iranian crisis, while it lasted, created an unprecedented occasion for British–American collaboration. Byrnes informed the country that the administration did not contemplate an alliance with Britain; yet the Iranian experience suggested strongly that Britain's historic concerns were becoming those of the United States. That same Anglo-American cooperation continued throughout the often-tumultous treaty negotiations of the Foreign Ministers which opened in Paris on 25 April and continued throughout the year. Closing in New York in December, the conference completed the long-sought treaties for the former German satellites.

Meanwhile, in March, Byrnes had requested the Joint Chiefs of Staff to consider the significance of Soviet pressures on Turkey. The JCS's response focused on Britain's role in sustaining America's world position:

> The defeat or disintegration of the British Empire would eliminate from Eurasia the last bulwark of resistance between the United States and Soviet expansion. . . . Militarily, our present position in the world is of necessity closely interwoven with that of Great Britain.

To the Joint Chiefs it was essential that the United States buttress the British Empire against possible Soviet aggression. In early April, Matthews advised the nation's military planners, 'If Soviet Russia is to be denied the hegemony of Europe, the United Kingdom must continue in existence as the principal power in Western Europe economically and militarily.' During the spring of 1946 the Joint Chiefs concluded that the USSR would be the likely adversary in another war. They declared that

> the consolidation and development of the power of Russia is the greatest threat to the United States in the foreseeable future. . . . United States foreign policy should continually give consideration to our immediate capabilities for supporting our policy by arms if the occasion should demand, rather than to our long term potential, which, owing to the length of time required for mobilization of the nation's resources, might not be sufficient to avert disaster in another war.[86]

This burgeoning compatibility between American and British concerns sealed the fate of the British loan. Hearings on the loan opened on 13 March before the Senate Banking and Currency Committee. Under-Secretary of State Dean G. Acheson assumed major responsibility for the loan's passage. Either the United States would accept its economic responsibilities, he warned, or it would witness the collapse of Europe. Acheson and the bankers he hailed before the committee justified the loan purely on economic grounds. When the hearings ended in April the opposition remained strong. Vandenberg's decision to support the loan turned on his anti-Soviet bias, but it secured enough Republican votes to assure Senate passage on 10 May by a vote of 46 to 32. The House did not approve the measure until mid-July. What mattered, observed Congressman Christian Herter, was the need of a British friend to meet the impending Soviet challenge. There was no future, James Reston of *The New York Times* noted in late May, 'in trying to break up the Anglo-American bloc or denying that it exists'.[87] The propensity of congressmen to laud the British loan as a bulwark against communism doomed the passage of a similar Soviet loan. The conditions set down in the proposed Soviet agreement were so demanding on the question of Eastern Europe that informed officials saw no possibility of a Soviet acceptance.[88] Convinced as well that Congress would not approve a Soviet loan, the administration dropped the issue.

Two trends, slowly destroying the illusion of one world, converged during the summer and autumn of 1946 to destroy the Grand Alliance. The first was the structuring of a bipolar world. Noting the early confrontations between Byrnes and Molotov in Paris, *U.S. News* declared on 24 May: 'A pronounced trend is developing toward two big blocs in the world.' What solidified the new bipolarism was the adoption by both the United States and the USSR of an intensely antagonistic diplomacy, reflecting the conviction of each that the other was its special adversary. Second, the United States deserted totally the role of mediator between Britain and the USSR and ventured fully into the arena of world politics as leader of the English-speaking bloc. For Britain the acceptance of that leadership came as a willing retreat from its traditional status. The United States alone could protect Britain's historic interests and thereby preserve whatever remained of its former role. The astute *London Observer* commented on 27 October: 'Our relations with America and Russia are not the same. Those with America, though our views and interests are far from identical, are easy and friendly, and we cannot view America as a potential menace to our existence. The same cannot, unfortunately, be said of Russia . . .'. The Kremlin, conscious of the burgeoning Anglo-American coalition it faced, tightened its posture in solitary defiance.

## NOTES

1. Robert L. Messer, *The End of an Alliance: James F. Byrnes, Roosevelt, Truman, and the Origins of the Cold War* (Chapel Hill: University of North Carolina Press, 1982), pp. 50–1; Martin F. Herz, *Beginnings of the Cold War* (Bloomington: Indiana University Press, 1966), pp. 80–5; Edward R. Stettinius, Jr, *Roosevelt and the Russians: The Yalta Conference*, ed. Walter Johnson (Garden City, NY: Doubleday, 1949), pp. 251–2.

2. Joseph Grew to Harriman, 27 Feb. 1945, *Foreign Relations of the United States, Diplomatic Papers* (Hereafter *FRUS*), *1945*: V (Washington: US Govt Printing Office, 1967), p. 483; Berry to Vyshinsky, 28 Feb. 1945, ibid., pp. 486–8; Berry to Stettinius, 28 Feb., 2, 7 March 1945, ibid., pp. 492–3, 502–3.

3. On Hungary, see Louis Mark, Jr. 'The View from Hungary', in Thomas T. Hammond (ed.), *Witnesses to the Origins of the Cold War* (Seattle: University of Washington Press, 1982), pp. 186–208. Everywhere in the regions of Soviet occupation, these witnesses agreed, the United States faced a no-win situation.

4. Harriman to Roosevelt, 15 March 1945, President's Secretary's File (PSF): Russia, Box 68, Franklin D. Roosevelt Library, Hyde Park (FDRL).

5. Messer, pp. 54–8.

6. See David Carlton, *Anthony Eden: A Biography* (London: Allen Lane, 1981), pp. 254–5.

7. See J. M. Mackintosh, *Strategy and Tactics of Soviet Foreign Policy* (London: Oxford University Press, 1962), pp. 6–7.

8. Warren F. Kimball, 'Naked Reverse Right: Roosevelt, Churchill, and Eastern Europe from TOLSTOY to Yalta – and a Little Beyond', *Diplomatic History*, 9 (Winter 1985), p. 18; Henry Butterfield Ryan, *The Vision of Anglo-America: The US–UK Alliance and the Emerging Cold War, 1943–1946* (Cambridge: Cambridge University Press, 1987), p. 91.

9. Martin Gilbert, *Winston S. Churchill, VII: Road to Victory, 1941–1945* (Boston: Houghton Mifflin, 1986), pp. 1230–1; Geir Lundestad, *The American 'Empire' and Other Studies of US Foreign Policy in a Comparative Perspective* (Oxford: Oxford University Press, 1990), p. 152; Ryan, p. 89.

10. Churchill to Roosevelt, 8 March 1945, Warren F. Kimball (ed.), *Churchill &*

Roosevelt: The Complete Correspondence (Princeton, NJ: Princeton University Press, 1984), III, pp. 547–51; Winston Churchill, The Second World War, VI: Triumph and Tragedy (Boston: Houghton Mifflin, 1953), pp. 421–3; Ryan, p. 92.

11. Messer, The End of an Alliance, p. 60.

12. Harriman to Stettinius, 24 Feb. 1945, FRUS, 1945: V, p. 124; Harriman to Stettinius, 27 Feb. 1945, ibid., pp. 129–30; Harriman to Stettinius, 1 Mar. 1945, ibid., p. 134; Churchill, pp. 362–3.

13. Charles E. Bohlen, Witness to History, 1929–1969 (New York: W. W. Norton, 1973), pp. 207–8; Harriman to Stettinius, 7 March 1945, FRUS, 1945: V, p. 145.

14. Robert Murphy, Diplomat Among Warriors (Garden City, NY: Doubleday, 1964), p. 227.

15. Roosevelt to Churchill, 11 Mar. 1945, Kimball, Churchill & Roosevelt, III, p. 562; Roosevelt to Churchill, 12 Mar. 1945, ibid., p. 563; Roosevelt to Churchill, 15 Mar. 1945, ibid., pp. 568–9.

16. Anthony Eden, The Reckoning (Boston: Houghton Mifflin, 1965), pp. 603, 606–7; Churchill to Roosevelt, 27 March 1945, FRUS, 1945: V, p. 189; Ryan, pp. 94–5.

17. Roosevelt to Stalin, 31 March 1945, PSF: Russia, Box 68, FDRL; Roosevelt to Stalin, 1 April 1945, FRUS, 1945: V, pp. 194–6.

18. Churchill to Roosevelt, 5 Apr. 1945, Kimball, Churchill & Roosevelt, III, p. 613; Roosevelt to Churchill, 6 Apr. 1945, ibid., p. 617.

19. Stalin to Roosevelt, 7 April 1945, Ministry of Foreign Affairs of the USSR, Correspondence Between the Chairman of the Council of Ministers of the U.S.S.R. and the Presidents of the U.S.A. and the Prime Ministers of Great Britain During the Great Patriotic War of 1941–1945 (New York, 1965), pp. 211–13.

20. Churchill to Roosevelt, 1 Apr. 1945, Winston Churchill, Memoirs of the Second World War (Boston: Houghton Mifflin, 1959), p. 936; Churchill to Roosevelt, 5 Apr. 1945, Map Room, Box 7, FDRL.

21. Stephen E. Ambrose, Eisenhower and Berlin, 1945: The Decision to Halt at the Elbe (New York: W. W. Norton, 1967), pp. 88–9; Forrest C. Pogue, 'The Decision to Halt at the Elbe', Kent Roberts Greenfield (ed.), Command Decision (New York: Harcourt, Brace, and Co., 1959), pp. 479–92.

22. On Harriman's growing concern regarding Soviet intentions during March and April, see Walter Isaacson and Evan Thomas, The Wise Men: Six Friends and the World They Made (New York: Simon & Schuster, 1986), pp. 247–50.

23. Stettinius to Harriman, 3 April 1945, Department of State File (DS/F) 711.61/4–345, National Archives, Washington, DC; Harriman to Stettinius, 4 April 1945, PSF: Russia, Box 68, FDRL; Harriman to Stettinius, 6 April 1945, DS/F 711.61/4–645, National Archives.

24. Minutes of the Secretary of State's Staff Committee, 20 April 1945, FRUS, 1945: V, p. 841.

25. Stettinius's calender notes, 13 April 1945, Thomas M. Campbell and George C. Herring (eds), The Diaries of Edward R. Stettinius, Jr., 1943–1946 (New York: New Viewpoints, 1975), p. 318; Harry S. Truman, Memoirs, I: Year of Decisions (Garden City, NY: Doubleday, 1955), pp. 26, 64; Harriman to Stettinius, 17 April 1945, FRUS, 1945: V, pp. 225–6; Kennan to Stettinius, 21 April 1945, ibid., pp. 229–34; William D. Leahy, I Was There (New York: Whittlesey House, 1950), p. 349.

26. Truman, p. 71; Walter Millis (ed.), The Forrestal Diaries (New York: Viking Press, 1951), p. 47.

27. Bohlen memorandum of Truman–Harriman conversation, 20 April 1945, FRUS, 1945: V, pp. 231–34; Truman, pp. 71–2.

28. Stettinius and Truman quoted in Truman, pp. 76–7; for the White House meeting on 23 April see Millis, pp. 50–1. That day the State Department urged the President to avoid any agreement with the USSR that did not guarantee a Polish government representative of all the democratic elements among the Polish people. See Dunn and Bohlen to Truman, 23 April 1945, Series 11, Box 721, Stettinius Papers, University of Virginia Library, Charlottesville. For the views of Stimson and Marshall see Millis, pp. 50–1; Truman, pp. 77–9; Bohlen's memorandum of conversation, 23 April 1945, *FRUS, 1945*: V, pp. 253–5; Henry L. Stimson and McGeorge Bundy, *On Active Service in Peace and War* (New York: Harper, 1948), p. 609.

29. Conversations with Molotov, 23 April 1945, Truman, pp. 81–2.

30. Stalin to Truman, 24 Apr. 1945, Ministry of Foreign Affairs, *Correspondence*, pp. 219–20.

31. W. Averell Harriman and Elie Abel, *Special Envoy to Churchill and Stalin, 1941–1946* (New York: Random House, 1975), p. 448.

32. Vandenberg Diary, 24 April 1945, Arthur H. Vandenberg, Jr, and Joe Alex Morris (eds), *The Private Papers of Senator Vandenberg* (Boston: Houghton Mifflin, 1952), p. 176; Leahy, p. 352.

33. Millis, p. 49; Forrestal to Homer Ferguson, 14 May 1945, ibid., p. 57.

34. Joseph C. Grew, *Turbulent Era: A Diplomatic Record of Forty Years, 1904–1945*, ed. Walter Johnson (Boston: Houghton Mifflin, 1952), II, p. 1446.

35. Winston S. Churchill, *Memoirs of the Second World War* (Boston: Houghton Mifflin, 1959), p. 948; Gilbert, *Road to Victory*, p. 1350.

36. Richard A. Best, Jr, *'Co-Operation with Like-Minded Peoples': British Influences on American Security Policy, 1945–1949* (New York: Greenwood Press, 1986), p. 22.

37. Richard Law quoted in Ryan, *The Vision of Anglo-America*, p. 27.

38. Michael S. Sherry discusses the views of American military leaders toward the Soviet Union in *Preparing for the Next War: American Plans for Postwar Defense, 1941–1945* (New Haven: Yale University Press, 1977), pp. 168, 185; Bohlen quoted in Fraser J. Harbutt, *The Iron Curtain: Churchill, America, and the Origins of the Cold War* (New York: Oxford University Press, 1986), p. 132; Harriman and Abel, *Special Envoy*, pp. 461–2; Melvyn Leffler, *A Preponderance of Power* (Stanford: Stanford University Press, 1992), pp. 33, 46–7.

39. Lippmann to George Fielding Eliot, 14 June 1945, John Morton Blum (ed.), *Public Philosopher: Selected Letters of Walter Lippmann* (New York: Ticknor and Fields, 1985), pp. 467–8.

40. Churchill to Truman, 11 May 1945, *Foreign Relations of the United States, Diplomatic Papers: The Conference of Berlin, 1945, I* (Washington, US Govt Printing Office, 1960), p. 6; Churchill to Truman, 12 May 1945, ibid., p. 9.

41. For Churchill's unsatisfactory meeting with Davies, see Martin Gilbert, *Winston S. Churchill, VIII: 'Never Despair', 1945–1965* (Boston: Houghton Mifflin, 1988), p. 24.

42. Bohlen, *Witness to History*, p. 215; Messer, *The End of an Alliance*, p. 82.

43. Bohlen's report of the Hopkins–Stalin conversations, 26–7 May 1945, *FRUS: Berlin, 1945*, I, pp. 26–8, 37–40. Quotation on p. 39.

44. Harriman to Truman, 8 June 1945, ibid., p. 61.

45. Hopkins was delighted with the list. See Hopkins to Truman, 31 May 1945, *FRUS, 1945*: V, p. 308. Leader of the London Poles Mikolajczyk and the British were equally convinced that an agreement based on the Declaration of Poland was now possible. See Schoenfeld to Stettinius, 2 June 1945, ibid., p. 316.

46. Harriman to Stettinius, 28 June 1945, ibid., p. 728. On the movement toward a

Polish settlement, see *The New York Times*, 14 June 1945, p. 1; Bohlen, p. 219; 'Solution in Poland', *The New Republic*, 113 (2 July 1945), p. 6.
47. White House Press Release, 5 July 1945, *FRUS: Berlin, 1945*, I, p. 735.
48. Messer, *The End of an Alliance*, pp. 6–7, 96.
49. Stalin to Truman, 27 May 1945, *FRUS, 1945*, V, pp. 547–8; Harriman to Stettinius, 30 May 1945, ibid., p. 548; memorandum of Elbridge Dubrow, 30 May 1945, quoted in Lynn Ethridge Davis, *The Cold War Begins: Soviet–American Conflict over Eastern Europe* (Princeton, NJ: Princeton University Press, 1974), pp. 283–4; Truman to Stalin, 2 June 1945, *FRUS, 1945*, V, p. 550.
50. Winston Churchill, *Triumph and Tragedy*, p. 636; Meeting of Foreign Ministers, 20 July 1945, *FRUS: Berlin, 1945*, II, pp. 152–5; James F. Byrnes, *Speaking Frankly* (New York: Harper, 1947), p. 73.
51. Bohlen, *Witness to History*, pp. 234–5; Leahy, *I Was There*, pp. 428–9; The Department of State *Bulletin*, 13 (5 Aug. 1945), p. 159.
52. For the evolution of US policy toward Germany after Yalta, see Richard J. Barnet, 'Annals of Diplomacy: Alliance, I', *The New Yorker*, 10 Oct. 1983, pp. 53–61.
53. Truman to Churchill, 24 June 1945, *FRUS: Berlin, 1945*, I, p. 612; Byrnes to Pauley, 3 July 1945, ibid., p. 633.
54. The Department of State *Bulletin*, 13 (5 August 1945), pp. 153–60; *FRUS: Berlin, 1945*, II, pp. 210–15; 'Potsdam', *London Observer*, 5 Aug. 1945, p. 4; Lippmann to Forrestal, 24 Sept. 1945, Blum, *Public Philosopher*, p. 475. Lippmann saw clearly that after Potsdam the commitment to curtailing German power belonged far more to the Soviet Union than to the Western allies. Germany's division and resulting misery, if unfortunate, was not the result of Potsdam but simply a consequence of the war.
55. Truman, 'The Berlin Conference', The Department of State *Bulletin*, 13 (12 August 1945), p. 213.
56. Truman quoted in Joseph M. Siracusa, *Safe for Democracy: A History of America, 1914–1945* (Claremont: Regina Books, 1993), p. 257.
57. Byrnes quoted in Truman, *Year of Decisions*, p. 87.
58. Stimson quoted in Messer, *The End of an Alliance*, p. 127.
59. The Department of State *Bulletin*, 13 (30 Sept. 1945), p. 478.
60. Byrnes, *Speaking Frankly*, pp. 97–101.
61. Ethridge to Byrnes, 7 Dec. 1945, *FRUS, 1945*: V, pp. 633–7; Byrnes, *Speaking Frankly*, p. 107; Millis, *Forrestal Diaries*, p. 124.
62. Eduard Mark, 'Charles E. Bohlen and the Acceptable Limits of Soviet Hegemony in Eastern Europe: A Memorandum of 18 October 1945', *Diplomatic History*, 3 (Spring 1979), pp. 206–9; Robert L. Messer, 'Paths Not Taken: The United States Department of State and Alternatives to Containment, 1945–1946', ibid., 1 (Fall 1977), pp. 301–4.
63. Truman's speech of 27 Nov. 1945, *Public Papers of the Presidents of the United States: Harry S. Truman, 1945* (Washington: US Govt Printing Office, 1961), p. 434; Byrnes's address of 31 October 1945, The Department of State *Bulletin*, 13 (4 Nov. 1945), pp. 709–11.
64. Walter Lippmann, 'Today and Tomorrow', *New York Herald-Tribune*, 30 October 1945, p. 25, quoted in Robert Max Berdahl. 'The Emergence of American Cold War Policy, 1945–1947', MA thesis, University of Illinois, 1961, pp. 65–6.
65. Ethridge memorandum, 7 Dec. 1945, *FRUS, 1945*: V, p. 637; Hickerson to Byrnes, 10 Dec. 1945, ibid., IV, p. 407; Joint Chiefs of Staff quoted in Leffler, *A Preponderance of Power*, p. 50.
66. Alfred J. Rieber argues that Moscow's concern for French independence from

the United States encouraged French Communists to work within the system and support policies that would strengthen French patriotism, reconstruction and unity. This permitted them to play a leading and constructive role in French politics. See Rieber, *Stalin and the French Communist Party* (New York: Columbia University Press, 1962), pp. 212–37.

67. For a brief survey of the Iranian question, see Joseph Marion Jones, *The Fifteen Weeks: An Inside Account of the Genesis of the Marshall Plan* (New York: Viking Press, 1955), pp. 48–52. The views of the Iranian ambassador are reported in Acheson to Harriman, 21 Dec. 1945, *FRUS, 1945*: VIII (Washington: US Govt Printing Office, 1969), p. 508.
68. Henderson quoted in Daniel Yergin, *Shattered Peace: The Origins of the Cold War and the National Security State* (Boston: Houghton Mifflin, 1977), p. 152.
69. Truman, *Year of Decisions*, pp. 522–3; 'What Is Happening in Iran', *The New Republic*, 113 (3 Dec. 1945), pp. 731–2.
70. Kennan in Moscow opposed the conference, convinced that Byrnes would achieve nothing substantial. See George F. Kennan, *Memoirs: 1925–1950* (Boston: Little, Brown, 1967), pp. 284–6; Byrnes, *Speaking Frankly*, p. 109.
71. The United States recognised the Groza regime of Romania in January 1946 when it admitted two members from opposition parties and promised free elections. Meeting resistance to its demands in Bulgaria, the United States did not recognise that country's government until October 1947.
72. Kennan, p. 284; Davis, *The Cold War Begins*, p. 332; Philip R. Mosely, *The Kremlin and World Politics, Studies in Soviet Policy and Action* (New York: Vintage Books, 1960), p. 217.
73. Byrnes, pp. 111–12. Some members of the press, no less than Harriman and Bohlen, believed Byrnes's concessions at Moscow essential, permitting the Big Three to move forward toward a general postwar settlement. See, for example, 'Concessions and Confidence', *Manchester Guardian*, 4 Jan. 1946, pp. 2–3; 'Good News from Moscow', *The New Republic*, 114 (7 Jan. 1946), pp. 3–4.
74. On American–British relations at Moscow see Harbutt, *The Iron Curtain*, pp. 120–3; James L. Gormly, *The Collapse of the Grand Alliance, 1945–1948* (Baton Rouge, La.: Louisiana State University Press, 1987), p. 133; Best, '*Cooperation with Like-Minded Peoples*', p. 26; Kennan, p. 286.
75. Ryan, *The Vision of Anglo-America*, pp. 55–6; Robin Edmonds, *Setting the Mould: The United States and Britain, 1945–1950* (New York: W. W. Norton, 1986), p. 99; Richard N. Gardner, *Sterling–Dollar Diplomacy in Current Perspective* (New York: Columbia University Press, 1980), passim; Vandenberg and Morris, *Private Papers of Senator Vandenberg*, pp. 230–1.
76. Ryan, p. 58; Edmonds, pp. 100–3.
77. Truman, *Year of Decisions*, p. 549; John Lewis Gaddis, *The United States and the Origins of the Cold War, 1941–1947* (New York: Columbia University Press, 1972), pp. 282–90; Gormly, p. 135.
78. Truman to Byrnes, 5 January 1946 (unsent), Robert H. Ferrell (ed.), *Off the Record: The Private Papers of Harry S. Truman* (New York: Harper and Row, 1980), pp. 79–80; Truman, p. 552.
79. Gormly, pp. 135–6, 176–7; Harbutt, p. 144.
80. Stalin, 'New Five-Year Plan for Russia', *Vital Speeches of the Day*, 12 (1 Mar. 1946), pp. 300–1.
81. Harriman and Abel, *Special Envoy*, p. 547; *Newsweek*, 18 Feb. 1946, p. 47; *Time*, 18 Feb. 1946, pp. 29–30; Douglas quoted in Millis, *Forrestal Diaries*, p. 134.
82. For Kennan's Long Telegram, see Kennan, *Memoirs: 1925–1950*, pp. 547–59.

83. For the Republican attacks on the Truman administration, see Bradford Westerfield, *Foreign Policy and Party Politics: Pearl Harbor to Korea* (New Haven: Yale University Press, 1955), pp. 204–9; *The New York Times*, 6 December 1945, p. 18; Clare Booth Luce in ibid., 13 Feb. 1946, p. 18. For examples of Catholic opinion, see Norman A. Graebner, *America as a World Power: A Realist Appraisal from Wilson to Reagan* (Wilmington: Scholarly Resources, 1984), pp. 134–5.

84. Vandenberg's address in Vandenberg and Morris, *Private Papers of Senator Vandenberg*, pp. 247–8; Byrnes's speech in The Department of State *Bulletin*, 14 (10 March 1946), p. 358. On American public opinion in the spring of 1946, see Martin Kriesberg, 'Dark Ages of Ignorance', Lester Markel (ed.), *Public Opinion and Foreign Policy* (New York: Harper, 1949), p. 54; Thomas G. Paterson, *On Every Front: The Making of the Cold War* (New York: W. W. Norton, 1979), pp. 119–21. Paterson notes that much of the American elite endorsed the tougher approach.

85. Churchill's address in *Vital Speeches of the Day*, 12 (15 Mar. 1946), pp. 329–32; Gaddis, pp. 307–9; Gormly, p. 152; Harbutt, *The Iron Curtain*, p. 212.

86. Best, *'Co-operation with Like-Minded Peoples'*, pp. 121–2; *FRUS, 1946*: I (Washington: US Govt Printing Office, 1972), pp. 1165–6.

87. David S. McLellan, *Dean Acheson: The State Department Years* (New York: Dodd, Meade & Co., 1976), pp. 92–5. For the loan debate in Congress, see Robert M. Hathaway, *Ambiguous Partnership: Britain and America, 1944–1947* (New York: Columbia University Press, 1981), pp. 244–7; Herter quoted in Gardner, *Sterling–Dollar Diplomacy*, p. 250; Reston quoted in *The New York Times*, 31 May 1946, p. 8.

88. John H. Crider in *The New York Times*, 21 April 1946; Thomas G. Paterson, 'The Abortive American Loan to Russia and the Origins of the Cold War, 1943–1946', *The Journal of American History*, 56 (June 1969), pp. 86–8.

# Index